Biofeedback

Studies in Clinical Efficacy

Biofeedback

Studies in Clinical Efficacy

Edited by

JOHN P. HATCH
JOHNNIE G. FISHER
and
JOHN D. RUGH

The University of Texas Health Science Center at San Antonio
San Antonio, Texas

Sponsored by the Biofeedback Society of America

PLENUM PRESS • NEW YORK AND LONDON

Library of Congress Cataloging in Publication Data

Biofeedback: studies in clinical efficacy.

"Sponsored by the Biofeedback Society of America."
Includes bibliographies and index.
1. Biofeedback training. 2. Medicine, Clinical. I. Hatch, John P. II. Fisher, Johnnie
G. III. Rugh, John. IV. Biofeedback Society of America. [DNLM: 1. Biofeedback
(Psychology). WL 103 B6143]
RC489.B53B568   1987   615.8'51   86-30358
ISBN 0-306-42347-2

© 1987 Plenum Press, New York
A Division of Plenum Publishing Corporation
233 Spring Street, New York, N.Y. 10013

Contributors

FRANK ANDRASIK

Pain Therapy Centers, Greenville Hospital System, Greenville, South Carolina

EDWARD B. BLANCHARD

Center for Stress and Anxiety Disorders, State University of New York at Albany, 1535 Western Avenue, Albany, New York

BERNARD T. ENGEL

Gerontology Research Center, Baltimore, Maryland, National Institute on Aging, National Institutes of Health, U.S. Department of Health and Human Services, Bethesda, Maryland, and Francis Scott Key Medical Center, Baltimore, Maryland

MICHAEL S. GLASGOW

Gerontology Research Center, Baltimore, Maryland, National Institute on Aging, National Institutes of Health, U.S. Department of Health and Human Services, Bethesda, Maryland, and Francis Scott Key Medical Center, Baltimore, Maryland

JOHN P. HATCH

Department of Psychiatry, The University of Texas Health Science Center at San Antonio, San Antonio, Texas

v

TIMOTHY J. HOELSCHER

Department of Psychiatry, Duke University Medical Center, Durham, North Carolina

JOHN S. JORDAN

Behavioral Physiology Laboratory, Department of Psychiatry, Duke University Medical Center, Durham, North Carolina

FRANCIS J. KEEFE

Department of Psychiatry, Duke University Medical Center, Durham, North Carolina

F. DUDLEY MCGLYNN

Department of Community Dentistry, College of Dentistry, University of Florida, Gainesville, Florida

WALLACE L. MEALIEA, JR.

Department of Community Dentistry, College of Dentistry, University of Florida, Gainesville, Florida

MARVIN M. SCHUSTER

The Johns Hopkins University School of Medicine and Division of Digestive Diseases, Francis Scott Key Medical Center, Baltimore, Maryland

RICHARD S. SURWIT

Behavioral Physiology Laboratory, Department of Psychiatry, Duke University Medical Center, Durham, North Carolina

WILLIAM E. WHITEHEAD

The Johns Hopkins University School of Medicine and Division of Digestive Diseases, Francis Scott Key Medical Center, Baltimore, Maryland

M. FISCHER-WILLIAMS

Wells Building, Suite 433, 324 East Wisconsin Avenue, Milwaukee, Wisconsin

STEVEN L. WOLF

Department of Rehabilitation Medicine, Emory University School of Medicine, Atlanta, Georgia

Reviewers

Steven M. Baskin, *Ph.D.*

Charles Burgar, *M.D.*

I. G. Burnside

Andrew Cannistraci, *D.D.S.,*
F.A.C.D.

Michael F. Cataldo, *Ph.D.*

Mary R. Cook, *Ph.D.*

Jeffrey R. Cram, *Ph.D.*

Jeffrey A. Cutler, *M.D.*

Lars Dahlstrom, *D.D.S., Odont. Dr.*

Robert Dale, *D.D.S.*

Donald J. Dalessio, *M.D.*

Douglas DeGood, *Ph.D*

Chulani K. Fernando, *M.A.,*
R.P.T.

William W. Finley, *Ph.D.*

Johnnie G. Fisher, *M.D.*

Robert Freedman, *Ph.D.*

Kenneth R. Gaarder, *M.D.*

Elliot Gale, *Ph.D.*

Robert J. Gatchel, *Ph.D.*

Janel Gauthier, *Ph.D.*

Charles Greene, *D.D.S.*

John P. Hatch, *Ph.D.*

Kenneth A. Holroyd, *Ph.D.*

Rolf G. Jacob, *M.D.*

John W. Largen, *Ph.D.*

James W. Maas, *M.D.*

Robert Moss, *Ph.D.*

Peter D. Neilson, *Ph.D.*

Jeffrey P. Okesen, *D.M.D*

Barbara Peavey, *Ph.D.*

H. C. Philips, *Ph.D.*

Thomas G. Pickering, *M.D.,*
D. Phil.

John D. Rugh, *Ph.D.*

Steve H. Sanders, *Ph.D.*

Joseph D. Sargent, *M.D.*

Keith W. Sedlacek, *M.D.*

David Shapiro, *Ph.D.*

A. Maureen Skelly, *M.Sc.,*
M.C.S.P.

Edward J. Snyder, III, *M.D.*

Edward Taub, *Ph.D.*

Dennis C. Turk, *Ph.D.*

Stephen M. Weiss, *Ph.D.*

Preface

The chapters of this book were prepared as task force reports under the aegis of the Biofeedback Society of America (BSA). The impetus for the present generation of task force reports can be dated back to 1982, when John D. Rugh, as President-Elect of the Society, announced that the updating of the task force reports would be given high priority during his term as President. An ad hoc Task Force Committee was appointed in 1983, and the committee set the following objectives: (1) solicit a widely based stream of input from all segments of the Biofeedback Society of America, (2) establish a peer review system to assure the highest degree of scholarship and an unbiased approach, (3) select for area authors only individuals who have profound knowledge of the area and who have demonstrated the ability to extend understanding by reviewing and criticizing the literature, (4) prepare all reports according to a standardized format, and (5) publish all the reports simultaneously.

Input came from several sources. Many people responded with ideas and suggestions to an announcement in the BSA Newsletter that the task force reports were being revised. In 1984, a symposium was conducted at the BSA annual meeting, which included round table discussions and dialogues between task force report authors and the BSA membership. A questionnaire soliciting suggestions about topic areas and authors was sent to all BSA officers, executive board members, committee chairpersons, and *Biofeedback and Self-Regulation* editorial board members. Finally, informal suggestions and advice were accepted by committee members and authors about every aspect of the project.

The peer review system that was established to review the task force reports was in most cases more rigorous than the treatment most peer reviewed journal articles would receive. A total of 40 individuals were involved in the review process. All chapters were reviewed by at least one physician who was regarded as an expert in the field. The reviewers were well aware of the importance that the task force reports would have for the field of biofeedback, and consequently they carried out their assignments in a very professionally responsible manner. Authors continued to rewrite their chapters until exacting standards were met.

Each of the authors demonstrated integrity and scientific stature, and all did an exceptional job of navigating an honest and unbiased course in the midst of frequently incomplete information and conflicting criticisms. Without the hours of effort these dedicated members of the biofeedback research community provided, completion of this book would have been utterly impossible.

All authors were provided specific instructions and a detailed chapter outline to be followed in preparing their task force report. This assured a consistent approach to all areas. The primary objective was to document the clinical efficacy of biofeedback in the context of its use in treating specific disorders. The authors were instructed to emphasize the strongest available scientific evidence pertaining to the clinical efficacy of biofeedback in the treatment of a particular disorder. They were also asked to consider clinical lore, case studies, and data from uncontrolled outcome studies, but only insofar as these sources materially added to the knowledge base and were not contradicted by stronger evidence. The chapter outline required that the following seven sections be included in each report: (1) introduction, (2) clinical efficacy, (3) specificity of effect, (4) mechanism of action, (5) cost-effectiveness, (6) future research, and (7) conclusions.

The primary objective of the task force reports was to document the clinical efficacy of biofeedback in the context of its use in treating specific disorders. Nonetheless, publication of the reports simultaneously in a single volume had the advantage of facilitating a synthesis of information from various areas of application. Such a synthesis of information should help to advance the body of knowledge covering the whole field of biofeedback.

JOHN P. HATCH

Contents

CHAPTER 6

Biofeedback in the Management of Chronic Pain Syndromes 211

FRANCIS J. KEEFE AND TIMOTHY J. HOELSCHER

CHAPTER 7

Behavioral Treatment of Raynaud's Syndrome 255

RICHARD S. SURWIT AND JOHN S. JORDAN

CHAPTER 8

CHAPTER 9

1

Biofeedback Treatment of Vascular Headache

EDWARD B. BLANCHARD AND FRANK ANDRASIK

INTRODUCTION

Description of the Disorder

This BSA (Biofeedback Society of America) Task Force Report on vascular headache will consider three kinds of headaches: (a) migraine headache; (b) combined migraine and muscle contraction headache; and (c) cluster headache. Although the Ad Hoc Committee on the Classification of Headache (1962) classified cluster headache as a subtype of "vascular headaches of the migraine type," Kudrow (1980) has argued persuasively that cluster headache is different from migraine headache and is a "primary headache disorder." Among his bases are the differences in family history and distribution of the disorder and differences in treatment responses to various drugs. We will follow Kudrow's (1980) convention in this chapter.

Migraine Headache. There are two primary varieties of migraine

This Task Force Report was reviewed by Drs. Steve Baskin, Janel Gauthier, John Hatch, John Largen, and Joseph Sargent. Some of their suggestions and criticisms have been incorporated into the final version while others were not. The authors take responsibility for the conclusions drawn in the final version.

EDWARD B. BLANCHARD • Center for Stress and Anxiety Disorders, State University of New York at Albany, 1535 Western Avenue, Albany, NY 12203. FRANK ANDRASIK • Pain Therapy Centers, Greenville Hospital System, Greenville, SC 29601. Support for the preparation of this paper came in part from grants from NINCDS, NS15235 and NS-00818.

headache: *classic migraine*, in which the headache *per se* is preceded by definite neurological symptoms, usually visual in nature, and *common migraine*, which does not have the prodrome. Common migraine accounts for 80% to 90% of migraine sufferers. In both subtypes there are "recurrent attacks of headache, widely varied in intensity, frequency and duration. The attacks of headache, widely varied in intensity, frequency and duration. The attacks are commonly unilateral in onset; are usually accompanied by anorexia and sometimes, with nausea and vomiting" (Ad Hoc Committee, 1962). Although the exact pathophysiological mechanisms are unclear and the subject of ongoing research and debate, it does seem "that cranial artery distention and dilation are importantly implicated in the painful phase."

Cluster Headache.   Cluster headache is also a vascular headache that is predominantly unilateral in onset and tends to be extremely painful but of relatively short duration (minutes to one to two hours). They typically occur in closely packed groups (or "clusters") separated by remissions of months to years. A relatively rare variant is *chronic cluster headache* in which there are no appreciable remissions.

Combined Headache.   In the case of combined headache the patient suffers from two distinct headache disorders: migraine headaches as described previously occur episodically and are superimposed on chronic muscle contraction or tension headache. We have categorized combined headache as a vascular headache because the few biofeedback treatment studies have tended to treat these patients as if they had migraine headache.

Epidemiology

Estimates of the prevalence of migraine headache range from 0.9% to 25.7% of the adult population (Bruyn, 1983). Bruyn (1983) argued that a fair but conservative estimate of prevalence is 2% of the adult population. It is generally accepted that female migraineurs outnumber males by about 2 to 1. There are no good epidemiological data on combined headache or cluster headache. It appears that in clinics specializing in headache diagnosis and treatment, the ratio of cluster headache to migraine headache is about 1 to 12 (Kudrow, 1980). Leviton (1978) has provided a concise summary of the epidemiology of chronic headache *per se* and concluded that headache is one of the most frequent reasons for individuals to seek help from a primary care physician; moreover, as much as 50% or more of the general population may suffer the occasional (at least one per month) severe headache.

Causes

The issue of causes of vascular headache is a murky one. There is general agreement that the proximal cause of the pain in vascular headache is the dilation of cranial arteries (Dalessio, 1980), especially the extracranial ones. However, the headache phase of the migrainous episode is believed to be preceded by vasoconstriction of the intracranial arterial system, leading to cerebral anoxia. There are many views of what physiological events initiate the vasoconstriction, including neurogenic, biochemical, and vasogenic theories (Dalessio, 1980).

More distal causes or factors that help to bring on a vascular headache include certain foods, psychosocial stress, changes in hormone levels, and exposure to environmental stressors, such as bright light, loud noise, and lack of sleep. The pathophysiologic mechanisms of migraine and cluster headache both involve dilation of the external carotid system; there, however, the similarity between these two headache disorders ends.

Conventional Therapy for Vascular Headache

The conventional therapies for vascular headache fall into three broad categories: (a) *abortive,* in which something is done to abort or end the headache after it has begun; (b) *prophylactic,* in which something is done on a regular basis to prevent the onset of headache; and (c) *palliative,* in which something is done to lessen the distress of the headache episode. All conventional therapies are pharmacological.

Migraine. The standard abortive treatment for migraine are ergot derivatives, substances that cause cranial artery vasoconstriction. Other abortive drugs are aspirin or acetaminophen. In the prophylaxis of migraine, both beta-adrenergic blocking agents, such as propranolol, and tricyclic antidepressants, such as amitriptyline, have been used successfully. Ergot derivatives are also used for prophylaxis. For palliation, various levels of analgesics, sedative-hypnotics, and antiemetics are used (Dalessio, 1980).

Combined Headache. Drug treatments tend to be similar to those used for migraine with the exception that abortive treatment is unlikely to be helpful.

Cluster Headache. The abortive treatments for cluster headache are well established and include ergot derivatives and inhalation of pure oxygen (Dalessio, 1980; Kudrow, 1980). Methylsergide, corticosteroids, and amitriptyline have been used for prophylaxis. There are some reports of successful prophylaxis with lithium salts (Kudrow, 1980). Palliation tends to be less successful because the onset of the headache is so rapid.

Previous Biofeedback Society of American (BSA) Task Force Report on Vascular Headache

The previous BSA Task Force Report on Vascular Headache (Diamond, Diamond-Falk, & DeVeno, 1978) was appropriately cautious in its conclusions:

> Biofeedback has proven to be a worthwhile therapeutic modality in the treatment of vascular headaches, *but many factors have yet to be explored* [italics added]. Future studies should also be keyed toward determining whether thermal biofeedback, electromyographic biofeedback, autogenic training, or combinations of these are effective. (p. 404)

The Task Force Report cited only one published controlled study of the biofeedback treatment of migraine, that of Friar & Beatty (1976). Several published uncontrolled studies were cited as well. Finally, several preliminary versions of two controlled studies that had been presented at BSA meetings were cited (Andreychuk & Skriver, 1975; Blanchard, Theobald, Williamson, Silver, & Brown, 1978). As will be obvious from the next section of this chapter, the body of published literature on which to base conclusions has grown enormously during the 6 years between that report (1978) and the time when this one was prepared (early 1985).

CLINICAL EFFICACY

The major purpose of this chapter is a critical evaluation of the efficacy issue; or more simply, the question as to whether biofeedback is helpful for vascular headache and if so, how strongly can one support that conclusion? To answer these questions, we have prepared several tables to summarize the existing published literature. We then examine the information in these tables to draw conclusions.

Migraine Headache

Table 1 summarizes methodological details and outcome information on eight uncontrolled, single-group outcome studies of the biofeedback treatment of migraine headache. To be included in this table, a report had to present information on at least nine patients who had pure migraine headache. Sample sizes range from 9 to 160 with a median of 16 patients.

Table A–1 in the Appendix summarizes numerous methodological details on 22 controlled group outcome studies of the biofeedback treatment of migraine headache. When one considers that only two of those studies had been published at the time of the preparation of the previous BSA Task Force Report on Vascular Headache, one can see that there has been almost an explosion of research since 1978.

This table also summarizes the outcome data and follow-up results from those 22 studies. In each instance we have calculated a percentage improvement score for each of several dimensions of migraine headache using the following formula:

$$\frac{\text{Baseline Headache Parameter} - \text{End of Treatment Headache Parameter}}{\text{Baseline Headache Parameter}} \times 100 = \text{Percentage Improvement}$$

When possible we have also tabulated the percentage of patients in each treatment group who were judged to be clinically improved (usually at least a 50% reduction in headache activity). This is the data base for the discussion of efficacy.

We have examined the efficacy issue in three ways: (a) the so-called box score approach in which the number of studies that show, or that fail to show, certain significant effects was tabulated; (b) the meta-analysis approach (Blanchard, Andrasik, Ahles, Teders, & O'Keefe, 1980; Glass, 1976; Smith & Glass, 1977) in which the average score for a group of patients who all received the same treatment becomes a single datum, and then comparisons were made across treatments by means of averages of these data and standard statistical procedures for comparing means. In both of these approaches, no judgments were made as to the quality or external validity (Cook & Campbell, 1979) of the studies.

In our third examination of the data base, we present the conclusions supported by a much smaller set of exemplary studies, or studies with a high degree of external validity. Factors that we believe contribute to external validity are (a) clear diagnostic criteria for inclusion and exclusion, (b) adequate sample sizes on which to base between group comparisons; (c) adequate lengths of training; (d) appropriate use of adjunctive procedures for home practice; (e) use of multiple, experienced therapists.

The Box Score Approach

In our view five different biofeedback treatments have sufficient data available to be included in this analysis: thermal biofeedback for hand warming combined with autogenic training (TBF-W + AT) and

TABLE 1. Summary of Single Group Outcome Studies of Biofeedback

		Sargent et al. (1973)	Mitch et al. (1976)	Medina et al. (1976)
Patient Characteristics	Age, X̄	N/A	34[a]	35[b]
	Range	21–63	21–50[a]	10–60[b]
	Sex M/F	N/A	8/12[a]	3/24[b]
	Years of HA, X̄	N/A	14[a]	N/A
Source	Physician referred	Yes	Yes	Yes
	Self-referred	Yes	Yes	
Numbered started		20	N/A	N/A
Number completed		19	20 (12)[a]	27 (14)[b]
% Dropout		5	N/A	N/A
Diagnosed by:		PI	Physician	Neurologist
Diagnostic criteria		N/A	N/A	N/A

Treatment	Temp. BF + autogenic trng.	Temp. BF + autogenic trng. (mainly at home)	Temp. BF + EMG BF autogenic trng.
No. of sessions–fixed	N/A(8–32)	6	2/wk.
Avg. for sample	N/A	N/A	8
Avg. length of session	N/A	N/A	45 min.
Fixed protocol	No	Yes	Yes
Training to criteria	Prob. Yes	No	No
Home practice	Daily with home temp. trainer	Daily with home temp. trainer	Daily with temp. trainer & relaxation
Duration of treatment	2–4 mos.	12 wks.	1 mon.
Baseline length	N/A	6 mos. (retrospective)	2–60 mos.
HA diary	Yes	Yes	Yes
Evidence of BF training	?	?	Yes, 2°F in 1 min.
Multiple trainers	N/A	2	N/A
Avg. exp. of trainers	N/A	N/A	N/A
Trainer effect	N/A	N/A	N/A
Trainer present or absent	N/A	N/A	Absent

possibly with other relaxation training (8 studies); thermal biofeedback for hand warming alone (TBF-W) (6 studies); thermal biofeedback for hand cooling (TBF-C) (4 studies); cephalic vasomotor biofeedback for temporal artery vasoconstriction (CVM) (5 studies); and frontal EMG biofeedback (EMG BF) with or without explicit adjunctive relaxation training (4 studies).

Treatment of Migraine Headache

Fahrion (1978)	Russ et al. (1979)	Strobel et al. (1981)	Blanchard et al. (1982c)	Diamond & Montrose (1984)
N/A[c]	45.1	N/A	42.7	N/A
N/A	24–61	N/A	19–68	6–72
N/A	N/A	N/A	6/24	33/129
>10 yrs.	19.9	N/A	N/A	N/A
Yes	Yes	Yes	Yes	Yes
No		No	Yes	
N/A	N/A	N/A	33	N/A
21 (11)[c]	9	45	30	281
N/A	N/A	N/A	9	N/A
Neurologist	PI	N/A	Neurologist & psychologist	Neurologist
N/A	N/A	N/A	Ad hoc committee	Ad hoc committee
Temp. BF + autogenic trng. + discussion + (EMG BF for mixed)	Temp. BF + autogenic trng. + EMG BF	Quieting response: temp. BF + EMG BF + breathing exer. + progress. relaxation + autogenics	10 sessions of progressive relaxation + (14 patients) 12 sessions Temp. BF + autogenics	Temp. BF + EMG BF + other
N/A	1–2 wk.	8	10–22	21 wk.–3/day
N/A	15.6	N/A	N/A	8–22
60 min.	45 min.	60 min.	50 min.	45 min.
No	Yes	Yes	Yes	Yes
Yes (95.5°F, 1°F/min.	No	No	No	Yes (4 °F rise)
Daily with tapes & temp. trainer	Daily— relaxation	Spec. daily practice	Daily with tape & in BF with therm.	Daily with temp. trainer
N/A	4–12 wks.	N/A	2–4 mos.	1 wk.–4 wks.
N/A	N/A	N/A	4 wks.	N/A
		N/A	Yes	Yes
Yes	Yes	N/A	N/A	?
N/A	N/A	N/A	Yes	Yes
No	N/A	N/A	1 yr.	N/A
N/A	N/A	N/A	N/A	No
—	N/A	N/A	N/A	Absent
Present	N/A			

Continued

Biofeedback versus No Treatment or Headache Monitoring

Thermal Biofeedback plus Autogenic Training (TBF-W + AT) Of the four (Blanchard et al., 1978; Gamble & Elder, 1983; Jessup, Neufeld, & Stenn, 1976; Sargent, Solbach, Coyne, Spohn, & Segerson, 1986) direct experimental comparisons of TBF-W + AT to headache monitor-

TABLE 1. (*Continued*)

	Sargent *et al.* (1973)	Mitch *et al.* (1976)	Medina *et al.* (1976)
Results (% reduction)			
HA Index	N/A	N/A	47
HA Frequency	N/A	45?	N/A
HA Intensity	N/A	75?	N/A
HA Duration	N/A	60?	N/A
Meds	N/A	55?	47
Global rating	63	55 or 75	N/A
% Sample Improved	12/19 = 63	9/12 = 75	5/14 = 36
Follow-up duration	1/22 mos.	6 mos.	13 mos.
Maintenance condition	1/mo. visit	None	1/mo. booster
% sample available	N/A	50	100
% reduction vs. BL	N/A	90	47
% reduction vs. end of treatment	N/A	N/A	N/A
HA diary or global rating	N/A	Global Rating	Diary

Note. N/A—Information not available in article.
[a] 12/20 pure migraine, 8/20 mixed HA.
[b] 14/27 pure migraine, 13/27 mixed HA.
[c] 11/21 pure migraine, 10/21 mixed HA.
[d] Migraine and mixed combined.

ing, two (Blanchard *et al.*, 1978; Sargent *et al.*, 1986) showed significantly greater improvement for treatment over headache monitoring.

Cephalic Vasomotor Biofeedback. In two (Bild & Adams, 1980; Gauthier, Doyon, Lacroix, & Drolet, 1983) of the three (Bild & Adams, 1980; Gauthier *et al.*, 1980; Knapp & Florin, 1980) comparisons of CVM to headache monitoring, the treated patients were significantly more improved than the untreated ones.

Frontal EMG Biofeedback. Of the four comparisons (Bild & Adams, 1980; Gamble & Elder, 1983; Lake, Raney, & Papsdorf, 1979; Sargent *et al.*, 1986) of EMG BF to headache monitoring, two (Lake *et al.*, 1979; Sargent *et al.*, 1986) found significant advantage for treatment over headache monitoring.

Thermal Biofeedback. For the five studies that involved thermal biofeedback for hand warming alone (TBF-W) (Gamble & Elder, 1983; Jessup *et al.*, 1976; Kewman & Roberts, 1980; Lake *et al.*, 1979) or thermal biofeedback for hand cooling alone (TBF-C) (Jessup *et al.*, 1976; Kewman & Roberts, 1980), none of these biofeedback treatments were significantly different than headache monitoring.

On balance, then, there appears to be some advantage for biofeedback training over headache monitoring alone, or for treatment over no treatment.

Fahrion (1978)	Russ et al. (1979)	Strobel et al. (1981)	Blanchard et al. (1982c)		Diamond & Montrose (1984)
			R	BF	
N/A	22	N/A	21	17	N/A
N/A	N/A	N/A	19	1	N/A
N/A	N/A	N/A	25	11	N/A
N/A	N/A	N/A	N/A	N/A	77/159 (48)
N/A	N/A	N/A	−18	4	82/160 (51)
71	66	44	N/A	N/A	51
15/21 = 71	5/9 = 56	20/45 = 44	15/30 = 50		81/160 = 51
6–13 (x = 10)	N/A	Up to 2 yrs.	1 year[d]		6 mos.–4 yrs.
N/A		3, 6, 12 mo. booster	Half 1/mo. boosters		N/A
N/A		58 @ 2 yrs.	59		N/A
71		N/A	71		51
N/A		N/A	0		N/A
Global Rating		Global rating	HA diary		Global rating

Biofeedback versus Attention-Placebo Conditions

There have been surprisingly few comparisons of biofeedback training to psychological placebo conditions (Friar & Beatty, 1976; Mullinix, Norton, Hack, & Fishman, 1978; Reading, 1983). (We might hasten to add that we have not classified studies that used thermal biofeedback to teach hand cooling as in Gauthier et al., 1981; Jessup et al., 1976; Kewman & Roberts, 1980; Largen, Mathew, Dobbins, & Claghorn, 1981, as involving an attention-placebo condition, following the reasoning of Gauthier et al., 1981, on this point. Because the training in hand cooling is teaching patients some degree of peripheral vascular system control, and possibly stabilization, we have viewed it as a psychophysiologically active treatment.) If the studies that have used this condition are taken as ones involving an attention-placebo condition (which was the purpose for its inclusion), then there are seven studies.

There have been no comparisons of TBF-W + AT to placebo; the two comparisons (Jessup et al., 1976; Largen et al., 1981) of TBF-W + AT to TBF-C failed to show any significant difference between the two conditions. For thermal biofeedback alone (TBF-W), the two direct comparisons (Gauthier et al., 1981: Kewman & Roberts, 1980) with psychological placebo failed to show any advantage for the biofeedback condition.

Likewise, the one comparison (Kewman & Roberts, 1980) of TBF-W to TBF-C failed to show any significant difference.

The one comparison of CVM to placebo (Friar & Beatty, 1976) showed a significant advantage for biofeedback training. The single comparison of EMG BF (Reading, 1983) to placebo, however, failed to show any significant advantage for the EMG biofeedback training.

In summary, there are a decided lack of studies comparing any form of biofeedback to psychological placebo. Of those which have been conducted, all but one have failed to show biofeedback superior to psychological placebo.

Biofeedback versus Relaxation Conditions

The next logical set of comparisons for evaluating the efficacy of biofeedback treatments is to compare various forms of biofeedback training to another nondrug self-regulatory treatment, relaxation training. This form of comparison has been relatively common. Of the six direct comparisons (Attfield & Peck, 1979; Daly, Donn, Galliher, & Zimmerman, 1983; Blanchard et al., 1978; Blanchard et al., 1982; Gamble & Elder, 1983; Sargent et al., 1986) of TBF-W + AT to some form of relaxation training, one (Blanchard et al., 1982) found TBF-W + AT superior to relaxation training whereas the other five found no difference. The three comparisons of TBF to relaxation found no significant differences between the pairs of treatments. There have been no comparisons of CVM to relaxation.

Thus the bulk of empirical evidence finds no advantage for biofeedback training over various forms of relaxation training.

Comparisons among Various Types of Biofeedback Training

There have been six direct comparisons of EMG biofeedback to either TBF-W + AT or TBF-W (Cohen, McArthur, & Rickles, 1980; Daly et al., 1983; Gamble & Elder, 1983; Lake et al., 1979; Reading, 1983; Sargent et al., 1986). In no case has one form of biofeedback been significantly better than another. Likewise, there have been three direct comparisons (Cohen et al., 1980; Elmore & Tursky, 1981; Gauthier et al., 1981) of TBF-W + AT or TBF-W to CVM. In one case (Elmore & Tursky, 1981) CVM led to significantly greater analgesic medication reduction than TBF-W; however, there were no significant differences in reduction of headache parameters. The other two comparisons yielded no differences. Finally, there were no differences found in the two comparisons (Bild & Adams, 1980; Cohen et al., 1980) of CVM and EMG BF for migraine headache.

Summary and Conclusions from Box Score Analysis

Although it seems fairly well established that any form of biofeedback training is usually superior to headache monitoring (or no treatment), it is not at all well established that biofeedback training is superior to psychological placebo. In fact, there have been no comparisons of TBF-W + AT to a psychologically credible, but psychophysiologically neutral, placebo condition. Moreover, it is generally the case that various forms of biofeedback training are not superior to relaxation training. Finally, there are generally no differences found in individual studies among the various types of biofeedback training.

These conclusions must be qualified by noting (a) that no account has been taken of the quality of the various studies, including sample size, and (b) that no account is taken of arithmetic differences between conditions that do not reach conventional levels of statistical significance. The latter point is considered in the next section whereas the former point is addressed in the third section.

Meta-Analysis Approach

Meta-analysis is a relatively new, and somewhat controversial (Blanchard *et al.*, 1980; Glass, 1976; Smith & Glass, 1977) alternative to the box score approach for summarizing the literature. In what has become its usual or standard form, the value of datum entered into the analysis from each condition of a study is the effect size, a dimensionless number that represents the ratio of change in a dependent variable to the variance in the study population. Effect size was initially created in part to have a common measure across psychotherapy studies that used a great variety of dependent variables. It also took into account the variance in the dependent variable.

In our use of the procedures of meta-analysis, we are following previously published reports in the headache literature (Blanchard & Andrasik, 1982; Blanchard *et al.*, 1980) and thus depart somewhat from the standard form. Rather than using an effect size, we have calculated a percentage improvement score (using the formula given earlier) for each group of patients in a study who received the same treatment. The use of the percentage improvement score ignores the differences in variance from study to study, thus weakening it to some degree. However, its use, calculated as described in the following, enabled us to include more studies than use of an effect size would have. Moreover, it keeps the measures to be analyzed and their means in clinically meaningful units.

The percentage improvement score is calculated for all headache

TABLE 2. Summary of Metaanalysis of

	Condition			
	Headache monitoring	Attention placebo	Thermal biofeedback alone	EMG biofeedback
Mean % improvement score	13.3^a	$25.8^{a,b}$	27.2^b	29.0^b
Number of studies	7	6	6	4

Note. Means that share a superscript do not differ at the .05 level.

parameters but preference (following the arguments of Blanchard *et al.*, 1980) is given to the parameters in the following descending order: headache index (a function that combines frequency and intensity), headache frequency, headache intensity, headache duration, headache medications used, percentage of sample improved, or global ratings of improvement at end of treatment. Only a single value from each group in each study was used in subsequent analyses. We have arbitrarily decided that a percentage improvement score must be based on at least four patients to be included. As a result of this restriction, one study (Gamble & Elder, 1983) was eliminated. In one other study (Attfield & Peck, 1979), insufficient information was reported to calculate percentage improvement scores for individual treatment conditions.

In Table 2 are summarized the mean percentage improvement scores for all treatment conditions for which there were at least four scores available. We have also included in this table the mean scores from the uncontrolled studies summarized in Table 1, both for studies using TBF-W + AT and for those combining TBF-W + AT and EMG BF.

These values were subjected to two one-way analyses of variance: (a) to compare the seven conditions from the controlled studies; and (b) to compare those seven conditions and the two conditions from the uncontrolled studies. For these analyses TBF-C, or biofeedback training in hand cooling, has been treated as an attention-placebo condition. When a significant overall F was found, we have made individual comparisons using *t* tests.

Comparison of Conditions in Controlled Studies. The comparison of the seven treatment conditions in the controlled studies revealed significant differences among the conditions, $F(6,33) = 3.78$, $p = .006$. In-

Biofeedback Treatment of Migraine Headache

Cephalic vasomotor biofeedback	Relaxation training	Thermal biofeedback + autogenic training	Uncontrolled studies of TBF + AT + EMG,BF	Uncontrolled studies of TBF + AT
43.2^c	48.3^{c,d}	48.5^{c,d}	41.0^c	64.8^d
5	4	8	4	4

dividual comparisons reveal that (a) headache monitoring is significantly poorer than all active treatments but not different than attention placebo conditions; (b) TBF-W alone and EMG BF are not significantly better than attention placebo; (c) CVM, various forms of relaxation, and TBF-W + AT are not different among themselves but are all superior to attention placebo, TBF-W, and EMG BF.

Comparisons among Conditions Including Uncontrolled Studies. In the second analysis, two conditions were added from Table 1 representing uncontrolled studies: TBF-W + AT and TBF-W + AT combined with EMG biofeedback. The one-way ANOVA revealed significant differences among the conditions, $F(8,39) = 4.80$, $p = .0004$. Individual comparisons revealed that, although the results from the uncontrolled studies of TBF-W + AT are arithmetically superior to the results from controlled studies, especially for TBF-W + AT, the pooled results from the uncontrolled studies are not significantly better than the results for TBF-W + AT from controlled studies. Otherwise the results remain essentially the same.

Summary and Conclusions from Meta-Analysis

This approach thus confirms to some extent the conclusions of the box score approach: TBF-W + AT, relaxation, and CVM biofeedback are superior to headache monitoring and do not differ among themselves. This approach further suggests that TBF-W + AT is superior to TBF-W alone, EMG BF, or attention-placebo conditions. It also suggests that relaxation alone and CVM biofeedback are superior to TBF-W alone, EMG BF or attention placebo.

The failure to find an advantage for TBF-W + AT from the uncontrolled studies over the average value of TBF-W + AT from the controlled studies suggests that the adaption of TBF-W + AT to the controlled conditions of an experiment have not "emasculated" this biofeedback treatment. The results also suggest that autogenic training, even in the very abbreviated versions used in many studies, makes an important contribution to treatment effectiveness.

Exemplary Studies Approach

Unlike the two previous approaches to analyzing the existing literature on the outcome of biofeedback treatment of migraine, another approach, which we have termed the exemplary study approach, takes into account the quality of the study. Although every experimental study can be faulted on some dimensions, it seems to us a truism that some studies are better than others. In trying to make this judgment we have selected several features as very important, all of which can be seen as related to either internal validity or external validity of the study (Cook & Campbell, 1979).

Internal Validity Factors. Several factors are critical for the internal validity of the study: (a) random assignment of subjects to conditions; (b) adequate sample size; (c) explicit diagnostic criteria; (d) use of multiple-trained therapists.

External Validity Factors. The external validity refers to how well the experimental conditions match actual clinical practice and how well the subject population matches the clinical population to which one wishes to generalize. The conditions are (a) adequate length of training in terms of number of sessions; (b) use of explicit home practice; (c) use of adjunctive relaxation techniques; (d) demographic characteristics of sample.

A major problem in many studies is small sample size. When one finds a significant difference among groups small in size, it probably indicates a robust effect. However, in the area of biofeedback treatment of migraine headache, a major finding has been the lack of significant differences among conditions. In the latter case, small sample sizes are a major problem because of the lack of statistical power. It may well be the case that many of the failures to find significant differences between conditions is due to a lack of sufficient power rather than being representative of the true state of nature. (Gamble & Elder, 1983, with a sample size of three subjects per condition across eight conditions is an example of this problem.) For our purposes, we propose that a study should have at least 10 subjects per condition to be considered adequate. Only eight met this condition. (Interestingly, four of these eight report some significant between group differences.)

Of the 22 controlled group outcome studies summarized in Table A–1 in the Appendix, four meet most of our criteria for exemplary studies and two others, though meeting fewer criteria, seem worthy of mention.

Sargent et al. 1986. By far the strongest study is that of Sargent *et al.* (1986). A total of 136 migraine patients diagnosed by the Ad Hoc Committee criteria were randomly assigned to one of four conditions: (a) thermal biofeedback combined with autogenic training and routine use of home thermal trainers; two thirds of the patients achieved an explicit learning criterion (1.5° F rise in 1 minute); (b) frontal EMG biofeedback combined with autogenic training; patients in this condition demonstrated significant physiological control of EMG; (c) autogenic training alone; (d) headache monitoring. The 22 treatment sessions were spread over 36 weeks.

The results showed all three treated groups reduced headache frequency significantly and significantly more than headache monitoring. However, despite sample sizes of 34 per condition, no significant differences were found among the three treated groups.

Blanchard et al. (1978). In this study 30 migraineurs, meeting explicit inclusion and exclusion criteria, were randomly assigned to one of three conditions: (a) thermal biofeedback combined with brief autogenic training; (b) training in progressive muscle relaxation; (c) headache monitoring. The 12 treatment sessions were spread over 6 weeks with a 3-month follow-up. Although the three therapists were very experienced in relaxation training, they were novices at the biofeedback training. No home thermal trainers were made available.

The results showed that both treated groups improved significantly and were significantly more improved than the headache monitoring group. The two treated groups did not differ at the end of treatment, or during follow-up, even when the group sizes were increased to 13 each by the addition of control subjects treated in the two active conditions.

Kewman & Roberts (1980). In this study 11 migraineurs were given thermal biofeedback alone to raise hand temperature whereas 12 were given thermal biofeedback to reduce hand temperature. A third group of 11 patients, selected because of prior knowledge about biofeedback treatment of migraine, monitored headaches. The training was conducted by untrained undergraduates. Active training was conducted under double blind conditions for 10 sessions over a 9-week period of time. Home practice instructions are unclear and no home practice device was available.

Results showed significant within—group improvement in all three groups with no significant between—group differences. It is not clear how well the two active treatment groups mastered the biofeedback task. A reanalysis of the results, based on actual temperature changes shown in the training [learners ($n = 11$) average increase in temperature of $0.7°$ C ($+1.26°$ F); nonlearners ($n = 7$) average increase in temperature of $0.3°$ C ($+0.54°$ F); and decreased temperature ($n = 5$), average decrease in temperature of $0.7°$ C ($-1.26°$ F)], showed significant improvement for the learners, nonlearners, and headache monitoring group, whereas the decrease-temperature group became worse. Moreover, the decrease-temperature group did significantly poorer than the other three groups combined. Unfortunately explicit comparisons of the learners and nonlearners (who, in fact, show some learning) with the decrease-temperature group were not reported.

Jurish et al. (1983). In the Jurish *et al.* (1983) study a combination of thermal biofeedback, autogenic training, and relaxation training was administered to 20 migraineurs, diagnosed by Ad Hoc Committee criteria, by four experienced therapists. Unfortunately, the experimental comparison is between two methods of treatment delivery: 16 individual sessions versus 3 sessions and programmed manuals and audiotapes. Both groups improved significantly.

Unpublished data (Appelbaum, Blanchard, Andrasik, & Evans, 1984) from our laboratory have replicated this finding and further found significantly greater improvement for both treated groups than for a headache monitoring control condition.

In the other two studies, Friar & Beatty (1976) assigned 10 migraineurs to cephalic vasomotor biofeedback whereas 10 others received an attention-placebo condition (training in finger vasomotor control). The patient population was fairly young, averaging 30 years. Training was fairly brief (nine sessions) and no home practice was included. Despite these problems, the active treatment group was significantly more improved on some measures than the control group.

Finally, in a large-scale effort, Cohen *et al.* (1980) assigned 42 vascular headache patients (both migraine and combined, diagnosed by Ad Hoc Committee criteria) to one of four conditions: (a) TBF-W ($n = 11$); (b) EMG BF ($n = 11$); (c) CVM biofeedback ($n = 10$) or (d) EEG alpha biofeedback ($n = 10$). There was no home training component and the trainers qualifications were not given. All patients received 16 biofeedback sessions over 8 weeks. Results showed no significant within-group improvement and no significant between-group differences.

Summary and Conclusions from Exemplary Study Approach

From these six studies, it also seems clear that TBF-W + AT (and also with adjunctive relaxation training) is consistently superior to headache monitoring (Blanchard *et al.*, 1978; Sargent *et al.*, 1986) but is not significantly superior to relaxation training (Blanchard *et al.*, 1978;

Sargent et al., 1986) or frontal EMG BF (Sargent et al., 1986). Relaxation training (Blanchard et al., 1978; Sargent et al., 1986) and EMG biofeedback are significantly superior to headache monitoring. TBF-W without home practice is not superior to headache monitoring (Kewman & Roberts, 1980) or to any other treatment. CVM BF is sometimes superior to placebo.

Overall Conclusions on Efficacy

There is some degree of congruence in the conclusions supported by these three different approaches to analyzing the outcome data (these conclusions are repeated at the end of this chapter): (a) treatment of migraine headache with almost any form of biofeedback or relaxation training is superior to headache monitoring; (b) TBF-W + AT is not consistently superior to relaxation training; (c) there are no consistent findings when various forms of biofeedback training are compared.

Comparisons of Biofeedback Therapy and Pharmacotherapy for Migraine Headache

Indirect Comparisons. As noted earlier, the standard medical treatment for migraine headaches is either abortive drugs or prophylactic drugs. A crucial efficacy question, in our opinion, is the comparison of biofeedback therapies with routine or standard pharmacotherapy. In a sense, 11 of the 21 of the studies cited in Table A–1 in the Appendix and 4 of the 8 in Table 1 are indirect comparisons of self-regulatory therapies and medication because most of the patients entered those studies taking various antiheadache medications. If the level of medication consumption is reduced significantly in groups receiving self-regulatory therapy, then this could be construed as evidence in favor of the self-regulatory therapy.

Although it is not always possible to determine the effects of individual treatment conditions on medication consumption, seven of nine studies TBF-W, with or without autogenic training and possibly with frontal EMG biofeedback, led to significant reductions in headache medication X for percentage reduction = 44%, range = 4% to 64%). Control conditions (TBF-C or placebo) led to a mean decrease of 53% in three instances. Finally, CVM led to significant reductions in three of four instances with average decrease of 48%.

Direct Comparisons. To the best of our knowledge there have been two direct comparisons of biofeedback and drugs in the treatment of migraine headache. In the first study, Sovak, Kunzel, Sternbach, & Dalessio (1981) compared propranolol plus occasional analgesics to 8 to 10 sessions of TBF-W + AT. The biofeedback group also used thermal biofeedback trainers for regular home practice. Patients were trained until they could produce a 1° C rise within 15 minutes. Treatment was spread over approximately 12 weeks. Evaluation was by means of a headache diary. All patients were female, ranging in age from 30 to 57, and diagnosed by neurologists. Twenty-nine patients were assigned to each condition. Nine patients in the drug condition failed to complete treatment as compared to one in the biofeedback condition [χ (1) = 7.73, $p < .01$].

Based on a reduction of at least 50% in frequency, intensity and/or duration of headache as measured by diary, improvement was found for 15 of 28 (53.6%) patients treated with biofeedback as compared to 9 of 20 (45%) treated with medication. The two treatments were thus equivalent in terms of efficacy.

In the second study Mathew (1981) compared a biofeedback based therapy alone to abortive and analgesic therapy, propranolol or amitriptyline. Various other combinations of these treatments were also tried. Patients consisted of 13 males and 166 females with an average age of 35.5 years.

The biofeedback therapy consisted of 10 sessions combining TBF-W, EMG BF, autogenic training, and other relaxation training. A home thermal biofeedback device was used. In this study 17 of 48 (35.4%) biofeedback treated patients dropped out as compared to 6 of 44 (13.6%) on propranolol. In all 28 of 131 (21.4%) drug treated patients dropped out. In this case there is a trend [χ (1) = 3.68, $p < .10$] for there to be a higher drop out rate among the biofeedback treated patients than among the three drug treated groups combined.

Degree of improvement based upon headache diary was as follows: biofeedback—35%; abortive drugs plus analgesics—20%; amitriptyline—42%; propranolol—62%. In this case biofeedback was significantly better than the combination of abortives plus analgesics but significantly poorer than propranolol.

There is thus no weight of evidence on either side of this issue: in one case propranolol is superior to biofeedback whereas in the other case it is no different. In one case the drug condition leads to significantly more drop outs whereas in the other case there is a trend for the opposite finding to obtain.

Taking the data from the Mathew (1981) study and the earlier indirect evidence, it does seem that thermal biofeedback combined with autogenic training and possibly other self-regulatory therapies is superior to the combination of ergot abortives plus analgesics.

Long Term Follow-Up

Although it is obvious that the ultimate goal of biofeedback treatment of vascular headache is relatively long-term, or permanent, relief from headache, there are only limited data available on this topic. There are a limited number of retrospective follow-up studies of the biofeedback treatment of vascular headache, including several on migraine, summarized in Table 3. Of more value, it seems to us, are prospective follow-up studies in which patients who received certain specifiable treatments are then followed-up for a period of time.

In Table 3 are summarized the prospective follow-up studies of migraine and combined headache for which follow-up was at least 6 months.

Of the nine studies, five come from controlled outcome studies, whereas the other four represent follow-up of uncontrolled studies. Only four of the studies represent follow-ups of 12 months or more (Andrasik, Blanchard, Neff, & Rodichok, 1984; Medina, Diamond, & Franklin, 1976; Silver, Blanchard, Williamson, Theobald, & Brown, 1979; Stroebel, Ford, Strong, & Szarek, 1981). For those four studies, an average of 80% of patients were available at 12 months who had been available at end of treatment.

If one combines the groups who received TBF-W, TBF-W + AT, or either of these two plus additional treatment, one finds in four out of five instances, there was continued improvement from end of treatment to the end of follow-up. For the two studies with EMG biofeedback (Lake *et al.*, 1979; Sargent *et al.*, 1986) there was also continued improvement. Of the other eight conditions, only three showed improvement while five showed some deterioration.

In four studies (Andrasik *et al.*, 1984; Cohen *et al.*, 1980; Lake *et al.*, 1979; Sargent *et al.*, 1986) booster treatment sessions were given during follow-up ranging from 1 to 4 per month over 8 months. For the most part booster treatments seem associated with good maintenance. In the one experimental test of booster treatments versus repeated contact, Andrasik *et al.* (1984) found an arithmetic advantage that did not reach statistical significance for booster treatments over repeated contacts without booster treatments for vascular headache patients treated with either relaxation or relaxation and TBF-W + AT.

Unpublished data from our laboratory reveal that the arithmetic advantage for booster treatments had disappeared at 2 years. It is probably the case that other events in the patients' lives played a larger role in the 18 months after the end of the booster treatments than did the 6 months of once per month boosters.

TABLE 3. Summary of Long-Term Follow-up

	Silver et al. (1979) (Blanchard et al. 1978)		Cohen et al. (1980)				Gauthier et al. (1981)				Sargent et al. (1986)			
Headache type	Migraine		Migraine				Migraine				Migraine			
Type of study	Controlled Group		Controlled group				Controlled group				Controlled group			
Treatment conditions	TBF + AT	Relax	TBF	EMG	CVM	EEG	TBF -W	TBF -C	Temp Art-C	Temp Art-W	TBF + AT	EMG + AT	AT	HA Mon
Length of follow-up	12 mos.		8 mos.				6 mos.				6 mos.			
Number of patients at end of treatment	13	13	11	11	10	10	6	6	6	6	34	34	34	34
Number of patients at end of follow-up	9	9	8	9	8	9	6	6	6	6	34	34	34	
%	69	69	73	82	80	90	100	100	100	100	100	100	100	100
Follow-up conditions	Daily HA diary for 3 months, brief contact at 1, 2, 3 mo., no contact 3 mo.–11 mo.		Daily HA diary for entire follow-up, booster treatment at 1, 2, 3, 6 mo.				No specific follow-up conditions				Daily HA diary for entire follow-up, 12 lab self-control sessions.			
% Improvement end of treatment	73	81	5	28	24	14	28	37	19	61	21	26	17	9
% Improvement BL-follow-up	57	86	25	29	11	10	50	55	33	21	21	26	17	9
% Improvement end of treatment-follow-up	−8	7	21	2	−17	−5	30	28	17	−104	8	10	7	5
Data source	1 mon. HA diary		1 mon. HA diary				4 wks. HA diary				4 wks. HA diary			
Diary Global rating														

Certainly, longer-term, prospective follow-up studies are needed to confirm the apparently good maintenance of headache relief found in these studies.

Patient Selection Factors

Compared to the number of studies of treatment outcome, there have been relatively few studies of patient selection factors, or prediction

of Biofeedback Treatments for Vascular Headache

Andrasik et al. (1984) (Blanchard et al., 1982c)		Mitch et al. (1976)	Fahrion (1978)	Medina et al. (1976)	Stroebel et al. (1981)	
Migraine & combined		Migraine & combined	Migraine & combined	Migraine & combined	Migraine	Combined
Single group with cross-over		Single group	Single group	Single group	Single group	
Relaxation + TBF + AT for relaxation failures		TBF + AT	TBF + AT	TBF + AT EMG, BF	TBF, + AT, EMG BF, Relaxation, QR	
12 mos.		6 Months	6–13 mos. x = 10 mos.	13 mos.	3 mos.—100%	75%—12 mos.
					6 mos.—88%	58%—24 mos.
Booster 21	Nonbooster 29	20	21	27		
16	21	10	N/A	27	45	131
76	72	50	N/A	100	79	
Booster—6 booster treatments at 1–6 mo, HA diary. Nonbooster—6 brief contacts at 1–6 mo., HA diary.		No specific follow-up conditions.	None reported.	1/mo. booster treatment	None reported, patients urged to practice regularly.	
		45	71	47	NR	NR
82	57	90?	71	47	64	61
+57	−62	N/A	N/A	N/A	N/A	N/A
		Global rating	Global rating	HA diary	Global rating	

of biofeedback treatment outcome. Two studies from the Diamond Headache Clinic provide some indirect information. In one retrospective study of 407 chronic headache sufferers (Diamond, Medina, Diamond-Falk, & DeVeno, 1979), including 123 patients with vascular headache, 255 with combined headache and 19 with muscle contraction headache, it was found that age, sex, and whether the patient had had a previous drug habituation problem all were significantly related to biofeedback treatment outcome for the entire sample of 407 patients. By inference we might hypothesize that these factors also hold for sufferers of purely vascular headache. Thus 60.1% of patients under 30 years were much improved as compared to 54.2% of patients between 31 and 46, and only 31.9% of those 46 and older. Females showed a larger percentage of improved patients than males. Finally, patients with previous drug habituation problems had a significantly poorer outcome than those who did not have a previous problem.

In a second study (Diamond & Montrose, 1984) on 395 chronic headache sufferers, including 281 with vascular headache, 74 with combination headache, and 25 with muscle contraction, the age effect and sex effect were replicated for the entire sample. Again females did better overall than males, and younger patients do better than older ones: 82.1% of patients under 21 years were improved versus 51.2% of patients 22 to 30, 51.6% of those 31 to 46, and 54% of patients 47 to 90 years.

Werder, Sargent, & Coyne (1981) reported on the relation of several demographic and psychological test (MMPI) variables to treatment outcome in a sample of 27 migraine sufferers, 15 combined headache, and 9 tension. Considering the whole sample, they found a significant effect of age with successful patients (at least 51% reduction in headache activity) significantly younger ($X = 35.9$ years) than unsuccessful ones ($X = 45.0$ years). Sex was not related to successful treatment outcome.

In a discriminant function analysis, Scale 3 (Hy) of the MMPI significantly discriminated between successful and unsuccessful patients. There was also a significant difference on Scale 1 (Hs). Further information revealed that 58% of unsuccessful patients had T scores of greater than 70 on Scale 1 and 74% on Scale 3 as compared to 28% and 44% of successful patients, respectively.

Another large scale effort by Ford, Stroebel, Strong, & Szarek (1981) on a sample of 209 headache patients (33 muscle contraction, 45 migraine, and 131 combined headache) yielded a statistically significant discriminant function that correctly classified 62.3% of patients using a number of variables. The authors rightly conclude that the level of correct classification is probably too low to be clinically useful.

The SUNY-Albany Studies. Over the past 5 years we have conducted a series of studies (Blanchard, Andrasik, Neff, Arena, et al., 1982c; Blanchard, Andrasik, Arena, Neff, Saunders, et al., 1983b; Blanchard, Andrasik, Arena, Neff, Jurish, et al., 1983a; Blanchard et al., 1985; Neff, Blanchard, & Andrasik, 1983) on identifying potential predictors of successful treatment outcome for chronic headache patients using relaxation training and/or biofeedback. We have found significant classification using discriminant function analyses for migraineurs receiving relaxation training and for a pooled set of migraineurs and combined headache sufferers receiving thermal biofeedback after failing a course of relaxation training. Potential predictors have included psychological tests, psychophysiological measures, and information from the headache history. Results, expressed as complex combinations of variables, showed 87.5% correct classification for vascular headache patients receiving biofeedback from headache history variables; 90.6% from psychological tests, and 84.8% from psychophysiological variables. When all three sets of predictors were combined, correct classification was 100%.

More recently (Blanchard *et al.*, 1985) we have attempted to provide information of more clinical utility by examining the ability of individual scores on individual variables to predict outcome. For migraineurs treated with the combination of thermal biofeedback, autogenic training, and relaxation training, age is a significant predictor: 55.6% of patients 30 or younger were improved as compared to 11.1% who were unimproved (less than 25% reduction in headache activity). For patients 49 years or older, only 46.7% were improved versus 33.3% who were unimproved. We also found that Scales 1, 3, and 8 of the MMPI and the Beck Depression Inventory aided in prediction. For example, 63.2% of patients with T scores of 63 or less on scale 3 were improved versus only 30% with scores of 64 or above.

In summary, age is a consistent indicator of potential treatment outcome with patients under 30 years doing well in biofeedback and those 50 years and over tending to do poorly. Otherwise Scales 1 (Hs) and especially 3 (Hy) of the MMPI tend to predict outcome, with patients with elevations tending to do more poorly.

SPECIFICITY OF EFFECTS AND MECHANISM OF ACTION

The previous review of clinical efficacy has addressed indirectly the issues of specificity of effect and mechanism of action, in that comparisons of active treatments to control conditions were summarized there. Thus, if thermal biofeedback alone had a specific effect on migraine headache rather than a generalized mobilization of expectancies for improvement (attention-placebo effect), one would find thermal biofeedback alone more efficacious than attention placebo. Such is not the case.

We can conclude on the basis of the outcome studies that TBF-W + AT has a stronger effect on migraine headache than the effects of attention placebo, thermal biofeedback alone, or relaxation of the musculature of face and head by frontal EMG biofeedback. However, one cannot firmly conclude that the effect of TBF-W + AT is different than that of generalized relaxation. Similar conclusions can be drawn for CVM biofeedback.

An alternative way to address the issues of specificity of effect and mechanism of action is to examine the potential relation between change in the physiological response targeted by the biofeedback training and

TABLE 4. Summary of Research on Relation of Biofeedback-Produced

	Jessup et al. (1976)		Friar & Beatty (1976)	Mullinix et al. (1978)	Lake et al. (1979)		
	TBF-W + AT	TBF-C + AT	CVM placebo	TBF-W placebo	TBF-W	TBF-W + RET	EMG
Was there change in the response system targeted?	+0.7°C	+1.0°C	Yes, reduced to 79% of BL.	Yes	Yes (37%)	Yes (29%)	Yes (85%)
Was the change in the response signficant?	No	No	Yes	?	No	No	Yes
Was there more change in the response system targeted than in other conditions?	No		Yes	Yes	NR	NR	NR
Was there a correlation between change in response and headache relief?	No	No	No	NR	No	No	No

Note. NR—not reported in article.
?—the answer on this point is unclear.
[a] Change in temp. for assigned groups NR; internal analysis based on temp change.
[b] Also r for % improvement and max. increase in temp. from BL to self control $r = 30$, $p < .10$; apparent better results with max. temp. > 96.5° F.
[c] For 7 patients with 40% + reduction, sig. corr. $r > .7$) between CVM and HA parameters.
[d] HA monitoring control also showed temp. increase.

headache relief. If there is a specific effect, one would expect to find more change in the physiological response targeted by the specific biofeedback training than in other treatment conditions. Moreover, one would expect to see some sort of dose–response relation such that greater physiological change was associated with more headache relief and vice versa. Carrying this line of reasoning a step further, the absence of a dose–response relation might imply the lack of a specific effect and likewise imply the mechanism of action is either some generalized relaxation or an attention placebo effect. The findings of the various studies on these issues are summarized in Table 4.

Examining Table 4, one can see that in almost every instance, there was change in the physiological response for which biofeedback was given. The exceptions were the lack of EEG alpha change in the Cohen et al. (1980) study, and the increase in hand temperature found by Jessup et al. (1976) in a group being trained to lower temperature.

Physiological Change and Headache Relief

Elmore & Tarsky (1981)		Largen et al. (1981)		Gauthier et al. (1981)				Blanchard et al. (1983)	Jurish et al. (1983)
CVM	TBF-W	TBF-W + AT	TBF-C + AT	TBF-W	TBF-C	Temp. Art inc.	Temp. Art dec.	TBF-W + AT	TBF − W + AT
Yes 36%	Yes +2.8°C	Yes + 1.0°C (+3.0°C)	Yes −0.9°C (−0.6°C)	Yes 109% increase (77%)	Yes 166% increase (67%)	Yes 71% increase (60%)	Yes 33% increase (53%)	Yes	Yes Self control of temp. +3.5°F.
Yes	Yes	Yes	Yes	Yes	Yes	No	No	Yes	Yes
CMV > TBF 36% vs. 8% on CVM TBF > CVM +2.8°C vs. −1.6°C		TBF > TBF			Not reported			N/A	N/A
	NR	No signficant correlation between temp. and HA change.		No signficant correlations between temperature change and HA change.				Significant corr.[b] between % improvement in HA and number sessions in which temp. increased. r = 30, p < .05	

However, on the more crucial question of whether there was more change in response in a group given biofeedback training for that response than in other groups, four studies failed to report it. For the other 13 studies, there was significantly more change in frontal EMG when it was targeted than in other conditions in all five instances. However, in only 5 of 11 instances did thermal biofeedback, with or without AT, lead to significantly more physiological change in the targeted group than found in other groups. Finally in five of six instances, there was more change in temporal artery vasomotor activity when it was targeted than found in comparison groups. Thus whereas investigators have been able to obtain reliably the differential targeted response change with EMG and CVM biofeedback, in less than half of the cases has this been true with thermal biofeedback.

The number of instances when there has been a significant correlation between change in a physiological response, trained through biofeedback and change in headache activity are very few: Blanchard, Andrasik, Neff, et al., (1983) found a low but significant correlation ($r = .30$) between the number of sessions in which there was any temperature increase and the percentage of reduction in headache activity. They also

TABLE 4. (*Continued*)

	Cohen et al. (1980)			Attfield & Peck (1979)		Kewman & Robers (1980)		
	TBF-W	EMG	CVM	EEG Alpha	TBF-W Relax	TBF-W		TBF-C
Was there change in the response system targeted?	Yes 1.2°C	Yes	Yes 6%	No	Yes	[a] TBF-W−1 +0.7°C	TBF-W −2 −0.3°C	TBF-C −0.7°C
Was the change in the response signficant?	Yes .05	?	Yes .05	No	?	NR	NR	NR
Was there more change in the response system targeted than in other conditions?	No	Yes	No	No	Yes TBF > relax.	TBD-W1 > TBF-W-2	>	TBF-C01 TBF-C10
Was there a correlation between change in response and headache relief?	No	No	No	No	No	NR; however, groups who increased temp. had more HA relief than TBF-C.		

Note. NR—not reported in article.
?—the answer on this point is unclear.
[a] Change in temp. for assigned groups NR; internal analysis based on temp change.
[b] Also r for % improvement and max. increase in temp. from BL to self control $r = 30$, $p < .10$; apparent better results with max. temp. > 96.5 °F.
[c] For 7 patients with 40% + reduction, sig. corr. $r > .7$) between CVM and HA parameters.
[d] HA monitoring control also showed temp. increase.

found a trend ($p < .10$) between the maximum volitional temperature increase and the percentage of reduction in headache activity ($r = .23$). In that report, *Blanchard, Andrasik, Neff, et al.* (1983c) also noted an apparent threshold effect in that patients who reached 96.6°F or higher tended to be more likely to be improved (85.7%).

Sargent *et al.* (1986) found no correlations for temperature and headache relief but did find significant (values not reported) correlations within the EMG biofeedback treated group between EMG levels and

Bild & Adams (1980)		Gauthier et al., (1983)		Gamble & Elder (1983)		Reading (1983)		Sargent et al. (1986)		
CVM	EMG	CVM	CVM	EMG	TBF – C temporal	EMG	TBF-W	TBF-W + AT EMG AT		
Yes 48% reduct.	Yes 19% reduct.	Yes at least 40%.	Yes at least 30%.	Yes	Yes	Yes	Yes	Yes	Yes	Yes
								Approximately 2/3 of all Ss could raise 1.5°F in 1 min. Also, avg, 2.7°F increase in feedback session.[d]		
Yes	Yes	Significant reduction in CVM variability in both groups. 36% 45%		Sig. Reduct.	Sig. Reduct.	Yes	No	Temp. increases significant. EMG decrease significant.		
CVM > EMG on vasomotor EMG > CVM on EMG		CVM-Constrict more successful than CVM-Dilate P < .05.		Those receiving FB reduced EMG more than those not receiving it.		Signficant decrease in EMG only for EMG BF group. Significant increase in temp. for all groups.		No Yes No EMG Group sig. better on EMG.		
NR	NR	No. significant correlation between change in CVM-variability and HA[c]		No correlation of change scores reported. Significant EMG & duration of HA (r = .42) and temporal temp. & duration (r = .58)		None reported.		No significant correlations of temp. change and HA change. Some correlations between HA variables and EMG levels with lag 1, but not lag 0.		

headache levels 4 weeks later (lag-1). Gamble & Elder (1983) report significant correlations between frontal EMG levels and duration of headache ($r = .42$) (implying longer headaches were associated with higher levels of EMG) and between temporal artery temperature and headache duration ($r = .58$).

Some further observations on the Sargent et al. (1986) study, contributed by Sargent are as follows:

> the greatest degree of hand temperature change occurred during the stabilization period [baseline] as contrasted to the practice period [feedback or other training]. There was no significant difference in magnitude of temperature change across the four groups: no treatment, autogenic phrases,

EMG biofeedback, and thermal biofeedback. Also all groups became significantly faster in raising hand temperature 1.5°F during the stabilization period
and reached the highest temperature in practice as the study pro-
gressed. . . . *All this indicates that all groups had hand temperature changes of
equal magnitude.* Thus, the possibility of a common physiological mechanism
[among the four conditions] may exist while the differences in training among
the groups may be psychological. (italics added)

Finally, we might note that in the Kewman & Roberts (1980) study,
based on their internal analysis, those groups that increased hand temperature (by as little as 0.3°C) had more headache relief than the group
whose hand temperature decreased (-0.7°C).

Two other studies related to this issue should be mentioned. Fahrion
(1979) strongly advocated training headache patients undergoing TBF-
W + AT to two criteria: the ability to increase temperature at the rate
of 1°F/min. and the ability to maintain hand temperature above 95.5°F
for 10 minutes. If one assumes that the 42 migraineurs he described in
his paper had, in fact, been trained to these criteria (this point is never
made explicitly), then one finds 81% of patients at least slightly improved
or better, and 59.5% at least moderately improved. This is slightly below
the average level of improvement found for TBF-W + AT in uncontrolled studies (see Table 1).

In another study on this topic, Libo & Arnold (1983) reported on
the follow-up of patients, including 7 with migraine headache and 15
with combined headache, who were given thermal biofeedback and/or
frontal EMG biofeedback. At a follow-up, conducted by a mail survey,
1 to 5 years after treatment, there was a significant relation between self-
reported improvement or symptom return and having reached certain
biofeedback training criteria. For the thermal biofeedback training, the
criterion was 95°F. Of the 54 patients who received thermal biofeedback,
46% reached criterion whereas 54% did not. Of those reaching criterion
96% (24/25) reported themselves as remaining improved whereas only
76% (22/29) of those who did not reach criterion were improved ($p = .04$).

Unfortunately there are a number of problems with this study that
reduce its value on this issue: (a) we do not know the specific results
for the vascular headache patients separately; (b) most patients received
thermal and EMG biofeedback and various forms of relaxation thus
clouding the issue of to what to attribute improvement; (c) a global self-
report of degree of improvement, at least by headache patients, markedly overestimates improvement calculated from a daily diary (Blanchard, Andrasik, Neff, Jurish, & O'Keefe, 1981), thus further clouding
interpretation of the results.

In sum, although the idea that, within the thermal biofeedback
training of vascular headache patients, the patients should be trained
to a certain temperature criterion level or be able to produce a specified

rate of temperature increase has its very vocal proponents, the empirical evidence to demonstrate that such training makes a clinical difference is weak at best. Clear, prospective, experimental evidence on this issue would help clarify mechanism issues, at least for the most popular biofeedback treatment for vascular headache.

Two other studies have attempted to elucidate the possible physiological basis for the effect of thermal biofeedback on migraine headache. In the first, Mathew, Largen, Dobbins, Meyer, Sakai, & Claghorn (1980) studied regional cerebral blood flow (rCBF) by means of 133Xe inhalation in 11 migraineurs. Six of the 11 were trained in hand warming using TBF + AT + relaxation training whereas the other 5 were trained in hand cooling. (As noted in Table 2 in the study by Largen et al., 1981, there were no differences in headache alleviation between the two conditions.) At a test session in which rCBF was measured, each group attempted to change hand temperature with the aid of biofeedback. The TBF-W group achieved a mean increase of 1.25°C whereas the TBF-C group achieved a mean decrease of 0.38°C; the temperature difference between the two groups was significant.

Results from the rCBF showed a significant increase in total left hemisphere CBF for the TBF-W and no difference for right hemisphere; the hemispheric changes for the TBF-C group were not significant. The difference between the two groups on left hemisphere CBF approached significance ($p = .08$). Of the 48 statistical tests done on the sample of 11 subjects for specific regional CBF changes, one was significant at the .01 level, one at .05, and one at .10. This level of significant findings is about what one would expect by chance.

Unfortunately, the Mathew et al. (1980) data present a dilemma since CBF data on much larger samples of headache patients from the same laboratory (Sakai & Meyer, 1978) show highly significant ($p < .001$) increases in total cerebral gray matter blood flow in migraineurs during a headache as opposed to during a headache-free state (approximately 31% greater). Thus the CBF effects of thermal biofeedback are the same as those of a headache, an increase in CBF. At one level, it seems difficult to attribute the therapeutic effectiveness of TBF-W to a physiological change that usually accompanies headache.

An alternative interpretation of these results, suggested by several of the reviewers of the Task Force Report, is that these results are consistent if one considers the stage of the migraine episode. It is clear that in classic migraine, the patient initially experiences a cerebral vasoconstrictive phase followed by the vasodilatory phase and the throbbing head pain. It has been assumed that sufferers of common migraine have the same blood flow changes.

Thus, if thermal biofeedback was used exclusively as an abortive technique, the warming of the hands and the attendant cerebral vasodilation might interrupt the prodromal, or vasoconstrictive phase, thus preventing the normal progression to a headache. Certainly there have been cases (Sargent, Green, & Walters, 1973) that reported of the ability of a patient to abort migraine headaches during the prodrome.

However, only 3 of 11 patients who completed treatment in the Largen *et al.* (1981) study had classic migraine. Only those three could have reliably used the hand warming or hand cooling in an abortive fashion; no data are presented that speak to this issue. Furthermore, because classic migraine accounts for only about 10% of the total migraine population, whereas roughly 50% to 60% benefit from TBF-W + AT treatment, it seems clear that more than just aborting of headache is involved in the beneficial outcome. Also no data exist, to the best of our knowledge, showing better outcome for classic migraine than for common migraine.

A final complication in this matter is that in a separate later report from Largen and his associates (Claghorn, Mathew, Largen, & Meyer, 1981), several significant correlations were reported between changes in some CBF parameters associated with hand warming and changes in headache parameters. This supports a potential specific mechanism even though there were no significant correlations between hand temperature parameters and headache changes (Largen *et al.*, 1981).

It seems obvious that much further research is needed to replicate and clarify these intriguing findings.

In the second study (Sovak, Kunzel, Sternbach, & Dalessio, 1978), 5 normal nonheadache subjects and 10 migraineurs were given a course of TBF-W + AT until they could reliably produce at least a 2°C increase in hand temperature within 15 minutes. Of the migraineurs, eight were rated as improved based on a reduction (of at least 50%) of headache activity measured by headache diary whereas two were unimproved. At a test session, peripheral blood flow was measured in the hand, superficial temporal artery, and supraorbital artery along with heart rate (HR) while patients rested quietly, volitionally increased hand temperature, or had hand temperature increased by a flow of very warm air.

Results showed a decrease in HR (about 4 BPM) for normals and successful migraineurs during volitional hand warming and an increase (about 5 BPM) for these groups during external hand warming. The two unsuccessful migraineurs showed no change in HR. Blood flow to the hands of the normals increased substantially more under both conditions than it did in either group of migraineurs.

With volitional (biofeedback-assisted) hand warming, blood flow (that is pulse volume) to both cranial sites decreased in the normals and successful migraineurs whereas it was essentially unchanged in the unsuccessful migraineurs. Under the external heating, pulse volume increased in the two cranial sites for the normals and for the unsuccessful migraineurs whereas the successful migraineurs exhibited a decrease in blood flow.

These results are interpreted by Sovak *et al.* (1978) and later by Dalessio, Kunzel, Sternbach, & Sovak (1979) as evidence that successful biofeedback training elicits a "conditioned adaptation-relaxation reflex" that represents "a retraining of the autonomic nervous system to produce a reduction in sympathetic tone" (Dalessio *et al.*, 1979, p. 2104).

Although the directions of group mean data are consistent with the authors' interpretation, inspection of the individual subject data, especially the pulse volume results, leads to a somewhat different interpretation. For example, although the group mean for the supraorbital pulse volume data shows an overall decrease, three of the eight successful migraineurs showed increases. For temporal artery pulse volume, data were missing for three of eight subjects. Of the remaining five, three showed decreases whereas two showed increases. It is thus not at all clear that the reported changes in cranial blood flow for the successful migraineurs are as clearcut as the article concludes.

We are thus left with what, in our opinion, are hints of what the physiological mechanisms might be in thermal biofeedback rather than compelling empirical evidence.

Childhood Migraine

Although headache is usually considered to be an illness of adults, it is clear that some children and adolescents suffer from migraine headache. It has been estimated (Bille, 1981) that childhood migraine afflicts 2.5% of children between the ages of 7 and 9 years with an increasing prevalence with advancing age up to 5.3% for children between the ages of 13 and 15 years. We have observed that many of our patients claim to have first had their migraine headaches as adolescents.

Bille (1981) in a 30-year follow-up study showed that 38% of children between the ages of 9 and 15 years continued to have migraine headaches over a 30-year period. Approximately 62% experienced a spontaneous remission during the years of adolescence and young adulthood. However, of that 62%, 35% (22% of the original sample) had a recurrence of migraine in the fourth decade of life.

As we will note later, there is evidence that younger migraineurs do better in TBF-W + AT than older ones (see p. 21). This finding extends down below young adulthood into childhood and adolescence. Over the past few years there have been a few small-scale uncontrolled and large-scale controlled outcome studies of the biofeedback treatment of childhood migraine. The large-scale controlled reports are summarized in Table 5.

Examining these five published studies of the biofeedback treatment

TABLE 5. Biofeedback Treatment of

	Diamond & Franklin (1975)	Werder (1978)	Labbe & Williamson (1984)	
Number of patients	32	4	28	
Age, $\bar{X}$	N/A	13.8	10.8	
Range	N/A	10–17	7–16	
Sex M/F	N/A	1/3	14/14	
Years of HA, $\bar{X}$	N/A	4	N/A	
Referred by:	N/A	Physician	Pediatrician, self-referral	
Diagnosed by:	Neurologist-PI	PI	Physician, specific inclusion criteria	
Treatment(s)	Autogenic training, relaxation, TBF, EMG, BF, regular home practice.	TFB + AT Home practice with temperature trainer.	TFB + AT HA monitoring Home practice in hand-warming	
Type of Study	Single-group Outcome	Single-group Outcome	Controlled Group Outcome	
BL Length	N/A	N/A	4 weeks	
HA Diary	N/A	Yes	Yes	
by whom:		Child	Child	
Number of sessions	N/A	5 or 6	10	
Length of treatment	N/A	N/A	7 Weeks	
Results			TBF + AT	Mon.
HA index	—	—	79%*	−4%
HA frequency	—	85%	66%	−2%
HA intensity	—	—	65%	−3%
HA duration	—	98%	64%	−11%
Meds	—	70%	96%	48%
Global rating	Yes	No		
% Sample Improved	26/32 = 81	4/4 = 100	13/14 = 93	1/14 = 7
Follow-up length	N/A	4 Months-2 Years	6 Months	
% sample	97	100	46	
Change in HA index	N/A	42%	−144%	
End of treatment			88% sample improved at	
to follow-up			end of treatment; only 62% of sample improved at follow-up.	

[a] Olness & MacDonald (1981) report they treated 15 children by a combination of thermal biofeedback and self-hypnosis, but they describe results for only 3 of these children. This study is not included in the table because of the limited available data

[b] One-half of children received booster treatments during follow-up

[c] Extrapolated from Figure 1, page 124.

Migraine Headache in Children[a]

Andrasik *et al.* (1984)			Mehegan et al. (1984)	Werder & Sargent (1984)
48			20	21
11.2			10.2	N/A
7–16			7–12	7–17
22/26			10/10	N/A
4.8			2.7	5.3
Pediatrician, self-referral			Pediatric neurologist	Physician
Pediatric neurologist, specific inclusion and exclusion ciriteria			Pediatric neurologist, specific inclusion criteria	Neurologist-PI
TBF & at home practice with temperature trainer	Relaxation home practice with cassette tape recordings	HA monitoring	EMG, BF, relaxation, and behavior therapy	TBF & AT, EMG, BF, Relaxation, self-awareness, and guided imagery— home practice with biofeedback trainers
Controlled Group Outcome			Group multiple baseline	Single-group Outcome
4 weeks			3, 6, 9, or 12 weeks	N/A
Yes			Yes	Yes
Child			Child	Child or parent
10			9	Mean of 7
8 wks.			10 wks.	Mean of 8 wks.
TBF + AT	REL	MON		
82%	45%	−5%	93%	N/A
N/A	N/A	N/A	79%	N/A
N/A	N/A	N/A	74%	N/A
N/A	N/A	N/A	84%	73[c]
N/A	N/A	N/A	83%	N/A
N/A	N/A	N/A	N/A	N/A
85	60	25	85	95
	6 mos.		12 mos.	24–36 mos.
	90		100	57
80%	65%	N/A	91%	92%
2%[b]	20[b]		−2%	19%

of childhood migraine, one finds a very high degree of improvement: the percentage of children displaying marked improvement by treatment's end ranges from 81% to 95%. This is considerably higher than the average for adults. We can conclude from these data that TBF-W + AT is superior to headache monitoring (Andrasik *et al.*, 1984; Labbe & Williamson, 1984) and that biofeedback might yield a slight edge to relaxation (Andrasik, *Attanasio*, Blanchard, *et al.*,1984). Beyond that, the research is not available to make empirically based statements. However, one might seriously entertain the idea that TBF-W + AT is the treatment of choice for childhood migraine, as Diamond and Franklin (1975) suggested.

Four of the five studies showed good maintenance of treatment effects out to as long as three years for available subjects. The Labbé and Williamson (1984) study presents somewhat contradictory data. They showed a substantial deterioration in headache abatement from the end of treatment to a follow-up 6 months later. The sample as a whole showed large deterioration; on an individual subject basis, their results showed 88% of the sample improved at end of treatment but only 62% by the 6-month follow-up. This represents a decline of 30%. Why this occurred is not clear.

In conclusion, one would hope for continued research in this area, and especially for comparisons of TBF-W + AT to other self-regulatory therapies, to drugs, and to good attention placebo conditions.

Combined Headache

When one turns from pure migraine headache to combined migraine and tension headache, one finds a marked drop-off in the level of available research evidence on efficacy. Instead of 21 controlled group outcome studies, one finds only 3, all of which are somewhat problematic. In Table 6 are summarized the group outcome studies with combined headache in which biofeedback has been used as a treatment. (We might note that several of the studies presented earlier in Table 1 included some patients with combined headache. However, because separate results for the patients with combined headache were not presented, these studies are not repeated in Table 6.)

From Table 6, one can see that combined headache has typically been treated with a combination of therapies. With regards to the biofeedback treatments, one study used only EMG biofeedback, two used only thermal biofeedback, and two used both EMG and thermal biofeedback. No study has used biofeedback alone. Relaxation training was included in all studies and autogenic training was always included with the thermal biofeedback. Overall level of headache reduction is remark-

TABLE 6. Summary of Group Outcome Studies of the Biofeedback Treatment of Combined Headache

		Bakal et al. (1981)	Strobel et al. (1981)	Mathew (1981)	Blanchard et al. (1982)	Jurish et al. (1983)
Patient Characteristics	Age, $\bar{X}$	36.2[b]	N/A	42.6	36.5	37.2
	Range	N/A	N/A	N/A	23–65	N/A
	Sex M/F	10/35	N/A	5/92	1/27	6/19
	Years of HA, $\bar{X}$	16.8	N/A	N/A	N/A	19.6
	Physician referred	Yes	Yes	Yes	Yes	Yes
Source	Self-referred	No	Yes	Yes	Yes	Yes
Number started		45	N/A	145	31	25
Number completed		45	131	97	28	20
% Dropout		0	N/A	33 (40 in BF)	10	20
Diagnosed by:		Neurologist	N/A	Neurologist	Neurologist & PI	Neurologist & PI
Diagnostic criteria		N/A	N/A	Ad hoc committee	Ad hoc committee	Ad hoc committee
Type of study		Single-group outcome (17 tension, 15 migraine, 13 combined HA)	Single-group outcome	Controlled-group outcome BF, abortive drugs, amitriptyline	Single-group outcome with crossover	Controlled group outcome clinic treatment vs. home treatment
Treatment(s)		HA monitoring-3 wks, relaxation training, EMG biofeedback, coping skills trng., imagery, cognitive restructuring.	EMG biofeedback, thermal BF, progressive relaxation, autogenic training, QR.	BF-EMG biofeedback, thermal biofeedback, progressive relaxation, autogenic training.	Progressive muscle relaxation, then thermal BF with autogenics for relaxation failures.	Progressive muscle relaxation, thermal BF + autogenics 10 sessions, 16 session in clinic vs. 3 sessions + home tapes.

Continued

TABLE 6. (*Continued*)

	12	8	10	R 10	BF-12	16 vs. 3
Number of sessions	12	8	10	R 10	BF-12	16 vs. 3
Average length of session	N/A	1 hour	1 hour	50 min.		50 min.
Fixed protocol	Yes	Yes	Yes	Yes		Yes
Training to criteria	No	NR	No	No		No
Home practice	Yes, relaxation with tape, coping skills homework.	Yes, relaxation exercises with tapes.	Yes, home temp. trainer.	R—audio tape BF—thermometer + relaxation tape.		Yes, thermometer and audio tape of relaxation.
Duration of treatment	16 wks.	NR	NR	R—8 wks. BF—9 wks.		8 Wks.
Baseline length	3 wks?	N/A	1 mo.	4 wks.		4 wks.
HA diary	Yes	?	Yes	Yes		Yes
Evidence of BF training	No	NR	No	Yes		Yes, in clinic-3.5°F rise in self-control by session 10.
Multiple trainers	N/A	N/A	N/A	Yes (6)		Yes (4)
Average experience of trainers	N/A	N/A	N/A	1 yr.		2 yrs.
Trainer effect	N/A	N/A	N/A	No		No
Trainer present or absent	N/A	N/A	N/A	R—present.	BF—absent.	Present in relaxation, absent in BF.
Results % Reduction			BF / Abortive / Amitrip	R	BF	
HA index	46%[a]	N/A	48 / 18 / 60	22*	53*	52[d]*
HA frequency	N/A	N/A	N/A / N/A / N/A	N/A	39*	N/A
HA intensity	N/A	N/A	N/A / N/A / N/A	14*		35*
HA duration	46*	N/A	N/A / N/A / N/A	30*	78*	138*
Meds	53*	N/A	N/A / N/A / N/A	15*	54	52
Global rating	N/A	60% at least moderately improved[c]	N/A / N/A / N/A	N/A		No
% sample improved	60	N/A		6/28 = 22	9/14 = 64	15/20 = 75

Table 6. (*Continued*)

	Bakal et al. (1981)	Strobel et al. (1981)	Mathew (1981)	Blanchard et al. (1982)	Jurish et al. (1983)
Follow-up duration	6 mos.	Up to 2 yrs.	3–4 mos.	1 yr.	N/A
Maintenance conditions	NR	NR	NR	Half received 6 boosters, half did not.	
% sample available	44.4	NR	NR	31/50 = 62	
% reductioon vs. BL	58	NR	BF 48	Booster—82 Nonbooster—57	
% reduction vs. end of treatment	21	NR		Booster— +57 Nonbooster— 62	
HA diary or global rating	Diary	NR	Diary	Diary	

Note: N/A—Not Available.
* % reduction is signficant
[a] No difference in outcome for different HA types.
[b] Characteristics of whole sample as of end of follow-up.
[c] As of last follow-up point.
[d] Combined results for two conditions that did not differ.

ably similar across the five studies, averaging 51.8%, with a range of 46% to 60%.

With regards to relative efficacy, a combined EMG, TBF-W + AT, and relaxation training Mathew (1981) is apparently superior to treatment with ergot abortives and analgesics but inferior to amitriptyline. Unfortunately, direct between-group comparisons were not made in the study. TBF-W + AT also is apparently superior to relaxation alone in the sequential comparison reported by Blanchard et al. (1982b). Nine of the 14 relaxation failures who subsequently received TBF + AT became improved (64%). In unpublished data from our laboratory, we (Appelbaum et al., 1984) have shown the combination of TBF-W + AT and relaxation superior to headache monitoring. There have been no comparisons of biofeedback therapy to placebo conditions for combined headache. Moreover, the one comparison of TBF-W + AT to relaxation is not a true experimental comparison (Blanchard et al., 1982b).

Thus on balance, preliminary evidence is very encouraging for biofeedback-based treatment of combined headache. However, well controlled studies remain to be done. The effects of the biofeedback training apart from various relaxation elements have not been determined.

Baskin (1985, personal communication) called attention to a potentially important issue in the study of treatment efficacy with combined headache, the problem of potential analgesic abuse and analgesic rebound headache. In his view much of the total headache activity found in patients diagnosed as combined headache is the result of so-called analgesic rebound, or a headache resulting from decreasing blood levels of analgesics. Patients may then treat this headache with new doses of analgesics, perpetuating the cycle. These analgesic rebound headaches may confound treatment outcome results.

Specificity and Mechanism

No work available.

Patient Selection Factors

The previous findings from the Diamond Headache Clinic (Diamond & Montrose, 1984; Diamond et al., 1979, p. 22) on migraine headache potentially apply, because the patient population included both migraine and combined headache.

SUNYA Headache Project. The SUNYA Headache Project prediction studies have treated combined headache as a separate population in the relaxation studies but merged results for the TBF-W + AT treatment condition. In the most recent study (Blanchard et al., 1985) for combined headache patients treated with relaxation, Scale 3 of the MMPI was the best predictor: 50% of patients scoring 59 or less were improved whereas 69% of patients scoring 64 or higher were unimproved (<25% reduction in headache).

For combined headache patients treated with relaxation and TBF-W + AT, age is a significant predictor and is radically different than for migraine or tension headache. For patients 40 years or older, 64% are improved as compared to only 14% who are unimproved. For patients 35 or younger, only 52% are improved versus 41% who are unimproved. Scale 3 of the MMPI is also a predictor: 73% patients with a T score of 54 or less were improved versus 53% with T scores of 70 or higher who were unimproved.

Long-Term Follow-up

Reported follow-ups of 2 years by Stroebel *et al.* (1981) and 1 year by Andrasik, Blanchard *et al.* (1984) reveal reasonably good maintenance of end of treatment effects, as noted in Table 3.

Summary

Combined headache is a prevalent but insufficiently studied disorder. Preliminary evidence suggests biofeedback-based combination treatments are efficacious, leading to an average reduction of about 52% in headache activity. The isolated effects of biofeedback have not been clearly evaluated although TBF-W + AT appears to be more efficacious than headache monitoring and relaxation training. Treatment effects apparently hold up well over time (up to 2 years).

Cluster Headache

As we noted earlier the evidence, in terms of number of studies, for clinical efficacy of combined headache is much smaller than that for migraine. When one turns to cluster headache, the evidence becomes smaller still. There is only one single-group outcome study (Blanchard, Andrasik, Jurish, & Teders, 1982) with more than 10 patients. The remainder of the reports are of one to five cases and are typically at the level of anecdotal case report. Nevertheless, the available research on the treatment of cluster headache with biofeedback is summarized in Table 7.

Of the five reports on the treatment of cluster headache by biofeedback, two are reports on single cases of secondary chronic cluster headache, two are anecdotal reports on small series (4 or 5 patients) and one report includes 11 patients. The two case reports are well documented and clearly show marked improvement in the single patient studied.

TABLE 7. Summary of Biofeedback Treatments for Cluster Headache

	Blanchard et al. (1982)	Adler & Adler (1975)	Fritz & Fehmi (1983)	Hoelscher & Lichstein (1983)	King & Arena (1984)
Number of cases	11	5	4	1	1
Sex M/F	7/4	N/A	N/A	Male	Male
Average age	44.5	N/A	N/A	61	69
Range	31–62	N/A	N/A	—	—
Years of HA	12.6	N/A	N/A	21	20
Episodic/Chronic	11/0	N/A	2/2	Secondary chronic	Secondary chronic
Length of BL	4 wks.	N/A	N/A	18 days	6 wks.
BL during HA	No	N/A	N/A	Yes	Yes
Treatment	10 sessions of progressive relaxation, followed by 12 sessions of TBF + AT (7 of 11 completed treatment.)	EMG, BF, followed by TBF accompanied by dynamic psychotherapy.	"Open focus," includes EEG biofeedback.	14 sessions of blood volume pulse biofeedback, constrict. & dilation over 7 wks.	TBF + AT plus marital contracting.

Number of sessions	22	5–60	N/A	14	7
Fixed protocol	Yes	No	NR	No	No
Home practice	Tape for Relaxation Therm. for TBF.	NR	NR	Practice at home what was done in lab.	Relaxation.
HA diary	Yes	NR	NR	Yes	Yes
Evidence of BF training	No	NR	NR	Yes	Yes, at least 2°F.
Number of therapists	4	1	NR	1	1
Length of follow-up	22–29 months	3½–5 years	NR	21 months	15 months
Results	3 of 7[a] who completed treatment were somewhat better—HA less severe, HA less frequent, could abort HA.	3 of 5 had at least 75% reduction in HA.	"Successful remission of pain episodes."	90%+ reduction in HA meds, 99% reduction in HA frequency.	From average 6/wk. PRN meds to none, 44% reduction in HA activity.

[a] 1 patient became chronic cluster.

The two small series report very good results with 60% (Adler & Adler, 1975) and 100% (Fritz & Fehmi, 1983) success rates. However, so few details are included that the value of these reports is diminished. For example, no patient characteristics and few details of treatment are given. Moreover, the method of evaluating outcome is not specified at all.

In the one medium size series (Blanchard, Andrasik, Jurish, & Teders, 1982), only 7 of the 11 patients completed treatment. Of these, three were somewhat improved at follow-ups of 2 to 2 1/2 years whereas one was markedly worse.

We are left with the following conclusions on the efficacy of biofeedback in the treatment of cluster headache: (a) there are no controlled evaluations of biofeedback as a treatment for cluster headache; (b) the one medium size uncontrolled series showed that 27% of cluster patients were somewhat better at a follow-up 2 to 2 1/2 years after treatment but no single patient could be called cured; (c) cephalic vasomotor biofeedback may be of some value in the treatment of chronic cluster headache.

Obviously, a great deal more research is needed before one could recommend biofeedback as a treatment for cluster headache.

COST-EFFECTIVENESS

There are virtually no data on the cost-effectiveness of biofeedback treatments of vascular headache. In one partially relevant study, Jurish *et al.* (1983) compared a clinic-based treatment, comprised of 16 individual treatment sessions in which thermal biofeedback and autogenic training were combined with training in progressive muscle relaxation, to a comparable largely home-based, self-administered treatment regimen, comprised of three individual treatment sessions augmented with audiotapes and manuals. Results showed the two treatments to be equally effective for migraine and combined headache patients. The home-based treatment program was significantly more cost effective.

Data from our laboratory (Blanchard, Jaccard, Andrasik, Guarnieri, & Jurish, 1985) is also relevant to this topic. We gathered retrospective medical cost data for the 2 years prior to patients beginning self-regulatory treatment for their chronic headaches. The patient sample, comprised of migraine, combined, and tension headache sufferers, received various combinations of biofeedback (thermal for the vascular patients, frontal EMG for the tension patients) and relaxation training. Similar cost data from follow-up 2 years after the completion of treatment showed that medical costs for headaches had been reduced by 94% ($\bar{X}$ pre $-$ \$955, $\bar{X}$ post $-$ \$55). These results would indicate that self-regulatory treatments for chronic headache may be cost-effective over a 2-year period, if treatment costs are under $900. Obviously, well-controlled evaluations are needed in this area.

FUTURE RESEARCH

There are four categories of future research needs in the area of the biofeedback treatment of vascular headache:

1. For both migraine and combined headache there needs to be additional controlled comparisons of biofeedback therapy with (a) credible placebo treatments; (b) other non-biofeedback-based self-regulatory treatments; and (c) appropriate prophylactic pharmacotherapy. In such comparisons, information should be gathered on efficacy and true cost-effectiveness. Such studies need to be conducted with sample sizes having sufficient power to deal meaningfully with possible findings of no significant difference.

2. For migraine and combined headache, there need to be more prospective, follow-up studies of lengths of at least 2 years or more.

3. There should be studies designed to optimize the self-regulatory treatment of chronic vascular headache. Assuming that thermal biofeedback combined with autogenic training is the best biofeedback treatment for vascular headache, we need, for example, empirical studies to test whether the addition of a cognitive therapy component would significantly improve overall efficacy.

4. There needs to be additional research to lead to a clearer understanding of the mechanisms, both psychological and psychophysiological, that are involved in the biofeedback treatments. Such understanding could lead to enhanced efficacy and/or to better matching of patients to treatment.

5. Finally, there needs to be research aimed at discovering whether there can be an appropriate, and perhaps optimal, blend of self-regulatory treatment with pharmacotherapy.

CONCLUSIONS

Migraine Headache

The strongest and most widespread evidence on efficacy is available for migraine headache. The following conclusions seem warranted.

1. Thermal biofeedback for hand warming combined with autogenic training is consistently superior to the mere daily monitoring of headaches.

2. Thermal biofeedback for hand warming combined with autogenic training is probably superior to thermal biofeedback alone or to frontal EMG biofeedback alone.

3. Thermal biofeedback for hand warming combined with autogenic training is possibly superior to psychological placebo treatments.

4. Thermal biofeedback for hand warming combined with autogenic training has not been shown to be consistently superior to various forms of relaxation training. However, TBF-W + AT does seem to convey an advantage over relaxation training in some cases.

5. Thermal biofeedback for hand warming combined with autogenic training is possibly superior to drug therapy consisting of ergot abortives and analgesics but has not been shown to be consistently superior to prophylactic drug therapy with propranolol.

6. The short-term headache relief effects of thermal biofeedback for hand warming combined with autogenic training appear to persist for at least 6 months and probably for at least 12 months.

7. Cephalic vasomotor biofeedback is consistently superior to daily headache monitoring.

8. Although only limited data are available, thermal biofeedback for hand warming combined with autogenic training may be the treatment of choice for childhood migraine.

9. The mechanisms by which thermal biofeedback combined with autogenic training work are unclear at this point.

Combined Headache

There are much less data available on the biofeedback treatment of combined headache than on the treatment of migraine. Thus, the one conclusion on this type of headache should be seen as tentative.

1. A combination thermal biofeedback for hand warming combined with autogenic training and with various forms of relaxation training is superior to daily headache monitoring and to relaxation training alone.

Cluster Headache

There are no controlled studies of the biofeedback treatment of cluster headache. The scant published evidence suggests:

1. Chronic cluster headache may be more responsive to treatment than episodic cluster headache.

2. A combination of thermal biofeedback for hand warming with autogenic training and relaxation training may be slightly beneficial.

REFERENCES

Ad Hoc Committee on the Classification of Headache. (1962). Classification of Headache. *Journal of American Medical Association, 179,* 717–718.

Adler, C. S., & Adler, S. M. (1975). Biofeedback psychotherapy for the treatment of headaches: A 5-year follow-up. *Headache, 16,* 189–191.

Andrasik, F., Attanasio, V., Blanchard, E. B., Burke, E., Kabela, E., McCarran, M., Blake, D. D., & Rosenblum, E. L. (1984, November). *Behavioral treatment of pediatric migraine headache.* Paper presented at the meeting of the Association for Advancement of Behavior Therapy, Philadelphia, PA.

Andrasik, F., Blanchard, E. B., Neff, D. F., & Rodichok, L. D. (1984). Biofeedback and relaxation training for chronic headache: A controlled comparison of booster treatments and regular contacts for long-term maintenance. *Journal of Consulting and Clinical Psychology, 52,* 609–615.

Andreychuk, T., & Skriver, C. (1975). Hypnosis and biofeedback in the treatment of migraine headache. *International Journal of Clinical and Experimental Hypnosis, 23,* 172–183.

Appelbaum, K. A., Blanchard, E. B., and Andrasik, F., & Evans, D. D. (1984, November). *A controlled evaluation of home-based vs. clinic-based treatment of chronic headache.* Paper presented at the 14th Annual Meeting of the Association for the Advancement of Behavior Therapy, Philadelphia, PA.

Attfield, M., & Peck, D. F. (1979). Temperature self-regulation and relaxation with migraine patients and normals. *Behaviour Research and Therapy, 17,* 591–595.

Bakal, D. A., Demjen, S., & Kaganov, J. A. (1981). Cognitive behavioral treatment of chronic headache. *Headache, 21,* 81–86.

Bild, R., & Adams, H. E. (1980). Modification of migraine headaches by cephalic blood volume pulse and EMG biofeedback. *Journal of Consulting and Clinical Psychology, 48,* 51–57.

Bille, B. (1981). Migraine in childhood and its prognosis. *Cephalalgia, 1,* 71–75.

Blanchard, E. B., & Andrasik, F. (1982). Psychological assessment and treatment of headache: Recent developments and emerging issues. *Journal of Consulting and Clinical Psychology, 50,* 859–879.

Blanchard, E. B., Andrasik, F., Jurish, S. E., & Teders, S. J. (1962). The treatment of cluster headache with relaxation and thermal biofeedback. *Biofeedback and Self-Regulation, 7,* 185–191.

Blanchard, E. B., Theobald, D. E., Williamson, D. A., Silver, B. V., & Brown, D. A. (1978) Temperature biofeedback in the treatment of migraine headaches. *Archives of General Psychiatry, 35,* 581–588.

Blanchard, E. B., Andrasik, F., Ahles, T. A., Teders, S. J., & O'Keefe, D. M. (1980). Migraine and tension headache: A meta-analytic review. *Behavior Therapy, 11,* 613–631.

Blanchard, E. B., Andrasik, F., Neff, D. F., Jurish, S. E., & O'Keefe, D. M. (1981). Social validation of the headache diary. *Behavior Therapy, 12,* 711–715.

Blanchard, E. B., Andrasik, F., Jurish, S. E., & Teders, S. J. (1982a). The treatment of cluster headache with relaxation and thermal biofeedback. *Biofeedback and Self-Regulation, 7,* 185–191.

Blanchard, E. B., Andrasik, F., Neff, D. F., Teders, S. J., Pallmeyer, T. P., Arena, J. G., Jurish, S. E., Saunders, N. L., & Rodichok, L. D. (1982b). Sequential comparisons of relaxation training and biofeedback in the treatment of three kinds of chronic headache or, the machines may be necessary some of the time. *Behaviour Research and Therapy, 20,* 469–481.

Blanchard, E. B., Andrasik, F., Neff, D. F., Arena, J. G., Ahles, T. A., Jurish, S. E., Pallmeyer, T. P., Saunders, N. L., Teders, S. J., Barron, K. D., & Rodichok, L. D. (1982c). Biofeedback and relaxation training with three kinds of headache: Treatment effects and their prediction. *Journal of Consulting and Clinical Psychology, 50,* 562–575.

Blanchard, E. B., Andrasik, F., Arena, J. G., Neff, D. F., Jurish, S. E., Teders, S. J., Barron, K. D., & Rodichok, L. D. (1983a). Prediction of outcome from the non-pharmacological treatment of chronic headache. *Neurology, 33,* 1596–1603.

Blanchard, E. B., Andrasik, F., Arena, J. G., Neff, D. F., Saunders, N. L., Jurish, S. E., Teders, S. J., & Rodichok, L. D. (1983b). Psychophysiological responses as predictors of response to behavioral treatment of chronic headache. *Behavior Therapy, 14,* 357–374.

Blanchard E. B., Andrasik, F., Neff, D. F., Saunders, N. L., Arena, J. G., Pallmeyer, T. P., Teders, S. J., Jurish, S. E., & Rodichok, L. D. (1983c). Four process studies in the behavioral treatment of chronic headache. *Behaviour Research and Therapy, 21,* 209–220.

Blanchard, E. B., Andrasik, F., Evans, D. D., Neff, D. F., Appelbaum, K. A., & Rodichok, L. D. (1985a). Behavioral treatment of 250 chronic headache patients: A clinical replication series. *Behavior Therapy, 16,* 308–327.

Blanchard, E. B., Andrasik, F., Appelbaum, K. A., Evans, D. D., Jurish, S. E., Teders, S. J., Rodichok, L. D., & Barron, K. D. (1985b). The efficacy and cost-effectiveness of minimal-therapist-contact, non-drug treatments of chronic migraine and tension headache. *Headache, 25,* 214–220.

Blanchard, E. B., Jaccard, J., Andrasik, F., Guarnieri, P., & Jurish, S. E. (1985). Reduction in headache patients' medical expenses associated with biofeedback and relaxation treatments. *Biofeedback and Self-Regulation, 10,* 63–68.

Bruyn, G. W. (1983). Epidemiology of migraine, "a personal review." *Headache, 23,* 127–133.

Claghorn, J. F., Mathew, R. J., Largen, J. W., & Meyer, J. S. (1981). Directional effects of skin temperature self-regulation cerebral blood flow in normal subjects and migraine patients. *American Journal of Psychiatry, 138,* 1182–1187.

Blanchard, E. B., Andrasik, F., Ahles, T. A., Teders, S. J., & O'Keefe, D. M. (1980). Cohen, M. J., McArthur, D. L., & Rickles, W. H. (1980). Comparison of four biofeedback treatments for migraine headache: Physiological and headache variables. *Psychosomatic Medicine, 42,* 463–480.

Cook, T. D., & Campbell, D. T. (1979). *Quasi-experimentation: Design and analysis issues for field settings.* Chicago, IL: Rand McNally.

Dalessio, D. J. (Ed.) (1980) *Wolff's headache and other head pain* (4th ed.). New York: Oxford University Press.

Dalessio, D. J., Kunzel, M., Sternbach, R., & Sovak, M. (1979). Conditioned adaptation-relaxation reflex in migraine therapy. *Journal of American Medical Association, 242,* 2102–2104.

Daly, E. J., Donn, P. A., Galliher, N. J., & Zimmerman, J. S. (1983). Biofeedback applications to migraine and tension headaches: A double-blinded outcome study. *Biofeedback and Self-Regulation, 8,* 135–152.

Diamond, S., & Franklin, M. (1975). Biofeedback: Choice of treatment in childhood migraine. In W. Luthe & F. Antonelli (Eds.), *Therapy in psychosomatic medicine* (Vol. 4, pp. 000–000). Rome: Autogenic Therapy.

Diamond, S., & Montrose, D. (1984). The value of biofeedback in the treatment of chronic headache: A four-year retrospective study. *Headache, 24,* 5–18.

Diamond, S., Diamond-Falk, J. R., & DeVeno, T. (1978). Biofeedback in the treatment of vascular headache. *Biofeedback and Self-Regulation, 3,* 385–408.

Diamond, S., Medina, J., Diamond-Falk, J., & DeVeno, T. (1979). The value of biofeedback in the treatment of chronic headache: A five-year retrospective study. *Headache, 19,* 90–96.

Elmore, A. M., & Tursky, B. (1981). A comparison of two psychophysiological approaches to the treatment of migraine. *Headache, 21,* 93–101.

Fahrion, S. L. (1977). Autogenic biofeedback treatment for migraine. *Mayo Clinic Proceedings, 52,* 776–784.

Ford, M., Stroebel, C., Strong, P., & Szarek, B. (1982, March). *Predictors of long-term successful outcome with Quieting Response training.* Paper presented at 13th Annual Meeting, Biofeedback Society of America, Chicago, IL.

Friar, L. R., & Beatty, J. (1976). Migraine: Management by trained control of vasoconstriction. *Journal of Consulting and Clinical Psychology, 44,* 46–53.

Fritz, G., & Fehmi, L. (1983). Cluster headaches: A cerebral vascular disorder treated with biofeedback-assisted attention training. *Proceedings of the 14th Annual Meeting of the Biofeedback Society of America* (pp. 82–83). Wheat Ridge, CO: Biofeedback Society of America.

Gamble, E. H., & Elder, S. T. (1983). Multimodal biofeedback in the treatment of migraine. *Biofeedback and Self-Regulation, 8,* 383–392.

Gauthier, J., Bois, R., Allaire, D., & Drolet, M. (1981). Evaluation of skin temperature biofeedback training at two different sites for migraine. *Journal of Behavioral Medicine, 4,* 407–419.

Gauthier, J., Doyon, J., Lacroix, R., & Drolet, M. (1983). Blood volume pulse biofeedback in the treatment of migraine headache: A controlled evaluation. *Biofeedback and Self-Regulation, 8,* 427–442.

Glass, G. V. (1976). Primary, secondary, and meta-analysis of research. *Educational Researcher, 10,* 3–8.

Jessup, B., Neufeld, R. W. J., & Stenn, P. G. (1976). *Autogenic training and hand temperature biofeedback in the treatment of migraine: A preliminary analysis.* Research Bulletin #390, ISSN 0316-4675. Department of Psychology, University of Western Ontario, London, Ontario, Canada.

Jurish, S. E., Blanchard, E. B., Andrasik, F., Teders, S. J., Neff, D. F., & Arena, J. G. (1983). Home- versus clinic-based treatment of vascular headache. *Journal of Consulting and Clinical Psychology, 51,* 743–751.

Hoelscher, T. J., & Lichstein. K. L. (1983). Blood volume pulse biofeedback treatment for chronic cluster headache. *Biofeedback and Self-Regulation, 8,* 533–541.

Kewman, D., & Roberts, A. H. (1980). Skin temperature biofeedback and migraine headache: A double-blind study. *Biofeedback and Self-Regulation, 5,* 327–345.

King, A. C., & Arena, J. G. (1984). Behavioral treatment of chronic cluster headache in geriatric patients. *Biofeedback and Self-Regulation, 9,* 201–208.

Knapp, T. W., & Florin, I. (1981). The treatment of migraine headache by training in vasoconstriction of the temporal artery in a cognitive stress-coping training. *Behavior Analysis and Modification, 4,* 267–274.

Kudrow, L. (1980). *Cluster headache: Mechanisms and management.* New York: Oxford University Press.

Labbé, E. L., & Williamson, D. A. (1984). Treatment of childhood migraine using autogenic feedback training. *Journal of Consulting and Clinical Psychology, 52,* 968–976.

Lake, A., Raney, J., & Papsdorf, J. D. (1979). Biofeedback and rational-emotive therapy in the management of migraine headache. *Journal of Applied Behavior Analysis, 12,* 127–140.

Largen, J. W., Mathew, R. J., Dobbins, K., Myer, J. S., & Claghorn, J. L. (1978). Skin temperature self-regulation and non-invasive regional cerebral blood flow. *Headache, 18,* 203–210.

Largen, J. W., Mathew, R. J., Dobbins, K., & Claghorn, J. L. (1981). Specific and non-specific effects of skin temperature control and migraine management. *Headache, 21,* 36–44.

Leviton, A. (1978). Epidemiology of Headache. In B. S. Schoenberg (Ed.), *Advances in Neurology* (Vol. 19, pp. 341–352). New York: Raven Press.

Libo, L. M., & Arnold, G. E. (1983). Does training to criterion influence improvement? A follow-up study of EMG and thermal biofeedback. *Journal of Behavioral Medicine, 6,* 397–404.

Mathew, N. T. (1981). Prophylaxis of migraine and mixed headache. A randomized controlled study. *Headache, 21,* 105–109.

Matthew, R. J., Largen, J. W., Dobbins, K., Meyer, J. S., Sakai, F., & Claghorh, J. L. (1980). Biofeedback control of skin temperature and cerebral blood flow in migraine, *Headache, 20*, 19–28.

Medina, J. L., Diamond, S., & Franklin, M. A. (1976). Biofeedback therapy for migraine. *Headache, 16*, 115–118.

Mehegan, J. E., Masek, B. J., Harrison, R. H., Russo, D. C., & Leviton, A. (1984). *Behavioral treatment of pediatric headache*. Unpublished manuscript.

Mitch, P. S., McGrady, A., & Iannone, A. (1976). Autogenic feedback training in migraine: A treatment report. *Headache, 15*, 267–270.

Mullinix, J., Norton, B., Hack, S., & Fishman, M. (1978). Skin temperature biofeedback and migraine. *Headache, 17*, 242–244.

Neff, D. F., Blanchard, E. B., & Andrasik, F. (1983). The relationship between capacity for absorption in chronic headache patients' response to relaxation and biofeedback treatment. *Biofeedback and Self-Regulation, 8*, 177–183.

Olness, K., & MacDonald, J. (1981). Self-hypnosis and biofeedback in the management of juvenile migraine. *Developmental and Behavioral Pediatrics, 2*, 168–170.

Reading, C. (1984). Psychophysiological reactivity in migraine following biofeedback. *Headache, 24*, 70–74.

Russ, K. L. Hammer, R. L., & Adderton, M. (1979). Clinical follow-up: Treatment and outcome of functional headache patients treated with biofeedback. *Journal of Clinical Psychology, 35*, 148–153.

Sakai, F., & Meyer, J. S. (1978). Regional cerebral hemodynamics during migraine and cluster headaches measured by the 133Xe inhalation method. *Headache, 18*, 122–132.

Sargent, J. D., Green, E. E., & Walters, E. D. (1973). Preliminary report on the use of autogenic feedback training in the treatment of migraine and tension headaches. *Psychosomatic Medicine, 35*, 129–135.

Sargent, J., Solbach, P., Coyne, L., Spohn, H., & Segerson, J. 1986. Results of a controlled, experimental, outcome study of non-drug treatments for the control of chronic migraine headaches. *Journal of Behavioral Medicine, 9*, 291–323.

Silver, B. V., Blanchard, E. B., Williamson, D. A., Theobald, D. E., & Brown, D. A. (1979). Temperature biofeedback and relaxation training in the treatment of migraine headaches: One year follow-up. *Biofeedback and Self-Regulation, 4*, 359–366.

Smith, M. L., & Glass, G. V. (1977). Meta-analysis of psychotherapy outcome studies. *American Psychologist, 32*, 752–760.

Sorbi, M., & Tellegen, B. (1984). Multimodal migraine treatment: Does thermal feedback add to the outcome? *Headache, 24*, 249–255.

Sovak, M., Kunzel, M., Sternbach, R. A., & Dalessio, D. J. (1978). Is volitional manipulation of hemodynamics a valid rationale for biofeedback therapy of migraine? *Headache, 18*, 197–202.

Sovak, N., Kunzel, M., Sternbach, R. A., & Dalessio, D. J. (1981). Mechanism of the biofeedback therapy of migraine: Volitional manipulation of the psychophysiological background. *Headache, 21*, 89–92.

Stroebel, C. F., Ford, N. R., Strong, P., & Szarek, B. L. (1981). Quieting response training: Five-year evaluation of clinical biofeedback practice. In *Proceedings of the Biofeedback Society of America 12th Annual Meeting* (pp. 78–81). Wheat Ridge, CO: Biofeedback Society of America.

Werder, D. S. & Sargent, J. D. (1984). A study of childhood headache using biofeedback as a treatment alternative. *Headache, 24*, 122–126.

Werder, D. S., Sargent, J. D., & Coyne, L. (1981, October). MMPI profiles of headache patients using self-regulation to control headache activity. Presented at the 1981 meeting of the American Association of Biofeedback Clinicians, Kansas City, MO.

Appendix

Table A-1. Summary of Control Group Outcome Studies of Biofeedback Treatment of Migraine Headache

Table A-1. Summary of Controlled Group Outcome Studies of Biofeedback Treatment of Migraine Headache

		Andreychuk & Skriver (1975)	Jessup et al. (1976)	Friar & Beatty (1976)	Blanchard et al. (1978)
Patient characteristics	Age, $\bar{X}$	N/A	39.3	30.4	38.7
	Range	N/A	20–61	19–54	21–77
	Sex M/F	4/24	6/27	3/16	5/25
	Years of HA, $\bar{X}$	N/A	16.1	N/A	N/A
Source	Physician referred	—	No	No	—
	Self-referred	Yes	Yes	Yes	Yes
	Advertising	Yes	Yes	Yes	Yes
Number started		33	37	20	37
Number completed		28	33	19	30
% Dropout		15.2	0	5	18.9
Diagnosed by		PI	Neurologist	PI & neurologist	PI
Diagnostic criteria	Ad hoc committee	No	N/A	No	Explicit inclusion and exclusion
	other	N/A	N/A	Explicit, drug response	
Biofeedback treatments					
Thermal only		—	—	—	—
Thermal & autogenic		9	13	—	10(13)
Thermal + autogenics + relaxation		—	—	—	—

50

TABLE A-1. (Continued)

	Mullinix et al. (1978)	Lake et al. (1979)	Attfield & Peck (1979)	Kewman & Roberts (1980)
Patient characteristics { Age, X̄	N/A	33.0	36.7	40
Range	N/A	20–56	23–44	21–75
Sex M/F	16/58	5/19	4/6	0/34
Years of HA, X̄ }	5/7	13.8	9.5	N/A
Source { Physician referred	Yes	?	Yes	Partly
Self-referred	—	Yes	—	Yes
Advertising }	—	Yes	—	Yes—partly
Number started	12	24	10	40
Number completed	11	24	10	34
% Dropout	8.3	0?	0	15
Diagnosed by:	PI	PI and neurologist	Neurologist	PI
Diagnostic criteria { Ad hoc committee	Explicit inclusion and exclusion	No	No	No
other }		Unclear	Explicit Inclusion	Explicit Inclusion Criteria
Biofeedback treatments				
Thermal only	6	5	5	11
Thermal & autogenic	—	—	—	—
Thermal + autogenics + relaxation	—	—	—	—

Continued

51

TABLE A-1. (Continued)

	Cohen et al. (1980)	Bild & Adams (1980)	Knapp & Florin (1980)	Largen et al. (1981)
Patient characteristics — Age, $\bar{X}$	42	37.7	41.7	38.1
Range	23–60	21–62	28–62	N/A
Sex M/F	10/40	5/14 4/2 EMG	1/19	0/11
Years of HA, $\bar{X}$	N/A	N/A	18.8	15.3
Source — Physician referred	Yes	Part	N/A	Yes
Self-referred	No	Part	N/A	Yes
Advertising	No	Yes	N/A	Yes
Number started	50	21	20	13
Number completed	42	19	20	11
% Dropout	16	10	0	15.4
Diagnosed by	PI & physician	PI	PI	Neurologist
Diagnostic criteria — Ad hoc committee		Yes	No	Yes
other	Yes (Migraine & Mixed)		Explicit inclusion criteria	
Biofeedback treatments				
Thermal only	11	—	—	—
Thermal & autogenic	—	—	—	—
Thermal + autogenics + relaxation	—	—	—	6

52

TABLE A-1. (*Continued*)

	Elmore & Tursky (1981)	Gauthier et al. (1981)	Blanchard et al. (1982)	Gauthier et al. (1983)
Patient characteristics — Age, $\bar{X}$	N/A	38.6	N/A	34.7
Range	N/A	21–65	28–69	20–48
Sex M/F	N/A	4/20	N/A	0/21
Years of HA, $\bar{X}$	N/A	N/A	N/A	22
Source — Physician referred	—	No	Yes	No
Self-referred	Yes	Yes	Yes	Yes
Advertising	Yes	Yes	No	Yes
Number started	23	24	18	21
Number completed	23	24	16	21
% Dropout	0%	0%	11%	0%
Diagnosed by:	PI	PI	PI & neurologist	PI
Diagnostic criteria — Ad hoc committee	No	No	Yes	No
other	N/A	Explicit inclusion & exclusion		Explicit, inclusion criteria
Biofeedback treatments				
Thermal only	11	6	—	—
Thermal & autogenic	—	—	—	—
Thermal + autogenics + relaxation	—	—	8	—

Continued

53

TABLE A-1. (*Continued*)

	Daly et al. (1983)	Jurish et al. (1983)	Gamble & Elder (1983)	Reading (1983)
Patient characteristics { Age, X̄	38.2	37.3	N/A (College students)	45.6
Range	N/A	N/A	N/A	N/A
Sex M/F	N/A	6/21	N/A	0/28
Years of HA, X̄	19.0	19.6	N/A	23.4
Source { Physician referred	No	Yes	N/A	Yes
Self-referred	Yes	Yes	N/A	No
Advertising	Yes	No	N/A	No
Number started	75	50	N/A	28
Number completed	23	10	N/A	28
% Dropout	31	20	N/A	0
Diagnosed by:	Physician	Neurologist & PI	PI	Neurologist or GP
Diagnostic criteria { Ad hoc committee	N/A	Yes	N/A (All classic	No
other	N/A	—	migraine?) (On no meds)	Explicit
Biofeedback treatments				
Thermal only	—	—	3	7
Thermal & autogenic	10	—	3	—
Thermal + autogenics + relaxation	—	10 10		—
		clinic home		

54

TABLE A-1. (*Continued*)

	Sorbi & Tellegen (1984)	Sargent et al. (1986)
Patient characteristics — Age, $\bar{X}$	40.3	35.7
Range	20–59	N/A
Sex M/F	5/16	22/114 (16.1)
Years of HA, $\bar{X}$	16.9	N/A
Source — Physician referred	Yes	60%
Self-referred	—	40%
Advertising	—	No
Number started	24	193
Number completed	21	136
% Dropout	12.5	29.5
Diagnosed by:	Physician & PI	PI
Diagnostic criteria — Ad hoc committee	Yes	Yes
other		
Biofeedback treatments		
Thermal only	—	—
Thermal & autogenic	—	34
Thermal + autogenics + relaxation	11[k]	—

Continued

55

TABLE A-1. (*Continued*)

	Andreychuk & Skriver (1975)	Jessup et al. (1976)	Friar & Beatty (1976)	Blanchard et al. (1978)
Frontal EMG only	—	—	—	—
Frontal EMG + relaxation	—	—	—	—
Thermal + frontal EMG	—	—	—	—
Thermal + frontal EMG + other	—	—	—	—
Cephalic vasomotor	—	—	10	—
Other	EEG Alpha (9)	—	—	—
Comparison conditions				
Pre-post assessment only	—	—	—	—
HA monitoring	(Hypnosis) (10)	—	—	—
Relaxation	10	7	—	10
Cognitive therapy	—	—	—	10(13)
Attention placebo	—	Hand cool + auto.	Vasoconstriction in hand	—
Other				
Number of sessions: fixed	10	8 (4 Feedback)	9	12
Average for sample	10	—	9	—
Average length of session	45 min.	20 min?	N/A	—

TABLE A-1. (*Continued*)

	Mullinix et al. (1978)	Lake et al. (1979)	Attfield & Peck (1979)	Kewman & Roberts (1980)
Frontal EMG only	—	6	—	—
Frontal EMG + relaxation	—	—	—	—
Thermal + frontal EMG	—	—	—	—
Thermal + frontal EMG + other	—	—	—	—
Cephalic vasomotor	—	—	—	—
Other	—	Thermal + RET 6	—	—
Comparison conditions				
Pre-post assessment only	—	—	—	—
HA monitoring	—	6	—	11
Relaxation	—	—	5	—
Cognitive therapy	—	—	—	—
Attention placebo	False feedback that indicated success.	—	—	12 taught[a] to lower temp.
Other	—	—	—	—
Number of sessions: fixed	9	8	6	10
Average for sample	N/A	45	6	10
Average length of session	N/A	60	30 min.	60 min.

Continued

57

TABLE A-1. (*Continued*)

	Cohen et al. (1980)	Bild & Adams (1980)	Knapp & Florin (1980)	Largen et al. (1981)
Frontal EMG only	11	6	—	—
Frontal EMG + relaxation	—	—	—	—
Thermal + frontal EMG	—	—	—	—
Thermal + frontal EMG + other	—	—	—	—
Cephalic vasomotor	10	7	4	—
Other	EEG Alpha 10	—	8 Cog + CVM	—
Comparison conditions				
Pre-post assessment only	—	—	—	—
HA monitoring	—	—	4	—
Relaxation	—	6	—	—
Cognitive therapy	—		8 Cog + 4 CVM	—
Attention placebo	—		—	(5) taught[a] hand cooling
Other	—		—	
Number of sessions: fixed	24(16)	10	10	12–16
Average for sample				N/A
Average length of session	40 min.	60 min.	60 min.	

58

TABLE A-1. (*Continued*)

	Elmore & Tursky (1981)	Gauthier et al. (1981)	Blanchard et al. (1982)	Gauthier et al. (1983)
Frontal EMG only	—	—	—	—
Frontal EMG + relaxation	—	—	—	—
Thermal + frontal EMG	—	—	—	—
Thermal + frontal EMG + other	—	—	—	—
Cephalic vasomotor	12	Temp. Art. Cool. 6	—	7 Constrict 7 Dilate
Other	—	—	—	—
Comparison conditions				
Pre-post assessment only	—	—	—	—
HA monitoring	—	—	—	7
Relaxation	—	—	8	—
Cognitive therapy	—	—	—	—
Attention placebo	—	TBF-C Temp. Art. Warm 6	—	—
Other	—	—	—	—
Number of sessions: fixed	9	8	12	16
Average for sample	9	—	—	—
Average length of session	45 min.	—	50 min.	60 min.

Continued

59

TABLE A-1. (*Continued*)

	Daly et al. (1983)	Jurish et al. (1983)	Gamble & Elder (1983)	Reading (1983)
Frontal EMG only	—	—	3	—
Frontal EMG + relaxation	10 (Auto)	—	3	7
Thermal + frontal EMG + other	—	—	3	—
Cephalic vasomotor	—	—	—	—
Other	—	—	—	skin conduct 7
Comparison conditions				
Pre-post assessment only	—	—	—	—
HA monitoring	—	—	—	3
Relaxation	10 PMR + Auto	—	—	3
Cognitive therapy	—	—	—	—
Attention placebo	—	—	—	false 7 EMG
Other	—	—	—	—
Number of sessions: fixed	9	16	7	10
Average for sample	—	3	—	—
Average length of session	30 min.	50 min.	60 min.	45 min.

TABLE A-1. (*Continued*)

	Sorbi & Tellegen (1984)	Sargent et al. (1986)	
Frontal EMG only	— —	—	—
Frontal EMG + relaxation	— —	34 — (Auto)	—
Thermal + frontal EMG	— —	—	—
Thermal + frontal EMG + other	— —	—	—
Cephalic vasomotor	— —	—	—
Other	— —	—	—
Comparison conditions			
Pre-post assessment only	—	—	—
HA monitoring	—	—	34
Relaxation	—	— 34 (Autogenics)	—
Cognitive therapy	10^c	—	—
Attention placebo	—	—	—
Other	—	—	—
Number of sessions: fixed	18	22 (6 feedback)	
Average for sample		—	
Average length of session	60 min.	20 min.	

Continued

TABLE A–1. (*Continued*)

	Andreychuk & Skriver (1975)	Jessup et al. (1976)	Friar & Beatty (1976)	Blanchard et al. (1978)
Fixed protocol	Yes	Yes	Yes	Yes
Training to criterion	No	No	No	No
Home practice—relaxation	Yes	Yes	No	Yes
Home practice—temp. trainer	No	No	No	No
Duration of treatment	10 wks.	8 wks.	3 wks.	6 wks.
Experimental design issues				
Random assignment	Yes	Yes	Yes	Yes
Matching of samples	No	No	Yes	Yes
Baseline length	6 wks.	4 wks.	30 days	4 wks.
Evidence of BF training	No	No	Yes	No
Use of HA diary	Yes	Yes	Yes	Yes
Credibility assessed	No	No	No	No
Therapist variables				
Multiple trainers	N/A	N/A	No	4
Average exp. of trainers	N/A	N/A	N/A	3 yrs. with relaxation, 1 mo. with BF.
Trainer effect	N/A	N/A	No	No
Trainer present or absent	N/A	Absent	Absent	Absent

TABLE A-1. (Continued)

	Mullinix et al. (1978)	Lake et al. (1979)	Attfield & Peck (1979)	Kewman & Roberts (1980)	
Fixed protocol	Yes	Yes	Yes	Yes	Yes
Training to criterion	No	No	No	No	No
Home practice—relaxation	Yes	Yes + RET	No	?	?
Home practice—temp. trainer	No	No	No	No	No
Duration of treatment	9 wks.	4 wks.	N/A	9 wks.	
Experimental design issues					
Random assignment	Yes	Yes	Yes	Yes	No
Matching of samples	No	No	No	No	No
Baseline length	5 wks.	4 wks.	N/A	6 wks.	
Evidence of BF training	No	Yes (85%) for EMG, poor (37% and 29%) for therm.	BR > REL on temp.	8/11	3/12
Use of HA diary	Yes	Yes	No	Yes	Yes
Credibility assessed	No	No	No	No	No
Therapist variables					
Multiple trainers	N/A	5	N/A	2	2
Average exp. of trainers	N/A	N/A	N/A	2	None
Trainer effect	N/A	No	N/A	No	No
Trainer present or absent	N/A	N/A	N/A	Present	Present

Continued

TABLE A-1. (*Continued*)

	Cohen et al. (1980)	Bild & Adams (1980)	Knapp & Florin (1980)	Largen et al. (1981)
Fixed protocol	Yes	Yes	Yes	Yes Yes
Training to criterion	No	No	No	No No
Home practice—relaxation	No	No	Use of BF procedures	Yes Yes
Home practice—temp. trainer	No	No	No	No
Duration of treatment	8 wks.	4 wks.	5 wks.	5 wks.
Experimental design issues				
Random assignment	Yes No	Yes	Yes	Yes
Matching of samples	No	No	Yes	Yes
Baseline length	8 wks. Yes Yes No	6 wks. —	4 wks.	5 wks. Yes
Evidence of BF training	Yes Yes	Yes	No	Yes
Use of HA diary	Yes	Yes	Yes	Yes
Credibility assessed	No	No	No	No
Therapist variables				
Multiple trainers	N/A	N/A	N/A	1
Average exp. of trainers	N/A	N/A	N/A	N/A
Trainer effect	—	—	N/A	No
Trainer present or absent	Absent	Absent	N/A	Absent

TABLE A-1. (*Continued*)

	Elmore & Tursky (1981)	Gauthier et al. (1981)	Blanchard et al. (1982c)	Gauthier et al. (1983)
Fixed protocol	No	Yes	Yes	Yes
Training to criterion	Yes	No	No	No
Home practice—relaxation	Practice lab.	In lab. strategies	Yes	Use BF procedure —
Home practice—temp. trainer	No	No	Yes	No
Duration of treatment	8 wks.	8 wks.	6–12 wks.	8 wks.
Experimental design issues				
Random assignment	Yes	Yes	No (Relax failures)	Yes
Matching of samples	No	Yes	—	Yes
Baseline length	1 mo.	4 wks.	4 wks.	5 wks.
Evidence of BF training	Yes	Yes Yes No No	Yes	Const. > dilation
Use of HA diary	Yes	Yes	Yes	Yes
Credibility assessed	—	Yes Yes Yes Yes	No	Yes C > D
Therapist variables				
Multiple trainers	1	2	4	2
Average exp. of trainers	N/A	N/A	1 year	N/A
Trainer effect	No	No	No	No
Trainer present or absent	Absent	N/A	Absent	N/A

Continued

TABLE A-1. (*Continued*)

	Daly et al. (1983)	Jurish et al. (1983)	Gamble & Edler (1983)	Reading (1983)
Fixed protocol	Yes	Yes	Yes	Yes
Training to criterion	No	No	No	No
Home practice—relaxation	Yes Yes	Rel. + BF	N/A	N/A
Home practice—temp. trainer	No	Yes	No	No
Duration of treatment	5 wks.	8 wks.	3 wks.	5 wks.
Experimental design issues				
Random assignment	?	Yes	Yes	Yes
Matching of samples	Yes	Yes	No	N/A
Baseline length	N/A	4 wks.	1 wk.	5 wks.
Evidence of BF training	2.5° F Yes No	3.5 F Yes	Yes, for EMG cond. only	Yes, for EMG FB
Use of HA diary	Yes	Yes	Yes	Yes
Credibility assessed	No	Yes	—	No
Therapist variables				
Multiple trainers	3	4	No	N/A
Average exp. of trainers	Brief	2 years	N/A	N/A
Trainer effect	N/A	No	No	N/A
Trainer present or absent	N/A	Mixed-Almost absent for TBF	N/A	N/A

TABLE A-1. (Continued)

	Sorbi & Tellegen (1984)	Sargent et al. (1986)
Fixed protocol	Yes	Yes
Training to criterion	No	No
Home practice—relaxation	Yes Yes	Yes Yes —
Home practice—temp. trainer	No	Yes EMG (8 weeks)
Duration of treatment	13 wks.	36 wks.
Experimental design issues		
Random assignment	Yes	Yes
Matching of samples	No	No
Base line length	4 wks.	4 wks.
Evidence of BF training	Yes, for TBF	Yes? ($1.5°F$ in 1 min. – 2/3 Patients)
Use of HA diary	Yes	Yes
Credibility assessed	—	No No No No
Therapist variables		
Multiple trainers	6	Yes (Blind to Hyp.)
Average exp. of trainers	N/A	N/A
Trainer effect	No	N/A
Trainer present or absent	N/A	Absent

Continued

TABLE A-1. (Continued)

	Andreychuk & Skriver (1975)			Jessup et al. (1976)			Friar & Beatty (1976)		Blanchard et al. (1978)		
	Therm.	Alpha.	Hyp.	Temp.	Temp.	Mon.	CVM	Control	Therm.	Relax.	Monitor
Results											
Within-group changes											
% reduction in HA index	65.3	27.7	53.4	50%	20	3	—	—	73	81	23
HA frequency	—	—	—	48	29	26	36	14	56	68	45
HA intensity	—	—	—	33%	19%	7%	6%	-16%	44	56	13
HA duration	—	—	—	51%	30%	10%	—	—	46	67	0
Meds	—	—	—	—	—	—	45	45	64	96	34
Global ratings	Not used			—	—	—	Not used		Not used		
% sample improved	N/A	N/A	N/A		N/A		N/A	N/A	54	85	N/A
Between-group comparisons	No significant between-group effects. Hi hypnotic suggestible did better. More Hi's in TBF group.			Signif. within-group change on freq., dur., intensity. No sig. between-group differences.			CVM > control on major migraine attacks only (one tail).		TBF = REL > HA monitoring.		
Follow-up											
Duration	None			None			None		12 months		
Maintenance conditions									None		
% sample available				69.2							

TABLE A-1. (*Continued*)

	Mullinix et al. (1978)		Lake et al. (1979)				Attfield & Peck (1979)		Kewman & Roberts (1980)		
	TBF	False TBF	Therm.	Therm. - RET	EMG	Mon	TBF	Relax.	TBF-W	TBF-C	Monitor
Results											
Within-group changes											
% reduction in HA index	21	8	32	25	26	17	—	—	—	—	—
HA frequency	—	—	—	—	—	—	No	No	14	21	19
HA intensity	—	—	—	—	—	—	No	Yes*	39*	22*	34*
HA duration	—	—	—	—	—	—	No	No	—	—	—
Meds	—		—	—	—	—	—	—			
Global ratings	Not used						Used		Not used		
% sample improved	2	1	67	33	100	17	N/A	N/A	N/A	N/A	N/A
Between-group comparisons	No sign. differences. TBF showed sig. more temp. increase.		EMG Gp. > monitoring on % sample improved. Otherwise, *no* sig. between-group effect.				N/A		No between-group differences. (Patients who actually decreased temp. (*n* = 5) were significantly worse than all others.)		
Follow-up											
Duration	None		3 mos.				None		None		
Maintenance conditions			1 booster session								
% sample available			100								

69

Continued

TABLE A-1. (Continued)

	Cohen et al. (1980)				Bild & Adams (1980)			Knapp & Florin (1980)				Largen et al. (1978)	
								CMV					
Results	TBF	EMG	CVM	EEG	EMG	CVM	Mon.	CVM	COG	COG	Mon.	TBF-W	TBR-C
Within-group changes													
% reduction in HA index	—	—	—	—	—	—	—						
HA frequency	5	28	24	14	36	63	17%	—	37*	—	N/A	66	54
HA intensity	2	5	−6	19	NS	NS	NS	—	34 ns	—	N/A	54	5
HA duration	12	4	−6	13	57*	74*	−5	—	39*	—	N/A	18	−3
Meds	—	—	—	—	−6%	45%	−21%	—	69*	—	N/A	65	36
Global ratings	—	—	—	—	—	—	—	Not used				Not used	81
% sample improved	N/A	N/A	N/A	N/A	3/6	6/7	1/6	N/A	N/A	N/A	N/A	5/6	2/5
Between-group comparisons	No sig. within-group changes. No sig. between-group differences.				No sig. differences between 2 treatments. CVM > Monitor for duration.			No sig. differences between treated patients and controls on HA reduction. Some subjective differences between treatments and controls.				No sig. between-group differences.	
Follow-up													
Duration	8 mos.				12 wks.							None	
Maintenance conditions	4-booster session				None								
% sample available	31				100								

TABLE A-1. (Continued)

	Elmore & Tursky (1981)		Gauthier et al. (1981)				Blanchard et al. (1982)		Gauthier et al. (1983)		
	TBF	CVM	TBF-W	TBF-C	Art	Art	TBF	Relax.	CVM-C	CVM-D	Mon.
Results											
Within-group changes											
% reduction in HA index											
HA frequency	38	56*	28*	37	19	61	—	—	37	52	-10
HA intensity	-27	-4	8	1	3	5	—	—	45	47	-19
HA duration	-35	-5	30*	31	33	49	—	—	41	60	5
Meds	2	53*	43*	48	30	59	—	—	-11	47	8
Global ratings	Not Used								Not Used		
% sample improved	N/A	N/A					1/8	1/8	N/A	N/A	N/A
Between-group comparisons	CVM > TBF on meds and on reactivity but on no HA parameters.		No significance between-group differences; no tests on within-group changes for specific groups.				1/8 relaxation failures helped by TBF.		Both treated groups improved more than control on Frequency and Intensity, but not on Duration or Meds.		
Follow-up											
Duration	None		6 months				None		None		
Maintenance conditions			None								
% sample available			100								

Continued

71

	Daly et al. (1983)			Jurish et al. (1983)		Gamble & Edler (1983)								Reading (1983)			
	TBF	EMG	Relax.	TBF+ R. Clin.	TBF+R Home	T	T+R	E	E+R	T+E	T+E+R	Mont. HA	R	TBF	EMG	SCL	False E
Results																	
Within-group changes																	
% reduction in HA index	N/A	N/A				—	—	—	—	—	—	—	—	—	—	—	E
HA frequency	N/A	N/A		33	32	89	91	64	76	89	98	10	6	(35% reduction in severe HA, 32% in moderate HA)			
HA intensity	N/A	N/A		13	42	—	—	—	—	—	—	—	—	—			
HA duration	N/A	N/A		N/A	N/A	—	—	—	—	—	—	—	—	—			
Meds	45			16	28	—	—	—	—	—	—	—	—	—			
Global ratings				Not used		—	—	—	—	—	—	—	—	—			
% sample improved	8/10	7/10	6/11	4/10	7/10	N/A	N/A	N/A	N/A	N/A	N/A	N/A	N/A	NA			
Between-group comparisons	No sig. differences between groups (no comparisons made on migraine).			No sig. between-group differences.		No sig. between-group differences. No sig. within-group changes reported.								No sig. between-group differences. No individual within-group data.			
Follow-up																	
Duration	3 months			None		None								None			
Maintenance conditions	None																
% sample available	100																

72

TABLE A-1. (Continued)

	Sorbi & Tellegan (1984)		Sargent et al. (1985)			
	TBR + AT Cog. Ther.	AT + Cog. Ther.	TEMP.	EMG	AUTO.	Mon.
Results						
Within-group changes						
% reduction in HA index	29*	51*	—	—	—	—
HA frequency	43*	53*	21	26	17	9
HA intensity	26*	27*	22	28	18	8
HA duration	6	2	—	—	—	—
Meds			—	—	—	—
Global ratings	50*	71*	—	—	—	—
% sample improved	N/A	N/A	N/A			
Between-group comparisons	No sig. between-group effects. Highly significant within-group effects for both conditions.		All 3 treated groups reduce significantly more than HA monitoring. Trend (.08) for TEMP to do better than EMG and AUTO combined.			
Follow-up						
Duration	7 mos.		6 mos?			
Maintenance conditions	None		12 contacts (self control)			
% sample available	100		100			

Continued

73

TABLE A-1. (*Continued*)

	Andreychuk & Skriver (1975)	Jessup et al. (1976)	Friar & Beatty (1976)	Blanchard et al. (1978)	
				Therm.	Relax.
% Reduction *vs.* BL				57	86
% Reduction *vs.* end of treatment				− 8	+ 17
HA diary or global rating				4-week HA diary	

TABLE A-1. (*Continued*)

	Mullinix et al. (1978)	Lake et al. (1979)				Attfield & Peck (1979)	Kewman & Roberts (1980)
	TBF	TBF + RET	EMG	Mon			
% Reduction vs. BL	29%	21%	54%	−18%			
% Reduction vs. end of treatment	0%	6%	28%	−20%			
HA diary or global rating		HA diary					

Continued

Table A-1. (*Continued*)

	Cohen et al. (1980)	Bild & Adams (1980)	Knapp & Florin (1980)	Largen et al. (1981)
% Reduction vs. BL	25 Freq. 29 11 10	70 Freq.		
% Reduction vs. end of treatment	21 Freq. 2 −17 −5	20 Freq.		
HA diary or global rating	HA diary		HA diary	

TABLE A-1. (*Continued*)

	Elmore & Tursky (1981)	Gauthier et al. (1981)			Blanchard et al. (1982c)	Gauthier et al. (1983)
% Reduction vs. BL	50 Freq.	55 Freq.	33 Freq.	40 Freq.		
	0 Dur.	57 Dur.	17 Dur.	39 Dur.		
% Reduction vs. end of treatment	30 Freq.	27 Freq.	17 Freq.	−104 Freq.		
	−43 Dur.	37 Dur.	−23 Dur.	−20 Dur.		
HA diary or global rating		HA diary	Dur.	Dur.		

Continued

TABLE A-1. (*Continued*)

	Daly et al. (1983)	Jurish et al. (1983)	Gamble & Edler (1983)	Reading (1983)
% Reduction vs. BL	N/A			
% Reduction vs. end of treatment	N/A			
HA diary or global rating	HA diary			

Note. N/A—Information not available.

[a] Raise and lower temperature conditions were double-blind. 91% T ↑ correct, 18% T ↓ correct in guessing direction.
[b] Also included 9 sessions of cognitive stress coping therapy.
[c] Also included 9 sessions of AT.

TABLE A-1. (*Continued*)

	Sorbi & Tellegen (1984)	Sargent et al. (1986)
% Reduction vs. BL	47 40	Same as above
% Reduction vs. end of treatment	25 −22	8 10 7 5
HA diary or global rating	HA diary	HA diary

2

Clinical Issues in Biofeedback and Relaxation Therapy for Hypertension

Review and Recommendations

MICHAEL S. GLASGOW AND BERNARD T. ENGEL

INTRODUCTION

Blood pressure (BP) is maintained by cardiac output and peripheral vascular resistance that, in turn, are modified by stroke volume, pulse rate, total blood volume, blood viscosity, elasticity of blood vessels, and humoral and neurogenic stimuli. Changes in one or more of these variables by pharmacological, behavioral, physiological, or environmental means normally affect BP only transiently because a variety of homeostatic reflexes, responding to the change, act to maintain a relatively stable mean arterial BP. When a homeostatic mechanism chronically maintains BP at abnormally high levels, it is sometimes due to a surgically or medically correctable condition (e.g., coarctation of the aorta, primary hyperaldosteronism, Cushing's syndrome, pheochromocytoma, or unilateral renal disease). However, more than 90% of all cases of chronically elevated BP are not secondary to one of these correctable conditions, and are therefore referred to as primary, or essential, hypertension

---

MICHAEL S. GLASGOW AND BERNARD T. ENGEL • Gerontology Research Center, Baltimore, National Institute on Aging, National Institutes of Health, U.S. Department of Health and Human Services, Bethesda, and the Francis Scott Key Medical Center, Baltimore, MD 21224.

(Whelton & Russell, 1984). The nature of essential hypertension (HBP) has been a topic of controversy for some time (Laragh, 1965). The tendency for an individual to develop HBP often runs in families, and population studies have demonstrated a familial resemblance at all levels of the BP continuum. Environmental stimuli also seem to play a significant role in most cases of HBP (Whelton & Russell, 1984). Predominantly environmental factors that have been implicated in the genesis of HBP are increased ingestion of sodium, excessive caloric intake, and emotional stress. Although BP has been demonstrated to rise in response to diets extremely high in sodium and to fall in response to diets extremely low in sodium, a relationship between dietary salt and HBP still has not been clearly established. Similarly, although weight reduction is often associated with BP reduction, even when dietary sodium and potassium are held constant, obesity is rarely the primary cause of HBP. Acute responses of BP to emotional stress also have not been shown to have a role in the etiology of chronic HBP. The role of other environmental factors (eg., alcohol consumption, cigarette smoking, heavy metal intake, and calcium content of water intake) is also unclear although there is evidence that some role exists in each case (Whelton & Russell, 1984). Because these environmental factors are not mutually exclusive in their influence on BP, the view that HBP has a multifactorial etiology is now gaining wide acceptance.

BP also can be regarded as a graded characteristic of the population like height or weight (Pickering, 1968). This view is supported by the observation that BP is continuously distributed, showing no obvious separation between hypertension and normotension. Furthermore, the failure of mortality figures to clearly separate hypertensive individuals from normotensive ones, makes classification of individuals as either hypertensive or normotensive very difficult. Nonetheless, patients with sustained elevation in BP are usually classified on the basis of average diastolic BP (DBP), being "labile" when this measure fluctuates around 90 mm. Hg., "mild" between 90 and 104 mm. Hg., "moderate" between 105 and 114 mm. Hg., and "severe" when DBP exceeds 114 mm. Hg. (Whelton & Russell, 1984).

Establishment of a BP level beyond which pharmacological treatment is indicated remains difficult. Because the side effects resulting from antihypertensive drug therapy often disrupt the patient's daily lifestyle and can be hazardous, the treating physician often faces a dilemma between the risks to the patient associated with HBP and those associated with antihypertensive drug therapy. Although it is clear that drug therapy reduces the risk of cardiovascular mortality among patients with DBP greater than 100 mm. Hg. (Australian National Study, 1980; HDFP, 1979; VA Cooperative Study Group, 1970) the value of drug treatment for milder forms of HBP still is not clear (Madhavan & Alderman, 1981;

McAlister, 1983; W.H.O./I.S.H., 1982). Intervention is often begun with patient education regarding diet (primarily salt restriction) and weight management when casual clinical BP determinations are regularly observed to be above 140/90 mm Hg. (Note: 86% of all patients with HBP have DBPs between 90 and 105 mm. Hg.; Alderman, 1980).

Data from the Hypertension Detection and Follow-up Program (HDFP) of the National Heart, Lung, and Blood Institute (NHLBI) suggest that DBP should be reduced to 90 mm Hg, or be reduced by 10 mm Hg if it is already below 100 mm Hg without medication (HDFP, 1979). A stepped-care protocol is recommended, wherein antihypertensive medications are prescribed in a stepwise sequence. The steps are as follows: Step 1, diuretic therapy; Step 2, addition of an antiadrenergic drug, such as reserpine or methyldopa if necessary (note: beta adrenergic blockers, such as propranalol, which also are popular for treatment of mild-to-moderate HBP, were not used in this study.); Step 3, addition of a vasodilator, such as hydralazine if necessary; Step 4, addition of the antiadrenergic drug, guanethidine, if necessary, with or without discontinuation of the medications from Steps 2 or 3; and Step 5, addition or substitution of other drugs as necessary (HDFP, 1979).

More recently (Brandt, 1983) the Assistant Secretary for Health, Department of Health and Human Services, issued an advisory on the treatment of mild hypertension recommending that treatment be initiated when DBP is between 90 and 94 mm Hg, and that the initial treatment should be nonpharmacologic as long as such treatment is effective at maintaining normal BP. This recommendation was based largely on results from the NHLBI's HDFP (1979) supporting vigorous pharmacological treatment of even mild HBP and their Multiple Risk Factor Intervention Trial (MRFIT, 1982), which reported a comparatively higher mortality among those with mild HBP if they also had ECG abnormalities at baseline and were treated pharmacologically for HBP.

Thus the therapeutic dilemma faced by the medical community continues. Physicians are called on to reduce patients' risks of cardiovascular diseases while contending also with the risks associated with antihypertensive drug therapy. The dilemma is further complicated by problems of poor compliance with drug therapy and adverse side effects associated with antihypertensive medications.

In June, 1984, the Joint National Committee on Detection, Evaluation, and Treatment of High Blood Pressure (JNC III) acknowledged the persistent difficulties associated with the assessment of HBP and recommended procedures to be followed when a patient over the age of 18 is found to have SBP > 140 or DBP > 89 mm Hg (average of two or more determinations on at least two clinic visits subsequent to the first-occasion measurement).

The JNC III advised that the goal of antihypertensive treatment should be to prevent the morbidity and mortality associated with HBP and that initiation of therapy should depend on the severity of BP elevation and presence or absence of other complications or risk factors.

Clearly a need for more effective nonpharmacologic interventions for HBP persists. However, in order for researchers in behavioral medicine to exert a meaningful influence on the development of standard guidelines for treating HBP, they must gain greater credibility within the medical community at large. In the following sections, recent progress toward this end will be assessed. Behavioral studies since the last Task Force Report (Blanchard, 1978; with addendum by Fahrion, 1979) that have examined the effectiveness of biofeedback and relaxation techniques for treating HBP will be reviewed critically and recommendations will be given for future research in this area.

CLINICAL EFFICACY

Assessment of the clinical efficacy of biofeedback and relaxation therapies for treating HBP necessarily requires a comparison of results obtained by these techniques with those obtained using standard antihypertensive drug regimens. Of course, it must first be demonstrated that a given behavioral treatment does, in fact, significantly lower BP when administered under controlled conditions. Then it must be demonstrated that the treatment effects are maintained in the patient's normal environment and for a duration comparable to that achieved with drug treatment. The sections that follow review current reports from the behavioral literature, dividing them into two categories; namely, laboratory research, those studies that test whether or not a defined behavioral treatment protocol is effective as a method of lowering BP, and clinical research, those studies that investigate whether or not the treatment effects of a given behavioral protocol are transferable to the patient's normal environment and are maintained for a meaningful period of time. A third section reviews the results of studies designed to compare pharmacologically treated groups of patients with behaviorally treated groups.

Laboratory Research

In general, those studies we call laboratory research (Table 1) do not include a follow-up period as part of their design. Typically, few patients are studied in a given report and the conditions, although usually well-controlled for purposes of the investigation, are not readily comparable to the conditions of otherwise similar studies. Their purpose

TABLE 1. Behavioral Treatment of High Blood Pressure: Laboratory Research

Reference	Treatment(s)	Cntl	Exp	Tot	Subject characteristics	Follow-up	Duration of training	Main finding(s)
			n					
Agras et al., 1982	Rel	18	12	30	Newspaper ad respondents Medically supervised for HBP Avg BP = .138/86	—	3 × 20 min.	expecting immediate results −17/−7 expecting delayed results −2/−6
Cottier et al., 1984	Rel	10	20	30	Aged 18–50, Mild HBP, unmedicated or no more than two drugs.	—	Ten 45-min. visits in 22 wks.	Decr. avg mean home BP by 3 mmHg (5–13 mmHg in patients with elevated sympathetic drive)
Datey, 1980	Rel, BF(GSR)	10	10	20	Medicated Pts w/HBP Avg BP = 158/103	—	3 × ½h/wk. × 8 wks.	−18/−7 decr. drug requirement by 33%
Davidson et al., 1979	Rel			6	Had surgically implanted myocardial markers 135:79	—	1h + 3 or 4½h practice sessions w/tapes	Physiological changes during Rel may be mediated through SNS + 4/−1
Frost & Holmes, 1980	BF (BP)			120	Psychology Students SBP = 90 − 150 No BP Meds	—	40 min.	Changes in SBP due to BF only limited
Gervino & Veazey, 1984	Rel			11	Asymptomatic, Sedentary females, aged 20–31 yrs.	—	20 min BID × 4 or 5 wks.	Rel reduced $\dot{V}O_2$, RER, SBP, RPP, f_R and RPE during submaximal aerobic exercise

Continued

Table 1. (*Continued*)

Reference	Treatment(s)	n			Subject characteristics	Follow-up	Duration of training	Main finding(s)
		Cntl	Exp	Tot				
Holroyd et al., 1982	BF(BP,EMG)			16	Ad respondents Avg SBP = 108	—	Trial sessions only	Hypnotizability not a factor in BP lowering ability Avg SBP = 109 w/BPBF
Libo & Arnold, 1983	BF(EMG,Temp)Rel			58	Outpatients in stress disorder clinic	1–5 yrs	4–16 (avg = 7) 1h sessions	Occasional post-therapy practice helps maintain therapeutic gains
McGrady et al., 1981	EMG-Aided Rel, Autogenics	16	22	38	Medic + nonmedic pts w/HBP (144/90)	—	2 × $\frac{1}{2}$h/wk. × 8 wks.	Decr. BP (−11/−6), musc tension, plasma aldosterone, & urine cortisol
Wallace et al., 1983	TM			112	TM practitioners Avg SBP = 112	—	5 yrs.	Practitioners have lower SBP than pop. norm + SBP (TM < 5 yrs)>SBP (TM > 5 yr)

BF = biofeedback; BID = twice per day; BP = blood pressure; Cntl = control; Combo = combined treatment; EMG = electromyogram; Exp = experimental; f_R = frequency or respiration (breaths/min); F/U = follow-up; GSR = galvanic skin resistance; h = hour(s); HBP = hypertension; HR = heart rate; Mon = monitor; n = number of subjects; Rel = relaxation; RER = respiratory exchange ratio (VCO₂/VO₂); RPE = rating of perceived exertion; RPP = rate pressure product (HR × SBP); Rx = treatment; TM = transcendental meditation; Tot. = total; VO₂ = oxygen uptake.

usually is to test some aspect of acute change in BP that, due to appropriate internal control, can be attributed to a specific intervention. Important criteria for evaluation of such studies are numbers of subjects, proper use of control groups, clear characterization of subjects, and training periods adequate to promote the learning of desired behaviors. Due to the absence of a standardized behavioral treatment for HBP, direct comparison of the studies in this category is very difficult. Furthermore, the paucity of attempts to reproduce the findings of one laboratory by other investigators limits the availability of data on which to base a selection of the most promising behavioral treatment modes or even to compare differences in mechanisms. Future research should address two major assumptions implicit in most such studies to date; namely, that acute changes in BP are appropriate indicators of the long-term changes that the treatment is supposed to produce, and that studies of normal (i.e., nonpatient) subjects provides information that is applicable to the hypertensive patient.

The report by Libo and Arnold (1983b) actually examines the follow-up period and is designed to test the importance of continued practice of relaxation, following EMG or thermal biofeedback therapy, in the maintenance of treatment effects. A variety of conditions typically encountered in a biofeedback practice were examined; however, only 12 of the 58 patients were included because of HBP. Therefore, even though 11 of the 12 patients with HBP (92%) showed improvement at the end of therapy and after a follow-up period of 1 to 5 years, it is not possible to draw sound conclusions from this study about the importance of continued relaxation practice to the long-term control of HBP.

Other studies listed in Table 1 examine the effects of behavioral intervention on physiological responsiveness to stimulation. Gervino & Veazey (1984) demonstrated reductions in oxygen uptake, respiratory exchange ratio, SBP, rate pressure product, breathing rate, and rate of perceived exertion during submaximal aerobic exercise. McGrady, Yonker, Tan, Fine, & Woerner (1981) found significant decreases in muscle tension, plasma aldosterone, and urinary cortisol coincident with reductions in BP following EMG feedback-assisted relaxation training. Similarly, Datey (1980) used GSR feedback to reinforce relaxation-induced BP reductions. In the Datey study, decreased responsiveness to the cold pressor test and Master's two-step exercise test were observed along with reductions in BP. The similarity of the studies by McGrady et al. (1981) and by Datey (1980) in terms of numbers of subjects, duration of training, and type of treatment is supportive of the reproducibility of their similar findings. However, whereas the Datey paper dealt with subjects all of whom were medicated, a small number of the subjects in the McGrady et al. study were nonmedicated. Because the importance of concurrent medication—regarding the potential for interaction between behavioral and pharmacological modes of treatment for HBP—is unclear, this suggests an area for further investigation. Neither of these studies used a baseline period of monitoring in order to determine pretreatment values.

The study by Wallace, Silver, Mills, Dillbeck, & Wagoner (1983) meets the criteria for a well-designed laboratory research paper. However, the extent to which the Transcendental Meditation (TM) and TM-Sidhi programs are comparable to the various forms of relaxation and biofeedback studied in the other works is not clear, and the self-selected nature of the subjects (mostly associated in some way with Maharishi International University and all practicing TM before recruitment into the study) leaves comparison of the results of this study with those of the other studies in this group open to question. The finding that practitioners of TM and TM-Sidhi experience beneficial effects on SBP that improve with extended experience in the programs, although well supported by the data, may not be generalizable to patients with HBP who do not otherwise elect to practice these disciplines.

The importance of expectation that BP will be lowered by relaxation instructions during training to increase or decrease BP, and individual differences in hypnotizability as a predictor of success at altering physiological responses also were investigated. Cottier, Shapiro, & Julius (1984) employed an interesting method of controlling for placebo effects during progressive muscle relaxation therapy for HBP. Thirty subjects with mild HBP were nonmedicated or taking no more than two antihypertensive drugs. All drug treatment was discontinued for the 22-week duration of the study, and all patients were placed instead on a placebo regimen, having been told that they would be given either a placebo or an active compound at some time in the study. Heart rate, 24-hour urinary sodium, ambulatory plasma renin activity, and resting plasma norepinephrine and epinephrine levels were used to index sympathetic nervous system activity. Home and clinic measurements were used to monitor BP. The authors concluded that relaxation therapy is time-consuming and not substantially better than placebo in unselected patients (reduction of mean BP = 3 mm Hg).

In general, the conclusions drawn from the other studies listed in Table 1 also were not convincingly supportive of behavioral therapy for HBP. Agras, Horne, & Taylor (1982) found that SBP, but not DBP, responded more rapidly to the lowering effects of relaxation among patients expecting immediate lowering; and Frost & Holmes (1980) found that instructions to increase, but not to decrease, SBP were effective even without BP feedback. Holroyd, Nuechterlein, Shapiro, & Ward (1982) were unable to demonstrate a relationship between hypnotizability of subjects and the success or failure of attempts to regulate BP by biofeedback of Korotkoff sounds. However, with the exception of Cottier *et al.* (1984), these studies employed short study sessions, and only the Frost and Holmes study used a large number of subjects. It should be noted also that the Holroyd *et al.* study was not restricted to BP responses and its subjects were not selected on the basis of BPs. Nonetheless, the finding of Cottier *et al.* (1984) that patients with elevated heart rate and plasma norepinephrine level tend to respond more favorably to BP reduction using relaxation (reduction of mean BP = 5–13 mm Hg), is potentially a very important clinical finding that merits more attention in future investigations.

Clinical Research

A valid clinical question regarding behavioral treatment for HBP relates to whether or not the treatment effects are maintained for extended periods following the completion of a course of therapy. That is, how does cessation of behavioral therapy for HBP compare with cessation of drug therapy? The VA Cooperative Study Group on Antihypertensive Agents (1975) found BPs returning to hypertensive levels in 42 of 60 patients (70%) within 18 months after substitution of a placebo medication for antihypertensive medications (hydrochlorothiazide, reserpine, and hydralazine) that had controlled BP for at least 2 years. BPs of 39 of the placebo patients (65%) returned to hypertensive levels within 6 months. In a study of 24 patients taking only diuretic antihypertensives—who, presumably, were less severely ill than the patients studied in the VA Cooperative Study—Levinson, Khatri, & Fries (1982) found that 54% returned to DBP levels >90 mm Hg within 6 months and 79% within 12 months following cessation of drug therapy. Therefore, it would seem that a behavioral treatment for HBP that can result in maintenance of normotensive BP levels for as long as 6 months following the active treatment (training) period would compare favorably, on this basis, with traditional forms of drug therapy for HBP. Behavioral studies that have addressed this question by including follow-up data have been designated as clinical research and are summarized in Table 2. The studies by Richter-Heinrich (1981), Richter-Heinrich, Homuth *et al.* (1982), Richter-Heinrich *et al.* (in press); and McGrady, Fine, Woerner, & Yonker (1983) had follow-up periods lasting at least 18 months. Four others had follow-up periods of at least 12 months (Agras, Southam, & Taylor, 1983; Bali, 1979; Goebel, Viol, Lorenz, & Clemente, 1980; and Goldstein, Shapiro, & Thananopavarn, 1984), and five (Agras, Schneider, & Taylor, 1984; Engel, Glasgow, & Gaarder, 1983; Goldstein, Shapiro, Thananopavarn, & Sambhi, 1982; Patel, Marmot, & Terry, 1981; Southam, Agras, Taylor, & Kraemer, 1982) report follow-up periods of at least 6 months. Treatment effects were maintained in all cases; although this was complicated

TABLE 2. Behavioral Treatment of High Blood Pressure: Clinical Research

Reference	Treatment(s)	n			Subject characteristics	Follow-up	Duration of training	Main finding(s)
		Cntl	Exp	Tot				
Agras et al., 1983 Southam et al., 1982	Rel + Ambulatory Monitoring	18	12	30	Clinic BP 144/97, Worksite BP 143/93, 67% Medicated	15 mos.	½ h/wk. × 8 wks.	Clinic Worksite Post Rx −16/−14 −9/−6 F/U −12/−14 −12/−8
Agras et al., 1984	Rel	11	11	22	Subsample from larger study who returned to baseline BP after lowering Avg DBP >90	6 mos.	10 × ½h in 8 wks	Initial F/U Retrain −11/−12 −6/−10 No retrain −12/13 −10/−8
Bali, 1979	Rel			18	Males w/moderate HBP (146−174/98−116)	1 yr.	1 h/wk. × 8 wks.	Rel decr BP for 1yr (−12/−9), also decr anxiety
Engel et al., 1981 1982 Glasgow et al., 1982 Engel et al., 1983	BF(BP),Rel, Mon, Combo	20	70	90	Medic + Nonmedic Borderline HBP (90 < DBP < 105 w/out Medication)	6 mos.	6 mos.	Cntl −7/−4 Rel −6/−4 BF(BP) −9/−8 Rel-BF(BP) −10/−6 BF(BP)-Rel −12/−10 All midday results

Study	Treatments	N		N total	BP levels	Follow-up	Sessions	Results
Goebel et al., 1980 (Prelim Report)	BF(BP,EMG), Rel, TA			80	Medicated BP levels not reported	1 yr.	12 wks.	All 4 treatments decr BP (−7/−4) + decr Meds (64%) Group differences inconclusive to date
Goldstein & Shapiro, 1982	BF(BP), Rel, Drugs, Mon			36	Mild HBP untreated 150-165/90-105	1-6 mos.	2/wk. × 8 wks.	Drug −15/−5 BF −4/−4 Rel +2/+5 Mon +4/+3
Goldstein et al., 1984	Rel, Rel + BF(EMG), Mon	14	27	41	Medic 134/87 Non-medic 139/94	1 yr.	10 wks.	Rel & Rel + BF(EMG) decr BP (−8/−4 in morning) Rel more effective in medicated pts
Hafner, 1982	Medit Medit + BF aided Rel, No Rx control	7	14	21	Pts w/HBP Medit 146/103 Medit + BF 160/107 Cntl 159/98	3 mos.	8 × 1h	Medit −15/−14 Medit + BF −22/−15 Cntl −9/−2
Luborsky et al., 1982	Rel, BF (BP), Med, Exercise			51	Drugs 145/101 Rel 142/99 BF(BP) 138/93 Exercise 138/101	3 mos.	3h/wk ×5-12 wks.	Drugs −19/−10 Rel −6/−4 BF(BP) −7/−6 All standing BPs
McGrady et al., 1983	EMG Aided Rel	16	13	29	Medicated 143/91	2 yrs.	1/wk. × 4 wks.	Pre-Post −13/−7 Pre-F/U −8/−5

Continued

TABLE 2. Behavioral Treatment of High Blood Pressure: Clinical Research
(*Continued*)

Reference	Treatment(s)	*n* Cntl	Exp	Tot	Subject characteristics	Follow-up	Duration of training	Main finding(s)
Patel *et al.*, 1981	BF(GSR) + Health Educ.	93	99	192	Nonmedicated Industrial Employees (145/87)	8 mos.	8 wks.	−20/−11 (8 wks); −22/−12 (8 mos) + decr plasma renin & aldosterone
Richter-Heinrich *et al.*, 1981 Richter-Heinrich, Homuth, *et al.*, 1982 Richter-Heinrich *et al.*, in press	BF(BP), Rel, Mon.	20	20	40	Nonmedic w/HBP; 20 placed on β-blocker 20 on Behav. Rx	4 yrs.	6–8 sessions in 14 days	Behav −16/−11 Drugs −20/−11
Seer & Raeburn, 1980	"TM-like"	13	28	41	Nonmedic 150/102	3 mos.	5 wks.	−5/−7 Mantra not essential

BF = biofeedback; BID = twice per day; BP = blood pressure; Cntl = control; Combo = combined treatment; EMG = electromyogram; Exp = experimental; f_R = frequency of respiration (breaths/min); F/U = follow-up; GSR = galvanic skin resistance; h = hour(s); HBP = hypertension; HR = heart rate; Mon = monitor; *n* = number of subjects; Rel = relaxation; RER = respiratory exchange ratio ($\dot{V}CO_2/\dot{V}O_2$); RPE = rating of perceived exertion; RPP = rate pressure product (HR × SBP); Rx = treatment; TM = transcendental meditation; Tot. = total; VO_2 = oxygen uptake.

by medication changes in Goldstein *et al.* (1982) and was incomplete at the writing of Goebel *et al.* (1980). Also, the subpopulation studied by Agras *et al.* (1984)—that is, subjects whose BPs returned to pretreatment levels after having successfully been treated using relaxation training—failed to demonstrate that retraining in relaxation might be effective for maintaining treatment effects in such individuals. In the study by Goldstein *et al.* (1984), the negative trends in BP actually continued throughout the one-year follow-up.

The papers by Richter-Heinrich and coworkers (Richter-Heinrich *et al.*, 1981; Richter-Heinrich, Homuth *et al.*, 1982; Richter-Heinrich *et al.*, in press) compare the effects on BP achieved using combinations of psychophysiological interventions and psychotherapy with those achieved using beta-blockers (Talinolol or Propranolol) or BP monitoring. The BP reductions of behaviorally treated subjects compared favorably with those of the medicated group after one year of treatment. However, the 4-year follow-up period involved only the behaviorally treated Therapy Group 1. Furthermore, at crossover, Therapy Group 2 (self-monitoring only in Phase 1) received a slightly altered behavioral "treatment package," and the pharmacologically treated group underwent changes in medications. Therefore, the value of comparisons based on these follow-up data is questionable.

McGrady and coworkers examined the lasting effects of EMG-assisted relaxation on SBP, DBP, forehead EMG, plasma aldosterone, and urinary cortisol. All of these variables were reduced after 16 sessions (McGrady *et al.*, 1981); and all but urinary cortisol showed significantly lower values at the 2-year follow-up (McGrady *et al.*, 1983). However, none of the patients had been aware of a potential follow-up study at the time of the original experiment, so there could have been some degree of self-selection among the follow-up patients favoring those who had found the treatment procedure appealing. Furthermore, additional training was provided at follow-up. The effect of this on follow-up BP levels is uncertain.

Behavioral Treatment Compared with Pharmacological Treatment

Behavioral and pharmacological treatments for HBP have been compared by many authors: for example, Weiss (1980); Luborsky, Ancona, Masoni, Scolari, & Longoni (1980–81); Luborsky *et al.* (1982); Andrews, Macmahon, Austin, & Byrne (1982); Glasgow, Gaarder, & Engel (1982); Goldstein *et al.* (1982); Richter-Heinrich *et al.* (1981); Richter-Heinrich, Homuth *et al.* (1982); Richter-Heinrich *et al.* (in press); and Vaitl (1982). In Luborsky *et al.* (1980–81), subjects treated with antihypertensive medications responded better even at moderate doses than did subjects treated with biofeedback, metronome-conditioned relaxation, or metronome-conditioned mild exercise. However, because some patients received comparable benefits from the behavioral treatments, the authors suggest that patients with HBP who are strongly motivated to try behavioral treatments should be encouraged to undergo such therapy before medical intervention is begun in order to determine whether this approach will be beneficial for them.

More negative conclusions were drawn by Vaitl (1982) who, using data from published reports, contrasted the depressor effects on DBP of relaxation and/or biofeedback with BP changes observed in multicenter drug intervention programs for mild HBP—defined as DBP $\leq$ 110 mm Hg, although few would classify DBPs $>$ 104 mm Hg as mild HBP. Separate linear regression analyses were made for both groups to determine change in DBP relative to pretreatment BP levels. Slopes and intercepts of the regression lines were compared with the "ideal" regression line ($y' = 90 - x$) representing reductions in DBP to 90 mm Hg. The conclusion was that relaxation and/or biofeedback should not be generally recommended as alternatives to pharmacotherapy. Rather, they are more appropriate as adjuncts to medical treatment.

Andrews et al. (1982) compared 37 reports of nonpharmacological treatments for HBP with standard drug treatment. Their finding was that drugs offered the most effective treatment for HBP, with weight reduction, yoga, and muscle relaxation producing small reductions in BP and meditation, exercise training, BP biofeedback, and salt restriction proving inferior and not different from placebo treatment.

Weiss (1980), in his review of the literature, noted that although biofeedback is often criticized for the low magnitude of BP reductions attributed to the procedure, evidence exists to suggest that combined behavioral approaches play a synergistic role in the treatment of HBP and that a combination of pharmacologic and behavioral treatments might show significant benefits over the use of drugs alone (cf. Patel, 1973; Patel & North, 1975).

Richter-Heinrich et al. (1981) studied a group of 40 hypertensives for a period of 3 months. Twenty subjects were treated psychophysiologically (relaxation and blood pressure biofeedback) and 20 were given a beta-blocker (Talinolol or propranolol). Behaviorally treated subjects were removed from all antihypertensive medications at least 14 days prior to hospitalization. After 3 months of treatment, including relaxation, BP feedback, BP monitoring, circulation and respiratory exercises, discussions of life-style, and psychotherapy, the psychophysiological treatments were found to be adequate to produce reductions in BP among some patients with mild HBP. It was necessary for other behaviorally treated subjects to begin drug therapy.

In a more recent study, Richter-Heinrich, Homuth, *et al.* (1982) reported comparable reductions in BP over a one-year period among 20 pharmacologically treated subjects and 20 behaviorally treated subjects, which contrasted with elevations in BP experienced by 8 control subjects who only monitored their BP for 3 months.

Still more recently, Richter-Heinrich *et al.* (in press) have compared a similar behavioral treatment group of 20 subjects with a self-monitoring control group ($n = 24$) and a pharmacological control group ($n = 20$ taking beta blockers, 10 on Talinolol and 10 on propranolol). In a crossover design, after 3 months, 21 of the self-monitoring group received a variation of the psychological treatment package (outpatient stress-management training instead of the individual psychotherapy). Self-recordings of BP, professional recordings of BP, pre- and posttherapeutic physiological stress testing, and psychological inventories were used to monitor the effects of treatments. During the initial 3 months, the BPs of the psychologically treated group decreased significantly whereas those of the self-monitoring group rose slightly only to decrease significantly and at a comparable rate to that of the first group upon crossing over to psychological treatment. After one year, the mean reductions in BP were 16/11 and 20/11 for the psychological group and the pharmacological group, respectively. They conclude once again that in certain patients with mild HBP a behavioral treatment can be successfully used in lieu of drug therapy.

In another study with a similar goal, but contrasting results, Luborsky *et al.* (1982) compared pharmacological treatment (mostly diuretics but following the stepped-care plan of the HDFP such that one subject also took propranolol and another also took methyl dopa), BP feedback (3 one-hour sessions per week for 5 weeks, in which BPs taken every 2 minutes for 40 minutes were graphically compared with the session's baseline, enabling patients to raise, lower, alternately raise and lower, and finally to lower BP), metronome-conditioned relaxation, and mild exercise. They found that 70% of medicated patients lowered their BP by at least 10 mm Hg whereas in the other three groups the percentages of patients achieving 10 mm Hg reductions were 36%, 31%, and 18%, respectively. These three groups were not different from one another but the behavioral treatments were significantly weaker in effect on BP than was medication. No patients were taking antihypertensive medications at the time of the study. However, 20 subjects who had been taking small doses of diuretics for HBP had this medication discontinued for at least 3 days prior to the start of the 2-week baseline. It is doubtful that 3 days' discontinuance of diuretic therapy is long enough to render subjects truly comparable in regard to their medical status for BP treatment during baseline (see Engel *et al.*, 1983).

Goldstein *et al.* (1982) compared the effects of BP feedback (cf. Shapiro, Tursky, Gershon, & Stern, 1969; Tursky, Shapiro, & Schwartz, 1972), relaxation (cf. Benson, Rosner, Marzetta, & Klemchuk, 1974a, b), and drug treatment (minimal dosage and medication for optimal BP control) to the effect of home monitoring (a control group). Thirty-six subjects, 35 to 60 years of age, with DBP = 90 − 105 mm Hg. and/or SBP = 150 − 165 mm Hg. were, on three initial visits to the laboratory, given psychological tests and instructions in home monitoring of BP. BP medications were gradually withdrawn over a period of a few months. In five baseline sessions (conducted over a period of $2\frac{1}{2}$ weeks) the investigators measured BP, heart rate, respiratory rate, skin conductance, and frontalis muscle EMG in Sessions 1, 2, and 4; and reactivity to mental arithmetic, white noise, and the cold pressor test in Sessions 3 and 5. During the 8-week treatment period, patients in each treatment modality were seen twice per week. Drug treatment was markedly superior to all other treatments for regulation of home BP. However, BP feedback was as effective as drugs for lowering DBP—but not SBP—in the laboratory. Follow-up reactivity sessions were conducted at 1,2,3, and 6 months following the treatment period on all patients except those on medication. During this time, SBP rose in all groups followed. DBP for the biofeedback group tended to remain at treatment levels whereas, by the 6-month test period, the relaxation and home monitoring groups showed increased DBPs. The authors note, however, that these results are complicated by the fact that as BPs rose, patients were placed back on their antihypertensive medications. Nonetheless, the relatively slow rise in BP after cessation of behavioral treatment compares with results obtained by the VA Cooperative Study Group (1975). Those authors claimed that a slow rise in BP over 6 months was indicative of a capability of arterial pressure to modify following long-term treatment. Otherwise, elevated pressures would have been expected to reappear promptly after stopping treatment. It is also of interest that the patients in the Goldstein et al. (1982) study monitored BP during the morning and evening only. In the light of our experience (Glasgow et al., 1982), we would expect greater effects of behavioral treatment to have been observed had afternoon pressures been monitored as well.

CLINICAL EXPERIENCE

Behavioral treatment of HBP will be judged by the medical community on the basis of how well reports of its therapeutic effectiveness have adhered to the rules of scientific methodology. Procedures for gathering data must be specified precisely and results must be reproducible by others. It is suggested by some that, in behavioral research, strict adherence to the scientific method has resulted in literature on biofeedback that underestimates its true therapeutic potential when used by experienced clinicians. For example, 14 responders (hospitals, clinics, and individual clinicians) to surveys conducted by Patricia A. Norris of the Menninger Foundation, and/or the American College of Physicians (Norris, personal communication) reported experiences with biofeedback treatment of HBP that were quite favorable (70% to 88% of patients improved with followups of from 6 months to 8 years). However, reports such as these, which provide almost no data, are testimonial rather than substantive in nature, and they do not gain widespread respect from physicians, who are more accustomed to pharmacological methods of treating HBP.

It has always been recognized, even among the most rigorous investigators, that the actual response(s) of a patient to treatment can often far exceed expectations based on research evidence. This is true of pharmacological interventions and behavioral ones; and, for lack of a more objective explanation, has been ascribed to such phenomena as the "clinical skill of the practitioner," the "art of medicine," the "healing touch," etc. We also acknowledge these extremely important aspects of patient care. However, it is the duty of scientific research to provide a firm basis upon which treatment procedures can be established, regardless of any additional personal attributes the provider or patient may or may not possess.

The frequent use of but two categories, "improved" and "failed to improve," in clinical accounts of behaviorally treated cases of HBP makes comparison of such reports with those discussed earlier quite difficult. Chronically elevated BP is of concern only insofar as it places one at greater risk of experiencing serious cardiovascular of cerebrovascular sequelae. Therefore, if one improves (i.e., achieves a lower BP), the risk of these serious consequences is reduced. However, the physician responsible for treating a patient's HBP is not typically inclined to experiment with biofeedback and/or relaxation techniques to see whether or not the patient improves—especially when BP can be reduced with certainty using drugs. There must be some established level of confidence that the physician can use to predict likelihood of improvement, and this must be based on the controlled experiences of many. This fact is basic to scientific methodology, and must remain basic to clinical practice also. Therefore, we strongly recommend that researchers investigating behavioral methods for treating HBP renew their efforts to follow the historical guidelines for sound research procedures.

SPECIFICITY OF EFFECT

Data pertinent to the question of whether a particular behavioral treatment for HBP is associated with greater reduction of BP because it contains more of some BP-specific active ingredient have been reviewed previously (Shapiro & Jacob, 1983). Results were equivocal, some studies demonstrating greater effectiveness of BP biofeedback and others favoring relaxation. To date, this question remains unanswered. In fact, the popularity of treatments that combine BP biofeedback with relaxation, or that use biofeedback to assist relaxation training, tends to add further to the complexity of this issue. In this section, we will discuss direct BP feedback separately from other behavioral treatments that are purported to affect BP secondary to a reduction in sympathetic nervous system (SNS) activity or muscle tension.

Direct Feedback of Blood Pressure

In his part of the previous Task Force Report that reviewed 8 studies (1971–1975) using beat-by-beat feedback of BP as described by Tursky et al. (1972), Blanchard (1978, p. 7) reported that seven of the studies had achieved "clinically and/or statistically significant decreases in BP." However, he asserted that these BP reductions (6 to 8 mm Hg relative to BP levels in baseline periods that ranged from no baseline to 26 sessions over a 6-week period—four of the studies having baselines of but 1, 1, 3, and 4 sessions, respectively) were borderline in "clinical meaningfulness." He did not justify his criteria for "clinical meaningfulness," nor did he define the term. However, he did note that the studies he reviewed typically did not include good follow-up data, nor did they adequately investigate the extent to which changes observed in the laboratory were transferable to the patient's natural environment. Noting the poor replicability of those studies that had obtained promising results, Blanchard concluded that direct feedback of BP was only marginally useful or effective for treatment of HBP. By Blanchard's assessment (p. 12), "only one study using the Tursky et al. (1972) constant cuff pressure technique obtained meaningful clinical results, after an adequate baseline, which held up during follow-up: Kristt & Engel (1975)." The greater magnitude of BP changes brought about during more recent studies involving direct feedback of BP, coupled with the maintenance of these reductions over more extended follow-up periods (cf. Tables 1 & 2), would suggest that the clinical usefulness of this form of BP treatment might be greater than it appeared to be in 1978.

In that earlier Task Force Report (Blanchard, 1978), the author suggested that self-control training (e.g., the use of a sphygmomanometer for home BP readings) and self-management techniques (e.g., home BP monitoring) offer the optimum strategy for controlling tonic physiological responses. He also advised that future work should use BPs measured by the patient at home, along with independent assessments made by the patient's personal physician, in order to obtain reliable BP data, and that home practice of techniques learned in the biofeedback laboratory should be encouraged in order to facilitate the transfer of training effects to the patient's natural environment. Notably, several recent studies employing some or all of these strategies (Glasgow et al., 1982; Richter-Heinrich et al., 1981, Richter-Heinrich, Homuth, et. al., 1982; Richter-Heinrich, in press) have in fact obtained more promising results using direct feedback of BP. The validity of home monitoring has been supported further by Cottier, Julius, Gajendragadkar, & Schork (1982).

Frost and Holmes (1980) were interested in the effect of clinical instructions on the regulation of BP. In a study of 120 patients, they found that instructions alone were effective at causing a person to raise SBP but not to lower it, whereas biofeedback (viewing a graphic strip chart recorder reflecting changes in BP) facilitated limited effects on both raising and lowering of SBP. Shoemaker and Tasto (1975) found a similar graphic form of BP feedback to be ineffective (cf. Blanchard, 1978).

As described earlier, Goldstein et al. (1982) compared the effects of medication, direct BP feedback, meditation, and self-monitoring in 36 patients with mild hypertension. Medication was found to be the superior treatment for SBP, but biofeedback produced a reduction in DBP comparable to that of drugs when measurements were taken in the laboratory. Glasgow et al. (1982) hypothesized that combinations of behavioral therapies might affect BP through different physiological mechanisms and, therefore, might act synergistically to lower BP more in combination than would either treatment used alone. The research design included a one-month baseline period of daily self-monitoring (morning, afternoon, and evening) and weekly professional monitoring of BP, followed by 6 months of continued monitoring along with behavioral treatment. Although a control group (C, $n = 20$) continued the baseline procedure for the full 7 months, the crossover design resulted in four treatment groups over two 3-month study phases (relax-relax, relax-feedback, feedback-relax, and feedback-feedback). The relax (R) condition was a combination progressive and meditative procedure and the feedback (F) condition was a constant cuff method of direct, beat-by-beat, feedback of SBP. Of 127 patients who completed baseline, 90 completed the entire study. R and F lowered BP acutely, that is, during the actual practice, and the extent of lowering improved with practice. The two behavioral treatments were equally effective at lowering SBP, but R was more effective at lowering DBP. Generalization of treatment effects was demonstrated by the long-term results that showed BP declining for at least 6 months with regular BP monitoring and patient-involved assessment of progress. The application of R and F together was more effective than either used alone, and the sequence FR was slightly, but not significantly, better than RF. The greatest reductions in

BP were observed during the afternoon hours when BP tended to be highest. Average long-term afternoon changes (measured as changes from the average level of BP during the one month baseline period) for the respective groups were as follows: CC (-7/-4), RR (-6/-4), FF (-9/-8), RF (-10/-6), FR (-12/-10). Average changes in clinically determined BPs (measured as the average change in clinic BP from the average of the last three BPs recorded in each patient's medical record prior to entering the study to the average BP during the final study phase) were: CC (-7/-6), RR (-6/-7), FF (-5/-6), RF (-8/-6) and FR (-14/-10). Only the FR group was significantly different from control. It was hypothesized that the combined effects of R and F are greater because of different mechanisms of action. However, appropriate laboratory studies should be done to test this further.

Goebel *et al.* (1980) attempted to isolate the effects of R from those of F by comparing four treatment groups (R only, R + EMG, BP feedback, and R + BP feedback) against a control group practicing transactional analysis. In this preliminary report (written after 4 years of a 6-year protocol), all treatment groups had significantly lowered BPs (-7/-4) and reduced their requirement for antihypertensive medication (64%); but the control group had not. Treatment group differences and hormonal analyses were awaiting completion of the full 6 years. Because pretreatment BP levels were not reported in this study, it is difficult to assess this magnitude of BP reduction in comparison with those reported by other investigators.

Electromyograph (EMG), EMG-Assisted Relaxation, Galvanic Skin Resistance (GSR)

The second treatment group (R + EMG) in the study by Goebel *et al.* (1980) is an example of the use of biofeedback putatively to aid in bringing about a general reduction in SNS activity and muscle tension, thereby reducing BP. However, adequate data to justify this rationale are not yet available (Richter-Heinrich, Lori, Knust, & Schmid, 1982), nor are there data to show that the patients in the Goebel study had abnormal SNS activities before treatment. Furthermore, there is little or no evidence to show that, even if the rationale is valid, reduction of SNS activity of this degree or nature is clinically useful.

Hafner (1982) compared BP changes among groups of hypertensive patients practicing meditation, meditation plus biofeedback (GSR or EMG)-assisted relaxation, or a no-treatment control procedure (sitting in a relaxed position for 30 minutes) in order to determine whether the combination of behavioral interventions is better than meditation alone. He found the behavioral treatments to be effective at reducing SBP and

DBP, but neither to be significantly better than the control procedure. Hafner investigated relatively few subjects (7 in each group) over a relatively short period of time (5 months including a 3-month follow-up), so his conclusion that the results clearly prove that biofeedback-aided relaxation does not enhance reduction of BP over that produced in association with meditation needs to be validated.

The most noted works involving biofeedback of other than BP for treatment of HBP have been those of Patel (1973), Patel and North (1975), and Patel *et al.* (1981). In the more recent study, Patel *et al.* (1981), 204 adult employees of a large industry, who were found to have two or more coronary risk factors (high serum cholesterol, high BP, or smoking 10 or more cigarettes per day), were randomly divided into a biofeedback group receiving training in relaxation and stress management and a control group. Everyone received health education literature on entry and a subsample from each group was tested for plasma renin activity and plasma aldosterone on entry, after 8 weeks of training, and at an 8-month follow-up. Training in breathing exercises, deep muscle relax-ation, and meditation was facilitated using a cassette tape in weekly one-hour sessions for 8 weeks. Relaxation was enhanced by the use of a multicircuit galvanic skin resistance feedback machine. Six subjects were trained at a time and were lent the tapes for use in home practice twice daily. After 8 weeks, subjects whose BPs had exceeded 140/90 showed average reductions of 19.6/10.6 as contrasted with control group reduc-tions of 8.2/3.6. At the 8-month follow-up, the treated subjects' average BP had been reduced by 22.4/11.5 compared with the control reductions at follow-up of 11.4/2.7. In addition, a significantly greater reduction in plasma renin activity and plasma aldosterone concentration was ob-served at 8 weeks but not at 8 months in the biofeedback group as compared with the control group. No correlation was observed between the changes in BP and plasma renin activity for either group. However, the correlation between plasma aldosterone and BP at 8 weeks was significant. The authors interpret this as a suggestion that different mechanisms are responsible for long-term maintenance of BP reduction and acute reduction. Our observations (Glasgow *et al.*, 1982) are con-sistent with this interpretation. Whereas relaxation and SBP feedback were equally effective at lowering SBP acutely, relaxation had a greater short-term effect on DBP. However, the long-term effects of SBP feed-back were slightly greater than those of relaxation, and those patients who received both treatments showed the greatest long-term effects (cf. Table 2).

An average reduction in mean BP of 10 mm Hg in 10 hypertensive subjects, coupled with a 33% reduction in medication requirements, was observed by Datey (1980) following the addition of relaxation training and GSR biofeedback to conventional drug treatment. Comparable changes were not seen in the 10 control subjects who did not receive behavioral treatment. However, it should be noted (Table 1) that the pretreatment BP levels of subjects in this study were relatively high (158/103 mm Hg). Therefore, a comparison of the observed BP reductions (-18/-7) with those observed in studies of patients with lower pretreatment BPs is of uncertain validity (cf. Agras & Jacob, 1979). Changes in the responsiveness of the experimental subjects to the cold pressor test and Master's two-step exercise test, not seen in the control subjects, led Datey to conclude that the behavioral treatments modified his subjects' responsiveness to stress. Although these tests do stress the individual physically, it is not clear that this form of acute stress is comparable to the "constant state of anxiety" that Datey suggested is the cause for modern day increases in the incidence of HBP. It is true that increasing skin resistance can be associated with an increased state of relaxation and, therefore, the GSR might serve as a valuable aid in relaxation training. However, the physiological link between acute changes in GSR and the chronic problem of HBP was not examined in the Datey study and no attempt was made to determine whether patients with HBP have characteristically low skin resistance. Valuable information should result from further investigation of the relationship between GSR and BP.

McGrady et al. (1981) showed reductions in BP, muscle tension, plasma aldosterone, and urinary cortisol in a group of subjects practicing EMG-assisted relaxation. They interpreted their results as indicating a reduction of muscle tension and BP mediated by reductions in responsiveness to stress involving the adrenal cortex. The Patel group and the McGrady group have both made admirable attempts to elucidate the mechanism(s) by which behavioral techniques are able to lower BP. However, the complexity of the physiological systems involved in BP homeostasis will require that additional studies be done in the laboratory before final conclusions can be drawn. The results of such studies should help to improve the efficacy of behavioral treatments for HBP, and enable practitioners more accurately to predict the type of behavioral treatment(s) that will be most effective with a given patient. However, it is likely that animal models ultimately will provide the best means for studying physiological mechanisms because the neurosurgical techniques required to assess hormonal function or regional hemodynamics are unacceptable in human research.

Skin Temperature Feedback

The use of skin temperature feedback from thermisters attached to a finger and/or a toe also has been put forth as an effective way to train hypertensive patients to regulate sympathetic outflow to the periphery and thereby putatively to lower BP and to minimize or eliminate the requirement for antihypertensive medication (Green, Green, & Norris, 1980). This form of biofeedback is usually recommended as part of "a multicomponent treatment program including cognitive explanations, effective relaxation procedures, home practice of relaxation and (often) home measurement of blood pressures by the subjects themselves" (Fahrion, 1979, p. 1). In this sense, thermal biofeedback is not obviously different from GSR, EMG, or even direct feedback of BP as they are often applied in the treatment of HBP. Each of these modalities also has been used successfully in training patients to lower BP, and each has been described as a major component in a clinical treatment protocol, but the effectiveness in the treatment of HBP of a multicomponent protocol involving thermal biofeedback from the hands and/or feet has been claimed to be preferable clinically (Fahrion, 1979). Libo and Arnold (1983a) suggest that training to criteria (i.e., EMG < 1.1 mV and/or skin temperature $> 95°$ F) is important for achieving good clinical results using these modalities.

Relaxation

The distinction between relaxation therapy for HBP and many of the other forms of behavioral treatment discussed earlier is not clear. In fact, most forms of biofeedback discussed earlier involve some form of directed relaxation therapy with instrumental assistance provided to aid the patient in learning either to relax musculature or to reduce skin resistance, presumably in order to reduce sympathetic nervous system activity and lower BP. Constant cuff BP feedback is an exception to this.

Most recent studies of relaxation and/or meditation for treatment of HBP have confirmed many of the earlier findings of Benson, Rosner, & Marzetta (1973). That is, to emit the relaxation response seems to be a skill that can be learned and refined with practice (Wallace et al., 1983), and the specifics of the particular method used—for example, focused with a mantra or unfocused (Seer & Raeburn, 1980)—is not as important as is regular practice and adherence to the basic elements of relaxation described by Benson (1975). Evidence generally supports the theory that the physiological changes that occur during the practice of relaxation are mediated through the sympathetic nervous system (Davidson, Winchester, Taylor, Alderman, & Ingels, 1979). The improvement of therapy for HBP using relaxation has evolved into efforts to enhance generalization of the effects of relaxation from the laboratory or other site of relaxation practice into the subject's natural environment. Approaches to this have included offering training at the worksite (Agras et al., 1983; Charlesworth, Williams, & Baer, 1984; Patel et al., 1981; Southam et al., 1982), and the development of shortened forms of the relaxation procedure, which can be used more frequently during the day and in a wider variety of circumstances (Glasgow *et al.*, 1982).

Thus, of the variety of behavioral approaches to BP reduction that we have reviewed, relaxation is the least specific in its effect. The BP lowering effects of relaxation range from very good to no better than control conditions (cf. Tables 1 & 2), quite possibly owing to subtle differences in approach to the procedure by different individuals (therapists or patients), to differences in the physical environments in which the treatments were administered and/or practiced, or to patient selection variables which have not been evaluated systematically.

MECHANISM OF ACTION

The physiological variables that interact to maintain BP were identified in the introduction. Although it is presumed that BP reductions achieved with behavioral treatment strategies operate through one or more of these variables, little progress has been made toward the elucidation of the mechanism(s) by which this occurs. In fact, little is known about the physiological mechanisms that elevate BP leading to sustained HBP. Because these are apt to be different in different individuals—as evidenced by differing levels of effectiveness of the various antihypertensive medications—behavioral treatments might also be differentially suitable for different patients.

Research in this area involving human subjects has naturally been limited to the assessment of plasma or urinary levels of hormones (plasma aldosterone, plasma renin, and urinary cortisol) as the titers of these substances change in association with a behavioral treatment procedure and concomitant BP reductions. For example, as noted in the previous section, the work of Patel *et al.* (1981) suggested different mechanisms of action for long- and short-term BP regulation using relaxation techniques and GSR feedback. This was based on different, time-related correlations between BP reductions and plasma renin and aldosterone. Similarly, McGrady *et al.* (1981) demonstrated the potential involvement of the adrenal cortex by measuring reductions in plasma aldosterone and urinary cortisol in association with reductions in muscle tension and BP. However, no causal relationship has yet been established between the levels of these hormones and HBP. Therefore, their value as indicators of successful BP intervention can be questioned.

Early reports (Benson, Greenwood, & Klemchuk, 1975; Wallace & Benson, 1972; Wallace, Benson, & Wilson, 1971) found the reductions in BP associated with the practice of relaxation to concur with reductions in breathing rate, heart rate, and oxygen consumption, suggesting that relaxation lowers BP primarily by reducing cardiac output. The recent work of Gervino & Veazey (1984) supports this. Conversely, reductions in BP attributed to BP feedback have been observed in the absence of changes in muscle tension (triceps brachii), EEG (alpha wave activity), heart rate, or breathing rate (Kristt & Engel, 1975), or in stroke index (Messerli, Decarvalho, Christie, & Froelich, 1979). These authors suggest that BP feedback lowers BP primarily by reducing the tension in peripheral vascular musculature.

Goebel *et al.* (1980) have sought further to isolate the hypotensive effects of relaxation from those of biofeedback. The projected number of subjects for this study was 130. Eighty subjects are included in this preliminary report, which tests the effects upon BP of (a) EMG-assisted R as opposed to R alone, (b) feedback of BP vs. cultivated low arousal (whether feedback assisted or not), and (c) R prior to BP feedback. The effects of R and BF on plasma renin activity, cortisol levels, aldosterone levels, and norepinephrine levels also are examined. Although the findings of this study are strengthened by its relatively long (2 to 26 weeks) "stabilization" (baseline) period, during which BP control is achieved through adjustments in medications, the adjustments were made weekly, which is probably too frequent to allow for stabilization of BP between changes in medication. Results of the 12-month follow-up were not available at this writing. Undoubtedly, much further laboratory research involving both human and subhuman subjects will be required to answer the many remaining questions about the physiological mechanisms by which BP can be regulated behaviorally.

The paper by Davidson *et al.* (1979) is another interesting study of the mechanism(s) of action whereby BP can be reduced by relaxation. Clearly, the subjects—six patients at 21 to 53 months after cardiac surgery who had implanted metallic myocardial markers—are not representative of the general population of patients with HBP, but the finding that training in deep muscle relaxation was accompanied by reductions in plasma norepinephrine and myocardial contractility adds support to the hypothesis that the physiological changes associated with relaxation are mediated through the sympathetic nervous system, at least in the heart.

Synergistic or Antagonistic Interactions between Behavioral and Pharmacological Treatments

Relatively little work has been published addressing the possibility that behavioral and pharmacological treatments might interact with one another in beneficial or adverse ways—a special concern when a stepped-care treatment plan is followed (Laughlin, 1981)—and the results which have been reported are mixed. In their recent study, Goldstein, Shapiro,

& Thananopavarn (1984) compared the effects on BP of relaxation, relaxation + EMG feedback, and self-monitoring among groups of pharmacologically treated patients with the effects on BP of the relaxation procedure in an unmedicated group. Greater reduction in BP was observed among the medicated group although the relaxation procedure lowered BP in all groups. The authors suggest that relaxation and medication may have had additive effects on BP. Charlesworth et al. (1984), studying the BP-lowering effects of a group stress management program conducted at the worksite, did not show differences in responsiveness to the procedures (including self-monitoring of BP, autogenic training, and relaxation directed by audio tapes for home practice) between medicated and unmedicated hypertensive subjects. Glasgow et al. (1982) found less responsiveness to behavioral therapy among patients currently undergoing only diuretic therapy for HBP (Medicated patients in the Goldstein et al., 1984, study were taking a variety of antihypertensive medications with a variety of sites of action.) It was suggested by Glasgow et al. (1982) that the effects on peripheral vascular resistance of thiazide diuretics may have been sufficient to prevent further reduction of vascular tone by relaxation or SBP feedback. Further investigation of possible interactions between antihypertensive medications and behavioral therapies is obviously warranted; but future work will have to contend with the wide variety of pharmacological mechanisms by which medications affect BP regulation, as well as the duration of their activity following discontinuation of medical treatment.

COST-EFFECTIVENESS

To date, research in behavioral medicine has not systematically compared the cost-effectiveness of behavioral treatment to that of pharmacological treatment for HBP. However, because the cost of medication could negatively influence patient compliance, better management of BP would likely result if the cost of therapy were reduced. As more is learned about the interaction of behavioral and pharmacological antihypertensive treatments, it is possible that a significant number of patients will be managed successfully on lower dosages of drugs, thereby reducing that component of the cost of care.

Because most of the behavioral treatments for HBP reviewed here were of relatively short duration (commonly one or two sessions per week for 8 weeks, cf. Table 2), and the cost of equipment needed was either a one-time expense or was nominal, it is likely that any behavioral treatment that effects a reduction in the requirement for antihypertensive medication would reduce the overall cost of treatment by minimizing the cost of medication and the cost of periodic medical evaluation requisite for patients taking antihypertensive drugs. Of course, the reduction in incidence of drug-related side effects, which would be expected to accompany reduced dosages, should further enhance the cost-effectiveness of antihypertensive treatment strategies that include effective behavioral components. Additional long-term benefits resulting from behavioral interventions at the worksite have been realized through reductions in health insurance costs (Charlesworth et al., 1984). This constitutes a monetary savings for both the patient and the employer.

Alternatively, the short duration of many behavioral treatment programs leaves them dependent, for their cost-effectiveness, upon the patient's learning of a skill that will be maintained for a long period of time without further professional intervention. In most cases, this would presume some continual activity on the part of patient in order to maintain learning and extend the duration of treatment effects. To date, no one has shown that compliance at this level of continued patient involvement would be widespread. Dropout rates from many studies suggest that it would not be. If one were to infer from this that maintenance of behavioral treatment effects will often require periodic (perhaps annual) repetition of the professional training regimen—and/or persistent efforts on the part of the therapist to motivate the patient to comply with the treatment protocol—then the monetary cost of behavioral therapy may be greater than what would be estimated on the basis of currently available data.

Further evaluation of the cost-effectiveness associated with efforts to manage HBP using behavioral techniques should attempt to determine its effect on (a) medication requirements for maintaining adequate control of BP, (b) incidence of side effects associated with antihypertensive drug therapy, (c) patient compliance with the overall treatment plan, (d) the overall cost of the treatment plan—including professional fees, laboratory tests, medications, and equipment purchased by the patient, and (e) corporate savings realized through effective utilization of the worksite as a point of intervention for treatment of large numbers of individuals.

FUTURE RESEARCH

Controlled Clinical Trial

We recommend the implementation of a large-scale controlled clinical trial (CCT). This would involve the establishment of standardized guidelines for measurement of BP (Kirkendall, Burton, Epstein, & Fries, 1967; Mancia, 1983; Manning, Kuchirka, & Kaminski, 1983) and standardized behavioral treatment protocols with appropriate periods for gathering baseline data. Of course it would also be necessary to specify guidelines for the duration of behavioral treatment(s), intertreatment intervals, alterations in drug dosage, and the duration of follow-up.

Considerable attention should be given in the CCT to the relative responsiveness to behavioral treatment of medicated and nonmedicated patients with HBP. Such data would facilitate comparison of the respective mechanisms of action associated with pharmacological and behavioral treatments and would provide a basis for standardization of clinical protocols involving combinations of treatment modalities. Also, more extensive studies of the relative levels of compliance with behavioral and pharmacological treatments are needed. One might speculate that a behavioral treatment with a small effect but a high level of compliance would provide a better means of managing HBP than would a drug treatment having a large effect but relatively poor compliance. Yet this remains to be proven.

Improved BP Measurement Technique

The therapeutic effect of BP monitoring has been reported under varied circumstances (Engel, Gaarder, & Glasgow, 1981; Gould, Mann, Davies, Altman, & Raftery, 1981), but the full therapeutic impact of regular monitoring on a patient's average BP level deserves further study. For example, what would be the expected outcome if a patient found to have hypertension were prescribed self-monitoring instead of medication for control of the condition? Clearly, the answer to this question has economic as well as therapeutic significance. Also, what is the likelihood of spontaneous recovery from a state of HBP following—or during—a finite period of treatment by either behavioral or pharmacologic means? Normal BP has been shown to persist for 12 to 18 months following cessation of effective antihypertensive drug therapy (Levinson et al., 1982; VA Cooperative Study Group on Antihypertensive Agents, 1975) and some behavioral techniques have led to maintenance of BP reductions for similarly long periods following cessation of treatment (cf. Table 2). Yet elucidation of this aspect of HBP treatment is far from adequate to provide guidelines whereby a physician could, with confidence, discontinue antihypertensive drug therapy without further objective evidence that control of BP will be sustained. Self monitoring of BP, by the patient, could provide sufficient data to establish this level of confidence (cf. Cottier et al., 1982), but improvements in indirect BP measurement technology also are necessary.

Blood pressure, by virtue of its inherent role in maintaining physiological homeostasis, varies greatly with changing environmental conditions (Laughlin, Sherrard, & Fisher, 1980). Therefore, casual clinical BP measurement may not provide the best sampling procedure. Although casual clinical BP determinations have been shown to predict morbidity and mortality (Kannel, 1975), Floras et al. (1981) found that the incidence of target organ damage actually was greater when clinic cuff BP measurements were more highly correlated with mean arterial blood pressure as determined by direct monitoring under ambulatory conditions. In 32 patients, mean arterial pressure was more than 10 mm Hg lower than cuff pressure and the incidence of cardiovascular target organ damage was less than that in 22 other patients whose mean cuff and ambulatory pressures were similar; yet the two groups of patients were not distinguishable by clinical examination, sympathetic nervous system activity, BP variability, or by the magnitude of BP rise during physical or mental exercise. The Floras group concluded that better predictability of cardiovascular morbidity and mortality would follow improvements in methodologies for estimating true arterial pressure and its daily fluctuations.

In a retrospective study, Perloff, Sokolow, & Cowan (1983) reviewed the course of 1,076 patients with HBP who had initially been evaluated using ambulatory BP and office BP measures. Ambulatory pressure was estimated using a portable electronic semiautomatic indirect BP recorder. Patients were classified by the difference between their mean ambulatory BP as observed with the portable recorder and that predicted by office measurements. Life-table analyses revealed a greater cumulative 10-year incidence of fatal and nonfatal cardiovascular events among patients whose ambulatory pressures were greater than predicted by office measurements than among patients whose ambulatory pressures were lower than predicted by office measurements. Because the office-determined BPs were similar between the two groups, this work casts further doubt on the validity of casual clinical BPs as predictors of cardiovascular morbidity and mortality resulting from HBP.

Other investigators have noted discrepancies between professionally determined BPs taken in an office or clinic setting and self-determined BPs taken at home or at the worksite (Engel et al., 1981; Laughlin et al., 1980) or by a portable, semiautomatic, ambulatory BP recorder (desCombes, Porchet, Waeber, & Brunner, 1984). The general finding has been that professionally determined BPs are higher and less reliable than self-determined BPs. For example, we (Engel et al., 1981) have reported that professionally determined BPs approximate self-determined BPs at the highest time of day (afternoons) and that the correlations between professionally determined BPs were 0.20 (diastolic) and 0.37 (systolic). The correlations among self-determined BPs (systolic and diastolic) were consistently above 0.90. Sokolow, Werdegar, Kain, &

Hinman (1966) reported that about 80% (cf. Figure 1 of Sokolow et al., 1966) of their patients had lower average daily BPs when measurements were recorded using their semiautomatic device than when BPs were recorded by a physician in an outpatient clinic.

Pickering, Harshfield, Kleinert, Blank, & Laragh (1982), and Pickering, Harshfield, Kleinert, & Laragh (1982) also have stressed the differences between BPs measured in the physician's office, at work, at home, and while asleep. To obtain their measurements, this group used a noninvasive ambulatory BP recorder and obtained BP readings every 15 minutes over a 24-hour period. In their study of 25 subjects with normal BP, 25 with borderline HBP, and 25 with established HBP they determined that both HBP groups showed consistently higher BPs in the physician's office as compared with their home readings. BPs at home and in the physician's office were similar among those with normal BP. They also found that pressures in the physician's office predicted the average 24-hour pressures among normal subjects and those with established HBP, but not among patients with borderline HBP. For those in the latter category, they suggest that 24-hour ambulatory monitoring might be better.

In another study from this group, Harshfield, Pickering, Kleinert, Blank, & Laragh (1982) recorded BP and heart rate at 15-minute intervals for 24 hours in 60 untreated patients with uncomplicated mild HBP. Again using an ambulatory monitoring technique that allowed patients to continue their normal daily routines, they found that although casual clinical BP determinations correlated with average 24 hour values ($R = 0.54$ for SBP, $R = 0.61$ for DBP), clinical measurements were actually poor predictors of 24 hour values on an individual basis. Using this same ambulatory monitoring procedure and equipment, Devereux et al., (1983) found left ventricular hypertrophy to be poorly related to clinical SBP ($r = .24$) and DBP ($r = .20$) and to home SBP ($r = .31$) and DBP ($r = .21$) but to be more closely related to BPs during recurring stress at work ($r = .50$ for SBP, $r = .39$ for DBP). This difference in correlation was significant ($p < .05$). Other studies (Agras, Taylor, Kraemer, Allen, & Schneider, 1980; Agras et al., 1983; Southam et al., 1982) also have made use of ambulatory monitoring in order to assess BP under a variety of conditions during a normal working day.

Engel et al. (1981) suggested that, in borderline patients, regular BP monitoring at different times of day would be advisable in determining a treatment plan. Because of the relatively high internal consistency observed among self-determined BPs as compared with that among professionally determined BPs, self-monitoring was recommended as way to obtain more reliable data in the borderline HBP group. It also was noted that several weeks are required for BP to approach an asymptote, even under conditions of frequent measurement. Therefore, extensive baseline periods are essential for establishing a basis from which to measure therapeutic change in BP, and for assessing the clinical status of patients to determine whether therapy is warranted. Furthermore, research is needed to compare semiautomatic BP monitoring, which requires the use of expensive equipment, with patient self-monitoring using a standard (properly calibrated) sphygmomanometer, which is relatively inexpensive.

Matching Patients with Behavioral Treatments

Shapiro and Goldstein (1982) have pointed out that research findings pertaining to the treatment of hypertension by behavioral methods have been inconsistent, owing largely to the variety of kinds of patients studied (borderline or established, medicated or nonmedicated, etc.) and the variety of behavioral techniques attempted (relaxation, blood pressure biofeedback, EMG feedback, skin temperature feedback, etc.). Each of these techniques has been reported to be successful in the regulation of blood pressure but the criteria for success have not been the same throughout the body of research. In fact, reports of successful lowering of BP have rarely been based on preestablished criteria. However, if one accepts the HDFP (1979) results as the standard for successful stepped-care intervention using traditional pharmacological methods (-9.9 mm Hg. DBP, only a 5.4 mm Hg reduction greater than that achieved by the referred-care group), then the results from 11 studies of biofeedback for control of BP, in which the average reduction of BP was 7.4/4.1 mm Hg. with a range of -1 to 23/0 to 21 mm Hg. (Pickering, 1982) are promising, and the results of the studies reviewed here are rather impressive (average BP reduction when some form of biofeedback was used in the treatment = 12/9 mm Hg., range = 4/4 to 22/15, cf. Table 2). Better matching of patients with HBP to behavioral treatments that are more suitable for them might lead to even more impressive reductions in BP, thereby clarifying the usefulness of behavioral treatments for those members of the medical community who remain skeptical.

The relative wealth of information about the physiological mechanisms that contribute to HBP has led to the development of pharmacological agents that affect specific variables to regulate BP. Similarly, it should become possible for one to match behavioral treatments more closely to the physiological problems contributing to HBP. So far, efforts to correlate patient variables with BP and with effectiveness of behavioral therapies have been negative (Goldstein et al., 1982; Holroyd et al., 1982), ambivalent (Luborsky et al., 1982), and positive psychologically (Richter-Heinrich et al., in press) and biochemically (McGrady et al., 1981; Patel et al., 1981). Clearly, much remains to be learned about the long-term effects of the various forms of behavioral treatment for HBP and about the ways in which these effects might differ in different patients.

Comparison of the Long-Term Effects of Behavioral and Pharmacological Treatments

We have used duration of follow-up as a basis for comparison among behavioral studies. This is a common practice, but it is not necessarily a valid one for comparison of behavioral studies with pharmacological ones. In consideration of the differences between pharmacological and behavioral treatments for HBP, one might propose that drug treatments are limited in the duration of their effects by the half-lives of the active ingredients used in therapy. Therefore, any lasting therapeutic benefit following cessation of drug treatment must be due to a restoration of physiological BP determinants to normotensive levels. The extent to which drug therapy contributes to such a recovery remains unclear— again the possibility of a spontaneous recovery. Similarly, when behavioral treatments are offered for HBP, it is unclear whether associated control of BP is limited by some half-life of treatment effectiveness, or whether—as most behavioral researchers assume to be the case—the behavioral treatment has reset the physiological determinants of BP to normotensive levels. Presumably, if the latter were true, traditional poststudy follow-up involving only repeated measures after a specified period of time would be inadequate. In order to be fully informative, attempts at follow-up should include procedures designed to account for changes in the psychosocial factors (major life changes, exercise, diet, etc.) that may bring about a relapse of HBP—perhaps similar to the original cause(s) of BP elevation.

Comment

In spite of the fact that behavioral treatment for HBP has had demonstrated effectiveness under many different circumstances and with many different types of patients, there remains a reluctance among most physicians to accept biofeedback and/or relaxation as reliable therapeutic tools. Frequently it is claimed that the statistically significant BP reductions achieved by these strategies are not clinically significant. Yet there is no widely accepted definition of a reduction in BP which is, or is not, clinically significant. Luborsky et al. (1980) defined a clinically significant reduction in BP as a decrease of more than 10% in mean BP, more than 10 mm Hg. in mean BP, and to a level less than 140/90 mm Hg. However, this definition is arbitrary and has not been generally accepted.

At one time the phrase *clinical significance* was used to refer to the complications of HBP. Thus, HBP was said to be a clinically significant disease because it increased the likelihood of, or caused, serious physical impairment (e.g., left ventricular hypertrophy). Today one frequently encounters the term in a context wherein its meaning is entirely different. For example, many authors have used the term pejoratively to characterize a treatment-induced change in BP that, depending on the author's intent, can mean either a "large and impressive effect" or a "small and unimpressive effect." Often, the latter interpretation is ascribed to a statistically significant outcome; for example, "The results were statistically significant but clinically insignificant." It should be very clear that this use of the concept of clinical significance is completely arbitrary and unsupported by empirical data. There is no epidemiological evidence to support the notion that there is a magnitude of reduction of BP that can be used to define the lower limit of therapeutic effectiveness. As we have noted, the behavioral studies reviewed here achieved BP reductions that compare favorably with the 5.4 mm Hg reduction in DBP taken to be clinically significant by the HDFP (1979). Yet there is still a great deal of ambiguity surrounding the measurement of BP and there is unequivocal evidence that BP varies considerably as a function of the conditions of measurement. Therefore, the frequent use of arbitrary criteria to define outcome effects is wholly unjustified and we urge journal editors to preclude their use. At the same time, we encourage investigators to carry out clinical trials designed to establish the relationship between therapeutic outcome and clinical effect.

Current research in the field of behavioral medicine has made clear the fact that BP can be reduced by strategies employing biofeedback and relaxation techniques. We have reviewed evidence that a variety of forms of behavioral treatment for HBP can be effective, and that their effectiveness can compare with that of medication in terms of overall efficacy in the management of HBP as well as duration of treatment effects. BP reductions ranging from 4 to 22 mm. Hg. systolic and from 1 to 15 mm. Hg. diastolic have reportedly been maintained from 6 to 48 months, sometimes accompanied by reductions in the requirement for antihypertensive medications (cf. Tables 1 and 2). However, the phrase *behavioral treatment for HBP* remains much less definitive than the phrase *pharmacological treatment for HBP*. For whereas the latter unmistakably connotes a situation wherein standard dosages of one or more of the approved drugs having antihypertensive activity will be prescribed, the former suggests only that some effort will be made to induce reduction of BP without the use of medication. Many of the studies we have discussed established rather strictly defined conditions under which the respective treatments were tested, but no evidence of standardization of protocols across studies exists, and reproducibility across laboratories of the various protocols has not been tested. Therefore, the evidence that has been put forth to suggest that behavioral therapies could be as practical for treatment of HBP as are the antihypertensive medications has failed to convince most physicians, and behavioral forms of treatment continue to command little attention from most providers of care for HBP. The failure of behavioral researchers to standardize methodology has detracted from the scientific import of the research on HBP and on the studies of clinical application. There are so many differences in methodologies that it is impossible to characterize the mechanisms underlying any of them. For example, a common faith among users of relaxation therapies is that they all operate through similar mechanisms (Benson, 1975). Yet, as far as we could determine, there are no systematic data to justify this faith.

Given the extent to which drugs have been tested before receiving approval for widespread clinical use, it is easy to understand why providers of therapy for HBP still tend to favor them over behavioral methods. Physicians believe that they understand the mechanism of action by which each of the drugs they prescribe affects BP, and that they can anticipate most of the side effects. Furthermore, there seems to be a prevailing assumption that once a certain titer of medication is reached in a patient, a level of BP control is established that can be regulated merely by adjusting drug dosages. By contrast, behavioral treatment of HBP is viewed as a "black box" in which a patient undergoes some process that affects BP in unclearly defined ways and to an unspecifiable extent. Application of such a treatment mode, therefore, is seen as requiring an inordinate and impractical amount of a provider's time without offering an assured outcome. Those conducting research in the behavioral treatment of HBP must overcome such barriers to its clinical use by establishing standardized procedures that have proven cost-effective for practical clinical use in the hands of many different therapists and in many different settings.

CONCLUSIONS

BP can be effectively reduced using biofeedback and/or relaxation techniques. The data we have reviewed show this clearly, but the variety of forms of behavioral interventions reported to be effective for some patients is still great, and selection of the behavioral treatment to be offered the patient is usually based on the therapist's preference or experience rather than a thoughtful clinical decision based on the patient's history and physical data. Frequently, behavioral therapies for HBP are offered merely as a component of a program of psychotherapy and/or counseling. Although this quite often results in a successful outcome, biofeedback and relaxation are still experimental forms of treatment with little known about the physiological mechanisms which they affect. Therefore, the extent to which they contributed to BP reduction is unclear.

BP is a continuous variable, dynamic in nature, that normally reflects the individual's responses to internal and external stimuli. The most common clinical procedures for estimating BP are not adequate for determining a patient's representative BP level. Therefore, an undisputed definition of the sustained level of BP that should be treated has not been established (JNC III, 1984). It is well known that many people respond to the process of auscultatory measurement of BP with pressure elevation. It is also probable that another subset of the population consists of individuals who respond to BP measurement with a reduction in pressure, leaving them at risk of cardiovascular morbidity due to HBP that is undetected by casual clinical measurements. Because direct arterial monitoring of BP is not practical for reasons that are obvious, better techniques for measuring a patient's BP indirectly are needed. We reviewed evidence supporting semiautomatic monitoring techniques as well as self-monitoring at various times of day and in various situations (e.g., the worksite) as improvements over casual clinical determinations alone. However, much remains to be done in the area of BP measurement in order to make assessment of individual BP levels more reliable and accurate, and to more clearly define a BP profile that predicts morbidity or mortality.

BP reductions accomplished by behavioral means are often sufficient in magnitude and duration to compare favorably with most pharmacological treatments. Nonetheless, the level of confidence in behavioral techniques for treatment of HBP remains low among physicians who presume relatively more reliable outcomes and predictable side effects to be associated with drug therapy. We suggest that three major obstacles may contribute to this prevailing negative attitude among physicians regarding behavioral treatment of HBP: (a) they do not know how to treat HBP behaviorally; (b) they can not afford the time they think is necessary for behavioral therapies; and (c) they do not have the necessary technology available in their facility.

It is difficult quantitatively to evaluate the absence of negative side effects reported for most behavioral forms of antihypertensive therapy.

However, this should be considered an advantage that these forms of treatment have over antihypertensive drugs. It is also difficult quantitatively to assess the negative effects of behavioral treatments. Clearly, they require more of the therapist's time during the training period and more commitment from the patient to practice enough to make the desired behavior become a full-time physiological response. The monetary cost is low, however, so the motivated patient and the skilled therapist can complement one another and enhance the likelihood of success. This is not required in drug therapy where patient compliance with dosage schedules usually will result in reduced BP. Unfortunately, systematic comparisons of compliance levels for behavioral and pharmacological forms of antihypertensive therapy are yet to be reported.

In many cases, behavioral treatments appear to act in harmoney (i.e., synergistically) with antihypertensive medications so as to reduce the dosage of medication required to maintain acceptable BP levels. However, explanations of the mechanism(s) whereby this occurs are only speculative at this time. It is also possible that some behavior–drug interactions are antagonistic and mutually incompatible. The current state of research in this area is in its infancy.

We also are far from an understanding of the ways in which the variety of behavioral approaches are similar or dissimilar in physiological effect. For example, it is not known whether a particular behavioral approach lowers BP by reducing cardiac output, peripheral resistance, or both. Also, it is only presumed that behavioral treatments that appear to lower the level of sympathetic nervous system activity are appropriate methods for treating HBP. In fact, it has not been proven that HBP is the result of abnormally high sympathetic nervous system activity. This should be accomplished before the claim is made that behavioral treatments affect the cause of HBP whereas drugs merely block physiological processes that follow the cause and lead to HBP.

Researchers interested in behavioral forms of antihypertensive treatment are making progress in answering many of these questions. However, it is very clear that any form of treatment for HBP that is presented to the medical community for widespread implementation will have to compare favorably with drug therapy on all comparison criteria; namely, clinical effectiveness (including ease of implementation, magnitude of BP reduction, long- and short-term side effects, and duration of effect), cost-effectiveness, appeal to the patient, and scientific verification of effectiveness. Although on a clinical level many therapists may continue to experience success at lowering their patient's BPs while reducing required dosages of antihypertensive medication, researchers will have to exercise a great measure of scientific rigor in their experiments in order to meet the last criterion.

REFERENCES

Agras, W. S., & Jacob, R. (1979). Hypertension. In O. F. Pomerleau & J. P. Brady (Eds.), *Behavioral medicine: Theory and practice.* (pp. 205–232), Baltimore, MD: Wiliams & Wilkins.

Agras, W. S., Taylor, C. B., Kraemer, H. C., Allen, R. A., & Schneider, J. A. (1980). Relaxation training: 24-hour blood pressure reductions. *Archives of General Psychiatry, 37,* 859–865.

Agras, W. S., Horne, M., & Taylor, C. B. (1982). Expectation and the blood-pressure-lowering effects of relaxtion. *Psychosomatic Medicine, 44,* 389–395.

Agras, W. S., Southam, M. A., & Taylor, C. B. (1983). Long-term persistence of relaxation-induced blood pressure lowering during the working day. *Journal of Consulting and Clinical Psychology, 51,* 792–794.

Agras, W. S., Schneider, J. A., & Taylor, C. B. (1984). Relaxation training in essential hypertension: A failure of retraining in relaxation procedures, *Behavioral Therapy, 15,* 191–196.

Alderman, M. H. (1980). The epidemiology of hypertension: Etiology, natural history, and the impact of therapy. *Cardiovascular Reviews and Reports, 1,* 509–519.

Andrews, G., Macmahon, S. W., Austin, A., & Byrne, D. G. (1982). Hypertension: Comparison of drug and non-drug treatments, *British Medical Journal, 284,* 1523–1526.

Australian National Study (1980). Report by the managmeent committee: The Australian therapeutic trial in mild hypertension, *Lancet, 1,* 1261–1267.

Bali, L. R. (1979). Long-term effect of relaxation on blood pressure and anxiety levels of essential hypertensive males: A controlled study, *Psychosomataic Medicine, 41,* 637–646.

Benson, H., Rosner, B. A., & Marzetta, B. R. (1973). Decreased systolic blood pressure in hypertensive subjects who practice meditation. *Journal of Clinical Investigation, 52,* 8a.

Benson, H., Rosner, B. A., Marzetta, B. R., & Klemchuk, H. P. (1974a). Decreased blood pressure in borderline hypertensive subjects who practiced meditation, *Journal of Chronic Diseases, 27,* 163–169.

Benson, H., Rosner, B. A., Marzetta, B. R., & Klemchuk, H. P. (1974b). Decreased blood pressure in pharmacologically treated hypertensive patients who regularly elicited the relaxation response. *Lancet, 1,* 289–291.

Benson, H. (1975). *The relaxation response.* New York: William Morrow & Co.

Benson, H., Greenwood, M. M., & Klemchuk, H. (1975). Relaxation response: Psychophysiological aspects and clinical applications. *International Journal of Psychiatry in Medicine, 6,*87–98.

Blanchard, E. B. (1978). *Biofeedback and the modification of cardiovascular dysfunctions.* Task Force Report. Wheat Ridge, CO: Biofeedback Society of America.

Brandt, E. N. (1983, November). Advisory on treatment of mild hypertension. *FDA Drug Bulletin, 13*(3), pp. 24–25.

Charlesworth, E. A., Williams B. J., & Baer, P. E. (1984). Stress management at the worksite for hypertension: Compliance, cost-benefit, health care and hypertension-related variables. *Psychosomatic Medicine, 46,* 387–397.

Cottier, C., Julius, S., Gajendragadkar, S. V., & Schork, M. A. (1982). Usefulness of home blood pressure determination in treating borderline hypertension. *Journal of the American Medical Association, 248,* 555–558.

Cottier, C., Shapiro, K., & Julius, S. (1984). Treatment of mild hypertension with progressive muscle relaxation: Predictive value of indexes of sympathetic tone. *Archives of Internal Medicine, 144,* 1954–1958.

Datey, K. K. (1980). Role of biofeedback training in hypertension and stress. *Journal of Postgraduate Medicine, 26,* 68–73.

Davidson, D. M., Winchester, M. A., Taylor, C. B., Alderman, E. A., & Ingels, N. B. (1979). Effects of relaxation therapy on cardiac performance and sympathetic activity in patients with organic heart disease, *Psychosomatic Medicine, 41,* 303–309.

des Combes, B. J., Porchet, M., Waeber, B., & Brunner, H. R. (1984). Ambulatory blood pressure recordings reproducibility and unpredictability. *Hypertension, 6,* C110–C115.

Devereux, R. B., Pickering, T. G., Harshfield, G. A., Kleinert, H. D., Denby, L., Clark, L., Pregibon, D., Jason, M., Kleiner, B., Borer, J. S., & Laragh, J. H. (1983). Left ventricular hypertrophy in patients with hypertension: Importance of blood pressure response to regularly recurring stress. *Circulation, 68,* 470–476.

Engel, B. T., Gaarder, K. R., & Glasgow, M. S. (1981). Behavioral treatment of high blood pressure: I. Analyses of intra- and interdaily variations of blood pressure during a one-month, baseline period. *Psychosomatic Medicine, 43,* 255–270.

Engel, B. T., Glasgow, M. S., & Gaarder, K. R. (1983). Behavioral treatment of high blood pressure: III. Follow-up results and treatment recommendations. *Psychosomatic Medicine, 45,* 23–29.

Fahrion, S. L. (1979, April 3) *Addendum: Cardiovascular task force study section report update on biofeedback assisted treatment of essential hypertension. Supplement to biofeedback and the modification of cardiovascular dysfunction.* Task Force Report. Wheat Ridge, CO: Biofeedback Society of America.

Floras, J. S., Jones, J. V., Hassan, M. O., Osikowska, B., Sever, P. S., & Sleight, P. (1981). Cuff and ambulatory blood pressure in subjects with essential hypertension. *Lancet, 2,* 107–109.

Frost, R. O., & Holmes, D. S. (1980). Effects of instructions and biofeedback for increasing and decreasing systolic blood pressure. *Journal of Psychosomatic Research, 24,* 21–27.

Gervino, E. V., & Veazey, A. E. (1984). The physiologic effects of Benson's relaxation response during submaximal aerobic exercise. *Journal of Cardiac Rehabilitation, 4,* 254–259.

Glasgow, M. S., Gaarder, K. R., & Engel, B. T. (1982). Behavioral treatment of high blood pressure: II. Acute and sustained effects of relaxation and systolic blood pressure biofeedback. *Psychosomatic Medicine, 44,* 155–170.

Goebel, M., Viol, G. W., Lorenz, G. J., & Clemente, J. (1980). Relaxation and biofeedback in essential hypertension: A preliminary report of a six-year project. *American Journal of Clinical Biofeedback, 3,* 20–29.

Goldstein, I. B., Shapiro, D., Thananopavarn, C., & Sambhi, M. P. (1982). Comparison of drug and behavioral treatments of essential hypertension. *Health Psychology, 1,* 7–26.

Goldstein, I. B., Shapiro, D., & Thananopavarn, C. (1984). Home relaxation techniques for essential hypertension. *Psychosomatic Medicine, 46,* 398–414.

Gould, B. A., Mann, S., Davies, A. B., Altman, D. G., & Raftery, E. B. (1981, December). Does placebo lower blood-pressure? *Lancet, 2,* 1377–1381.

Green, E. E., Green, A. M., & Norris, P. A. (1980). Self-regulation training for control of hypertension. *Primary Cardiology, 6*(3), 126–137.

Hafner, R. J. (1982). Psychological treatment of essential hypertension: A controlled comparison of meditation, and meditation plus biofeedback. *Biofeedback and Self-regulation, 7,* 305–316.

Harshfield, G. A., Pickering, T. G., Kleinert, H. D., Blank, S., & Laragh, J. H. (1982). Situational variations of blood pressure in ambulatory hypertensive patients. *Psychosomatic Medicine, 44,* 237–245.

Holroyd, J. C., Nuechterlein, K. H., Shapiro, D., & Ward, F. (1982). Individual differences in hypnotizability and effectiveness of hypnosis or biofeedback. *International Journal of Clinical and Experimental Hypnosis, 30,* 45–65.

Hypertension Detection and Follow-up Program Cooperative Group (1979). Five-year findings of the hypertension detection and follow-up program I. Reduction in mortality of persons with high blood pressure, including mild hypertension. *Journal of the American Medical Association, 242,* 2562–2571.

Joint National Committee on Detection, Evaluation, and Treatment of High Blood Pressure (1984). The 1984 Report of the Joint National Committee. *Archives of Internal Medicine, 144,* 1045–1057.

Kannel, W. B. (1975). Role of blood pressure in cardiovascular disease. *Angiology, 26,* 1–14.

Kirkendall, W. M., Burton, A. C., Epstein, F. H., & Fries, E. D. (1967). Recommendations for human blood pressure determination by sphygmomanometers. American Heart Association Committee Report, *Circulation, 36,* 980–988.

Kristt, D. A., & Engel, B. T. (1975). Learned control of blood pressure in patients with high blood pressure. *Circulation, 51,* 370–378.

Laragh, J. H. (1965). Recent advances in hypertension. *American Journal of Medicine, 39,* 616–645.

Laughlin, K. (1981). Enhancing the effectiveness of behavioral treatments of essential hypertension. *Physiology and Behavior, 26,* 907–913.

Laughlin, K. D., Sherrard, D. J., & Fisher, L. (1980). Compariosn of clinic and home blood pressure levels in essential hypertension and variables associated with clinic home differences. *Journal of Chronic Diseases, 33,* 197–206.

Levinson, P. D., Khatri, I. M., & Freis, E. D. (1982). Persistence of normal BP after withdrawal of drug treatment in mild hypertension. *Archives of Internal Medicine, 142,* 2265–2268.

Libo, L. M., & Arnold, G. E. (1983a). Does training to criterion influence improvement? A follow-up study of EMG and thermal biofeedback. *Journal of Behavioral Medicine, 6,* 397–404.

Libo, L. M., & Arnold, G. E. (1983b). Relaxation practice after biofeedback therapy: A long-term follow-up study of utilization and effectiveness. *Biofeedback and Self-Regulation, 8,* 217–227.

Luborsky, L., Crits-Christoph, P., Brady, J. P., Kron, R. E., Weiss, T., & Engelman, K. (1980, September) Antihypertensive effects of behavioral treatments and medications compared [Letter to the editor]. *New England Journal of Medicine,* p. 586.

Luborsky, L., Ancona, L., Masoni, A., Scolari, G., & Longoni, A. (1980–81). Behavioral vs pharmacological treatments for essential hypertension. *International Journal of Psychiatry in Medicine, 10,* 33–40.

Luborsky, L. Crits-Christoph, P., Brady, J. P., Kron, R. E., Weiss, T., Cohen, M., & Levy, L. (1982). Behavioral versus pharmacological treatments for essential hypertension—A needed comparison. *Psychosomatic Medicine, 44,* 203–213.

Madhaven, S., & Alderman, M. H. (1981). The potential effect of blood pressure reduction on cardiovascular disease. A cautionary note. *Archives of Internal Medicine, 141,* 1583–1586.

Mancia, G. (1983). Methods for assessing blood pressure values in humans. *Hypertension, 5*(Suppl 3), 5–13.

Manning, D. M., Kuchirka, C., & Kaminski, J. (1983). Miscuffing: inappropriate blood pressure cuff application. *Hypertension 68,* 763–766.

McAlister, N. H. (1983). Should we treat "mild" hypertension? *Journal of the American Medical Association, 249,* 379–382.

McGrady, A. V., Yonker, R., Tan, S. Y., Fine, T. H., & Woerner, M. (1981). The effect of biofeedback-assisted relaxation training on blood pressure and selected biochemical parameters in patients with essential hypertension. *Biofeedback and Self-Regulation, 6,* 343–353.

McGrady, A., Fine, T., Woerner, M., & Yonker, R. (1983). Maintenance of treatment effects biofeedback-assisted relaxation on patients with essential hypertension. *American Journal of Clinical Biofeedback, 6,* 34–39.

Messerli, F. H., Decarvalho, J. G. R., Christie, B., & Frohlich, E. D. (1979). Systemic haemodynamic effects of biofeedback in borderline hypertension. *Clinical Science, 57,* 437s–439s.

Multiple Risk Factor Intervention Trial Research Group, Risk factor changes and mortality results (1982). *Journal of the American Medical Association, 248,* 1465–1477.

Patel, C. (1973). Yoga and biofeedback in the management of hypertension. *Lancet, 2*(1837), 1053–1055.

Patel, C., & North, W. R. (1975). Randomized controlled trial of yoga and biofeedbck in the management of hypertension. *Lancet, 2*(1925), 93–95.

Patel, C., Marmot, M. G., & Terry, D. J. (1981). Controlled trial of biofeedback-aided behavioural methods in reducing mild hypertension. *British Medical Journal, 282,* 2005–2008.

Perloff, D., Sokolow, M., & Cowan, R. (1983). The prognostic value of ambulatory blood pressures. *Journal of the American Medical Association, 249,* 2792–2798.

Pickering, G. (1968). *High blood pressure* (2nd ed.). New York: Grune & Stratton.

Pickering, T. G., (1982). Nonpharmacologic methods of treatment of hypertension: Promising but unproved. *Cardiovascular Reviews and Reports, 3,* 82–88.

Pickering, T. G., Harshfield, G. A., Kleinert, H. D., Blank, S., & Laragh, J. H. (1982). Blood pressure during normal daily activities, sleep, and exercise: Comparison of values in normal and hypertensive subjects. *Journal of the American Medical Association, 247,* 992–996.

Pickering, T. G., Harshfield, G. A., Kleinert, H. D., & Laragh, J. H. (1982). Ambulatory monitoring in the evaluation of blood pressure in patients with borderline hypertension and the role of the defense reflex. *Clinical and Experimental Hypertension, A4*(4&5), 675–693.

Richter-Heinrich, E., Homuth, V., Heinrich, B., Schmidt, K-H., Wiedemann, R., & Gohlke, H-R. (1981). Long term application of behavioral treatments in essential hypertensives. *Physiology and Behavior, 26,* 915–920.

Richter-Heinrich, E., Lori, M., Knust, U., & Schmidt, K. H. (1982). Comparison of blood pressure biofeedback and relaxation training in essential hypertension. In E. Richter-Heinrich & N. E. Miller (Eds.), *Biofeedback—Basic Problems and Clinical Applications* (107–120). New York: North-Holland.

Richter-Heinrich, E., Homuth, V., Gohlke, H. R., Heinrich, B., Schmidt, K. H., Wiedemann, R., & Heine, H. (1982). Effectiveness of behavioral treatment methods compared to pharmacological therapy and self recordings of blood pressure in essential hypertensives (preliminary report). *Activitas Nervosa Superior,* Suppl. **3,** 422–427.

Richter-Heinrich, E., Homuth, V., Heinrich, B., Knust, U., Schmidt, K. H., & Wiedemann, R. (in press). A long-term controlled study of behavioral treatment in essential hypertension. *Activitas Nervosa Superior.*

Seer, P., & Raeburn, J. M. (1980). Meditation training and essential hypertension: A methodological study. *Journal of Behavioral Medicine, 3,* 59–71.

Shapiro, A. P., & Jacob, R. G. (1983). Nonpharmacologic approaches to the treatment of hypertension. *Annual Review of Public Health, 4,* 285–310.

Shapiro, D., & Goldstein, I. B. (1982). Biobehavioral perspectives on hypertension. *Journal of Consulting and Clinical Psychology, 50,* 841–858.

Shapiro, D., Turksy, B., Gershon, E., & Stern, M. (1969). Effects of feedback and reinforcement on the control of human systolic blood pressure. *Science, 163,* 588–590.

Shoemaker, J. E., & Tasto, D. L. (1975). The effects of muscle relaxation on blood pressure of essential hypertensives. *Behavioral Research and Therapy, 13,* 29–43.

Sokolow, M., Werdegar, D., Kain, H. K., & Hinman, A. T. (1966). Relationship between level of blood pressure measured casually and by portable recorders and severity of complications in essential hypertension. *Circulation, 34,* 279–298.

Southam, M. A., Agras, W. S., Taylor, C. B., & Kraemer, H. C. (1982). Relaxation training: Blood pressure lowering during the working day. *Archives of General Psychiatry, 39,* 715–717.

Tursky, B., Shapiro, D., & Schwartrz, G. E. (1972). Automated constant-cuff pressure system to measure average systolic and diastolic blood pressure in man. *IEEE Transactions in Biomedical Engineering, 19,* 271–276.

VA Cooperative Study Group on Antihypertensive Agents (1970). Effects of treatment on morbidity in hypertension: Results in patients with diastolic blood pressures averaging 90 through 114 mm Hg. *Journal of the American Medical Association, 213,* 1143–1152.

VA Cooperative Study Group on Antihypertensive Agents (1975). Return of elevated blood pressure after withdrawal of antihypertensive drugs. *Circulation, 51,* 1107–1113.

Vaitl, D., (1982). Psychological management of essential hypertension. *Contributions to Nephrology, 30,* 87–91.

Wallace, R. K., Benson, H., & Wilson, A. F. (1971). A wakeful hypometabolic physiological state. *American Journal of Physiology, 221,* 795–799.

Wallace, R. K., & Benson, H. (1972). The physiology of meditation. *Scientific American, 226,* 84–90.

Wallace, R. K., Silver, J., Mills, P. J., Dillbeck, M. C., & Wagoner, D. E. (1983). Systolic blood pressure and long-term practice of the transcendental meditation and tm-sidhi program: Effects of tm on systolic blood pressure. *Psychosomatic Medicine, 45,* 41–46.

Weiss, S. M. (1980). Biobehavioral approaches to the treatment of hypertension. *Journal of the South Carolina Medical Association, Suppl. 9,* 38–43.

Whelton, P. K., & Russell, R. P. (1984). Systemic hypertension. In A. M. Harvey, R. J. Johns, V. A. McKusick, A. H. Owens, & R. S. Ross (Eds.), *The principles and practice of medicine* (21st ed., pp. 278–297). Norwalk, CT: Appleton-Century-Crofts.

W.H.O./I.S.H. Mild Hypertension Liaison Committee (1982). Trials of the treatment of mild hypertension: An interim analysis. *Lancet, 1,* 149–156.

3

Temporomandibular Disorders and Bruxism

Wallace L. Mealiea, Jr., and Dudley McGlynn

Introduction

Temporomandibular (TMJ) disorders are characterized by facial pain and functional disturbances of the masticatory system. Traditionally these disorders have been the concern of dentistry. However, in concert with the biofeedback and behavioral medicine movements, TMJ disorders have become of interest to nondental clinicians. One purpose of the present chapter is to review applications of biofeedback to patients suffering from TMJ problems. The behavior known as bruxing involves excessively forceful clenching and/or grinding of the teeth. Bruxing has been a traditional concern of psychology and psychiatry as well as dentistry and bruxing probably is related to TMJ disorders in some patients. A second purpose of this chapter is to review biofeedback applications in the treatment of bruxism.

Temporomandibular Disorders

The masticatory system consists of the mandible, periodontia, and teeth; the muscles of mastication, the temporomandibular joints, and much of the central nervous system (see Dubner, Sessle, & Storey, 1978). Although fine-grain clinical descriptions of masticatory system disorders are variable (Travell & Simons, 1983), the so-called TMJ syndrome entails the three cardinal symptoms of outwardly radiating preauricular pain,

Wallace L. Mealiea, Jr., and F. Dudley McGlynn • Department of Community Dentistry, College of Dentistry, University of Florida, Gainesville, FL 32610.

clicking or popping sounds in the TMJ, and various limitations in functional jaw movements. TMJ patients sometimes present with tenderness in the area of the TMJ, subluxation/dislocation of the mandible, tinnitus, and dizziness.

Bruxism

The term *bruxism* refers to dysfunctional or parafunctional clenching, gnashing, and/or grinding of the teeth. Bruxing can occur primarily during the day (diurnal bruxism), primarily during sleep (nocturnal bruxism), or during both periods (Reding, Rubright, & Zimmerman, 1966). A body of data exists supporting the view that diurnal and nocturnal bruxing are fundamentally different behaviors (cf. Rao & Glaros, 1979; Reding, Zepelin, Robinson, Smith, & Zimmerman, 1968). Diurnal bruxing usually takes the form of clenching and involves the masseter and temporalis muscles. Nocturnal bruxing usually takes the form of lateral grinding and involves the lateral and medial pterygoid muscles also (Dubner *et al.*, 1978; Hamada, Kotani, Kawazoe, & Yamada, 1982). Excessive force is the clinically significant factor in both varieties of bruxing and it produces clinical problems or signs, such as wear, attrition, and mobility of the teeth; bulging masseter muscles; occlusal disharmony; and facial pain (Alling & Mahan, 1977; Meklas, 1971; Ramfjord & Ash, 1983).

Etiology of Temporomandibular Disorders

Because of the writing of Costen (1934), the view became popular early on that a unique TMJ syndrome exists that is characterized by relatively homogeneous symptoms occurring within the masticatory system. Because of the writing of Laskin (1969), the view has persisted that a related myofascial pain-dysfunction (MPD) syndrome exists that has similarly identifiable symptoms. Hence the literature on the etiology of temporomandibular disorders has, until recently, been comprised of competing explanations of one syndrome or the other.

One historically prominent etiological view is that occlusal interferences can produce the symptoms of TMJ syndrome by affecting the TMJ, by producing muscular hyperactivity, etc. (cf. Ramfjord, 1961). Carlsson and Droukas (1984) reviewed the various clinical, experimental, and epidemiologic literatures on the occlusal interference theory and characterized them as inconclusive. Our own study of the same literatures suggests that occlusal interferences might well be causally involved in TMJ disorders. However, their action probably is not monolithic and their ordinal position in a causal chain could not be argued persuasively on the basis of available data (also see Weinberg, 1979).

A second historically prominent etiological view is that emotional stress can produce the symptoms of TMJ syndrome by leading to mandibular muscle hyperactivity (e.g., Moulton, 1966; Schwartz, 1956). The currently popular version of this type of thinking is Laskin's (1969) MPD syndrome wherein emotional stress leads to noxious muscular hyperactivity, fatigue, and spasm. There is a sizable literature on the relationship between stress and mandibular muscle activity among TMJ patients (see Yemm, 1979). The literature is not conclusive and is not uniformly indicative that a unique relationship exists. Again, the causal role of stress is not likely to be monolithic.

Improved etiological understanding was begun in the middle of the last decade (e.g., Rugh & Solberg, 1976) with the introduction of the multifactorial etiology concept. According to this view, numerous etiological factors (e.g., intracapsular, extracapsular, psychophysiologic) can participate in producing TMJ symptoms. The causes of the symptoms are rarely monolithic. It is now known that a host of etiological factors can interact to produce TMJ symptoms and that a TMJ syndrome as such probably does not exist (see McNeill et al., 1980, for one contemporary taxonomy).

Etiology of Bruxism

A thorough review of the etiology of bruxism has been presented recently (McGlynn, Cassisi, & Diamond, 1985) and only an overview of the literature will be offered here. Historically, etiological theories of bruxism have paralleled closely those of the TMJ and MPD syndromes. Some etiological factors that have received frequent mention are local dental conditions, such as missing or elongated teeth, occlusal disharmony, emotional stress, untoward personality traits, occupational factors, and psychodynamics. It was suggested over 50 years ago (Tischler, 1928) that interactions between dental factors and stress produce the bruxing habit. More recently Ramfjord and Ash (1983) have argued that bruxing reflects a multifactor interaction of anatomic, physiological, and psychological variables.

In principle, multifactorial etiological thinking is sound because it promotes relatively comprehensive diagnosis and treatment and because it doubtless is true in some ways. As it is currently formulated, however, the multifactorial etiology concept is so general as to be of little enduring value. Obviously much work remains in delineating the etiologies of bruxism satisfactorily. This is true for both diurnal and nocturnal bruxism. A related need exists for a consensually endorsed taxonomy of bruxist activities and for an improved understanding of the relationships between bruxing and TMJ disorders.

Dental Treatments for Bruxism and TMJ Disorders

Dental therapy for TMJ disorders has consisted primarily of drug therapy, occlusal stabilization splints, occlusal equilibration, and oral surgery. A variety of medication has been used to treat TMJ patients, including minor tranquilizers such as Valium, major tranquilizers such as Stelazine, and tricyclic antidepressants such as Elavil. Patients are most commonly treated with minor tranquilizers to induce muscle relaxation and with tricyclic antidepressants if underlying depression seems to be a component of the problem. Although medication does frequently alleviate some of the symptoms of the syndromes, particularly muscular tension and pain, the symptoms often return shortly after discontinuation of drug therapy (Ramfjord & Ash, 1983). Weak maintenance of treatment gains, side effects, and the potential for abuse render drug therapy useful mainly as a temporary treatment during acute phases and as a treatment for depression.

By far the most common TMJ treatment used by dentists is some type of intraoral appliance. Variously called a bite splint, a night guard, or an occlusal splint, the device is fabricated in acrylic from an articulator-mounted casting of the patient's dentition. The splint is retained by wire or hard acrylic clasps and is worn by patients at night and sometimes during the day. The purpose of the splint is to help the patient's bite return to normal occlusal balance by distributing the forces of nonfunctional oral-motor movements over a maximum area of tooth surface. This prevents excessive force on individual teeth and the occurrence of occlusal trauma. Some research has indicated that occlusal splints do reduce masseter muscle activity during clenching behavior and do produce muscular activity levels that more nearly reflect the levels of non-TMJ subjects (Fuchs, 1975; Hamada et al., 1982; Kawazoe, Kotani, Hamada, & Yamada, 1980). However, other research is less positive. For example, Clark, Beemsterboer, Solberg, and Rugh (1979) showed that splints reduced nocturnal EMG activity in 52% of subjects, whereas they increased EMG levels in 20% of subjects. Few studies have been really sound methodologically and, in general, the treatment-outcome research literature is inconclusive (Okeson, Moody, Kemper, & Calhoun, 1983). However, occlusal splint therapy is reversible and the splints do protect the teeth.

Another common therapy used by dentists is occlusal equilibration. The term *equilibration* means permanent balancing of occlusion by grinding away interfering tooth structure. The dentist creates casts of the patient's teeth and, having studied the casts on an articulator, decides which teeth have occlusal interferences that are to be removed.

Occlusal adjustment is considered by some dental authorities (Dawson, 1974; Ramfjord & Ash, 1983) as the treatment of choice for TMJ disorders and bruxism. However, as with bite splint therapies, good treatment outcome data are not available. Also as with bite splint therapy, the effectiveness of occlusal adjustment may be related to the demand characteristics of the clinical setting and the influence of the placebo effect (Goodman, Greene, & Laskin, 1976; Greene & Laskin, 1972). A cautionary note concerning occlusal adjustment has been stated by Marbach (1976), who warned his dental colleagues that the act of grinding a patient's teeth not only removes tooth structure, but also can traumatize the TMJ and produce the very symptoms of pain and dysfunction that are the object of therapy. It also should be noted that the effects of equilibration are not reversible. Therefore, more detailed study of occlusal adjustment is required before a definitive statement can be made about the propriety of the approach (cf. Clark et al., 1979).

Surgery is the most invasive therapy for TMJ disorders and is performed on a small number of patients. Those suffering pain from chronic dislocation of the condyle or other internal derangement of the TMJ, trauma to the jaw, and posttraumatic arthralgia are among the most common surgery candidates. However, prior to surgical intervention it is customary to treat TMJ patients conservatively for at least one year with analgesics, anti-inflammatory medications and muscle relaxants.

Psychological Treatments for Bruxism

A recent review of psychological treatments for bruxism is available elsewhere (McGlynn et al., 1985). Hence treatments other than biofeedback are mentioned only briefly here.

Psychoanalysis and insight-oriented psychotherapy have from time to time been suggested as treatments for bruxist patients, but virtually no data exist to support such a view. Limited treatment-outcome data do exist vis-à-vis muscular relaxation training, massed negative practice, habit reversal, and aversive punishment.

Muscular relaxation has been studied as a component procedure in three multiple-treatment studies using bruxist subjects (Heller & Forgione, 1975; Moss et al., 1982; Rosenbaum & Ayllon, 1981). These studies were uniformly problematic methodologically; relaxation was not studied alone; and procedurally weak relaxation regimens were used. Hence, currently it is not possible to characterize the effects of thorough training in progressive muscle relaxation on bruxing or TMJ symptoms.

Dunlap (1932) suggested that nervous habits, such as tics, could be treated by having patients voluntarily practice them. This negative practice would fatigue the muscles of habit expression and reduce the frequency of the behavior. There have been individual case reports in which bruxism seemingly was treated successfully with a massed practice protocol. There also have been several group-outcome studies of massed negative practice as a treatment for bruxism (e.g., Ayer & Levin, 1973, 1975; Heller & Forgione, 1975; Rugh, 1976). Confident conclusions based on the existing literature cannot be offered because the experiments were methodologically problematic and their outcomes contradictory (see McGlynn *et al.*, 1985).

Azrin and Nunn (1973) described a behavior modification technique, habit reversal, for the elimination of nervous habits and tics. Basically, the procedure alerts the patient to occurrences of the behavior, provides a means of interrupting their antecedents, initiates competing behaviors, and redirects contingent social attention from unwanted habits to more appropriate behaviors. There is a small but promising literature on habit reversal in the modification of diurnal bruxing (Azrin & Nunn, 1977; Azrin, Nunn, & Frantz-Renshaw, 1982; Rosenbaum & Ayllon, 1981). It should be noted that diurnal bruxers can sometimes alter the habit simply on being told by a dentist that it is important to do so (Ramfjord & Ash, 1983).

Aversive punishment has been used to reduce diurnal bruxing in special populations, such as psychiatric patients and retarded individuals. Three promising studies have appeared but much more information is needed to formulate clinical guidelines for response-contingent punishment of diurnal bruxism (see McGlynn *et al.*, 1985).

CLINICAL EFFICACY

The previous overview of existing treatments for TMJ disorders and bruxism indicates that they are diverse in origin and that most enjoy some degree of apparent success (Marbach, 1976). This situation reflects not only the generally poor quality of therapy-outcome research, but also the equivocality of our understanding of these disorders (Greene, 1976; Marbach, 1976). Although a satisfactory conceptualization of etiology is not available, a fairly consistent pattern of anxiety, pain, and muscular tension does emerge in these disorders. That these components coexist in many TMJ patients does not necessarily mean that they are etiological factors. However, they are factors that may be amenable to a biofeedback-based treatment protocol. The use of biofeedback is consistent with Rugh and Solberg's (1976) recommendation that, given the current knowledge base, the clinician's focus should not be finding and eliminating the cause of the symptoms. Rather, clinicians should attempt to provide patients with the skills needed to cope with their symptoms and thus have more productive lives.

Applications to TMJ Syndromes

Electromyographic (EMG) biofeedback consists of measuring the electrical activity of a patient's contracting muscles and providing the patient with information about muscle activity through the use of visual, auditory, or other modes of feedback. The primary goal for the patient is learning to either increase or decrease the muscular activity on demand. Because excessive muscular tension is believed to be associated frequently with TMJ disorders, the use of EMG biofeedback to reduce muscular tension has strong face validity. Budzynski and Stoyva (1973) first showed that normal individuals could, with EMG biofeedback information, decrease the EMG activity of their masseter muscles when compared to normal subjects not given feedback. Audio and visual feedback from masseter activity were equally effective in reducing muscular tension as compared to a bogus feedback and a no-feedback protocol. The authors suggested the possible use of EMG feedback for the treatment of TMJ disorders.

Following this demonstration, a number of uncontrolled case studies and group clinical outcome studies used masseter EMG biofeedback to treat TMJ or MPD patients. Gessel (1975) reported a study in which 23 MPD patients (22 females, 1 male) were given from 3 to 14 sessions of laboratory training in relaxation using auditory feedback of masseter/temporalis EMG activity. The patients' task was to lower the tone. If no improvement was indicated by the sixth session, feedback training was terminated and the patient was given a tricyclic antidepressant. According to self-report, biofeedback training produced "satisfactory control of symptoms" in 15 of 23 MPD patients, four patients later responded positively to the medication, and four subjects did not respond to either form of therapy.

Dohrman and Laskin (1976) reported a group experiment in which 24 MPD patients (16 males and 8 females) were assigned to either an auditory EMG biofeedback group ($n = 16$) or a placebo group ($n = 8$) for 12 training sessions. Twelve of the 16 biofeedback-treated subjects and four of the eight placebo subjects showed significant improvement of clinical symptoms and required no further treatment.

In two case studies and one group clinical trial, Carlsson and his colleagues (Carlsson & Gale, 1976, 1977; Carlsson, Gale, & Ohman, 1975) reported the successful treatment of TMJ pain patients with EMG biofeedback. The patients were trained to differentially tense and relax masseter muscles by observing a meter that provided feedback of EMG activity. The first case (1975) involved a 21-year-old female who reported no TMJ pain after ten 30-minute EMG training sessions and no pain on 6-month follow-up. The second case (1976) was a 59-year-old female who reported no TMJ pain after nine training sessions and no pain at one-year follow-up. The group clinical trial (1977) involved 11 TMJ patients (6 male, 5 female) who were treated for 6 to 18 sessions. At the end of training, 8 of the 11 patients reported no pain. Five of the 11 claimed to be symptom free at the end of one year.

Peck and Kraft (1977) used EMG biofeedback-assisted relaxation training to treat three groups of pain patients: 18 tension headache sufferers, 8 patients with back pain, and 6 female TMJ pain patients. Following a 2-week baseline period for self-monitoring pain, the patients were given an average of ten 30-minute biofeedback treatment sessions using a tone and a visual meter. Training was followed by four more weeks of pain monitoring. All groups, including the TMJ patients, showed slight decreases in EMG activity over treatment sessions; however, these reductions were not correlated with pain relief among the TMJ patients. At the 4-week posttreatment assessment, two patients reported slight decreases in TMJ pain, one patient reported no change, and three patients reported increased TMJ pain. The authors noted that these patients were long-term chronic TMJ sufferers who had not responded to other forms of therapy.

As with muscular relaxation training, EMG biofeedback has often been used as a component or comparison procedure in studies of multifaceted treatments for TMJ pain. Berry and Wilmot (1977) reported that masseter EMG feedback "relieved" symptoms among 31 of 35 mandibular dysfunction patients, 25 of whom received other treatments along with auditory feedback training. Gale (1979), Majewski and Gale (1983), and Gelb and Gale (1983) reported various clinical comparisons between effects on facial pain of masseter EMG biofeedback training and progressive relaxation training specific to the facial muscles. In general, both approaches yielded reliable improvements in symptoms of pain and did not differ in effectiveness.

Olson (1977) presented data on the treatment of 15 MPD patients who had been unresponsive to drug and bite plate therapy. The patients were divided into three groups for 12 treatment sessions: (a) auditory masseter EMG feedback ($n = 5$); (b) auditory frontalis EMG feedback ($n = 4$); and (c) auditory frontalis EMG feedback plus psychotherapy ($n = 6$). No cross-group comparisons were made; however, all groups showed decreased EMG activity over sessions. Patients in the masseter EMG group reported slight decreases in pain, whereas in the frontalis

EMG group one patient reported remission of pain and three reported no change. In the masseter EMG/psychotherapy group two patients reported total remission of pain, three a reduction in pain, and one no change in pain. Olson concluded that psychotherapy with EMG biofeedback is more effective than is EMG biofeedback alone with MPD patients. However, such a conclusion is obviously premature.

Stenn, Mothersill, and Brooke (1979) evaluated a combined progressive relaxation training, sensory awareness training, and coping skills training protocol for treating 13 MPD patients. Six of the patients were also randomly assigned to receive masseter EMG feedback as a component of their relaxation training. Seven weekly training sessions followed a one-week baseline period of self-monitoring of pain by each subject. Masseter EMG levels showed significant reductions across treatment sessions and at a 3-month follow-up. There were no differences in masseter EMG levels between the feedback and nonfeedback subjects. A posttreatment rating of pre- to posttreatment differences in pain behavior by an experimentally blind physician also showed uniform decreases in symptoms, and no differences between the biofeedback and nonbiofeedback patients. The authors concluded that both masseter biofeedback and cognitive behavior modification procedures were effective treatments for MPD.

Moss, Wedding, and Sanders (1983) reported a series of single-case studies designed to compare the efficacy of masseter EMG feedback with progressive relaxation training in treating TMJ dysfunction. The first patient, a 58-year-old female, suffered from chronic pain of the jaw and shoulder. Her protocol consisted of (a) a one-week baseline for recording subjective intensities of pain and tension; (b) a 2-week relaxation training phase, consisting of instructions to use a relaxation tape twice daily; (c) a 3-week phase of continued relaxation plus eight 30-minute masseter EMG feedback sessions; and (d) and additional 3-week phase of continued relaxation training plus eight 30-minute trapezius EMG feedback sessions. Treatment outcome data were gathered during the week immediately after the end of treatment and again 4 weeks later. These data indicated that taped relaxation training was responsible for improvements in subjective jaw pain and tension ratings.

Trapezius EMG feedback, however, did influence subjective ratings of shoulder pain. Four more TMJ pain patients also were treated with varying sequences of EMG feedback sessions and taped relaxation training. The results for pain and tension ratings were mixed. One patient improved with taped relaxation training. Two patients improved during both relaxation and EMG feedback training. One patient showed no training effect at all. Moss *et al.* (1983) concluded that some support exists for the use of relaxation training as a treatment for some TMJ patients; however, weak support for EMG biofeedback training should prompt more research before routine applications to TMJ dysfunction are undertaken. However, several methodological problems reduce the force of this conclusion vis-à-vis biofeedback therapy.

The reviewed studies of masseter EMG biofeedback therapy are provocative in that they suggest biofeedback to have considerable potential as a treatment for facial pain syndromes. However, the few attempts at controlled experimental evaluation of the approach resulted in only modest support. All of the research in the area suffers from limitations imposed by the contemporary knowledge base. Hence biofeedback management of TMJ disorders has not yet have received a fair series of experimental tests.

Applications to Bruxism

The relationship between bruxing and increased muscle activity has led to the widespread use of electromyography (EMG) for the assessment and treatment of nonfunctional oral-motor behavior. EMG is used to measure nonfunctional oral-motor behavior at microvolt levels outside the range of those associated with functional oral motor behavior (Dubner et al., 1978; Solberg, Clark, & Rugh, 1975). In addition, EMG is used to detect nonfunctional behaviors during times when no functional oral-motor behaviors are occurring. The development of inexpensive portable EMG devices that amplify, filter, intergrate, and record EMG activity made it possible to monitor and treat bruxing patients outside of a clinic setting, and corresponding increase in published studies reflects the use of these instruments (McGlynn et al., 1985; Rugh, 1978).

The application of biofeedback techniques to bruxism derived from the work of Mowrer and Mowrer (1938), who used response-contingent noise to attenuate nocturnal enuresis. Various researchers have sought to eliminate nocturnal and diurnal bruxing with response-produced signals. Early reports of the use of nocturnal alarms to treat bruxing rested on intraoral bite plates and records of audible grinding to define bruxing and regulate signal delivery (e.g., Heller & Strang, 1973). Solberg and Rugh's (1972) development of a portable biofeedback device for signal delivery based on suprathreshold EMG established the foundation for commonly used EMG biofeedback alarms.

Kardachi and Clarke (1977), in a prospective group study, used a nocturnal EMG-activated tone to treat nine bruxist patients. Bruxing was quantified in single night-long time-intensity units and was recorded usually for 7 baseline nights before the nocturnal feedback treatment. True auditory feedback of suprathreshold masseter/temporalis muscle activity was provided by a tone proportional in intensity to the intensity, frequency, and duration of the EMG recording. The signal did not awaken the patients; however, when viewed as a series of A-B single-subject experiments, the nocturnal feedback tone markedly reduced durations of bruxing in eight of nine cases.

In a comparatively well-controlled study, Kardach, Bailey, and Ash (1978) compared EMG-contingent auditory feedback to randomly delivered tones, to occlusal equilibration, and to mock occlusal equilibration as treatments for nocturnal bruxism among 20 bruxist males and females 18 to 39 years of age. Bruxing was quantified and recorded as noted earlier. True auditory feedback of masseter/anterior temporalis muscle activity above a 100 μv threshold constituted treatment for four patients. Control feedback of a noncontingent tone sounded six to eight times per hour served as treatment for four patients. Occlusal equilibration performed according to orthodox criteria was the treatment for four patients. Mock equilibration, grinding nonopposing and nonsupporting tooth surfaces, was used as a control treatment with four patients. A fifth group of four bruxist patients served as (temporarily) untreated controls. Nocturnal feedback produced an average 70% reduction in bruxing during treatment but was followed by rebounds in three of four patients when the treatment was withdrawn. The control feedback procedure produced no significant change in mean bruxist activity. The effects of equilibration on bruxing were more complex. Two subjects showed immediate increases in bruxing followed by reductions to or below the initial baseline level. Two subjects showed immediate decreases in bruxing followed by rebounds to or toward the initial baseline levels. Mock equilibration produced a slight decrease in bruxing in all four subjects. The four untreated patients turned out to have unexpectedly low bruxing values to begin with. Kardachi et al. concluded tentatively that nocturnal feedback is preferred over equilibration in the treatment of nocturnal bruxism.

Funch and Gale (1980) used a nocturnal EMG-activated auditory signal to treat a 27-year-old female with a 4-year bruxing history. Daily levels of stress, exercise, EMG activity, and sleep were recorded during five 10-day baseline periods that alternated with two 10-day treatment periods. During the first treatment period, a tone was sounded through an earphone whenever the EMG criterion was exceeded during sleep. During the second treatment period, the tone served also as a prompt to get out of bed, walk to a nearby desk, and record the time and quality of sleep. Bruxing episodes were tallied and bruxing durations were measured as seconds of bruxing per hour of sleep. Bruxing during sleep did decrease during the first treatment period. When the EMG-activated tone served also to prompt self-recording of sleep variables, bruxing decreased significantly. However, bruxing rebounded over pretreatment baseline levels when treatment was withdrawn and the rebound was stable over a 2-month follow-up period.

Rugh and Johnson (1981) used a nocturnal EMG-activated tone to treat five 20- to 39-year-old subjects who reported nocturnal grinding and associated muscular fatigue. Their purpose was to determine whether the nocturnal alarm protocol reduced the durations of bruxist events or their frequencies. Auditory feedback of suprathreshold masseter muscle tension was provided by a tone that remained on whenever 20 μV or greater EMG activity was occurring. All five subjects' home monitoring showed demonstrable lowering of bruxing durations between baseline recording and a period following nocturnal feedback treatment. Data for frequencies of bruxing episodes showed no such improvement.

Clark, Beemsterboer, and Rugh (1981) used a nocturnal EMG-activated tone coupled with an arousal task to treat 10 nocturnal bruxing patients of 19 to 34 years of age. Auditory feedback was done following Rugh and Johnson (1981) and the feedback tone served also to prompt getting out of bed, crossing the room, and recording of time and sleep quality. Using home-monitored recordings of nightly suprathreshold-EMG duration to define bruxing, mean bruxing during 7 to 14 days after nocturnal feedback was significantly less than mean bruxing during 10 to 12 days before nocturnal feedback. This was true for 9 of 10 patients and, in contrast to previous studies, there were no rebounds following treatment withdrawal. This latter finding might derive from the selection by Clark *et al.* of patients without clinically significant malocclusion.

Piccione, Coates, George, Rosenthal, and Karzmark (1982) used masseter EMG-activated nocturnal alarms to treat bruxing in two female patients. A time-lagged baseline-treatment-baseline-treatment (reversal) design was used in which participation of one patient preceded participation of the other by one week. Bruxing incidents were defined when masseter EMG activity met specific amplitude, duration, and rhythmicity criteria during the course of all-night polysomnographic recordings. An alarm sounded when these criteria were exceeded at which time the patients were to get out of bed, walk across the room, and record sleep data. Bruxing was measured by tallying the number grinds in each incident and by recording their durations. Treatment did not have a positive effect for either subject. For one, bruxing was variable during the first feedback period and basically did not improve. A marked rebound occurred during the subsequent return-to-baseline condition, and the second feedback period served only to reduce the rebound to just above the initial baseline levels. For the second subject, bruxing increased slightly from the first baseline to the first feedback period, increased further in the subsequent return-to-baseline condition, and dropped to the initial baseline level during the second feedback period. Of concern here is that neither subject was demonstrably bruxing during the initial baseline period.

Moss *et al.* (1982) used masseter EMG-activated nocturnal alarms and correlated arousal tasks to treat two female patients with 3- and 7-year bruxing histories. Using independent single-subject designs, they treated the patients in multiple phases. For the first patient, the phases were as follows: (a) baseline recording, (b) soft tone termination and reset automatically, (c) soft tone requiring manual termination and reset, (d) loud buzzer terminated and reset automatically, (e) loud buzzer requiring manual termination and reset, (f) return-to-baseline conditions, and (g) loud buzzer requiring manual termination and reset. Using nightly frequencies and nightly durations of bruxing incidents as separate measures of bruxism, the most beneficial effects were produced by loud noises that could only be escaped manually. For the second patient, the phases were as follows: (a) baseline recording, (b) progressive relaxation training, (c) return to baseline, and (d) loud buzzer requiring manual termination and reset, (e) return to baseline, and (f) loud buzzer requiring manual termination and reset. The loud buzzer requiring manual termination and reset produced immediate decreases in bruxing duration and frequency. Relaxation training had no effect.

Casas, Beemsterboer, and Clark (1982) compared four procedures: (a) stress-reduction behavioral counseling, (b) nocturnal EMG feedback, (c) combined counseling plus feedback, and (d) an assessment-wait-reassessment control regimen. Subjects were 16 bruxist males and females who presented to a TMJ clinic. The nocturnal EMG feedback treatment was the same as that used by Rugh and Johnson (1981). Nocturnal EMG activity was chart recorded by patients for approximately 10 nights before treatment was begun and 10 nights after treatment had ended. Bruxing was quantified in the form of duration units per hour of sleep. There was no difference between the three treatment groups with respect to pre- to posttreatment bruxing activity. However, all treatment groups demonstrated pre- to posttreatment reductions in suprathreshold masseter EMG values compared to the control group. Changes on questionnaire reports of daytime clenching/nocturnal grinding behaviors taken before and 2 months after treatment pointed to nocturnal EMG feedback as the treatment of choice for nocturnal grinding and, perhaps, to behavioral counseling as a potentially better approach to diurnal bruxism.

The literature on the use of EMG-activated nocturnal alarms to treat bruxing shows variable outcomes and is difficult to characterize accurately. Part of the variability problem relates to methodological weaknesses, such as inadequate control groups, small experimental samples, unreliable measures of bruxing behavior, and incomplete technical reporting (see following). Part of the problem relates to procedural differences across studies, differences in patient-selection criteria, feedback parameters during treatment, and the requirement of signal-cued arousal behaviors. In general, suprathreshold EMG-contingent auditory feedback is best viewed as a promising approach to *managing* nocturnal bruxing when the auditory signal also serves as an instruction to perform some psychomotor task that requires wakefulness. The rebound problem stands in the way of viewing nocturnal feedback as a viable *treatment* strategy. This is particularly true insofar as the duration of rebound effects following feedback withdrawal has not been assessed satisfactorily. Nocturnal feedback can be of value alongside occlusal splints in the context of a multifaceted treatment program.

Critique and Overview of the Literature

New areas of clinical therapy-outcome research routinely evolve through identifiable stages. Retrospective reports of success with individual patients or small patient cohorts appear. These are followed by reports of prospective group clinical trials with larger cohorts of patients and, ulitimately, by randomized groups experiments comparing treated versus untreated samples. The literature on biofeedback applications to facial pain and bruxing has had a characteristic evolution. Table 1 summarizes the methodological characteristics of the literature just reviewed. As can be readily seen, there is a need for continued methodological evolution toward treatment versus no-treatment comparisons in which treatments are not confounded, demand/placebo effects are controlled, and outcome measures are accurately representative of adaptively relevant naturalistic pain behavior.

There is no definitive experimental support for the use of biofeedback-assisted masseter-area relaxation training alone or in combination with other treatments. As noted earlier, this state of affairs reflects the absence of adequate research protocols and might not mirror the weaknesses of a biofeedback approach. Some clearly promising clinical reports have, in fact, appeared. There is some meaningful experimental support for the use of EMG-activated nocturnal alarms for the management of bruxism. Here again, however, the state of evolved research paradigms forestalls strong claims of clinical efficacy. The problem of contrast-like rebounds when alarms are discontinued also seems to exist. Virtually nothing is known confidently about how patient and/or syndrome variables interact with procedure, setting, and therapist variable to yield differential outcomes clinically.

Within such constraints, some recommendations for treatment can be made to the biofeedback practitioner. EMG biofeedback training as

TABLE 1. Biofeedback Management of TMJ Disorders and Bruxing

Syndrome	N	Treatment	Research design	Assessment	Success	Follow-up
TMJ						
Berry & Wilmot (1977)	35	EMG feedback "Occlusal (Covers)"	none	self-report	yes	none
Carlsson, Gale, & Ohman (1975)	1	EMG feedback	none	self-report	yes	6-month maintained treatment gains
Carlsson & Gale (1976)	1	EMG feedback	none	self-report	yes	12-month maintained treatment gains
Carlsson & Gale (1977)	11	EMG feedback	GT	self-report dental examination	yes	12-month maintained treatment gains
Dohrmann & Laskin (1976)	24	EMG feedback ($n = 16$) Placebo ($n = 8$)	GT	self-report Masseter EMG activity incisal opening	yes	none
Gessell (1975)	23	EMG feedback	GT	self-report	yes	none

Continued

TABLE 1. (*Continued*)

Syndrome	N	Treatment	Research design	Assessment	Success	Follow-up
Gelb & Gale (1983)	51	EMG feedback (*n* = 32) EMG feedback/taped home relaxation training (*n* = 19)	GT	self-report	yes-no differences between groups	none
Moss, Wedding, & Sanders (1983)	3	EMG feedback Progressive relaxation	SS	self-report Masseter EMG activity	marginal	1 month— mixed
Olson (1977)	15	EMG feedback— Masseter (*n* = 5) EMG feedback— Frontalis (*n* = 4) EMG feedback/ Psychotherapy (*n* = 6)	GT	self-report Masseter and frontalis activity	yes-no group comparisons	none
Peck & Kraft (1977)	6	EMG feedback	none	self-report Masseter EMG activity	no	4-week— mixed
Stenn, Mothersill, & Brooke (1979)	13	EMG feedback Progressive relaxation/ coping skills/ sensory awareness—(*n* = 6), Progressive relaxation/ coping skills/sensory awareness (*n* = 7)	GT	self-report blind-physician rating Masseter EMG activity	yes, but no difference between feedback and nonfeedback subjects	3-month maintained treatment gains

Bruxism

Study	N	Treatment	Design	Measure	Results	Follow-up
Casas, Beemsterbcer, & Clark (1982)[a]	16	1)Stress-reduction behavioral counseling 2)Nocturnal EMG feedback 3)Counseling & feedback 4)Wait—control	CT	Masseter EMG activity & self-report questionnaire	1)yes 2)yes 3)yes 4)no	2 month
Cleark, Beemsterboer, & Rugh (1981)[a]	10	Nocturnal alarm-cued arousal task	SS	Masseter EMG activity	yes-9 subjects no-1 subject	Maintained gains for 6 or 7 subjects assessed
Clarke & Kardachi (1977)[a]	7	Nocturnal feedback	none	Masseter/ Temporalis EMG activity	yes-4 subjects no-3 subjects	none
Funch & Gale (1980)	1	1)Nocturnal alarm 2)Nocturnal alarm-cued arousal task	SS	Masseter EMG	1)no 2)yes	rebound
Kardachi, Bailey, & Ash (1978)[a]	20	1)Nocturnal feedback 2)Randomly delivered nocturnal tones 3)Equilibration 4)Mock equilibration	CT	Masseter/ Temporalis EMG activity	1)yes 2)no 3)marginal 4)marginal	see text

Continued

TABLE 1. (*Continued*)

Syndrome	N	Treatment	Research design	Assessment	Success	Follow-up
Moss, Hammer, Adams, Jenkins, Thompson, & Haber (1982)	2	1)Soft alarm, automatic termination 2)Soft alarm, manual termination 3)Loud alarm, automatic termination 4)Loud alarm, manual termination 5)Progressive relaxation	SS	Masseter EMG activity	1)marginal 2)marginal 3)marginal 4)yes 5)no	see text
Piccione, Coates, Rosenthal, George, & Karzmark (1982)[a]	2	Nocturnal alarm-cued arousal task	SS	Masseter EMG activity	no	none
Rugh & Johnson (1981)[a]	5	Nocturnal feedback	none	Masseter EMG	marginal	none
Rugh & Solberg (1977)[b]	15	Portable EMG feedback alarm	none	Masseter EMG activity	yes-10 subjects no-5 subjects	none

[a] Nocturnal bruxing.
[b] Diurnal bruxing.
GT—Group trial; SS—Single subject; CT—Control-Treatment.

a sole form of treatment is not indicated. Possibly a combination of biofeedback with progressive relaxation training and/or behavioral counseling offers most to the patient. The use of feedback-cued nocturnal alarms for managing bruxing should incorporate arousal tasks.

Notwithstanding the implications of Table 1, the data on biofeedback applications to these syndromes certainly are no worse than the data on other applicable treatment techniques (cf. Okeson *et al.*, 1983). Even if clinical decisions were derived solely from scientific evidence, it would not be necessary to prefer other approaches to biofeedback methods. Compared to other data, the case reports and early experiments on biofeedback clearly do permit judicious applications to TMJ disorders and bruxism. This is particularly so because EMG biofeedback training is noninvasive and there is no indication that it compounds the problem.

SPECIFICITY OF EFFECT

The preceding review of the literature provided no definitive experimental support for the global clinical efficacy of biofeedback approaches vis-à-vis TMJ disorders. Therefore, it is not currently possible to pinpoint specific or active clinical effects within the global effects of biofeedback therapy. An argument for active therapy effects requires a demonstration of clinical effects in the presence of controls over demand/placebo influences. Although some of the experimenters contributing to the literature have shown sensitivity to these issues (e.g., Kardachi *et al.*, 1978), no study has incorporated the array of controls and measures required for arguments in terms of active effects (see especially Kazdin & Wilcoxon, 1976).

MECHANISM OF ACTION

Nothing substantive can be said about the therapeutic mechanism of biofeedback training for TMJ disorders. This is true for at least three reasons. First, there are no adequate or consensually endorsed accounts of therapeutic biofeedback effects in general. In their seminal review of biofeedback training and assessment paradigms, Raczyznski, Thompson, and Sturgis (1982) delineated a half dozen theoretical explanations of therapeutic biofeedback mechanisms. They noted, in addition, that all of the explanatory models are post hoc. Second, there is no adequate or consensually endorsed account of the etiology of the TMJ disorders aside from the view that it is complex and multifactorial. The multifactorial view of TMJ disorders also is post hoc and it rests on a knowledge base that is largely nonexperimental. Third, there is the state of affairs, noted earlier, that active or specific effects have not been produced. Theoretical accounts of therapy mechanisms are tied to active experimental effects, as opposed to nonspecific influences. Hence, there are virtually no trustworthy data from which to erect microstructures for therapeutic mechanisms. In brief, theories of both therapy mechanism and syndrome mechanisms are post hoc and no data exist describing the range of therapy-outcome phenomena over which underlying mechanisms would be expected to manifest influence.

The therapeutic mechanism of nocturnal alarms in the modification of bruxism is not clear either. The bulk of data seems to suggest that they operate by waking people up, not by teaching or conditioning patients to brux less frequently.

COST-EFFECTIVENESS

The literature on EMG biofeedback approaches to treating TMJ disorders and bruxism has not yet evolved to a point that allows confident description of normative treatment effects. As noted earlier, the literature concerning therapy outcomes for dental approaches to these syndromes is not qualitatively superior. The current literature on EMG biofeedback approaches to treating TMJ disorders does suggest, albeit tentatively, that biofeedback regimens should be used to supplement, not replace, the clinical methods of the dental profession. Therefore, concern over relative cost-effectiveness among various treatment approaches is superfluous.

FUTURE RESEARCH

The application of biofeedback to TMJ disorders and bruxism affords exceptional opportunities for laboratory and clinical researchers. All relevant questions about etiology, pathophysiology, biofeedback-treatment outcomes, specificity of biofeedback effects, mechanisms of therapy effects, etc. are in need of more trustworthy answers than we now have. Four major substantive directions for research in the short-term future are discussed in the following.

Only during the last decade have behavioral psychologists begun to pay systematic attention to TMJ disorders and bruxism. Therefore, realistically adequate research methodologies have not yet evolved. Some methodological guidelines for the short-term future also are offered.

Substantive Problems

Clinical Outcome

As noted, truly sound behavioral research has yet to document reliably robust effects for either biofeedback treatment or orthodox dental therapies on TMJ disorders. Clearly the major thrust of research for the next few years should be carefully evaluating the global effects of dental and biofeedback treatments. With regard to biofeedback, research is needed in which replicable prototype procedures are used along with sophisticated assessments of TMJ and bruxing problems and of their adjustive consequences.

Active Effects

Research in the short-term future also should determine the extent to which clinically beneficial effects form biofeedback-based treatments mirror the influence of demand/placebo factors in the professional care and assessment contexts. Some reports (e.g., Goodman et al., 1976; Greene & Laskin, 1972) point to robust clinical influence from demand/placebo factors among patients with TMJ problems. An accurate characterization of the effects of demand/placebo factors within biofeedback-based treatments would be valuable for a variety of reasons. Research is needed in which real and bogus biofeedback treatments are compared using sophisticated measures of TMJ pain and dysfunction as well as convergent measures of demand/placebo influence (cf. Kazdin & Wilcoxon, 1976).

Interactions with Syndrome Variables

Most reports of biofeedback applications describe the participants globally as TMJ patients, MPD patients, or bruxers. This routine classification of TMJ disorders leaves much to be desired; it is not empirically derived; it is a disjunctive-concept system; it is used inconsistently, etc. While undertaking clinical-outcome research, scientists and clinicians should in the immediate future provide as much information as possible concerning the fine grain of the etiological factors, of the resulting symptoms, and of their adaptive consequences in individual cases. Systematic empirical work toward an improved taxonomy for TMJ disorders is no less important than work on therapy outcomes. An improved nomenclature for syndrome variables might, in time, result from the confluence of routinely detailed clinical-research reports and formal taxonomic efforts. In the meantime, therapy outcome research might be organized around a taxonomy such as that proposed by McNeill et al. (1980).

Applications of Disregulation Theory

Homeostasis within the masticatory system depends on the integration of several participating systems, for example, the nervous system, the muscles of mastication, the TMJs, and the teeth and their supporting structures. According to contemporary disregulation theory (Schwartz, 1979), psychophysiological disturbances in the system would arise, in general, from a chronic ("tonic") and/or situational ("phasic") loss of homeostasis or disregulation among the participating systems. Yemm (1979) presented a potentially heuristic multifactor typology for bruxing and other forms of muscular hyperactivity. *Habitual activity* he related to the structure and form of masticatory system. Facial muscle activity is initiated and maintained to reduce or ameliorate the effects of abnormal morphological characteristics. *Hyperactivity in chewing* he related to the function of the masticatory system. Local hyperactivity during chewing is produced by occlusal development or restorataive changes, by tooth loss, and by inflammatory and other degenerative disease processes. *Stress-induced muscle activity* refers to hyperactivity of psychophysiological origin. *Nocturnal hyperactivity* is a disorder of arousal similar to other sleep disturbances. Yemm's four-part typology for muscular hyperactivity accords well with a "tonic and/or phasic disregulation" approach in which, for example, Yemm's "habitual activity" mirrors Schwartz' "tonic disregulation." Hence, therapy-outcome research using Yemm's typology could contribute to the development of disregulation theory as it applies to bruxing and the facial musculature. Data concerning differential biofeedback outcomes across Yemm's syndrome categories would also be of interest to clinicians, taxonomists, and biofeedback theorists.

Methodological Approaches

As noted, the major thrust of research during the next few years should be careful evaluation of global biofeedback-based treatment effects among patients with TMJ disorders. The principal hazards to accomplishing this careful evaluation are encountered at the level of assessment. Hence, some perspectives on the problem of adequate assessment are reviewed in the following.

Therapy-outcome research using biofeedback-based interventions poses special problems from the vantage point of design logic. The chapter concludes with some perspectives on between-groups, within-subjects, and hybrid experimental designs.

Systematic Behavioral Assessment

Biofeedback-therapy researchers working with TMJ disorders are concerned with sequential assessment at four levels: (a) changes in mandibular muscle tension in the training environment and in the presence of exteroceptive EMG feedback; (b) changes in mandibular muscle tension in the training environment but without exteroceptive feedback; (c) changes in mandibular muscle tension in the natural environment; and (d) changes in the naturalistic pain experiences and pain/dysfunction behaviors that prompt individuals to seek treatment. All too frequently an omission at some assessment level has confused interpretation of findings. Hence routine reporting of four-level assessment is needed.

The late 1970s witnessed the participants in the behavioral assessment movement attempt to bring the assumptions and practices of clinical assessment into accord with those of clinical behavior therapy (Goldfried, 1977). Out of this movement has evolved a relatively systematic statement of general assessment strategy based on the postulate that behaviors are situation specific and on the corollaries that problematic conduct must be sampled in adequate amounts and in representative subsets of the natural environment (cf. Linehan, 1980). Behavioral assessment issues come into play at each of the previously noted assessment stages but are most prominent at Stages c and d. An explicit connection between biofeedback therapy outcome research and the methods of behavioral assessment also is needed.

As noted, clinical biofeedback therapy for TMJ patients is concerned not only with mandibular muscle hyperactivity but also with pain and dysfunction as they impact on patients' lives. In turn, realistically adequate assessment of therapy effects requires evaluations of perceived pain and pain behaviors and of the consequences of the adjustments these problems require. A strong case can be made for three-channel assessment in this arena, that is, for the assessment of pain reports and pain behaviors in addition to mandibular muscle hyperactivity.

Finally, research involving Yemm's (1979) typology (or disregulation theory) will require development of integrated, multidisciplinary, assessment protocols in which tonic and phasic parameters can be evaluated separately. Basically, this will involve adequate time sampling of tonic conditions and/or deliberate production of phasic disregulation. Some advances already have been made in developing clinical assessment prototypes along these lines. Rugh (1977), for example, reported a laboratory-based psychophysiological evaluation for bruxers that is consistent with psychophysiological-disregulation thinking . Obviously much work remains vis-à-vis the thorough-going assessment of TMJ conditions and their impacts on life-styles. It is equally obvious that meaningful therapy-outcome research hinges on advances at the level of assessment.

Hybrid Experimental Designs

Research on biofeedback applications to TMJ disorders mirrors two empirical traditions. Randomized groups experiments are couched in the actuarial tradition. Intrasubject replication experiments derive from the experimental analysis of behavior. As noted, therapy-outcome research using biofeedback-based interventions poses special problems from either perspective. Given the sample-size requirements of true actuarial research, the multisession nature of biofeedback treatments, and the work involved in meaningful behavioral assessment, the between-groups comparison paradigm dramatically restricts scientific access and clearly requires prohibitive amounts of work. Intrasubject replication methodology, on the other hand, suffers from the problem of generality and from other problems in specific instances.

Between-groups and within-subjects comparisons stress, differentially, the nomothetic versus idiographic purposes of researchers. Standing squarely between the two orthodox approaches is research that undertakes within-subject manipulations of independent variables *and* between-subject comparisons of dependent variables. Designs using multiple baselines across several subjects exemplify this hybrid approach and represent a beneficial compromise between the demands of actuarial methodology and the problems of behavior-analytic methodology. Taken alone, however, multiple baselines across subjects designs are not without shortcomings; for example, ethical problems in witholding treatment until several other patients successively have achieved baseline stability or interpretive problems posed by raw visual inspection of some data sets. Hence, identical interventions and intrasubject phase manipulations for successive, not simultaneous, patients might be used as a general approach to therapy-outcome research. When coupled with adequate assessment, this can be a persuasive strategy that does not require large samples but does address the problem of generality. Rules for evaluating a general class of "systematically cumulative intrasubject experiments" would ultimately evolve out of work along these lines (see also, Delprato & McGlynn, 1986).

In their excellent review of biofeedback assessment and training paradigms, Raczynski *et al.* (1982) articulated an experimental approach that could easily serve as a basic model for work with TMJ disorders. Following their protocol would divide, systematically, for assessing masseter-area EMG control during pretreatment, then biofeedback, then no-feedback, and self-control phases of training; their protocol would also provide for assessing EMG control in the natural environment. Raczynski *et al.* issued a cogent call for thorough assessment of psychophysiological disorders in terms of patterns of disregulation. It is a small step to add systematic, multidisciplinary assessment in terms of Yemm's (1979) heuristic typology and/or the taxonomy of McNeill *et al.* (1980).

Comprehensive evaluation of biofeedback therapy for TMJ disorders and bruxism involves assessing pain behaviors and life-style impacts of therapy, not just control over masseter-area EMGs. Realistic approaches to performing such an evaluation require hybrid experimental tactics. As supplemented by bona fide behavioral assessment of pain behaviors and their consequences, the Raczynski *et al.* (1982) protocol would serve as a basis for "systematically cumulative intrasubject experiments" on biofeedback therapy for TMJ disorders.

Conclusions

This review of biofeedback applications shows the following: (a) TMJ disorders and bruxism are poorly understood in terms of etiology and classification; (b) biofeedback mechanisms are poorly understood and theories of biofeedback-based therapy effects are uniformly post hoc; (c) experimental evidence is only modest that biofeedback is an effective treatment for temporomandibular problems but biofeedback is clinically competitive with other therapy modes and is not incompatible with some of them; (d) the failure to find clinically unambiguous biofeedback-based therapy effects reflects weaknesses in research methodology not in weaknesses in the power of biofeedback approaches; (e) research methodologies are evolving that, in principle, will allow for careful clinical evaluation of biofeedback approaches; and (f) applications of biofeedback to temporomandibular disorders and bruxism are excellent areas for optimistic research in the short-term future.

References

Alling, C. C., & Mahan, P. E. (1977). *Facial pain*. Philadelphia PA: Lea & Febiger.

Ayer, W. A., & Levin, M. P. (1973). Elimination of tooth grinding habits by massed practice therapy. *Journal of Periodontology, 44*, 569–571.

Ayer, W. A., & Levin, M. P. (1975). Theoretical basis and application of massed practice exercises for the elimination of tooth grinding habits. *Journal of Periodontology, 46*, 306–308.

Azrin, N. H., & Nunn, R. G. (1973). Habit-reversal: A method of eliminating nervous habits and tics. *Behaviour Research and Therapy, 11*, 619–628.

Azrin, N. H., & Nunn, R. G. (1977). *Habit-control: Stuttering, nail biting, and nervous habits.* New York: Simon & Schuster.

Azrin, N. H., Nunn, R. G., & Frantz-Renshaw, S. E. (1982). Habit reversal vs. negative practice treatment of self-destructive oral habits (biting, chewing or licking of the lips, tongue or palate). *Journal of Behavior Therapy and Experimental Psychiatry, 13,* 49–54.

Berry, D. C., & Wilmot, G. (1977). The use of a biofeedback technique in the treatment of mandibular dysfunction pain. *Journal of Oral Rehabilitation, 40,* 255–260.

Budzynski, T., & Stoyva, V. (1973). An electromyographic feedback technique for teaching voluntary relaxation of the masseter muscle. *Journal of Dental Research, 52,* 116–119.

Carlsson, G. E., & Droukas, B. C. (1984). Dental occlusion and the health of the masticatory system. *Journal of Craniomandibular Practice, 2,* 141–147.

Carlsson, S. G., & Gale, E. N. (1976). Biofeedback treatment for muscle pain associated with the temporomandibular joint. *Journal of Behavior Therapy and Experimental Psychiatry, 7,* 383–385.

Carlsson, S. G., & Gale, E. N. (1977). Biofeedback in the treatment of long-term temporomandibular join pain. An outcome study. *Biofeedback and Self-Regulation, 2,* 161–171.

Carlsson, S. G., Gale, E. N., & Ohman, A. (1975). Treatment of temporomandibular joint syndrome with biofeedback training. *Journal of the American Dental Association, 91,* 602.

Casas, J. M., Beemsterboer, P., & Clark, G. T. (1982). A comparison of stress-reduction behavioral counseling and contingent nocturnal EMG feedback for the treatment of bruxism. *Behaviour Research and Therapy, 20,* 9–15.

Clark, G. T., Beemsterboer, P., & Rugh, J. D. (1981). The treatment of nocturnal bruxism using contingent EMG feedback with an arousal task. *Behaviour Research and Therapy, 19,* 451–455.

Clark, G. T., Beemsterboer, P., Solberg, W. K., Rugh, J. D. (1979). Nocturnal electromyographic evaluation of myofascial pain dysfunction in patients undergoing occlusal splint therapy. *Journal of the American Dental Association, 99,* 607–611.

Costen, J. B. (1934). Syndrome of ear and sinus symptoms dependent upon disturbed function of the temporomandibular joint. *Annals of Otolaryngology, Rhinology, Laryngology, 43,* 1.

Dawson, P. E. (1974). *Evaluation, diagnosis, and treatment of occlusal problems.* St. Louis, MO: C.V. Mosby.

Delprato, D. J., & McGlynn, F. D. (1986). Innovations in behavioral medicine. In M. Hersen, R. M. Eisler, & P. M. Miller (Eds.), *Progress in behavior modification, 20,* 67–122.

Dohrmann, R. J., & Laskin, D. M. (1976). Treatment of myofascial pain dysfunction syndrome with EMG biofeedback. *Journal of Dental Research, 55.* (Abstract No. 751, B249)

Dubner, R., Sessle, B. J., & Storey, A. T. (1978). *The neural basis of oral and facial function.* New York: Plenum Press.

Dunlap, K. (1932). *Habits: Their making and unmaking.* New York: Liveright.

Fuchs, P. (1975). The muscular activity of the chewing apparatus during night sleep. *Journal of Oral Rehabilitation, 2,* 35.

Funch, D. P., & Gale, E. N. (1980). Factors associated with nocturnal bruxism and its treatment. *Journal of Behavioral Medicine, 3,* 385–397.

Gale, E. N. (1979). The effectiveness of biofeedback treatment for temporomandibular joint pain. *Journal of Dental Research, 58.* (Abstract No. 496, A217)

Gelb, M. L., & Gale, E. N. (1983). Effects of home practice on biofeedback treatment of TMJ/MPD pain. *Journal of Dental Research, 62,* (AADR Abstract No. 152, B186).

Gessel, A. H. (1975). Electromyographic biofeedback and tricyclic antidepressants in myofascial pain-dysfunction syndrome: Psychological predictors of outcome. *Journal of the American Dental Association, 91,* 1048–1052.

Goldfried, M. R. (1977). Behavioral assessment in perspective. In J. D. Cone & R. P. Hawkins (Eds.), *Behavioral assessment: New directions in clinical psychology* (pp. 147–166). New York: Brunner-Mazel.

Goodman, P., Greene, C. S., & Laskin, D. M. (1976). Response of patients with myofascial pain-dysfunction syndrome to mock equilibration. *Journal of the American Dental Association, 92,* 755.

Greene, C. S. (1976). The relationship between research and clinical practice in treatment of myofascial pain-dysfunction. *Alpha Omegan, 18,* 74–80.

Greene, C. S., & Laskin, D. M. (1972). Splint therapy for the myofascial pain-dysfunction (MPD) syndrome: A comparative study. *Journal of the American Dental Association, 84,* 624–628.

Hamada, T., Kotani, H., Kawazoe, Y., & Yamada, S. (1982). Effect of occlusal splints on the EMG activity of masseter and temporal muscles in bruxism with clinical symptoms, *Journal of Oral Rehabilitation, 9,* 119–123.

Heller, R. F., & Forgione, A. G. (1975). An evaluation of bruxism control: Massed negative practice and automated relaxation training. *Journal of Dental Research, 54,* 1120–1123.

Heller, R. F., & Strang, H. R. (1973). Controlling bruxism through automated aversive conditioning. *Behaviour Research and Therapy, 11,* 327–329.

Kardachi, B. J. R., Bailey, J. O., & Ash, M. M. (1978). A comparison of biofeedback and occlusal adjustment on bruxism. *Journal of Periodontology, 49,* 367–372.

Kardachi, B. J. R., & Clarke, N. G. (1977). The use of biofeedback to control bruxism. *Journal of Periodontology, 48,* 639–642.

Kawazoe, Y., Kotani, H., Hamada, T., & Yamada, S. (1980). Effect of occlusal splints on the electromyographic activities of masseter muscles during maximum clenching in patients with myofascial pain-dysfunction syndrome. *Journal of Prosthetic Dentistry, 43,* 578.

Kazdin, A. E., & Wilcoxon, L. A. (1976). Systematic desensitization and nonspecific treatment effects: A methodological evaluation. *Psychological Bulletin, 83,* 729–758.

Laskin, D. M. (1969). Etiology of the pain-dysfunction syndrome. *Journal of the American Dental Association, 79,* 147.

Linehan, M. (1980). Content validity: its relevance to behavioral assessment. *Behavioral Assessment, 2,* 147–159.

Majewski, R. F., & Gale, E. N. (1983). The effectiveness of relaxation training for TMJ/MPD patients. *Journal of Dental Research, 62.* (AADR Abstract No. 150, 186)

Marbach, J. J. (1976). A holistic approach to the treatment of facial pain. *Alpha Omegan, 32,* 132–137.

McGlynn, F. D., Cassisi, J. E., & Diamond, E. L. (1985). Diagnosis and treatment of bruxism: A behavioral dentistry perspective. In R. J. Daitzman (ed.), *Diagnosis and intervention in behavior therapy and behavioral medicine* (Vol. 2, pp. 28–87). New York: Springer.

McNeill, C., Danzig, W. M., Farrar, W. B., Gelb, H., Lerman, B. D., Moffett, B. C., Pertes, R., Solberg, W. K., & Weinberg, L. A. (1980). Craniomandibular (TMJ) disorders— The state of the art. *Journal of Prosthetic Dentistry, 44,* 434–437.

Meklas, J. G. (1971). Bruxism . . . diagnosis and treatment. *The Journal of the Academy of General Dentistry, 11,* 31–36.

Moss, R. A., Hammer, D., Adams, H. E., Jenkins, J. O., Thompson, K., & Haber, J. (1982). A more efficient biofeedback procedure for the treatment of nocturnal bruxism. *Journal of Oral Rehabilitation, 9,* 125.

Moss, R. A., Wedding, D., & Sanders, S. H. (1983). The comparative efficacy of relaxation training and masseter EMG feedback in the treatment of TMJ dysfunction. *Journal of Oral Rehabilitation, 10,* 9–17.

Moulton, R. E. (1966). Emotional factors in non-organic temporomandibular joint pain. *Dental Clinics of North America, 10,* 609–620.

Mowrer, O. H., & Mowrer, W. (1938). Enuresis: A method for its study and treatment. *American Journal of Orthopsychiatry, 8,* 436–459.

Okeson, J., Moody, P. M., Kemper, J. T., & Calhoun, T. C. (1983). Evaluation of occlusal splint therapy. *The Journal of Craniomandibular Practice, 1,* 47–52.

Olson, R. E. (1977). Biofeedback for MPD patients non-responsive to drug and biteplate therapy. *Journal of Dental Research, 56B,* (Abstract No. 64, B12).

Peck, C. L., & Kraft, G. H. (1977). Electromyographic biofeedback for pain related to muscle tension. *Archives of Surgery, 112,* 889.

Piccione, A., Coates, T. J., George, J. M., Rosenthal, D., & Karzmark, P. (1982). Nocturnal biofeedback for nocturnal bruxism. *Biofeedback and Self-Regulation, 7,* 405–419.

Raczynski, J. M., Thompson, J. K., & Sturgis, E. T. (1982). An evaluation of biofeedback assessment and training paradigms. *Clinical Psychology Review, 2,* 337–348.

Ramfjord, S.P. (1961). Bruxism, a clinical and electromyographic study. *Journal of the American Dental Association, 62,* 21.

Ramfjord, S. P., & Ash, M. M. (1983). *Occlusion* (3rd ed.). Philadelphia: W. B. Saunders.

Rao, S. M., & Glaros, A. G. (1979). Electromyographic correlates of experimentally induced stress in diurnal bruxists and normals. *Journal of Dental Research, 58,* 1872–1878.

Reding, G. R., Rubright, W. C., & Zimmerman, S. O. (1966). Incidence of bruxism. *Journal of Dental Research, 45,* 1198–1204.

Reding, G. R., Zepelin, H., Robinson, J. E., Smith, V. H., & Zimmerman, S. O. (1968). Sleep patterns of bruxism: A revision. *Psychophysiology, 4,* 396.

Rosenbaum, M. S., & Ayllon, T. (1981). Treating bruxism with the habit-reversal technique. *Behaviour Research and Therapy, 19,* 87–96.

Rugh, J. D. (1976). Variables involved in extinction through repeated practice therapy (Doctoral dissertation, University of California, Santa Barbara, 1975). *Dissertation Abstracts International, 36,* 4738B-4739B. (University Microfilms No. 76-6582).

Rugh, J. D. (1977). A behavioral approach to diagnosis and treatment of functional oral disorders: Biofeedback and self-control techniques. In J. D. Rugh, D. B. Perlis, & R. I. Disraeli (Eds.), *Biofeedback in dentistry: Research and clinical applications* (pp. 126–137). Phoenix, AZ: Semantodontics.

Rugh, J. D. (1978). Electromyographic analysis of bruxism in the natural environment. In P. Weinstein (Ed.), *Advances in behavioral research in dentistry.* Seattle, WA: University of Washington Seminar Series.

Rugh, J. D., & Johnson, R. W. (1981). Temporal analysis of nocturnal bruxism during EMG feedback. *Journal of Periodontology, 52,* 263–265.

Rugh, J. D., & Solberg, W. K. (1976). Psychological implications in temporomandibular pain and dysfunction. *Oral Sciences Review, 7,* 3–30.

Schwartz, G. E. (1979). The brain as a health care system. In G. C. Stone, F. Cohen, & N. E. Adler (Eds.), *Health psychology—A handbook: Theories, applications, and challenges of a psychological approach to the health care system* (pp 341–359). San Francisco: Jossey-Bass.

Schwartz, L. (1956). A temporomandibular joint pain dysfunction syndrome. *Journal of Chronic Diseases, 3,* 284.

Solberg, W. K., Clark, G. T., & Rugh, J. D. (1975). Nocturnal electromyographic evaluation of bruxism patients undergoing short-term splint therapy. *Journal of Oral Rehabilitation, 2,* 215–223.

Solberg, W. K., & Rugh, J. D. (1972). The use of bio-feedback devices in the treatment of bruxism. *Journal of the Southern California Dental Association, 40,* 852–853.

Stenn, P. G., Mothersill, K. J., & Brooke, R. I. (1979). Biofeedback and a cognitive behavioral approach to treatment of myofascial pain dysfunction syndrome *Behavior Therapy, 10,* 29.

Tischler, B. (1928). Occlusal habit neuroses. *Dental Cosmos, 60,* 690–694.

Travell, J. G., & Simons, D. (1983). *Myofascial pain and dysfunction: The trigger point manual,* Baltimore, MD: Williams & Wilkins.

Weinberg, L. A. (1979). The etiology, diagnosis, and treatment of TMJ dysfunction-pain syndrome. Part I: Etiology. *Journal of Prosthetic Dentistry, 42,* 654.

Yemm, R. (1979). Causes and effects of hyperactivity of jaw muscles. In *Oral motor behavior: Impact on oral conditions and dental treatment.* (pp. 256–279). Washington, DC: U.S. Department of Health, Education, & Welfare.

4

The Use of Biofeedback in Disorders of Motor Function

STEVEN L. WOLF AND M. FISCHER-WILLIAMS

INTRODUCTION

Most physical therapeutic interventions are applied to patients with movement limitations resulting from weakness, central nervous system dysfunction, or a breakdown in appropriate integration of sensory information to effect purposeful motion. Inevitably clinicians in physical medicine and rehabilitation make use of their observational abilities and palpatory skills to instruct patients to improve motor performance. These instructions are often combined with a variety of neuromuscular reeducation techniques. In this framework clinicians typically provide verbal cues to a patient and, based on the clinician's interpretation of the patient's response, offer further information. In short, the clinician serves as a feedback interface to the patient.

At best this interaction between clinician and patient takes several seconds to complete. A basic tenet of motor learning theory dictates that enhanced movement is facilitated by the speed and accuracy with which information is provided to the learner. The advent of electromyographic (EMG) biofeedback has been seen as a viable form of treatment to enhance motor function among individuals with musculoskeletal or neuromuscular disorders. The information offered to patients through EMG

STEVEN L. WOLF • Department of Rehabilitation Medicine, Emory University School of Medicine, 1441 Clifton Road NE, Atlanta, GA 30322. M. FISCHER-WILLIAMS • Wells Building, Suite 433, 324 East Wisconsin Avenue, Milwaukee, WI 53202.

feedback is continuous and virtually instantaneous. The content of this information is dictated by the placement of recording sensors (electrodes) and the electronic processing of muscle signals.

In a Biofeedback Society of America Task Force Report on Physical Medicine and Rehabilitation offered by Fernando and Basmajian (1978) a suggestion was made that biofeedback might offer new hope for patients with movement limitations. Whereas the authors predicted that EMG feedback techniques would become used routinely, they also recognized that such techniques would add to, rather than replace, available clinical tools. Several recommendations were made by Fernando and Basmajian, and these recommendations should still be followed by conscientious practitioners today. The purpose of this chapter is to update information on clinical efficacy of EMG biofeedback in the treatment of several disorders including stroke, cerebral palsy, spinal cord injury, spasmodic torticollis, and musculoskeletal pathology. Information gathered in the past 6 years regarding the specificity of biofeedback effects and the mode of action of this modality on human physiology will be presented where appropriate.

MUSCLE BIOFEEDBACK APPLICATIONS TO NORMAL SUBJECTS

Introduction

The application of EMG biofeedback to patients with movement disorders has probably had enormous appeal to clinicians because the outcome of such applications could be readily assessed through overt changes in motor behavior. Therefore, in the past 15 years numerous studies have addressed specific patient populations. A more basic issue of whether normal individuals can utilize information about covert muscle activity to effect an appropriate change (increase or decrease in muscle responses) should ostensibly precede such clinical studies. Whereas the early work on single motor unit control by Basmajian (1974) would suggest unique muscle control capabilities, only a few well controlled studies addressing the ability of a normal individual to modify muscle responses appropriately have been published.

The ability of normal individuals to control muscle activity with appropriate feedback has been addressed primarily by Middaugh. Previously Middaugh (1978) had used EMG feedback to improve the ability of normal human subjects to make a prolonged voluntary contraction of the seldom-used left abductor hallucis muscle, which is responsible for moving the great toe away from the adjacent digit. In her 1982 study, each of 10 normal subjects was instructed to produce 12 sustained, 30-second contractions of this muscle. Six contractions were attempted in each of two sessions. EMG feedback and nonfeedback trials were counterbalanced. EMG activity proved to be significantly greater when muscle contractions occurred in the presence of EMG feedback. This improvement with feedback was presumably due to the increased motor unit recruitment early in the contraction but with little preceptual awareness on the part of subjects. Middaugh, Miller, Foster, and Ferdon (1982) concluded that the EMG feedback provided precise information concerning very minor muscle contractions. The behavior of normal individuals, provided feedback to augment muscle activity, appears to be similar to performances undertaken by paretic patients (Middaugh & Miller, 1980).

Another unique application of EMG feedback to normal individuals was provided by LeVeau and Rogers (1980). These investigators trained individuals to differentiate selectively muscle activity between vastus medialis (VM) and vastus lateralis (VL), two muscles of the quadriceps mass. Ten subjects received EMG biofeedback training sessions 5 days a week. Each session lasted one-half hour. This study investigated whether VL could indeed be trained to contract independently of VM. During the first 2 weeks subjects concentrated on decreasing VL activity. During the final week they tried to increase VM activity. Significant differences were found in the change of muscle activity levels of VL during the first 2 weeks, in VM during the 3rd week, and in the difference between VM and VL from the 1st to the 3rd weeks. Clearly then, normal individuals are capable of differentiating muscle responses among two muscles having a similar function and innervated by the same nerve.

Specificity of Effect

These studies suggest that normal individuals have the ability to control muscle activity in a seldom-used muscle and to differentiate activity among muscles whose firing patterns are usually concurrent. Unfortunately these studies lack information on transfer of training and on long-term maintenance of activity patterns. However, such issues are irrelevant for the purposes of demonstrating normal human control over specific muscles when precise information is provided. The application of these findings to athletes, dancers, and musical performers has yet to be ascertained. The data cited above certainly suggest that EMG biofeedback may enhance motor learning among individuals without concomitant neuromuscular pathology.

BIOFEEDBACK APPLICATIONS TO STROKE (CARDIOVASCULAR ACCIDENT) PATIENTS

Introduction

In 1981 approximately 500,000 people sustained a cerebrovascular accident, or stroke, in the United States. The mean age of such individuals ranged between 44 and 55 years, but increasingly younger persons are being affected (Robins & Baum, 1981). Furthermore, approximately 30% of initial stroke victims will survive for at least 5 years (Baum & Robins, 1981). Given improvements in preventive and restorative measures, it is expected that this survival rate will increase. Consequently, methods for rehabilitating individuals following stroke to enhance quality of life and vocational opportunities should become increasingly creative and efficacious.

Lesions producing the clinical syndromes of stroke involve numerous causative agents and consequently assume different definitions. McCormick (1975) groups the conglomerate of symptoms used to define stroke under the heading *neurovascular diseases*, which he defines as

> disorders attributable to structural and functional alterations of the blood vessels (arteries, veins, capillaries and their subtypes) of the nervous system . . . and includes vascular disease not only of the brain (cerebrovascular disease) but of the spinal cord, the spinal roots, the peripheral and the autonomic nervous systems and membraneous coverings of the nervous system.

Indeed stroke has long been recognized as the result of cerebral hemorrhage, infarction, and thrombo-embolism. Therefore stroke results primarily from a mass change in hemodynamic blood flow. As a result, blood supplied to specific areas of the central nervous system can be compromised. Failure to oxygenate sufficiently these areas will result in necrosis or deactivation of localized cerebral tissue. It is this situation that leads to the traumatic loss in precise homeostasis among motor and sensory systems with many of the more obvious clinical signs (spasticity, inapproprioception, dyskinesia) consequently prevailing.

Sites of cerebrovascular accidents are numerous. Such accidents can occur in a variety of foci, including internal carotid artery, small leptomeningeal vessels, vertebral artery, the "three vessel border zone" (anterior, middle, and posterior cerebral arteries), or at the major cerebral vessels (Romanul, 1976). The development of physical signs of stroke are predicated on the type of lesion (nonvascular, hemorrhagic, or ischemic). Levy (1975) notes that ischemic brain infarction is characterized by abrupt onset of deficits involving movement, sensation, and language but without headache or coma, whereas intracerebral hemorrhage causes a sequence beginning with a progressively intensifying headache and ending in coma within 6 to 24 hours.

Several elements of pathophysiology may occur with a stroke. The patient's ability to think (cognition) may be impaired. Muscle strength and coordination, sensibility, or appreciation of skin sensation and position sense, and visual preception may all be compromised. Occasionally only some of these functions are limited. Generally the more severe the communication limitation, the more severe the consequence of stroke. Additional problems resulting from stroke include a patient's inability to verbalize (expressive aphasia). Lesions in cerebral areas 22 and 42 may result in a patient's inability to comprehend verbalizations (receptive aphasia). Cerebrovascular accidents, therefore, produce stroke in an accompanying montage of clinical deficits, the extensiveness of which are contingent on the size and location of the lesion and the completeness of the stroke.

Clinical Efficacy

The rehabilitation of the stroke patient should encompass a comprehensive team approach because so many physiological systems may be disrupted. Aside from medical and pharmacological therapy a barrage of problems must be addressed. A stroke patient typically is hypertensive and stressed, restricted in affect and motivation, limited in mobility and possibly speech or articulation, and in need of psychosocial and vocational guidance. Whereas extensive work has dealt with physical rehabilitation through exercise programs (Basmajian, 1978) and application of traditional modalities (Rusk, 1971), a more comprehensive approach to total management is evolving. This management concept involves recognition that the patient can play a vital role in contributing to changes in his physical and psychological behaviors. Perhaps it was this recognition that made the interface of EMG biofeedback modalities and the possibility of self-regulation of muscle activity an intriguing approach within rehabilitation.

Hence, a rash of research efforts using EMG biofeedback for this patient population has emerged with very promising results. Before unequivocal statements can be made, however, such efforts must be subjected to critical analysis and several key issues contributing to efficacy must be assessed. The time following a stroke should be controlled within explicit experimental parameters or the results may be unclear. Shahani, Connors, and Mohr (1977) provided specific data on the location of the cerebral lesion in an acute stroke population. Several other studies (Basmajian, Gowland, & Brandstater, 1982; Middaugh & Miller, 1980; Takebe & Basmajian, 1976) presented combined data on acute (less than 6 months following insult) and chronic (greater than one year following insult) clients. Biofeedback studies performed on patients with acute stroke are difficult to assess because one cannot isolate specificity of EMG effect from spontaneous recovery or ongoing central nervous system plasticity. Even if such studies could include a no-treatment acute stroke population, they would still be open to criticism because of the impossibility of controlling for the interaction between the location of the injury and the amount of spontaneous recovery. With this reality in mind, Basmajian et al., (1982) attempted to group acute stroke patients by stage of neuromuscular recovery. For the 37 acute stroke patients assessed in that study, a technique that combined biofeedback and behavioral interventions appeared more effective than conventional physical therapy. Using behavioral (relaxation) and feedback procedures was most effective in enhancing motoric function for patients who were either at an advanced neuromuscular stage of recovery, within 4 to 5 months after stroke, or who had shown less recovery within 3 months following cerebral insult.

Studies in which acute and chronic stroke patients are grouped together involve analytical problems because specific treatment effects must be differentiated from spontaneous recovery (Fish et al., 1976). To address this problem large numbers of both acute and chronic stroke patients need to be studied in group design experiments. Results of such studies could be examined by duration of injury and by treatment choice. To date experimental biofeedback studies on stroke clients have had insufficient sample sizes to allow such analyses.

Thus far EMG biofeedback studies among stroke patients have failed to reveal a relationship between outcome and age, sex, duration of previous rehabilitation, presence of expressive aphasia, or site of cerebral insult (Middaugh & Miller, 1980; Wolf, Baker, & Kelly, 1979). Findings, therefore, should be viewed with caution. Repeated and more extensive studies must result in similar conclusions before one can convincingly state that these variables do not influence treatment effect. As an example, left versus right cerebral injury and outcome must be examined more closely in biofeedback experiments simply because the type and location of stroke may profoundly influence factors such as spatial orientation, cognition, and awareness of limb activities.

Similarly, whereas the existence of receptive aphasia among stroke patients has been shown to minimize the effect of EMG biofeedback training (Shiavi, Champion, & Freeman, 1979; Wolf et al., 1979; Wolf, Baker, & Kelly, 1980), the amount of proprioceptive loss and its effect on treatment outcome still require additional systematic evaluation. Wolf et al., (1979) indicated that proprioceptive loss may negatively influence the efficacy of treatment to the hemiplegic upper extremity; their treatment procedure, however, always involved training the lower extremity prior to the upper extremity. Consequently the observations made by this group may have been influenced by an ordering effect with patients becoming more resistant to upper extremity treatment. In the few cases in which only the upper extremity was treated, proprioceptive loss did not influence outcome. Skelly and Kenedi (1982) provided data suggesting that the initial limitation of active shoulder range of motion rather than loss of sensation may influence the specificity of biofeedback training to shoulder musculature.

Many studies (Gianutsos, Eberstein, & Krasilowsky, 1979; Mroczek, Halpern, & McHugh, 1978; Prevo, Visser, & Vogelaar, 1982; Wolf et al., 1979, 1980) have provided extensive details on general training procedures. Most studies however have failed to provide precise information regarding how stroke patients have been trained in biofeedback. In addition, such factors as electrode type, electrode placement, feedback displays or devices, shaping procedures, and sequencing of muscle by treatment have not been provided.

The amount of time for treatment and the total number of sessions needed to effect appropriate neuromusculature changes with feedback are unclear. With respect to these issues at least two studies (Brudny et al., 1974; Middaugh et al., 1982), offered far more feedback sessions than would be clinically realistic. On the other hand, in one study (Lee, Hill & Johnston, 1976) experimental sessions were limited to one day and contraction efforts were as short as 20 seconds. Experimental protocols that fail to parallel clinical reality with respect to duration and total number of treatments may fail to convince clinicians of the importance or value of biofeedback applications to stroke patients. As a ground rule, the number of muscle biofeedback sessions, whether offered separately or integrated within a therapeutic exercise plan, should not exceed a reasonable number of therapy treatments that third-party payers would be willing to reimburse for inpatient and outpatient services. This number has varied considerably based on geographical considerations and unique or individualized aspects of health insurance. Among chronic stroke patients receiving outpatient biofeedback, clearly 45 to 60 minute sessions at two to three times per week appear to be the maximum realistic achievement or productive goal levels for clinician and patient.

Many biofeedback studies on stroke patients have reported improvement in range of motion or strength at the wrist, joint (Mroczek et at., 1978), shoulder (Hurd, Pegram, & Nepumuceno, 1980; Skelly & Kenedi, 1982) or ankle (Basmajian, Kukulka, & Narayan, 1975; Binder, Moll, & Wolf, 1981; Burnside, Tobias, & Bursill, 1982; Hurd et al., 1980; Santee, Keister, & Kleinman, 1980; Swann, vanWieringen, & Fokkema, 1974; Takebe & Basmajian, 1976; Teng, McNeal, & Kralj, 1976). Measurements of muscle strength and range of motion to assess improvement may be unreliable, especially if undertaken by the investigator (Fernando & Basmajian, 1978; Hume, 1981) and might best be done by tained evaluators blind to the purposes of such studies (see following). Quantification of integrated EMG during active or passive muscle movement may be amenable to statistical analyses but in and of itself provides limited information concerning function. The degree of statistical significance may not always be related to the magnitude of clinical improvement. Therefore muscle tests, quantification of EMG or range of motion, although appropriate for data acquisition, may have limited clinical significance. For example, might a significant increase in active ankle dorsiflexion range of motion after feedback training mean that the stroke patient ambulates more effectively? Or does an increase in active wrist extension imply a greater ability for the stroke patient to manipulate his environment? Few studies have addressed such questions, and hence we may have reached a shortcoming in extrapolating physiological measures to quantified functional changes.

Therefore, it seems inescapable that the process of acquiring information from feedback training must be intimately linked to outcome. Basmajian et al., (1975) developed a scale used by others in performing feedback research (Hurd et al., 1980). Although these scales have value, they fail to provide quantitative measures that can be easily interpreted objectively. Much the same can be implied for the scale developed by Brudny and his colleagues (Brundy et al., 1974; Brundy, Korein, & Grynbaum, 1976) to assess functional changes in the upper extremities of stroke patients following feedback training. More recently Basmajian et al. (1982) made use of an upper extremity functional scale listing activities in order of complexity on 10-point incremental scales.

Perhaps it would be more meaningful to measure functional activity by continuous rather than discreet values. Three such measures of practical significance are time, distance, and force and all have been utilized in recent studies (Wolf & Binder-Macleod, 1983a, b). By undertaking correlational analyses that relate biofeedback treatment to functional tasks measured by time, distance, or force, data having importance to researchers and clinicians can be generated using either parametric or nonparametric tests of significance. Such analyses have been applied to only a few studies on stroke patients receiving biofeedback to the lower (Binder et al., 1981) or upper (Basmajian et al., 1982; Prevo et al., 1982) extremities. Future studies should include practical yet important functional scores to convince clinicians and third-party payers of the efficacy of this modality. Only a few feedback studies applied to stroke patients have made use of evaluators who are not the investigators (Binder et al., 1981; Burnside et al., 1982; Wolf & Binder-Macleod, 1983a, b). Often this approach may be impractical in a clinical setting but it is preferable to maintain objectivity in the research designs.

Several studies (Brudny *et al.*, 1974; Brudny *et al.*, 1976; Burnside *et al.*, 1982; Wolf *et al.*, 1980) have provided meaningful follow-up on treatment outcomes. Data from such studies have all concluded that patients who do not sustain further medical complications will maintain the beneficial effects of feedback. Recently studies by Wolf and Binder-Macleod (1983a, b) among chronic stroke populations have delineated, in controlled test situations, those neuromuscular factors predictive of successful intervention in the treatment of the lower and upper extremities for such patients. Evaluations were undertaken blindly and those patients with the least flexion synergy and greatest isolated extension movements, particularly in the digits, gained the greatest upper extremity functional independence. Among patients receiving biofeedback to improve gait, virtually all patients developed enhanced lower extremity function when compared to control conditions. It is hoped that future studies will attempt to expand as well as reproduce these findings.

Specificity of Effect

To date few studies have addressed the issues of transfer of treatment effect. It has yet to be determined whether more activities can be accomplished after feedback training than after other forms of treatment in locations other than the clinical environment. For cost effectiveness and to strengthen training effects, home practice with biofeedback instrumentation may be valuable. Only one anecdotal report has included this procedure as a phase of treatment (Johnson & Garton, 1973). This approach, unfortunately, is difficult to incorporate in experimental protocols because control over frequency or accuracy of home training is virtually impossible.

Mechanisms

Few clinical research studies on feedback applications to stroke patients have addressed the issue of mode of action. Not knowing how feedback can successfully improve neuromuscular function among stroke patients should not imply a lack of clinical effectiveness. When one considers that the complex neurophysiology underlying simple motor tasks is unclear, it should not be surprising that explanations involving the integration of sensory and motor behaviors to effect functional changes among stroke patients using feedback have not been elucidated.

Brudny, Korein, & Grynbaum (1977) have proposed two mechanisms that might account for how neurological patients most appropriately use auditory and visual representations of muscle activity to improve motor control. These mechanisms are (a) over-riding (relevant information entering the central nervous system at a higher level than the locus of pathology); and (b) by-pass (using subcortical structures in a feed-forward mode). Wolf (1983) suggested that auditory and visual information representative of muscle activity could activate central synapses previously underused in executing motor commands. Such information would be continuously processed by the cerebellum and/or sensory and motor cortices and available to responsive motor cells unaffected by the cerebrovascular accident. Following continued training stroke clients could improve performance by establishing new sensory engrams while simultaneously eliminating one or both forms of feedback. Undoubtedly the ultimate discovery of how new functions may be unmasked will invoke mechanisms that may involve transfer of function to intact neural structures, use of alternative pathways, or sprouting of axonal collaterals to form new synapses.

Future Research

Although this critique of feedback applications in stroke patients is comprehensive, the evidence from controlled studies suggests tremendous potential in application of this modality to stroke patients. In reviewing more than 30 research articles on this subject one is impressed by the gains made in both acute and chronic stroke populations even in the absence of rigorous controls desired by purists and ardent researchers. Considerable work still lies ahead in the following areas: specifying treatment protocols; reproduction of outcomes from specific biofeedback training strategies; quantification of function; prolonged follow-up analyses; and use of more sophisticated methods, for example cranial computed tomography and digital intravenous subtraction angiography to identify more clearly neural substrates responsive to biofeedback intervention.

BIOFEEDBACK APPLICATIONS TO CEREBRAL PALSY PATIENTS

Introduction

Cerebral palsy (CP) is a term that denotes multiple forms of motor abnormalities resulting from brain damage during embryonic and neonatal development (Milner-Brown & Penn, 1979). Recent statistics (National Institutes of Health, 1976) reveal that approximately 750,000 American citizens are afflicted with this disorder and 15,000 babies are born each year with brain damage leading to cerebral palsy.

This disease can assume various patterns, each with unique pathological features. Towbin (1960) has delineated specific characteristics of CP. The clinical picture is one in which spasticity, athetosis (slow, involuntary movement of limb or limb segments), and even ataxia (a dissociation of coordinated muscle movements) may occur concurrently or independently. Most brain insults leading to the diagnosis of CP are confined and tend to be nonprogressive. As a result, the clinical manifestations of CP are usually static and unaltered. On occasion CP can be associated with other disease processes, most notably epilepsy and mental retardation.

Generally the pathogenesis of CP can be attributed to any one of three primary causes. First, brain lesions represent a sequence of systemic disorders in the fetus or newborn infant that can result from anoxia, premature birth, or erythroblastosis or systemic sepsis (Towbin, 1955). Local trauma to the brain resulting in mechanical injury to the head, circulatory disorders, or hydrocephalus represent a second pathogenic factor. Third, hereditary or induced developmental defects of the brain may retard growth and differentiation.

The CP child represents an individual with delayed motor development caused by involuntary movement patterns, inappropriate progression of postural mechanisms, and a general imbalance of voluntary control over limb musculature. The apparent weakness in some muscle groups may be due to abnormal postural reflexes that impede intentional movements. Invariably the dysfunction in posture can be related to a failure to develop appropriate reflex behavior or to progress appropriately from one postural reflex to a more advanced one (Bobath & Bobath, 1975). Postural disorders may be observed in spastic, athetoid or ataxic forms of CP.

Typically treatment is provided in physical therapy sessions designed to induce normal reflex behavior and appropriate changes in muscle tone. The intent is to reduce hyperactive stretch reflexes and allow the patient to gain coordinated limb movements and head control. Included within therapeutic approaches are appropriate positioning and postural procedures, significant handling of the infant, and many exteroceptive stimuli, including vibration, thermal inputs, and stretch of tightened musculature. A major limitation to conventional physiotherapeutic approaches occurs when profound mental retardation accompanies sensorimotor imbalance.

Clinical Efficacy

A limited number of studies on feedback intervention to improve motor dysfunction in CP patients has been published. Usually most applications involve the presentation of additional reinforcers significant to the CP individual. Limited numbers of controls have been provided and most studies lack sufficient follow-up data.

The best controlled study was presented by Cataldo, Bird, and Cunningham (1978), who studied three choreo-athetotic CP individuals and employed between- and within-session controls, including reversals of baseline. These patients attempted exact muscle changes with and without feedback. The data showed that feedback enhanced muscle control and that generalization of feedback effects to times when there was no feedback and to untrained muscles prevailed. Unfortunately hospital staff were not able to observe noticeable changes in adaptive functioning outside of the feedback sessions among two of the clients. The third, an older patient, was able to produce generalized relaxation and more enhanced voluntary movements. An important consideration for assessing the effectiveness of the feedback interventions for a CP individual, as is the case with stroke injured patients, is the identification of dependent variables that have concomitant functional correlates.

Force feedback was provided by Seeger and Caudrey (1981) in the form of load sensitive sole inserts into the shoes of four CP children. Two of the four children showed improvement in symmetry of limb loading during the gait cycle. Two-year follow-up (Seeger & Caudrey, 1983) indicated that the therapy gains had been lost. This loss of improvement over time suggests that informational content should be gradually withdrawn and other reinforcers introduced.

EMG feedback to enhance wrist extension in a CP woman was successful (Asato, Twiggs, & Ellison, 1981). Music was provided to facilitate appropriate motor responses when EMG activity exceeded a prescribed level. One-year follow-up on this patient indicated that wrist extensor movements had been maintained.

Neilson and McCaughey (1983) studied four young athetoid patients to determine whether stretch reflex sensitivity from the biceps brachii muscle could be reduced and whether controlled shortening contractions about the elbow could be produced in the presence of EMG feedback. A visual tracking task requiring voluntary motion about the elbow was employed to assess improvement in functional control of elbow movement. Following a 3-month baseline recording period patients were seen for three one-hour sessions per week over an 18-month period. With training each patient's favorite music could be heard when the appropriate goal was achieved. All four patients learned to suppress involuntary muscle activity during tonic stretch reflex responses. Consequently it can be said that patients learned to regulate spasticity of the elbow and tonic stretch reflex sensitivity. On the other hand only one of the patients improved in the accuracy of elbow movements.

Skrotzky, Gallenstein, & Osternig, (1978) used EMG feedback exclusively to help four CP patients with spastic diplegia improve ankle range of motion and motor function. Patients were given two treatments per day for 10 consecutive days. Substantial increases in active range of motion about the ankle were obtained from all four patients. This acquisition of movement was maintained by two patients for a posttreatment interval of 4 to 9 weeks.

The problem of head control is quite common among cerebral palsied patients. Two studies have dealt with this issue using head position feedback, rather than EMG feedback, to control the orientation of the head in space. Walmsley, Crichton, & Droog (1981) presented pilot data obtained from five CP children. The head control device consisted of a series of mercury switches that, when maintained in circuitry, activated an electric buzzer. Taped music and verbal encouragement were used as feedback for correct performance. Each child received 24 treatments with a maximum of 2-day intervals between successive sessions. The criterion for improvement was maintenance of head position within a training angle of 35°. Three children improved in head control, one showed no change, and the performance in one child worsened. Leiper, Miller, Lang, & Herman (1981) employed a head position feedback device to assist five quadriparetic CP children to improve head control in sitting positions and during movement. First, each child wore the head position monitor in the classroom for three sessions of 30 minutes duration without feedback. Feedback training was gradually introduced and given daily for 9 weeks. All children improved in their capability to stabilize the head and neck during feedback intervention. Three of the children were able to self-monitor for up to one hour while maintaining the head within the required zone at least 80% of the time. No longterm follow-up data were provided.

Specificity of Effect

It would appear that electromyographic or position feedback is a viable interface for improving movement or head control among CP patients. Clearly more well-defined and controlled studies are required. The apparent discrepancy of long-term success must be more clearly related to the magnitude of pathology among CP clients. Results will continue to appear mixed until intervention is more closely related to precise classification of pathophysiology among CP patients. In addition, studies that compare feedback intervention to other therapeutic approaches are nonexistent and will be required if the efficacy of biofeedback as a treatment modality for this patient group is to be realized.

Biofeedback Applications to Spinal Cord Injured Patients

Introduction

The incidence of traumatic spinal cord injury (SCI) in the United States is 30 to 35 persons per million, or 7 to 8 thousand per year (Young & Northup, 1979). At present the best estimate of traumatic SCI individuals is about 150,000. Seventy percent of SCI events appear related to trauma and 30% to disease. The total SCI population, in America, approximates 200,000. Eighty-two percent of SCI patients are men, with the distribution somewhat balanced among occurrences of quadriplegia (53%) and paraplegia (47%). SCI occurs most commonly during one's productive years at a median age of 23.

Auto accidents account for approximately 36.5% of SCI occurrences. Other etiological factors include fall (15.8%); gunshot wound (11.6%); diving accidents (10.6%); and motorcycle accidents (6.2%). Collectively these data depict a situation with profound physical and psychological consequences. Given the age of the SCI population and the psychophysiological impairments resulting from spinal cord trauma, the need for comprehensive medical and psychosocial intervention is imperative.

Approximately 20% of patients who sustain injury to the vertebral column will also be subjected to neural involvements of varying magnitude. Among cervical vertebral injuries the flexor injury is the most common. These injuries occur from blows to the back of the head. A severe force can tear all the ligaments that provide added support to the vertebral column. The extensor injury is caused by forces directed to the face. These forces cause the back of the head to move abruptly toward the vertebral column thus stretching the ligament providing stability to the anterior aspects of the vertebral column. Widening of the intervertebral space between cervical vertebrae may cause spinal cord damage without fracture dislocation. Fracture dislocations at the lowest thoracic level and upper lumbar level may impinge on the spinal cord if the posterior vertebral elements and body undergo extensive destruction.

The segmental nature of the spinal cord blood supply does not permit adequate collateral circulation. As a result even a presumably localized contusion may have profound effects on the extensiveness of blood loss and subsequent functional impairment. In the acute phase the contused spinal cord will appear quite swollen and hemorrhagic. If significant blood loss has occurred, neural tissue will become demyelinated, vacuolized, and degenerative. If the cord is cut as a consequence of foreign body invasion or fractured dislocation, the entire cord is rarely transected in total; some element of continuity persists. The cord may become cavitated and connective tissue will replace myelin debris. Whether this or any other type of lesion causes total or partial spinal cord injury is debatable on both anatomical and clinical grounds.

Additionally, it is generally acknowledged that SCI will compromise activities within the autonomic nervous system. The loss of nerve fibers that subserve visceral functions produce marked effects on the vaso-motor system, leading to profuse sweating. This visible autonomic behavior may accompany bowel activity, retention of urine, or bladder wall contractions.

Ultimately, potential SCI patient abilities are dependent on the degree to which voluntary control returns to extremity musculature. During the first half year following SCI, somatic reflexes and muscle activity often return to those limbs supplied by peripheral nerves below the level of the lesion. The reflex magnitude of muscle activity is often grossly exaggerated because activity cannot be modulated properly. This occurrence is due to the fact that the cord lesion has disrupted fibers that descend from the brain stem and cerebrum to inhibit activity in those neurons in which transmission of nerve impulses are still preserved. The resulting disproportionate activity is referred to as spasticity. The presence of spasticity must be clearly differentiated from frequently occurring muscle spasms that are often set off by external stimuli causing reflex patternings of muscle group contractions (Stauffer, 1977). Changes in body position inducing proprioceptive or tactile stimuli, and unconscious maneuvers are classical methods of inducing muscle spasms in SCI individuals.

Extensor spasticity usually begins about 6 months after SCI and increases during the first year. Such spasticity often is of therapeutic benefit because it helps to maintain muscle bulk; joint range of motion; and varying degrees of mobility. Flexor spasticity appears to be more prevalent during the first 3 to 6 months following SCI and if not addressed through proper continuous patient repositioning can lead to hip, knee, and truck flexor contractures. Often persistent spasticity that interferes with a patients function, rehabilitation, and independent living can be treated surgically if all other pharmacological and medical measures have failed. These techniques may include selective paralysis of muscles with nerve blocks by anesthetic agents, phenol, or thermal-lysing agents; tendon lengthening; peripheral surgical nerve lesions; or rhizotomies of appropriate ventral or dorsal spinal roots.

More than any other neurol disorder SCI can lead to complications that compound all existing physical and psychological hardship. These complications include (a) development of bedsores and skin ulceration due to insensibility and prolonged pressure to circumscribed areas; (b) amputation of limbs due to infection and osteomyelitis secondary to pressure sore; (c) osteoporosis due to inactivity and non-weight bearing; (d) thrombophlebitis; (e) urinary infection; (f) ossification at joints; (g) pathological fractures; and (h) surgery to alleviate spasticity.

Traditional rehabilitation provides the SCI patient with a variety of treatment possibilities most of which are offered as part of a comprehensive rehabilitation program. These treatments include progressive exercises (with group mat exercise programs); wheel chair transfer training; vibration; ball gymnastics; hydro gynmastics; moist heat; massage; passive and active range of motion; revision of the home environment to facilitate the activities of daily living; gait training; and orthotics.

Clinical Efficacy

Recently biofeedback has been incorporated into some rehabilitation programs for the SCI patient. Among such interventions are blood pressure feedback when first training patients to assume an upright posture. This chapter deals primarily with muscle biofeedback designed to enable the patient to alter muscle responses by either strengthening weak muscles or reducing spasticity or stretched induced hyeractive responses in other muscles.

Within the past 6 years only a few reports of EMG feedback applications to spinal cord injured patients have been published. Wolf *et al.*, (1982) provided a comprehensive feedback training paradigm to five paraplegic patients. Computer generated electromyographic measures were made at baseline and following 15-treatment-session intervals through 60 sessions. All patients had been wheelchair bound with varying degrees of spinal cord impairment. When feedback was provided to the exclusion of all other therapeutic interventions, the outcomes indicated that the magnitude of EMG and functional change were quite variable. All five patients learned to either inhibit or suppress spontaneous clonic episodes, events that were perceived as exceptionally functional by the patients. There were no changes in sensory status as a result of feedback training. It was concluded that EMG biofeedback could be helpful to chronic spinal cord injured paraplegic patients who have partial cord injury with muscle sparing. It was suggested that feedback be integrated within a comprehensive therapeutic exercise regimen.

Nacht, Wolf, and Coogler (1982) provided data in a case history format when feedback was applied during the acute phase of spinal cord injury. The treatment goal for this paraplegic patient was to strengthen and facilitate muscle groups below the level of the injury. EMG feedback training was first given to hip musculature three times a week with a total of eight sessions over a 2-week period, during which time the patient was immobile. Feedback training led to appreciable increases in muscle activity. Functional changes during this period of immobilization could not be demonstrated. The benefit of this novel approach was primarily to provide the clinician with information about the return and activation of muscle while simultaneously permitting the patient to pursue a therapeutic program with feedback when other activities could not be undertaken.

Finley (1983) used contemporary electrophysiological recording techniques to operantly condition the short latency cervical somatosensory evoked potential among five quadriplegic patients. Patients were conditioned to increase the N14 potential. The increase in amplitude of this potential was usually associated with an increase in the N19 and P22 amplitudes. The functional implications of this form of conditioning for inherent signals generated within the neuraxis have yet to be determined. The unique aspect of this work, however, resides in the demonstration that somatosensory potential responses among spinal cord injured patients can be shaped. It is hoped that this technique may lead to either enhanced function or reduction in pain often associated with spinal cord injury.

Specificity of Effect

Considerable work using control paradigms is required before EMG feedback can be considered a viable tool in the treatment of SCI individuals. Appropriate experimental designs encompassing reasonably large numbers of SCI patients have yet to be devised. Anecdotal reports not contained herein would suggest that, at the very least, feedback may be used as an adjunct to provide knowledge of information about muscle activity to both therapist and patient, thereby facilitating appropriate motor responses within therapeutic exercise regimens.

BIOFEEDBACK APPLICATIONS TO PATIENTS WITH SPASMODIC TORTICOLLIS

Introduction

Spasmodic torticollis (wry neck) is the most common type of torsion dystonia. It is characterized by hyperactivity in the upper trapezius and contralateral sternomastoid muscles. This hyperactivity produces a sustained deviation of the head to one side. This head posture is often characterized by periodic turning presumably due to increased muscle spasms that alternate with relative quiescence of muscle activity. Often spasm can be briefly overcome by voluntary effort or by cutaneous contact with various aspects of facial skin. Over time patients lose awareness of the precise position of the head in space.

A simulation of torticollis-like activity can be obtained in animal models with lesions primarily located in the pontine and mesencephalic tegmentum (Foltz, 1959). Although abnormal responses to vestibular stimuli have been suggested as a cause of spasmodic torticollis, no specific pathological lesions have been found in man.

The exact incidence and etiology of this problem are unclear. Most cases appear to be sporadic and often associated in onset with psychological trauma. Occasionally, among individuals developing spasmodic torticollis, family members will exhibit scoliosis or torsion spasm, thereby suggesting a possible genetic factor in the etiology (Gilbert, 1977). Often trauma to the head or neck may precede occurrence of this condition (Sheehy & Marsden, 1980). The condition is often exacerbated during periods of emotional stress.

Treatment may consist of pharmocological or surgical intervention. Diazepam and related drugs or Lioresal are often prescribed. Major tranquilizers are often ineffective and may exacerbate spasms. Surgical disruption of the sternomastoid muscle may provide benefit for limited periods of time. Often the upper three cervical motor roots and the spinal accessory nerve may be severed to alleviate the distortion (Scoville & Bettis, 1979). Physical therapeutic interventions that emphasize range of motion may be helpful, provided such treatment also centers about patient recognition of stressors that exacerbate abnormal head posture.

Clinical Efficacy

Initial reports by Brudny et al., (1974) and Korein et al., (1976) were positive when EMG biofeedback was introduced to train patients to reduce hyperactive sternomastoid or trapezius muscle activity. These reports provided follow-up data that indicated improvement among 32 of 55 patients. At follow-up many of these patients had retained their ability to control head position in space. Cleeland (1973) reported on EMG biofeedback treatment among 52 patients who were followed for a mean time of 30 months. Of these patients 11 showed minimal or no improvement, 18 showed moderate improvement, and eight were described as markedly improved. Fifteen patients were lost at follow-up. These studies lacked adequate controls and did not provide quantitative measures of improvement. The variability in rate of improvement among patients in these studies may be attributed to differing unique problems involved in the specificity of diagnosis.

Gildenburg (1981) obtained satisfactory results in 21 of 29 patients with spasmodic torticollis. Seventeen patients with significant psychiatric impairment were excluded from treatment. Improvement was obtained through relaxation training, transcutaneous electrical nerve stimulation, dorsal column stimulation, or cervical and spinal accessory nerve root sections. Only four patients of the original 46 were given biofeedback therapy. Gildenburg concluded that there is no specific satisfactory treatment for all patients with spasmodic torticollis.

Specificity of Effect

Clearly more definitive diagnoses and assessment of neurological and psychological problems are required before a decision is made on the appropriateness of patient selection for feedback intervention. Furthermore, based on a report by Martin (1982), one can conclude that EMG biofeedback training among spasmodic torticollis may appear moderately effective. Martin does acknowledge, however, that further research is required to determine whether there is a specificity of effect.

Thus, although feedback training designed to reduce hyperactivity in spasmodic neck musculature appears promising, control studies with quantified physiological and physical data are required. To date there is no evidence that clearly suggests improvement is attributable solely to a biofeedback intervention. Furthermore more discrete data are required to help characterize spasmodic torticollis patients into subgroups that can be successfully interfaced with biofeedback in a predictable manner.

BIOFEEDBACK APPLICATIONS TO PATIENTS WITH MUSCULOSKELETAL DISORDERS

Introduction

Many musculoskeletal disorders are characterized by muscle weakness and movement limitations. Such symptoms may result from prolonged immobilization (for example, following casting) or after orthopedic interventions to restore joint integrity, reduce fractures, or repair, transplant, or transfer muscle. Unlike neuromuscular conditions involving the central nervous system, the situation with musculoskeletal pathology involves primarily restoration of strength and mobility without concern for significant proprioceptive or cutaneous loss, or for the patient's ability to integrate adequately sensory stimuli with motor behavior. It is perhaps for this reason that few reports have been provided concerning the efficacy of EMG biofeedback in the treatment of musculoskeletal pathology.

Clinical Effects

Placement of electrodes on weak muscles for the purpose of amplifying and presenting visual and auditory representations of activity provides immediate knowledge of effort to clinician and patient. Keying on these signals enables the patient to recruit motor units from the underlying muscle(s) at a greater rate and in greater numbers. An example of this possible effect from EMG feedback applications is demonstrable in the work of Lucca and Recchiuti (1983) who showed that a group of women performing isometric exercises with biofeedback produced greater gains in peak torque than isometric exercise alone or without exercise control. The findings from LeVeau and Rogers (1980) presented earlier to demonstrate differential training between quadriceps muscle components has clear implications for therapeutic interventions among patients with patello-femoral joint problems. By training vastus medialis to contract independently from vastus lateralis, alignment of the patella during knee extension and flexion movements might be more controlled. Malalignment of the patella occurs with a hypermobile kneecap and in patients with chondromalacia and certain types of arthritis. If differential training of the quadriceps muscles can be demonstrated in these patient populations one will be able to ascertain whether EMG feedback used in this manner can prevent or minimize abnormal patella movements.

Specificity of Effect

Undoubtedly in the future additional applications of EMG feedback to enhance performance for athletes or to improve body mechanics secondary to orthopedic problems will be forthcoming. To date only the few controlled studies mentioned earlier (plus numerous anecdotal reports) attest to the benefits of feedback intervention for patients with musculoskeletal disorders.

FUTURE RESEARCH

Based on the contents of this chapter, several recommendations for future clinical research can be made. These recommendations include:

1. Additional research in both animal and human models to discover mechanisms of motor control. In the context of clinical research, vehicles such as somatosensory evoked potentials, positron emission tomography, and cerebral blood flow studies should be employed to uncover data with implications for further understanding modes of action.

2. Multi-institutional studies should be undertaken to provide larger populations for controlled data acquisition.

3. Patients should be categorzed under specific clinical entities rather than by symptomatology alone.

4. Research studies should separate treatment effects from other reinforcement variables that can account for improvement.

5. Additional research within patient populations that delineate results from feedback versus no-feedback (control) paradigms should be examined.

6. Caution should be exercised in identifying changes in physiolog ical data and relating these to changes to function. Both types of variables, however, should be quantified.

7. Clear delineation of professional training and capabilities for application of EMG feedback to rehabilitation patients should be undertaken.

CONCLUSIONS

The publications cited in this task force report and chapter suggest that biofeedback applications have growing utility in the treatment of neuromuscular and musculoskeletal disorders. Most studies have addressed the application of EMG feedback to stroke patients. Of the 35 reports 16 have reported control groups. Nine of these 16 control group studies have been reported since 1980. Delineation of patient characteristics among chronic stroke clients amenable to successful feedback intervention is now available. Additional studies that incorporate new interinstitutional data and are designed to test for specificity of training and generalization of results outside of the clinical environment appear warranted.

The literature discussing EMG feedback applications to other patient categories is somewhat limited. Imaginative planning with collaboration among physiatrists, neurologists, psychologists, physical therapists, and other biofeedback professionals should be blended to reflect the specific interests of members within these disciplines. Considerable data obtained under controlled conditions are required to delineate more clearly the efficacy of feedback applications among patients with a variety of neuromuscular and musculoskeletal disorders. It is suggested that a primary reason for the apparent paucity of biofeedback literature on applications to patients with musculoskeletal pathology arises from a lack of appreciation for the apparent benefits that immediate knowledge of results of muscle activity may have in facilitating the therapeutic process. Undoubtedly clinicians have sensed these apparent benefits without recognizing the need to document them adequately.

A difficulty confronting biofeedback practitioners applying this modality to rehabilitation populations is clarifying the relationship between research approaches and clinical utility of findings. Undoubtedly, in the clinical environment, there are factors that cannot be controlled collectively with respect to the most important variables and at the same time remain cost-effective in approach. Even if such variables as clinician-patient interactions could be indisputably defined, their relative importance may be altered when considered across different diagnoses, or even within a specific patient population. For example, such factors as family support, the psychosocial milieu in which the patient resides, and the environment in which biofeedback training is undertaken will vary considerably for all patients, irrespective of feedback training or the diagnostic entity being studied. Attempts to control for these virtually intangible effects would require multitudes of patients. Such numbers are virtually impossible to treat in a data retrieval system that would also be cost-effective.

Hence, the research community must recognize that clinical efficacy may be based on more than controlled variables structured within research designs. This statement is particularly true in rehabilitation applications of EMG feedback because of the excessive intimacy of the clinician-patient interaction. In very few phases of medical management is the personal contact and direct, ongoing communication between clinician and patient more critical than in the physical therapeutic realm.

ACKNOWLEDGMENTS

The authors wish to thank Drs. Alan Mandel and Susan Middaugh for the materials they provided to us. We also acknowledge the diligent typing efforts of Gloria Bassett.

REFERENCES

Asato, S., Twiggs, D. G., & Ellison, S. (1981). EMG biofeedback training for a mentally retarded individual with cerebral palsy. *Physical Therapy*, *61*, 1447–1452.

Basmajian, J. V. (1978). Conscious control and training of motor units and motor neurons. *Muscles alive: Their functions revealed by electromyography* (2nd ed., pp. 114–130). Baltimore, MD: Williams & Wilkins.

Basmajian, J. V. (Ed.). (1978). *Therapeutic exercise* (3rd ed.). Baltimore, MD: Williams & Wilkins.

Basmajian, J. V., Kukulka, C. G., & Narayan, M. G. (1975). Biofeedback treatment of foot-drop after stroke compared with standard rehabilitation technique: Effects on voluntary control and strength. *Archives Physical Medicine and Rehabilitation*, *56*, 231–236.

Basmajian, J. V., Gowland, C., & Brandstater, M. E. (1982). EMG feedback treatment of upper limb in hemiplegic stroke patients: A pilot study. *Archives of Physical Medicine and Rehabilitation, 63,* 613–616.

Baum, H. M., & Robins, M. (1981). Survival and prevalence. *Stroke, 12,* 59–68.

Binder, S. A., Moll, C. B., & Wolf, S. L. (1981). Evaluation of electromyographic biofeedback as an adjunct to therapeutic exercise in treating the lower extremities of hemiplegic patients. *Physical Therapy, 61,* 886–893.

Bobath, B., & Bobath, K. (1975). *Motor development in the different types of cerebral palsy.* London: Heinemann.

Brudny, J., Korein, J., Levidow, L., Grynbaum, B., Lieberman A., & Friedmann, K. (1974). Sensory feedback therapy as a modality of treatment in central nervous system disorders of voluntary movement. *Neurology, 24,* 925–932.

Brudny, J., Korein, J., & Grynbaum, B. B. (1976). EMG feedback therapy: Review of 114 patients. *Archives of Physical Medicine and Rehabilitation, 57,* 55–61.

Brudny, J., Korein, J., Grynbaum, B. B. (1977). Sensory feedback therapy in patients with brain insult. *Scandinavian Journal of Rehabilitation Medicine, 9,* 155–163.

Burnside, I. G., Tobias, S., & Bursill, D. (1982). Electromyographic feedback in the remobilization of stroke patients: A controlled trial. *Archives of Physical Medicine and Rehabilitation, 63,* 217–222.

Cataldo, M. F., Bird, B., & Cunningham, C. (1978). Experimental analysis of EMG feedback in treating cerebral palsy. *Journal of Behavioral Medicine, 1,* 311–322.

Cleeland, C. S. (1973). Behavioral techniques in the modification of spasmodic torticollis. *Neurology, 23,* 1241–1247.

Fernando, C. K., & Basmajian, J. V. (1978). Biofeedback in physical medicine and rehabilitation. *Biofeedback and Self-Regulation, 3,* 435–455.

Finley, W. W. (1983). Operant conditioning of the short-latency cervical somatosensory evoked potential in quadriplegics. *Experimental Neurology, 81,* 542–588.

Fish, D., Mayer, N., Herman, R. (1976). Letter to the editor: Biofeedback. *Archives of Physical Medicine and Rehabilitation, 57,* 152.

Foltz, E. L. (1959). Experimental spasmodic torticollis. *Journal of Neurosurgery, 16,* 55–59.

Gianutsos, J., Eberstein, A., & Krasilowsky, G. (1979). EMG feedback in the rehabilitation of upper extremity function: Single case studies of chronic hemiplegics. *International Neuropsychological Society Bulletin, Symposium Issue,* 1–12.

Gilbert, G. J. (1977). Familial spasmodic torticollis. *Neurology, 27,* 11–13.

Gildenberg, P. L., (1981). Comprehensive management of spasmodic torticollis. Seminar of Spinal Cord Stimulation, New York 1980. *Applied Neurophysiology, 44,* 233–243.

Hume W. I. (1981). *Biofeedback* (Vol. 3, pp. 9–16). New York: Human Sciences Press. 1981, 9–16.

Hurd, W. W., Pegram, V., & Nepumuceno, C. (1980). Comparison of actual and simulated MG biofeedback in the treatment of hemiplegic patients. *American Journal of Physical Medicine, 59,* 73–82.

Johnson, H. E., & Garton, W. H. (1973). Muscle re-education in hemiplegia by use of electromyographic device. *Archives of Physical Medicine and Rehabilitation, 54,* 320–323.

Korein, J., Brudny, J., Grynbaum, B., Sachs-Frankel, G., Weisinger, M., & Levidow, L. (1976). Sensory feedback therapy of spasmodic torticollis and dystonia: Results in treatment of 55 patients. In R. Eldridge & S. Fahn (Eds.), *Advances in Neurology* (Vol. 40). New York: Raven Press.

Lee, K.- H., Hill, E., & Johnston, R. (1976). Myofeedback for muscle retraining in hemiplegic patients. *Archives of Physical Medicine and Rehabilitation, 57,* 588–591.

Leiper, C. I., Miller, A., Lang, J., & Herman, R. (1981). Sensory feedback for head control in cerebral palsy. *Physical Therapy, 61,* 512–518.

LeVeau, B. F., & Rogers, C. (1980). Selective training of the vastus medialis muscle using EMG biofeedback. *Archives of Physical Medicine and Rehabilitation, 60,* 1410–1415.

Levy, L. L. (1975). Examination and diagnosis. In S. Licht (Ed.), *Stroke and its rehabilitation* (pp. 78–105). Baltimore, MD: Waverly Press.

Lucca, J. A., & Recchiuti, S. J. (1983). Effect of electromyographic biofeedback on an isometric strengthening program. *Physical Therapy, 63,* 200–203.

Martin, P. R. (1982) Spasmodic torticollis: A behavioral perspective. *Journal of Behavioral Medicine, 5,* 249–273.

McCormick, W. F. (1975). The pathology of strokes. In S. Licht (Ed.), *Stroke and its rehabilitation* (pp. 46–77). Baltimore: Waverly Press.

Middaugh, S. J. (1978). EMG feedback as a muscle re-education technique: A controlled study. *Physical Therapy, 58,* 15–22.

Middaugh, S. J., & Miller, M. C. (1980). Electromyographic feedback: Effect on voluntary muscle contractions in paretic patients. *Archives of Physical Medicine and Rehabilitation, 61,* 24–29.

Middaugh, S. J., Miller, M. C., Foster, G. & Ferdon, M. B. (1982). Electromyographic feedback: Effects on voluntary muscle contractions in normal subjects. *Archives of Physical Medicine and Rehabilitation, 63,* 154–160.

Milner-Brown, H. S., & Penn, R. D. (1979). Pathophysiological mechanisms in cerebral palsy. *Journal of Neurology, Neurosurgery, and Psychiatry, 42,* 606–618.

Mroczek, N., Halpern, D., & McHugh, R. (1978). Electromyographic feedback and physical therapy for neuromuscular retraining in hemiplegia. *Archives of Physical Medicine and Rehabilitation, 59,* 258–267.

Nacht, M. B., Wolf, S. L., & Coogler, C. E. (1982). Use of electromyographic biofeedback during the acute phase of spinal cord injury. *Physical Therapy, 62,* 290–294.

National Institutes of Health. (1976). *Neurological and communicative disorders: Estimated numbers and cost* (DREW Publication No. (NIH)77-152. Bethesda, MD.

Neilson, P. D., & McCaughey, J. (1982). Self-regulation of spasm and spasticity in cerebral palsy. *Journal of Neurology, Neurosurgery, and Psychiatry, 45,* 320–330.

Prevo, A. J. H., Visser, S. L., & Vogelaar, T. W. (1982). Effect of EMG feedback on paretic muscles and abnormal co-contraction in the hemiplegic arm, compared with conventional physical therapy. *Scandinavian Journal of Rehabilitation Medicine, 14,* 121–131.

Robins, M., & Baum, H. M. (1981). Incidence. In F. D. Weinfeld (Ed.), *Stroke* (pp. 45–55).

Romanul, R. (1976). Some anatomical and pathophysiological aspects of clinical importance in stroke. In F. J. Gillingham, C. Mawdsley, & A. E. Williams (Eds.), *Stroke* (pp. 167–177). London: Churchill-Livingstone.

Rusk, H. A. (1971). *Rehabilitation medicine* (3rd ed.). St. Louis, MO: C. V. Mosby.

Santee, J. L., Keister, M. E., & Kleinman, K. M. (1980). Incentives to enhance the effects of electromyographic feedback training in stroke patients. *Biofeedback and Self-Regulation, 5,* 51–56.

Scoville, W. B., & Bettis, D. B. (1979). Motorics of the head and neck: Surgical approaches and their complications. *Acta Neurochirurgica (Wien), 48,* 47–66.

Seeger, B. R., & Caudrey, D. J. (1983). Biofeedback therapy to achieve symmetrical gait in children with hemiplegic cerebral palsy: Long-term efficacy. *Archives of Physical Medicine and Rehabilitation, 64,* 160–162.

Seeger, B. R., Caudrey, D. J., & Scholes, J. R. (1981). Biofeedback therapy to achieve symmetrical gait in hemiplegic cerebral palsied children. *Archives of Physical Medicine and Rehabilitation, 62,* 364–368.

Sheehy, M. P., & Marsden, C. D. (1980). Trauma and pain in spasmodic torticollis. *Lancet, 1,* 777–778.

Shahani, B. T., Connors, L., & Mohr, J. P. (1977). Electromyographic audiovisual feedback training effect on the motor performance in patients with lesions of the central nervous system. *Archives of Physical Medicine and Rehabilitation, 58,* 519.

Shiavi, R. G., Champion, S. A., & Freeman, F. R. (1979). Efficacy of myofeedback therapy in regaining control of lower extremity musculature following stroke. *American Journal of Physical Medicine, 58,* 185–194.

Skelly, A. M., & Kenedi, R. M. (1982). EMG biofeedback therapy in the re-education of the hemiplegic shoulder in patients with sensory loss. *Physiotherapy, 68,* 34–38.

Skrotzky, K., Gallenstein, J. B., & Osternig, L. R. (1978). Effects of electromyographic feedback training on motor control in spastic cerebral palsy. *Physical Therapy, 58,* 547–551.

Stauffer, E. S. (1977). Long-term management of traumatic quadriplegia. In D. S. Pierce & V. H. Nickel (Eds.), *The total care of spinal cord injuries* (pp. 81–102). Boston, MA: Little, Brown.

Swann, D., vanWieringen, P. C. W., & Fokkema, S. D. (1974). Auditory electromyographic feedback therapy to inhibit undesired motor activity. *Archives of Physical Medicine and Rehabilitation, 55,* 251–254.

Takebe, K. & Basmajian, J. V. (1976). Gait analysis in stroke patients to assess treatments of foot-drop. *Archives of Physical Medicine and Rehabilitation, 57,* 305–310.

Teng, E. L., McNeal D. R., & Kralj, A. (1976). Electrical stimulation and feedback training: Effect on the voluntary control of paretic muscles. *Archives of Physical Medicine and Rehabilitation, 57,* 228–233.

Towbin, A. (1955). Pathology of cerebral palsy. I. Developmental defects of the brain as a cause of cerebral palsy. *AMA Archives of Pathology, 59,* 397–411.

Towbin, A. (1960). *The pathology of cerebral palsy.* Springfield, IL: Charles C Thomas.

Walmsley, R. P., Crichton, L., & Droog, D. (1981). Music as a feedback mechanism for teaching head control to severely handicapped children: A pilot study. *Developmental Medicine and Child Neurology, 23,* 739–746.

Wolf, S. L. (1982). *Biofeedback rehabilitation of the incomplete spinal cord injured patient*Regional Rehabilitation Research and Training Center Grant No. G008003042). Washington, DC: National Institute of Handicapped Research

Wolf, S. L. (1983). Electromyographic biofeedback applications to stroke patients: A critical review. *Physical Therapy, 63,* 1448–1445

Wolf, S. L., & Binder-Macleod, S. A. (1983a). Electromyographic biofeedback applications to the hemiplegic patient: Changes in upper extremity neuromuscular and functional status. *Physical Therapy, 63,* 1393–1403.

Wolf, S. L., & Binder-Macleod, S. A. (1983b). Electromyographic biofeedback applications to the hemiplegic patient: Changes in lower extremity neuromuscular and functional status. *Physical Therapy, 63,* 1404–1413.

Wolf, S. L., Baker, M. P., & Kelly, J. L. (1979). EMG biofeedback in stroke: Effect of patient characteristics. *Archives of Physical Medicine and Rehabilitation, 60,* 96–102.

Wolf, S. L., Baker, M. P., & Kelly, J. L. (1980). EMG biofeedback in stroke: A 1-year follow up on the effect of patient characteristics. *Archives of Physical Medicine and Rehabilitation, 61,* 351–355.

Young, J. S. & Northup, N. E. (1979). Statistical information pertaining to some of the most commonly asked questions about SCI. *Model Systems' SCI Digest, 1,* 11–33.

5

Biofeedback in the Treatment of Gastrointestinal Disorders

WILLIAM E. WHITEHEAD AND MARVIN M. SCHUSTER

The following is an update of the 1978 report of the task force on biofeedback for gastrointestinal disorders. It details new applications of biofeedback in the areas of fecal incontinence, irritable bowel syndrome, rumination syndrome, and esophageal motility disorders; and it reports new data on the efficacy of previously published biofeedback applications for digestive disorders.

Unlike other chapters in this volume, this chapter will consider several different disorders sequentially and independently. We will begin at the caudal end of the gastrointestinal tract because fecal incontinence is the gastrointestinal disorder for which the efficacy of biofeedback has been most clearly established.

FECAL INCONTINENCE

Introduction

Fecal incontinence refers to the passage of any fecal matter in socially inappropriate places one or more times per month after the age of 5 years (Medical Research Council, MRC, 1978). The prevalence of fecal

Preparations of this report was supported in part by Research Career Development Award MH00133 form the National Institute for Mental Health.

WILLIAM E. WHITEHEAD AND MARVIN M. SCHUSTER • The Johns Hopkins University School of Medicine and Division of Digestive Diseases, Francis Scott Key Medical Center, Baltimore, MD 21224.

incontinence is inadequately documented, but is estimated at 0.1% (Brocklehurst, 1972) to 1.5% (Milne, 1979; Thomas, Plymat, Blannin, & Meade, 1980) of the population. Fecal incontinence is most prevalent at the two ends of the life span: an estimated 1.5% of children aged 7 to 8 years are fecally incontinent (Bellman, 1966; Schaefer, 1979), but the prevalence declines by age 10 and remains low until about age 60. The prevalence of bowel incontinence in elderly people living in the community is unknown. However, the National Nursing Home Survey shows that 30% of nursing home residents are fecally incontinent (Van Nostrand et al., 1979). Fecal incontinence is three to four times more common in male children than in female children (Levine & Bakow, 1976; Lowery, Srour, Whitehead, & Schuster, 1985), whereas the prevalence among old people does not differ with sex.

Several subtypes of fecal incontinence exist.

Sensory or Motor Impairment of the Sphincter Mechanism. The anal canal is surrounded by the striated, external anal sphincter muscle. Distension of the rectum causes a subjective sensation of urgency to defecate, which is normally accompanied by a brief, voluntary contraction of the external anal sphincter. Thus, continence depends on the ability to perceive rectal distension, the ability to squeeze the perianal muscles appropriately, and motivation to do so (Whitehead, Orr, Engel, & Schuster, 1981).

Fecal incontinence is frequently the result of injury to the spinal cord or to the nerves that travel from the spinal cord to the rectum, external anal sphincter, and pelvic floor muscles (Schuster, 1975; Whitehead & Schuster, 1983). Such neurological impairments can interfere with the ability to perceive rectal distension or to contract the external anal sphincters. The commonest causes of such neurological damage are spinal cord injuries or the birth defect, myelomeningocele; systemic diseases, such as diabetes; and complications of anorectal surgery or of rectal disease.

Biofeedback training either to improve sensory discrimination of rectal distension or to improve the strength of contraction of the external anal sphincters is considered the treatment of choice for this type of fecal incontinence, as explained in the following. Alternative treatment consists of habit training in which the patient is instructed to empty his bowel at frequent, regular intervals and to use a high fiber diet to solidify the stools. This may reduce the likelihood of fecal incontinence. Surgery to establish a colostomy may be performed if all other measures fail to control fecal incontinence.

Diarrhea-Related Fecal Incontinence. Approximately 25% of patients with diarrhea associated with irritable bowel syndrome report at least occasional fecal soiling (Enck, Steckler, Whitehead, Tucker, & Schuster,

1984). This is apparently due to a forceful colonic contraction overwhelming an otherwise adequate sphincter. Biofeedback is possibly useful as an adjunctive treatment for this type of incontinence. The usual treatment is to give a hydrophylic bulking agent to reduce the water content of the stools or to give antidiarrheal medications, such as Lomotil and Immodium.

Noncompliance of the Rectum to Distension. The rectum is normally very elastic (compliant); it stretches readily to store fecal matter until defecation can take place. In individuals who have had rectal disease (e.g., ulcerative proctitis) or an operation in which the bowel from higher up is pulled down through the anal canal, scar tissue may develop around the rectal area and reduce the compliance of the rectum. This contributes to fecal incontinence by causing rapid transit of fecal matter into the anal canal. This type of fecal incontinence can not be treated with biofeedback. Standard treatments include habit training to keep the rectum relatively empty and drugs such as Lomotil and Immodium to slow bowel transit.

Overflow Incontinence. The most common type of fecal incontinence in children is that which is associated with chronic constipation and fecal impaction. The patient develops a mass of hard stool in the rectum that (a) reduces the ability to feel the movement of new stool into the rectum, and (b) reflexly dilates the internal anal sphincter, thereby permitting the loss of liquid stool and small amounts of hard stool from the rectum. Because of the frequent loss of small amounts of liquid stool, encopretic patients and their parents may assume that they have diarrhea. However, a physical examination will reveal constipation in approximately 90% of encopretic children (Levine & Bakow, 1976; Lowery et al., 1985).

Bellman's (1966) studies document that childhood encopresis is often associated with fearfulness on the part of the child, with coercive toilet training, and with a disturbed mother–child relationship. These psychological factors apparently interact with constipation to produce soiling. However, habit training programs that do not deal with the psychological symptoms directly but that concentrate on the control of constipation are successful in approximately 80% of children (e.g., Levine & Bakow, 1976; Lowery et al., 1985; Young, 1973).

Overflow incontinence is not associated with any neurological impairment that requires biofeedback training of specific physiological responses. It is possible that nonspecific biofeedback (arousal reduction training) used as part of a stress management training program could contribute to the treatment of encopresis in anxious children, but this has not so far been investigated.

Mobility Impairment. Physical illness or disability that makes it difficult or painful to get to the toilet quickly is a major contributing factor to fecal incontinence in old people. Data from the National Nursing Home Survey (Van Nostrand *et al.*, 1979) showed that 60% of the nursing home residents who were in restraints and 41% of those in wheelchairs were fecally incontinent compared to only 17% of those who were able to walk with a cane or walker. Biofeedback has not been suggested as a treatment for this type of fecal incontinence.

Social Indifference. The fecal incontinence that occurs in senile, psychotic, and severly retarded individuals appears to be due in part to confusion about or indifference toward social conventions. The National Nursing Home Survey (Van Nostrand *et al.*, 1979) showed that 56% of patients with mental illness, chronic brain syndrome, or senility were fecally incontinent compared to 21% of residents without these diagnoses. Biofeedback is not an appropriate treatment for this group of patients. There is no currently accepted treatment that is effective.

Clinical Efficacy

Three distinct types of biofeedback have been described for the treatment of fecal incontinence secondary to sensorimotor impairment: manometric (balloon) biofeedback, EMG biofeedback, and saline enema retention. These are described in the following.

Manometric Biofeedback. The manometric biofeedback procedure was first described by Engel, Nikoomanesh, and Schuster (1974). It requires inserting a tube into the anal canal and rectum to which three balloons are attached. These balloons are positioned so that one of them lies at the opening of the anus to the outside and senses contractions of the external anal sphincter, one balloon lies at the top of the anal canal and senses contraction or relaxation of the internal anal sphincter, and one balloon lies in the rectum where it is used to stimulate the rectum by distending it. The rectal balloon can also be used to record intraabdominal pressure changes and contractions of the rectum. These three balloons are attached to pressure transducers via polyethlene tubing, and pressures inside the balloons are recorded on a polygraph that is visible to the patient. The polygraph is used as the biofeedback device.

Rectal distension produces a reflex inhibition (opening) of the internal anal sphincter that normally closes after 20 to 40 sec. In order to avoid incontinence, the individual must contract the external anal sphincter during the initial stages of this internal anal sphincter inhibition and do so until (a) the rectum can stretch to accommodate an increased volume and (b) the internal sphincter can begin to close. Biofeedback training consists of having the patient watch the tracing and attempt to contract the external anal sphincter appropriately in response to any rectal distension. Normally the therapist begins with large rectal distensions that are easily perceived, that is, 50 ml of air is added to the rectal balloon and immediately withdrawn. When the patient is consistently responding appropriately to a large, 50 ml balloon distension, the volume of rectal distension is reduced to 40 ml and the process repeated. In this way the volume of distension is reduced until the patient is responding to distensions of 10 ml or less. Verbal encouragement and shaping of more appropriate responses is used throughout. Two to four such biofeedback training sessions are provided at 2- to 8-week intervals, and the patient is instructed to practice squeezing the sphincter muscles 50 times daily between sessions to increase strength.

Minor modifications in this procedure have been found helpful in special populations: (a) when working with patients with spinal cord injuries that render the external anal sphincter muscles extremely weak, it is advisable to begin by teaching the patient to contract the sphincter in the absence of any rectal distension and to work up to larger and larger distensions as the patient is able to respond appropriately (Wald, 1981b, 1983; Whitehead, Parker, Masek, Cataldo, & Freeman, 1981; Whitehead et al., 1986). The reason for this modification is that rectal distension may cause a dilation of the whole anal canal, which makes it difficult to discriminate the intially very weak external sphincter responses. (b) When working with children younger than 10 years, it is helpful to combine biofeedback with tangible reinforcement in order to maintain the child's attention on the task. Tokens such as marbles that can later be exchanged for toys can be used for children aged 8 to 10 whereas the youngest children respond best to snack foods such as corn chips (Whitehead, et al., 1986). (c) When impaired sensation for rectal distension is a contributing cause of incontinence, treatment should include specific sensory discriminatin training. This involves gradually reducing the volume of rectal distension from volumes that are clearly distinguishable to volumes that are just below the threshold for subjective sensation (Wald & Tunuguntla, 1984).

The initial report by Engel et al. (1974) described six patients with mixed etiologies. Four of these patients became continent as a result of biofeedback, and the remaining two were significantly improved. Subsequently, Cerulli, Nikoomanesh, and Schuster (1979) reported data for a consecutive series of 50 patients treated with this technique. When all etiologies were combined, 72% of patients showed a good response to treatment, defined as at least a 90% decrease in the frequency of incontinence. However, outcomes differed as a function of etiology of incontinence. The best outcomes were achieved in patients whose bowel incontinence occurred as the result of anorectal surgery (92% good responders), and the poorest results were in patients with spinal cord injuries (45% good responders).

Comparable outcomes have been reported by other laboratories. Goldenberg, Hodges, Hersh, and Jinich (1980) treated 12 patients with various etiologies and achieved good results in 10 (6 became continent). Wald (1981a) reported good results in 12 of 17 adults with mixed etiologies. Ten children with inperforate anus repair and 40 with functional encopresis (overflow incontinence) were treated with this technique by Olness, McParland, and Piper (1980); they reported that 7 of 10 imperforate anus cases and 38 of 40 with overflow incontinence were substantially improved or continent. Whitehead, Burgio, and Engel (1985) used manometric biofeedback to treat 13 geriatric patients, and reported that six became continent and an additional four experienced at least a 75% decrease in the frequency of incontinence. Wald and Tunuguntla (1984) reported that 8 of 11 incontinent diabetic patients had a reduction in fecal soiling after biofeedback to improve discrimination of rectal discrimination and/or to improve the strength of sphincter contractions.

Fecal incontinence secondary to spinal cord injury was found by Cerulli et al. (1979) to be the most difficult subgroup to treat. This is particularly unfortunate because myelomeningocele is a common birth defect that is almost always accompanied by bowel and bladder incontinence. Consequently, three studies have concentrated on the treatment of children with myelomeningocele. Whitehead, Parker, et al. (1981) provided a modified form of biofeedback to eight children with myelomeningocele. They first trained the child to contract the perianal muscles in the absence of any rectal distension and then gradually increased the volume of rectal distension as the child learned to respond appropriately. This modified procedure resulted in continence for five children and significant improvements in one other. These results were well maintained as follow-up a year later. Wald (1981b) used a similar procedure to treat eight children with myelomeningocele and reported that four of them were improved by at least 75%. Subsequently, Wald (1983) extended his series by adding another seven patients. Three of these seven showed at least a 75% reduction in the frequency of incontinence.

It appeared from these studies that 50% to 75% of children with fecal incontinence secondary to myelomeingocele could benefit from biofeedback training. However, in the Whitehead, Parker, et al. (1981) study, and possibly also in the Wald (1981b, 1983) studies, biofeedback was combined with instructions to the family to have the child attempt bowel movements in the toilet on a daily basis. Whitehead et al. (1986) attempted to assess the relative contribution of such habit training and biofeedback training to clinical outcomes. They found that overall, patients who received only behavior modification for 3 months showed as much clinical improvement as patients who received behavior modification plus biofeedback. This suggests that previous reports have overestimated the value of biofeedback in this population because they have not controlled for nospecific treatment effects. However, a subgroup of patients (27%) were identified for whom biofeedback provided additional, specific benefit. These were children who had spinal cord lesions below L2 and who initially had two or more bowel movements per day. The combination of behavior modification and biofeedback resulted in a greater than 50% reduction in the frequency of incontinence for 64% of patients, and results were well maintained at follow up one year later.

As the previous discussion suggests, manometric biofeedback has been reported in several independent studies to produce significant clinical improvement in approximately 75% of patients. Moreover, these results are well maintained at follow-up 1 to 3 years later. The only diagnostic group for which biofeedback appears to be of limited value are children with fecal incontinence secondary to myelomeningocele. On the strength of these reports, manometric biofeedback is regarded to be the treatment of choice for fecal incontinence associated with sensorimotor impairment.

EMG Biofeedback. For patients with sphincter weakness (but not sensory impairment) as a cause of fecal incontinence, EMG biofeedback offers an alternative to manometric biofeedback. Haskell and Rovner (1967) were the first to report using sphincter EMG biofeedback. While doing needle EMG tests to assess neurological damage, they discovererd that patients could make use of the auditory and viusal displays on clinical EMG machines to improve sphincter control. Out of 38 patients with normally innervated sphincters whom they studied, 71% achieved continence; but only 38% of 16 patients with partially denervated sphincters reported improvement. This technique was subsequently abandoned, perhaps because rigid needle electromyography is painful.

MacLeod (1979, 1983) discovered that better results could be achieved if one used an anal plug with metal plates on its surface to detect the external anal sphincter EMG and attached this to a conventional EMG biofeedback instrument (which filters out the smooth muscle EMG activity and selectively amplifies the striated external anal sphincter muscle activity). In his first series of 17 patients MacLeod (1979) reported that six became continent, and four rated themselves as substantially improved. These improvements were maintained at follow-up 1 to 2 years later. In a subsequent series of 50 patients, MacLeod (1983) reported that 72% of his patients achieved at least a 90% improvement and that all improvements were maintained at follow up one year later.

Direct comparisons between manometric and EMG biofeedback have not been reported. EMG biofeedback has the advantage that the equipment is less expensive and more readily available, and the feedback displays from most EMG biofeedback instruments are less confusing to young patients than the polygraph displays used in manometric bio-feedback. The disadvantage of the EMG biofeedback procedure as currently implemented is that it does not offer a convenient way of improving awareness of rectal distension or of teaching the patient to coordinate sphincter contractions with rectal distensions. However, a modified anal EMG probe has been developed[1] that will permit a balloon-tipped catheter to be passed through the plug and situated in the rectum. This will permit the therapist to stimulate the rectum with balloon distension and to monitor intraabdominal pressure with an inexpensive pressure gauge.

Saline Enema Biofeedback. A novel biofeedback approach to the treatment of fecal incontinence was reported in a case study by Schiller, Santa Ana, Davis, and Fordtran (1979). Their patient was a woman whose incontinence was associated with diarrhea. They infused saline into the rectum at a constant rate and provided feedback on the volume already infused. The patient's goal was to reach a target of 1500 ml before leaking. After 10 sessions, the patient had increased the volume of saline she could hold by 700%, and her incontinence ceased despite continued diarrhea. The investigators demonstrated that these clinical improvements were not associated with an increase in external sphincter strength; they were presumably mediated by an increase in the compliance of the rectum. No other published reports have used this technique, and it must be regarded as potentially useful but of unproven efficacy.

Specificity of Effect

Manometric Biofeedback. Although manometric biofeedback has been reported by several independent investigators to be effective in approximately 75% of patients with a sensorimotor type of fecal incontinence, it should be noted that no studies have been published that include concurrent control groups. It is usually assumed that control groups are unnecessary because the outcome measure (frequency of incontinence) is objective. However, biofeedback is frequently combined with other recommendations to the patient, such as changing diet to avoid constipation, establishing a regular time to attempt a bowel movement, and performing sphincter squeezing exercises. These recommendations may have contributed to the apparent success of biofeedback training in published trials.

Two studies have addressed the specificity of manometric biofeedback training effects in fecally incontinent patients. Whitehead *et al.*

[1] Farrall Instruments, Inc. P.O. Box 1037, Grand Island, Nebraska 68802

(1985) placed 18 geriatric patients on a habit training program for 4 weeks before beginning biofeedback and reported that only two became continent without biofeedback. These patients had shown sphincter weakness before beginning habit training. An additional six patients became continent or had less than one bowel accident per month when provided with biofeedback, and an additional four improved bowel control by at least 75%.

A second test of the specificity of manometric biofeedback was reported by Latimer et al., (1984). They used a single-subject experimental design to test the effectiveness of what they viewed as the three principal components of manometric biofeedback training: exercise of the external sphincter, training in discrimination of rectal distension, and training in how to synchronize the external sphincter contraction with the internal sphincter relaxation. Eight patients were randomly assigned to two treatment protocols: (a) baseline, followed by sphincter exercise, baseline, sensory discrimination training, baseline, and then synchrony training; or (b) baseline, followed by sensory discrimination training, baseline, sphincter exercise, baseline, and synchrony training. Each phase of each treatment protocol lasted 4 weeks. Visual feedback was provided only during synchrony training, but verbal feedback and instruction were provided by the experimenter on a trial-by-trial basis during sphincter exercise and discrimination training. All eight patients in this study improved, but the treatment components could not be shown to have differential effects. This may have occurred because (a) the verbal feedback available for appropriate responses during all phases of the treatment may have constituted adequate feedback, (b) several subtypes of fecal incontinence were mixed together, or (c) there were nonspecific components of the treatment that accounted for its efficacy that have not yet been identified. Additional research on the component analysis of biofeedback with more homogenous samples of patients would be helpful in resolving questions about the specific value of manometric biofeedback for fecal incontinence. Nothing is known about the specificity of EMG biofeedback or saline enema biofeedback training.

Mechanism of Action

Manometric biofeedback training is believed to reduce the frequency of fecal incontinence through three specific physiological mechanisms: (a) by increasing the strength of contraction of the external anal sphincter muscle, (b) by increasing the ability to discriminate weak distensions of the rectum, and (c) by relearning to coordinate external anal sphincter contractions with internal sphincter relaxation following rectal distension. EMG sphincter biofeedback is believed to operate through the first of these mechanisms also. The mechanism for saline enema biofeedback is unknown.

Cost-Effectiveness

Manometric biofeedback and EMG biofeedback appear to be cost-effective alternatives to conventional treatments for sensory motor fecal incontinence for the following reasons: (a) biofeedback training typically requires two to four outpatient visits. (b) Training effects are well maintained for 1 to 3 years. (c) With the exception of surgery to establish a colostomy, alternative treatments for sensory motor incontinence are regarded as ineffective.

Future Research

Future research on biofeedback for fecal incontinence should include concurrent control groups in which patients are given all elements of the treatment package except access to information feedback. The non-specific elements of the treatment against which the effects of biofeedback training have to be judged are (a) use of a regularly scheduled time to attempt a bowel movement, (b) use of enemas or suppositories to control constipation, (c) increases in the fiber content of the diet, and (d) prescribed sphincter exercises without biofeedback training. It will also be helpful for defining the indications and contraindications for biofeedback training if future clinical trials specify and/or restrict the types of fecal incontinence that are being investigated.

Additional research is needed to identify biofeedback or other behavioral training procedures which may benefit patients with incontinence associated with diarrhea and incontinence associated with decreased rectal compliance. The saline enema biofeedback procedure may be useful for these types of incontinence.

IRRITABLE BOWEL SYNDROME

Introduction

Definition. Irritable bowel syndrome (IBS) has traditionally been defined by the presence of abdominal pain and altered bowel habits in the absense of any known pathophysiological changes adequate to explain these symptoms (Whitehead, Engel, & Schuster, 1980). However, there has been a growing concern in the last 8 years that these criteria are too imprecise and that they have hampered understanding of the disorder by including too heterogeneous a group of patients into this diagnostic category.

Additional diagnostic criteria were proposed by Manning, Thompson, Heaton, and Morris (1978) in an attempt to improve the precision of the diagnosis. They compared the responses of patients with a clinical diagnosis of IBS to patients with organic gastrointestinal disorders and concluded that reliable diagnosis could be based on the presence of two or more of the following four symptoms:

1. Pain eased after a bowel movement, often
2. Looser stools with onset of pain
3. More frequent bowel movements with the onset of pain
4. Visible distension of abdomen or feeling of distension

Manning *et al.* (1978) found that 91% of IBS patients had two or more of these four symptoms whereas only 30% of non-IBS patients did. The utility of these diagnostic criteria was supported by a subsequent study by Thompson and Heaton (1980) and a study by Bolin, Davis, and Duncombe (1982). However, Enck *et al.* (1984) found that the Manning criteria did not reliably distinguish patients with IBS from patients with lactose (milk) intolerance, which is believed to be a separate clinical entity; and Spiegel, Johannes, Shapiro, Malley, and Hendrix (1984) found that these criteria did not distinguish IBS from inflammatory bowel disease. Thus it is clear that the Manning criteria must be combined with physical examination and laboratory tests to avoid including patients with other types of gastrointestinal diseases.

Although self-reports of chronic constipation and diarrhea are usually thought to typify IBS, bowel habits appear not to be abnormal except during infrequent, symptomatic periods. For example, both Thompson and Heaton (1980) and Drossman, Sandler, McKee, and Lovitz (1982) reported that a group of patients who reported loose or watery bowel movements on more than 25% of occasions and a group who reported straining at stools on more than 25% of occasions showed little overlap with the group who experienced abdominal pain relieved by a bowel movement (a symptom thought to be central to IBS). This was true despite the fact that IBS patients were more likely to report looser stools and more frequent stools with the onset of pain and also significantly more likely to report abdominal distension and a feeling of incomplete evacuation (Manning *et al.*, 1978).

A major shortcoming of the Manning criteria is that they do not include any psychological symptoms. More than half of IBS patients report that psychological stress makes their symptoms worse (e.g., Chaudhary & Truelove, 1962; Drossman *et al.*, 1982; Fava & Pavan, 1976–1977; Hislop, 1971), and the majority of IBS patients are found to have clinically significant symptoms of anxiety, depression, and/or hysterical traits (e.g., Esler & Goulston, 1973; Latimer et al., 1981; Palmer, Stonehill, Crisp, Waller, & Misiewicz, 1974; West, 1970). Studies that have applied DSM-III criteria (American Psychiatriac Association, 1980) find diagnosable psychiatric disorders (chiefly hysteria, depression, and anxiety disorder) in 72% to 100% of IBS patients (Latimer et al., 1981; Liss, Alpers, & Woodruff, 1973; Young, Alpers, Norland, & Woodruff, 1976). Thus, psychological symptoms would appear to be important criteria to include in a definition of IBS.

In light of these observations, Whitehead and Schuster (1985) proposed the following as conservative diagnostic criteria for IBS:

1. Abdominal pain that is (a) relieved by a bowel movement often, (b) occurs at least six times per year, and (c) lasts at least 3 weeks per occasion.

2. Presence of at least two of the remaining Manning criteria: (a) loose stools at the onset of pain, (b) more frequent bowel movements with the onset of pain, (c) distension of the abdomen, (d) mucus passed by rectum, and (e) frequent feeling of incomplete evacuation.

3. Association of abdominal pain with anxiety or depression as demonstrated by (a) symptom diary demonstrating a temporal correlation of abdominal pain with sujective stress, and/or (b) psychometric tests demonstrating anxiety or depression scores at least two standard deviations above normal values.

4. Exclusion of physical disease and lactose malabsorption as a cause of bowel symptoms.

Epidemiology. The irritable bowel syndrome accounts for 22% (Harvey, Salih, & Read, 1983) to 50% (Ferguson, Sircus, & Eastwood, 1977) of all visits to gastroenterologists, and it has a prevalence of 8% (Whitehead, Winget, Fedoravicius, Wooley, & Blackwell, 1982) to 17% (Drossman et al., 1982) in the United States. It is more common in women than in men by a ratio of approximately 2:1 (Whitehead, et al., 1982).

Pathophysiology. Patients with IBS are usually found to have excessive contractile activity in the distal colon, especially if the colon has been stimulated with food, injections of cholocystokinin, balloon distension, or psychologically stressful interviews (e.g., Whitehead et al., 1980). These contractions are associated with momentary increases in abdominal pain (Holdstock et al., 1969), and they are believed to be responsible for the abdominal distension and constipation frequently associated with IBS (Connell, 1962).

Psychophysiological Mechanism. Four distinct models have been proposed to account for the observed relationship between psychological symptoms and bowel symptoms in IBS. There are currently insufficient data to choose among these theories.

Latimer's (1983) model emphasizes the relative independence of physiological events (e.g., colon motility), subjective symptoms (e.g., pain), and behavior. He proposed that many IBS patients misperceive or mislabel normal bowel physiology and behave inappropriately in response to these perceptions. This theory was supported by data showing that a mixed group of psychiatric outpatients without bowel symptoms had levels of colon motility that were intermediated between normal subjects and patients with IBS (Latimer et al., 1981).

Almy's (1951) theory proposes that the excessive colon motility that is the presumed basis for bowel symptoms in patients with IBS is a normal physiological response to emotional arousal. His theory is based on experimental observations that emotionally stressful interviews provoke increases in colon motility in normal subjects that are qualitatively similar to the colonic motility seen in IBS. Neither Latimer's nor Almy's theories suggest that there is any biological difference between IBS patients and normal subjects; the principal determinants of symptoms are psychological events.

By contrast, Snape, Carlson, and Cohen (1976) proposed a strong biological theory of IBS. They found that IBS patients showed a smooth muscle EMG abnormality characterized by an increased proportion of slow waves in the 2 to 4 cpm frequency range relative to all slow waves. This EMG finding was present even during asymptomatic periods. These findings were replicated by one other research group (Taylor, Darby, & Hammond, 1978) but not by two other groups (Latimer et al., 1981; Welgan, Meshkinpour, & Hoehler, 1985), and the hypothesis remains controversial. Bueno, Fioramonti, Frexinos, and Ruckebush (1980) have also proposed a biological theory of IBS, namely that constipated patients show an increased incidence of short spike bursts (2–10 sec in duration) whereas patients with diarrhea show a decreased incidence of long spike bursts (greater than 6.4 sec).

Whitehead et al. (1980) proposed an intermediate theory, namely that there is a biological basis for IBS that predisposes some people to react excessively with colon motility in response to a variety of stimuli. These stimuli include emotional arousal but also many stimuli that have no psychological significance, such as food and colonic distension. The 2 to 4 cpm myoelectric abnormality described by Snape et al. (1976) may constitute the biological substrate for this hyperreactivity in IBS patients. Whitehead et al. (1982) presented data that suggest that this biological predisposition may be learned.

Conventional Treatment of IBS. Standard treatment for IBS includes one or more of the following: high fiber diet, antispasmodic medications such as dicyclomine, antidepressants and/or tranquilizers, and emotional support. None of these treatments have been shown to be effective in controlled trials (Almy, 1977; Whitehead, 1985). However, brief psychotherapy was shown to be superior to placebo treatment by Svedlund, Sjodin, Ottosson, and Dotevall (1983). The aims of psychotherapy were to modify maladaptive behavior, to find new solutions to problems, and to teach coping skills.

Clinical Efficacy

Two types of biofeedback have been used to treat IBS: specific biofeedback aimed at reducing colon motility and nonspecific biofeedback aimed at teaching the patient to reduce emotional arousal.

Specific Biofeedback. Bowel sound biofeedback provided with an electronic stethescope was the first biofeedback treatment described for IBS. Furman (1973) taught five patients with IBS to increase and decrease alternately the volume of bowel sounds and reported that all of them improved as they acquired this ability. However, other investigators (e.g., Weinstock, 1976) have been unable to replicate these findings, and the technique has fallen into disuse.

Direct feedback of colonic contractions detected with a balloon on a rectal tube was used by Bueno-Miranda, Cerulli, and Schuster (1976) to teach 21 IBS patients to inhibit contractile activity. Two thirds of the group were able to reduce colon motility in a single 2-hour session, and they retained this skill when retested 8 weeks later. Clinical improvements were not reported for these patients.

A direct comparison between the balloon-feedback procedure described by Bueno-Miranda *et al.* (1976) and a stress management procedure involving progressive muscle relaxation training and systematic desensitization was made by Whitehead (1985). The groups were small (four in each group), but a crossover design was used, and abdominal pain and colon motility were tested before and after treatment. The stress management procedure appeared to produce greater reductions in symptoms of abdominal pain and was better tolerated by patients than repeated insertion of a rectal tube.

Nonspecific Biofeedback. The use of biofeedback to teach IBS patients how to relax was first described in an abstract by Weinstock (1976). He attempted to treat 12 IBS patients with bowel sound biofeedback and failed. Nine of these patients were then switched to forehead EMG biofeedback three times weekly plus home practice of progressive muscle relaxation exercises. All nine were said to have improved.

A controlled trial was subsequently reported by Giles (1978). He randomly assigned 40 patients with functional bowel disorders (diagnostic criteria not specified) to four groups: forehead EMG biofeedback alone, psychotherapy alone (training in how to identify stressors and how to solve personal problems), a combined biofeedback and psycho-therapy group, and a no-treatment control group. EMG biofeedback was the most effective treatment for reducing the frequency of loose bowel movements, but the combined treatment was most effective for decreasing psychological symptoms associated with IBS. Schneider (1983) reported an additional uncontrolled study from the same laboratory in which EMG biofeedback was combined with psychotherapy in the treatment of IBS. A total of 58 IBS patients have been treated with this protocol, and 68% to 73% were judged to be greatly improved or asymptomatic.

The study by Giles (1978) provides the strongest support to date for the efficacy of EMG biofeedback in IBS. However, it cannot be considered conclusive because the diagnostic criteria were not given and the outcome measures (responses to items on the Hopkins Symptom Checklist) were relatively weak for evaluating the effects of treatment on bowel symptoms.

Clinical Lore.   An informal survey of biofeedback clinicians that was conducted by Patricia Norris indicates that many biofeedback therapists are using forehead EMG biofeedback and/or thermal biofeedback (hand warming) to teach stress management skills to patients with IBS. Results reported in this informal survey are consistent with the outcomes of research studies cited earlier: 60% to 90% of patients were said to be improved by these procedures.

Specificity of Effect

Biofeedback training to modify directly the motility of the distal colon via bowel sound feedback or pressure recordings from intracolonic tubes has not as yet been shown to make a specific contribution to the treatment of IBS. The nonspecific forehead EMG biofeedback used by several investigators appears to be effective, but it has not been compared to other, nonbiofeedback stress management procedures. EMG biofeedback is usually combined with other psychotherapeutic techniques aimed at reducing stress reactions. Therefore, no specific value for biofeedback in the treatment of IBS has been established.

Mechanism of Action

The specific biofeedback procedure proposed by Bueno-Miranda *et al.* (1976) and tested by Whitehead (1985) directly modifies the motility of the distal colon. However, the clinical value of this technique has not been established.

Forehead EMG biofeedback is believed to contribute to the management of IBS by teaching the patient a technique for controlling anxiety and associated autonomic arousal. It is usually combined with systematic desensitization (Whitehead, 1985) or other psychotherapeutic procedures (Giles, 1978; Schneider, 1983) aimed at reducing situational anxiety.

Cost-Effectiveness of Biofeedback

The successful treatment program used by Giles (1978) and Schneider (1983) involved approximately 10 visits. In view of the relative ineffectiveness of conventional treatments for IBS (Almy, 1977), and in view of the large numbers of patients visits occasioned by IBS (Ferguson, Sircus, & Eastwood, 1977; Harvey et al., 1983), forehead EMG biofeedback combined with psychotherapy should be considered a cost-effective treatment.

Future Research

Large-scale clinical trials are needed that compare forehead EMG biofeedback and colonic manometric (pressure) biofeedback to other stress management procedures and to placebo treatment in order to determine the specific value of biofeedback for this disorder. Additional research on the psychophysiological mechanism of symptoms and on direct biofeedback to modify the pathophysiological mechanism of abdominal pain may also result in improved treatment techniques.

INFLAMMATORY BOWEL DISEASE AND OSTOMY

Ulcerative Colitis. This is a disorder involving inflammatory changes in the mucosa and to a lesser extent the submucosa of the colon. The disease occurs primarily in the left colon and rectum, although the entire colon may be involved. Major symptoms are diarrhea, rectal bleeding, abdominal pain, and weight loss due to anorexia (Hamilton, Bruce, Abdourhaman, & Gall, 1979). The most serious complication is colon cancer, which is 7 to 11 times more common than in people without ulcerative colitis. The probability of developing cancer increases with the length of time the disease has been present and reaches 50% after approximately 25 years. For this reason, the colon is sometimes removed prophylactically after the disease has been present for 10 years (Kirsner & Shorter, 1982). However, pathologists are developing improved criteria for rating the severity of precancerous tissue changes, and many patients elect to have an annual colonoscopy with multiple biopsies as an alternative to prophylactic colectomy.

The incidence of ulcerative colitis is approximately 7 to 9 per 100,000. It is 2 to 4 times more common in Jews than in non-Jews and also 2 to 4 times more common in caucasians than in black Americans (Monk, Mendeloff, Siegel, & Lilenfeld, 1967).

The etiology of ulcerative colitis is unknown, although recent research findings suggest an immune deficiency and/or autoimmune process (Kirsner & Shorter, 1982). Ulcerative colitis is frequently considered a psychosomatic disorder (e.g., Alexander, French, & Pollock, 1968; Engel, 1954), and there is evidence that supportive psychotherapy can alter the course of the disease favorably (Grace, Pinsky, & Wolff, 1954). No biofeedback treatment for this disorder has been published. However, in the clinical lore collected in Patricia Norris' survey, reference was made to nine patients with ulcerative colitis or Crohn's disease who were treated with a stress management biofeedback procedure. Half were said to benefit. Similarly, the 1978 task force report described a clinician's successful treatment of four patients with ulcerative colitis by means of biofeedback and mental imagery.

Crohn's Disease. This is a disease characterized by lesions that begin under the mucosa and penetrate outward into the muscle wall of the intestine. It may occur in any part of the gastrointestinal tract but is most commonly found in the small intestine. The principal symptoms are diarrhea, abdominal pain, anorexia with weight loss, and fever. The most serious complication is the development of bowel obstruction due to edema or scarring. This carries a risk of causing the bowel to perforate and contaminate the abdomen with bacteria. A more frequent complication is the development of fistulous tracks (channels) that connect one part of the bowel to another part or connect the bowel to the skin surface or to the bladder (Hamilton *et al.*, 1979). There is also an increased risk of cancer when Crohn's disease has been present for more than 20 years (McIllmurray & Langman, 1975).

Crohn's disease has a pattern of incidence similar to ulcerative colitis, although it is less common. It has an annual incidence of 3.5 per 100,000 females and 4.5 per 100,000 males. It is 2 to 4 times more common in Jews than in non-Jews and 2 to 4 times more common in caucasians than in blacks (Monk *et al.*, 1967).

The etiology of Crohn's disease is unknown, and like ulcerative colitis, immune factors have been implicated in its etiology. Kirsner and Shorter (1982) regard ulcerative colitis and Crohn's disease as different manifestations of the same disease.

Crohn's disease is also sometimes thought to be exacerbated by psychological factors, although the evidence for this is weak (Latimer, 1978). There are no published accounts of biofeedback or other psychological treatments for Crohn's disease.

Ileostomy and Colostomy   When the colon is removed due to ulcerative colitis or other disease, the terminal end of the small intestine may be brought through the abdominal wall to form an ileostomy. An appliance (bag) is fitted over the stoma to collect the discharge from the intestine. When only part of the colon is removed, the distal end of the colon may be brought through the abdominal wall to form a colostomy.

Ileostomies and colostomies create a number of cosmetic problems for the patients who have them. Among these are the appearance of the bag and the possibility of spilling fecal matter if the bag breaks or becomes detached from the body. An Italian group has investigated the use of biofeedback to teach patients with colostomies to pinch off the stoma with the surrounding abdominal wall muscles in order to preserve continence and avoid wearing a bag (Reboa, Picardo, Giusto, & Riboli, 1982). They inserted an hourglass-shaped plug into the stoma that contained perfusion ports to record the pressure with which the surrounding muscles were contracted. The device also included a balloon to distend the bowel below the stoma. During 12 20-min biofeedback sessions five patients were taught to recognize distensions of the bowel and to squeeze in response to these distensions. Clinical improvement was rated as good to excellent in four of five patients.

These encouraging results warrant further, controlled studies. Such biofeedback training is likely to be more effective for patients with colostomies than for patients with ileostomies because colostomies discharge stools that are more formed, and there is less peristaltic activity in the colon than in the small intestine.

CONSTIPATION DUE TO OUTLET OBSTRUCTION

A type of constipation that is due to outlet obstruction—that is, failure of the anal canal to relax to allow stool to pass out of the rectum—was described by Martelli, Devroede, Arhan, and Duguay (1978). The prevalence of this type of constipation is unknown. Denis, Cayron, and Galmiche (1981) described a biofeedback procedure for this disorder that they used successfully in a single case. The technique involved recording pressures in the upper and lower anal canal with a three-balloon tube similar to that described for the treatment of fecal incontinence by Engel *et al.* (1974) and having the patient attempt to relax while watching the pressure recording. The authors reported that their patient was able to reduce the amplitude of spontaneous variations in pressure in the upper anal canal and also that she could reduce the amplitude of the prolonged contraction that occurred in the upper anal canal secondary to rectal distension. This was associated with the development of an ability to defecate normally and without pain.

An apparently different type of outlet-obstruction constipation was treated with biofeedback by van Baal, Leguit, and Brummelkamp (1984). Diagnostic studies in their patient suggested that the internal sphincter inhibitory reflex was normal but that the external anal sphincter was spastic and prevented stool from passing through the anal canal. The authors introduced a single balloon attached to a tube into the rectum and inflated it with 100 ml of air. Pressure inside the ballon was displayed on an oscilloscope, and the patient was instructed to increase intraabdominal pressure by contracting the abdominus rectus muscles and simultaneously to relax the external sphincter. During this maneuver, the balloon was slowly pulled out of the rectum through the anal canal. An urge to defecate was stimulated with an enema or suppository prior to these sessions. After three weeks of daily training, the patient was able to defecate normally following a suppository, and results were well maintained at follow-up 6 months later.

These two innovative biofeedback procedures have only been described as single-case studies, so their value cannot be assessed. If outlet obstruction proves to be a genuine and frequent contributing cause of constipation, there will be a need for further development of biofeedback procedures such as these.

PEPTIC ULCER DISEASE

Introduction

Peptic ulcers are ulcers in the stomach (gastric ulcers) or the small intestine adjacent to the stomach (duodenal ulcers). The principal symptoms are gnawing hunger pains that are most severe a few hours after eating and that are relieved by eating or by antacids. The major complications of peptic ulcer, which may be fatal, are bleeding and perforation of the gastrointestinal wall with possible infection of the abdominal cavity.

Peptic ulcers are common, affecting an estimated 10% of the population (Pflanz, 1971). Duodenal ulcers make up about 75% of all peptic ulcers, and it is duodenal ulcers for which there is the clearest evidence of a relationship to psychological stress. Duodenal ulcers are about twice as common in men as compared to women, but gastric ulcers occur in equal proportions of males and females (Bonnevie, 1975a,b). Peptic ulcer disease is the 14th leading cause of death in the United States (National Center for Health Statistics, 1974). However, its incidence has been declining in the last 10 years.

Many different physiological events may contribute to the development of peptic ulcers, but there is general agreement that the most common proximal causes are increased secretion of hydrochloric acid and pepsin and/or impaired protection of the stomach and intestinal wall by mucus. Standard treatments for peptic ulcer are histamine 2 blockers, such as cimetidine and ranitidine, which inhibit acid secretion (Winship, 1978), and antacids that neutralize acid secretion (Peterson *et al.*, 1977). Both therapies have been shown to promote the healing of peptic ulcers in controlled trials.

Clinical Efficacy

The report of the 1978 Task Force on Gastrointestinal Biofeedback (Whitehead, 1978) reviewed several studies in which biofeedback training was used to alter gastric acid secretion (Gorman, 1976; Moore & Schenkenberg, 1974; Welgan, 1974, 1977; Whitehead, Renault, & Goldiamond, 1975). The report concluded (a) it is possible to train human subjects to alter gastric acid secretion, but (b) this is not a cost-effective treatment alternative to medical management with cimetidine, ranitidine, or large-dose antacids. No new studies have been published since 1978, and these conclusions stand.

The 1978 report also summarized studies showing that biofeedback training can be used to teach subjects to alter the phasic (Deckner, Hill, & Bourne, 1972) and tonic (Walker, Lawton, & Sandman, 1978) components of the electrogastrogram, which was described as an indirect measure of gastric motility. Since then Whitehead and Drescher (1980) reported using biofeedback to teach normal subjects to increase the frequency of 3 cpm gastric contractions. Gastric contractions were measured as pressure change in the stomach that were detected by having subjects swallow a nasogastric tube. This study reinforces the conclusion of the 1978 task force report that gastric motility can be modified using biofeedback training. However, the clinical relevance of such training to the treatment of peptic ulcer or other disorders has not been established.

Nonspecific biofeedback used to teach relaxation and self-management skills appears more promising. Beaty (1976) described treating three peptic ulcer patients with forehead EMG biofeedback training, home practice of progressive relaxation exercises, and training in the use of relaxation to cope with stress. All three patients reported symptomatic relief. Similarly, Aleo and Nicassio (1978) combined forehead EMG biofeedback with cognitive behavior therapy techniques (use of positive statements, such as "I can handle this situation," and use of distracting mental imagery to control reaction of stressors). They reported the duodenal ulcers were healed in 3 of 4 patients and reduced in size in the fourth.

Although these clinical reports suggest that nonspecific biofeedback combined with coping skills training may have a beneficial effect in peptic ulcer disease, they provide only weak evidence for efficacy. No control group was included in either study, and this is particularly important because approximately 75% of peptic ulcers heal spontaneously within a 6-week period (Scheurer et al., 1977). Also, any behavioral treatment for peptic ulcer disease must compete with cheap, effective pharmacological treatments. Histamine 2 blockers (cimetidine and ranitidine) (Winship, 1978) and antacids (Peterson et al., 1977) have been demonstrated to be effective.

Gastroesophageal Reflux

Esophageal reflux is a common gastrointestinal disorder characterized by burning chest pain that is usually worse after meals, during exercise, or when bending over. It may be accompanied by difficulty in swallowing, nausea and vomiting, and choking due to aspiration of refluxed material into the lungs (Henderson, 1980). These symptoms result from the reflux of acidic gastric contents up through the lower esophageal sphincter and into the esophagus. Prolonged exposure of the esophagus to gastric acid irritates the wall of the esophagus causing the burning sensation, and it may also provoke spastic motility of the esophagus. Standard treatment for gastroesophageal reflux is to give antacids and to recommend that the patient sleep with the head of the bed elevated to promote gravity drainage of the esophagus during sleep.

Two physiological mechanisms are believed to contribute to the occurrence of gastroesophageal reflux: the smooth muscle sphincter that separates the esophagus from the stomach (lower esophageal sphincter) is found to be abnormally weak (diminished resting tone) in 71% of patients with reflux. The second contributing mechanism may be hiatal hernia, in which the stomach balloons up through the diaphragm and compromises the mechanical valve ordinarily created by the short segment of the esophagus that extends below the diaphragm. Hiatal hernia is found in 83% of patients with gastroesophageal reflux, including many who also have diminished lower esophageal sphincter pressures (Henderson, 1980).

There is no evidence to suggest that reflux esophagitis is caused or exacerbated by psychological stress or that it is associated with psychopathology. However, Schuster, Nikoomanesh, and Wells (1973) described a biofeedback procedure that enabled patients to learn to increase lower esophageal sphincter pressure. The clinical efficacy of this procedure was not evaluated, and no new studies have been reported since the 1978 Task Force Report. Additional research is needed to establish the value of this procedure for treating gastroesophageal reflux.

Standard treatment for reflux esophagitis includes (a) antacids to neutralize stomach acid, (b) histamine 2 blockers, such as cimetidine and ranitidine, to inhibit acid secretion, and/or (c) sleeping with the head of the bed elevated to promote gravity drainage of the esophagus during sleep. These measures are usually effective. However, in severe, treatment-resistant cases, a surgical procedure called fundal plication may be performed in which the stomach is gathered over the end of the esophagus and sewn to it to provide a mechanical valve that prevents reflux. This form of treatment has been recommended for severe gastroesophageal reflux in retarded individuals who are not able to cooperate with conventional treatment (Wesley, Coran, Sarahan, Klein, & White, 1981).

DIFFUSE ESOPHAGEAL SPASM

There exists a spectrum of esophageal motility disorders that include excess numbers of contractions, contractions that are nonperistaltic, and contractions of greater than normal amplitude and duration. These motility disorders tend to occur together and to be referred to as diffuse esophageal spasm, although there is disagreement on the classification of esophageal motility disorders. The symptoms of esophageal spasm are intermittent chest pain and dysphagia in which food seems to become stuck in the body of the esophagus (Castell, 1976). The sharp chest pains produced by esophageal spasm are often mistaken for angina, a mistake that is reinforced by the fact that nitroglycerine, the smooth muscle relaxant normally given for angina, also relieves esophageal spasm. Esophageal spasm is reported to be common, but the exact prevalence is not known.

The etiology of diffuse esophageal spasm is unknown. Histological studies of the esophagus reveal no abnormalities in the myenteric nervous system, but there are reports that some patients show a denervation-type hyperresponsivity to cholinergic stimulation suggestive of vagal nerve degeneration (Mellow, 1977).

Although the role of psychological factors in diffuse esophageal spasm is controversial, there is abundant evidence that psychological stressors can provoke esophageal motility disorders (Faulkner, 1940;

Jacobson, 1927; Rubin, Nagler, Spiro, & Pilot, 1962; Stacher, Steinringer, Blau, & Landgraf, 1979; Wolf & Almy, 1949). An association between esophageal motility disorders and the presence of psychopathology has also been established (Clouse & Lustman, 1983). In blind psychiatric interviews, psychiatrists assigned DSM-III diagnoses to 84% of patients with esophageal motility disorders compared to only 31% of patients with normal esophageal motility. The psychiatric diagnoses most frequently encountered were depression, anxiety, phobia, and somatization disorder.

Latimer (1976) described a biofeedback treatment for diffuse esophageal spasm in a single-case study. His anxious, depressed patient was initially treated with progressive muscle relaxation training with the result that the frequency of painful esophageal spasm decreased from 10 hours per week to one hour per week. However, food continued to become stuck in the patient's esophagus occasionally, and the motility of her esophagus continued to be abnormal. Biofeedback of esophageal contractions was then used to teach her to swallow twice in close succession in a manner that was found empirically to inhibit the spasm of the lower esophagus. This resulted in a substantial further reduction in the frequency of her symptoms that was well maintained at follow-up 6 months later. This innovative approach to treatment warrants further investigation.

GLOBUS SENSATION

Globus sensation or globus hystericus refers to the feeling of a lump in the throat that often accompanies strong emotion. In extreme cases, the patient may feel unable to swallow. Globus is a common complaint that is acknowledged by 18% (Watson, Sullivan, Corke, & Rush, 1978) to 46% (Thompson & Heaton, 1982) of the population, but it is usually benign and does not result in a request for treatment.

The pathophysiological mechanism of globus sensation is disputed. Malcomson (1968) and Freeland, Ardran, and Emrys-Roberts (1974) have argued that the sensation occurs secondary to reflux exophagitis, whereas others (Lehtinen & Puhakka, 1976; Watson & Sullivan, 1974) suggest that the symptoms are due to spasm of the striated muscles that form the upper esophageal sphincter. In any case, there is epidemiological evidence to suggest that these symptoms occur more often in anxious individuals and that they are precipitated by psychological stress or strong emotion (Lehtinen & Puhakka, 1976; Thompson & Heaton, 1986).

In a case report, Haynes (1976) outlined a biofeedback treatment for upper esophageal dysphagia that was presumably related to globus. His patient reported that constriction of the throat muscles prevented her from swallowing and that these symptoms were worse when she was distressed. Haynes used forehead EMG biofeedback to teach this patient to relax and reported a complete remission of symptoms. No published studies have attempted to replicate this approach to treatment.

RUMINATION SYNDROME

Rumination syndrome refers to the regurgitation of previously ingested food into the mouth where it is rechewed and reswallowed or spit out. It is apparently rare in the general population, but is reported to occur in 6% to 10% of retarded residents of institutions (Ball, Hendrickson, & Clayton, 1974; Singh, 1981). Rumination may result in death in 15% to 20% of retarded children (Einhorn, 1972; Kanner, 1972) as a result of dehydration, malnutrition, or aspiration of food into the lungs. In adults of normal intelligence rumination appears to be benign.

The regurgitation that makes rumination possible is a voluntary act, although it is sometimes done without apparent awareness. It involves a brisk contraction of the abdominal wall muscles to force the food up the esophagus, and it may also be preceeded by stimulating the throat to elicit a gag reflex. Regurgitation and rumination appear to occur as self-stimulatory behaviors. There are case reports that suggest that rumination can become a response to anxiety in adults of normal intelligence (Kanner, 1936), but this is poorly documented.

Two psychological approaches have been used successfully to treat rumination syndrome in infants: increased holding; and punishment with electric shock, lemon juice injected into the child's mouth, or time out from social interaction (Pazulinec & Sajwaj, 1983). These procedures were reviewed in the 1978 Task Force Report. They work well for infants and retarded individuals, but they are not practical for adults.

Johnson (1980) described a biofeedback procedure for an adult ruminator that appears very promising. Having noted that regurgitation in this patient was always preceeded by a brisk contraction of the abdominal wall muscles, Johnson used EMG biofeedback of abdominus rectus muscle activity to teach his patient to relax these muscles and then to eat while keeping these muscles relaxed. This resulted in rapid elimination of reflux. Shay, Rosenthal, and Johnson (1983) subsequently replicated these results in a group of five patients. This biofeedback procedure appears to be appropriate and effective for the rare adult ruminator, but the procedure cannot as yet be considered to be of proven value.

CONCLUSIONS

1. Biofeedback by means of the three-balloon rectal tube is currently the treatment of choice for fecal incontinence secondary to weakness of the external anal sphincter and/or impairment of sensation for rectal distension. This treatment has not been tested against alternative treatment in controlled trials, but multiple replications by independent investigators show that it is effective and cost-effective.

2. EMG biofeedback by means of an anal plug electrode to detect contractions of the external anal sphincter appears also to be effective for fecal incontinence, and it provides a less costly alternative to manometric (balloon) biofeedback because the equipment is less expensive. However, more extensive clinical trials are required to firmly establish the value of EMG biofeedback for fecal incontinence.

3. Current research suggests that forehead EMG biofeedback may have value as adjunctive treatment for irritable bowel syndrome when combined with psychotherapeutic strategies to teach the patient how to cope with psychological stressors. Additional research is needed to establish the specific value of biofeedback in the treatment of this disorder.

4. For peptic ulcer disease, specific biofeedback to alter gastric acid secretion or gastric motility does not appear to be a cost-effective alternative to pharmacological treatment with cimetidine, ranitidine, or antacids. Uncontrolled studies suggest that nonspecific biofeedback, such as forehead EMG biofeedback training, may be a useful adjunct to stress management training, but more research is needed to prove this.

5. Innovative biofeedback treatment procedures have been reported for (a) control of the discharge from a colostomy, (b) treatment of constipation due to outlet obstruction, (c) treatment of adult rumination syndrome, (d) dysphagia associated with upper esophageal sphincter muscles, (e) esophageal spasm, and (f) gastroesophageal reflux. However, effectiveness has not yet been demonstrated for these applications.

ACKNOWLEDGMENTS

Carol Schneider and Ned Snyder made valuable contributions to the report.

REFERENCES

Aleo, S., & Nicassio, P. (1978). Auto-regulation of duodenal ulcer disease: A preliminary report of four cases. *Proceedings of the Biofeedback Society of America (Ninth Annual Meeting).* Denver, Colorado: Biofeedback Society of America. Pp. 278–281. Abstract.

Alexander, F., French, T. M., & Pollock, G. H. (1968). *Psychosomatic specificity, Vol. 1.* Chicago, IL: University of Chicago Press.

Almy, T. P. (1951). Experimental studies on the irritable colon. *American Journal of Medicine, 9,* 60–67.

Almy, T. P. (1977). Wrestling with the irritable colon. *Medical Clinics of North America, 62,* 203–210.

American Psychiatric Association. (1980). *Diagnostic and statistical manual of mental disorders* (3rd ed.). Washington, DC: Author.

Ball, T. S., Hendricksen, H., & Clayton, J. A. (1974). A special feeding technique for chronic regurgitation. *American Journal of Mental Deficiency, 78,* 486–493.

Beaty, E. T. (1976). Feedback assisted relaxation training as a treatment for peptic ulcers. *Biofeedback and Self-Regulation, 1,* 323–324.

Bellman, M. (1966). Studies on encopresis. *Acta Paediatrica Scandinavica, 56* (Suppl. 170).

Bennett, J. R., & Hendrix, T. R. (1970). Diffuse esophageal spasm: A disorder with more than one cause. *Gastroenterology, 59,* 273–279.

Binder, V., Both, H., Hansen, P. K., Hendriksen, C., Kreiner, S., & Torp-Pedersen, K. (1982). Incidence and prevalence of ulcerative colitis and Chrohn's disease in the county of Copenhagen, 1962 to 1978. *Gastroenterology, 83,* 563–568.

Blum, A. L., Peter, P., & Krejs, G. J. (1975). Pathogenesis and aetiology of ulcer disease. Part II. Duodenal ulcer. *Acta Hepato-Gastroenterologica, 22,* 123–128.

Bolin, T. D., Davis, A. E., & Duncombe, V. M. (1982). A prospective study of persistent diarrhoea. *Australian and New Zealand Journal of Medicine, 12,* 22–26.

Bonnevie, O. (1975a). The incidence of gastric ulcer in Copenhagen County. *Scandanavian Journal of Gastroenterology, 10,* 231–239.

Bonnevie, O. (1975b). The incidence of duodenal ulcer in Copenhagen County. *Scandanavian Journal of Gastroenterology, 10,* 385–393.

Brocklehurst, J. C. (1972). Bowel management in the neurologically disabled. The problems of old age. *Proceedings of the Royal Society of Medicine, 65,* 66–69.

Bueno-Miranda, F., Cerulli, M., & Schuster, M. M. (1976). Operant conditioning of colonic motility in irritable bowel syndrome (IBS). *Gastroenterology. 70,* 867. Abstract.

Bueno, L., Fioramonti, J., Frexinos, J., & Ruckebusch, Y. (1980). Colonic myoelectrical activity in diarrhea and constipation. *Hepato-Gastroenterology, 27,* 381–389.

Castell, D. O. (1976). Achalasia and diffuse esophageal spasm. *Archives of Internal Medicine, 136,* 571–579.

Cerulli, M. A., Nikoomanesh, P., & Schuster, M. M. (1979). Progress in biofeedback conditioning for fecal incontinence. *Gastroenterology, 76,* 742–746.

Chaudhary, N. A., & Truelove, S. C. (1962). The irritable bowel syndrome: A study of the clinical features, predisposing causes, and the prognosis in 130 cases. *Quarterly Journal of Medicine, 31,* 307–323.

Clouse, R. E., & Lustman, P. J. (1983). Psychiatric illness and contraction abnormalities of the esophagus. *New England Journal of Medicine, 309,* 1337–1342.

Connell, A. M. (1962). The motility of the pelvic colon. II. Paradoxical motility in diarrhoea and constipation. *Gut, 3,* 342–348.

Deckner, C. W., Hill, J. T., & Bourne, J. R. (1972). Shaping of human gastric motility. *Proceedings of the 80th Annual Meeting of the American Psychological Association.* Washington, DC: American Psychological Association.

Denis, P., Cayron, G., & Galmiche, J. P. (1981). Biofeedback: The light at the end of the tunnel? Maybe for constipation. *Gastroenterology, 80,* 1089–1090.

Drossman, D. A., Sandler, R. S., McKee, D. C., & Lovitz, A. J. (1982). Bowel patterns among subjects not seeking health care: Use of a questionnaire to identify a population with bowel dysfunction. *Gastroenterology, 83,* 529–534.

Engel, B. T., Nikoomanesh, P., & Schuster, M. M. (1974). Operant conditioning of rectosphincteric responses in the treatment of fecal incontinence. *New England Journal of Medicine, 290,* 646–649.

Engel, G. L. (1954). Studies of ulcerative colitis. I. Clinical data bearing on the nature of the somatic process. *Psychosomatic Medicine, 16,* 496–501.

Einhorn, A. H. (1972). Rumination syndrome (merycism or merycasm). In H. L. Barnett (Ed.), *Pediatrics* (pp. 1576–1578). New York: Appleton-Century-Crofts.

Enck, P., Steckler, I., Whitehead, W. E., Tucker, H., & Schuster, M. M. (1984). Lactose intolerance versus irritable bowel syndrome: Physiological and psychological comparison. *Gastroenterology, 86,* 1070.

Esler, M. D., & Goulston, K. J. (1973). Levels of anxiety in colonic disorders. *New England Journal of Medicine, 288,* 16–20.

Faulkner, W. B., Jr. (1940). Severe esophageal spasm: An evaluation of suggestion-therapy as determined by means of the esophagoscope. *Psychosomatic Medicine, 2,* 139–140.

Fava, G. A., & Pavan, L. (1976–1977) Large bowel disorders. I. Illness configuration and life events. *Psychotherapy and Psychosomatics, 27,* 93–99.

Ferguson, A., Sircus, W., & Eastwood, M. A. (1977). Frequency of "functional" gastrointestinal disorders. *Lancet, 2,* 613–614.

Freeland, A. P., Ardran, G. M., & Emrys-Roberts, E. (1974). Globus hystericus and reflux oesophagitis. *Journal of Laryngology, 88,* 1025–1031.

Furman, S. (1973). Intestinal biofeedback in functional diarrhea: A preliminary report. *Journal of Behavior Therapy and Experimental Psychiatry, 4,* 317–321.

Giles, S. L. (1978). Separate and combined effects of biofeedback training and brief individual psychotherapy in the treatment of gastrointestinal disorders. *Dissertation Abstracts International, 39,*(5-B), 2495.

Goldenberg, D. A., Hodges, K., Hersh, T., & Jinich, H. (1980). Biofeedback therapy for fecal incontinence. *American Journal of Gastroenterology, 74,* 342–345.

Gorman, P. J. (1976). Cephalic influences on human gastric acid secretion and their voluntary control through feedback training. *Dissertation Abstracts International, 36,* 6413-B. (University Microfilms No. 76-6661).

Grace, W. J., Pinsky, R. H., & Wolff, H. G. (1954). The treatment of ulcerative colitis. II. *Gastroenterology, 26,* 462–468.

Groen, J., & Bastiaans, J. (1951). Psychotherapy of ulcerative colitis. *Gastroenterology, 17,* 344–352.

Hamilton, J. R., Bruce, G. A., Abdourhaman, M., & Gall, D. G. (1979). Inflammatory bowel disease in children and adolescents. *Advances in Pediatrics, 26,* 311–341.

Harvey, R. F., Salih, S. Y., & Read, A. E. (1983). Organic and functional disorders in 2000 gastroenterology outpatients. *Lancet, 1,* 632–634.

Haskell, B., & Rovner, H. (1967), Electromyography in the management of the incompetent anal sphincter. *Diseases of the Colon and Rectum, 10,* 81–84.

Haynes, S. N. (1976). Electromyographic biofeedback treatment of a woman with chronic dysphagia. *Biofeedback and Self-Regulation, 1,* 121–126.

Heefner, J. D., Wilder, R. M., & Wilson, I. D. (1978). Irritable colon and depression. *Psychosomatics, 19,* 540–547.

Henderson, R. D. (1980). *Motor disorders of the esophagus* (2nd ed.) Baltimore, MD: Williams & Wilkins.

Hislop, I. G. (1971).Psychological significance of the irritable colon syndrome. *Gut, 12,* 452–457.

Holdstock, D. J., Misiewicz, J. J., & Waller, S. L. (1969). Observations on the mechanism of abdominal pain. *Gut, 10,* 19–31.

Jacobson, E. (1927). Spastic esophagus and mucous colitis: Etiology and treatment by progressive relaxation. Archives of Internal Medicine, 39, 433–445.

Johnson, L. F. (1980). 24-hour pH monitoring in the study of gastroesophageal reflux. Journal of Clinical Gastroenterology, 2, 387–399.

Kanner, L. (1936). Historical notes on rumination in man. Medical Life, 43, 26–61.

Kanner, L. (1972). Child psychiatry (4th ed.). Springfield, IL: Charles C Thomas.

Karush, A., Daniels, G., Flood, C., O'Connor, J., Druss, R., & Sweeting, J. (1977). Psychotherapy in chronic ulcerative colitis. Philadelphia, PA: W. B. Saunders.

Kirsner, J. B., & Shorter, R. G. (1982). Recent developments in "nonspecific" inflammatory bowel disease. New England Journal of Medicine, 306, 775–785, 837–848.

Latimer, P. R. (1978). Crohn's disease: A review of the psychological and social outcome. Psychological Medicine, 8, 649–656.

Latimer, P. R. (1981). Biofeedback and self-regulation in the treatment of diffuse esophageal spasm: A single-case study. Biofeedback and Self-Regulation, 6, 181–189.

Latimer, P. R. (1983). Functional gastrointestinal disorders: A behavioral approach. New York: Springer.

Latimer, P., Sarna, S., Campbell, D., Latimer, M., Waterfall, W., & Daniel, E. E. (1981). Colonic motor and myoelectrical activity: A comparative study of normal subjects, psychoneurotic patients, and patients with irritable bowel syndrome. Gastroenterology, 80, 893–901.

Latimer, P. R., Campbell, D., & Kasperski, J. (1984). A components analysis of biofeedback in the treatment of fecal incontinence. Biofeedback and Self-Regulation, 9, 311–324.

Lehtinen, V., & Puhakka, H. (1976). A psychosomatic approach to the globus hystericus syndrome. Acta Psychiatrica Scandanavica, 53, 21–28.

Levine, M. D., & Bakow, H. (1976). Children with encopresis: A study of treatment outcome. Pediatrics, 58, 845–852.

Liss, J. L., Alpers, D., & Woodruff, R. A., Jr. (1973). The irritable colon syndrome and psychiatric illness. Diseases of the Nervous System, 34, 151–157.

Lowery, S. P., Srour, J. W., Whitehead, W. E., & Schuster, M. M. (1985). Habit training as treatment of encopresis secondary to chronic constipation. Journal of Pediatric Gastroenterology and Nutrition, 4, 397–401.

MRC. (1978, December) Ad hoc meeting of faecal incontinence. Medical Research Council of Great Britain.

MacLeod, J. H. (1979). Biofeedback in the management of partial anal incontinence: A preliminary report. Diseases of the Colon and Rectum, 22, 169–171.

MacLeod, J. H. (1983). Biofeedback in the management of partial anal incontinence. Diseases of the Colon and Rectum, 26, 244–246.

Malcolmson, K. G. (1966). Radiological findings in globus hystericus. British Journal of Radiology, 39, 583–586.

Manning, A. P., Thompson, W. G., Heaton, K. W., & Morris, A. F. (1978). Towards positive diagnosis of the irritable bowel. British Medical Journal, 2, 653–654.

Martelli, H., Devroede, G., Arhan, P., & Duguay, C. (1978). Mechanisms of idiopathic constipation: Outlet obstruction. Gastroenterology, 75, 623–631.

McIllmurry, M. B., & Langman, M. J. S. (1975). Large bowel cancer: Causation and management. Gut, 17, 815–820.

Mellow, M. (1977). Symptomatic diffuse esophageal spasm: Manometric follow-up and response to cholinergic stimulation and cholinesterase inhibition. Gastroenterology, 73, 237–240.

Milne, J. S. (1976). Prevalence of incontinence in the elderly age groups. In E. L. Willington (Ed.), Incontinence in the Elderly (pp. 9–21). London: Academic Press.

Monk, M., Mendeloff, A. I., Siegel, C. I., & Lilienfeld, A. (1967). An epidemiological study of ulcerative colitis and regional enteritis among adults in Baltimore. I. Hospital incidence and prevalence, 1960 to 1963. Gastroenterology, 53, 198–210.

Moore, J. G., & Schenkenberg, T. (1974). Psychic control of gastric acid: Response to anticipated feeding and biofeedback training in a man. *Gastroenterology, 66,* 954–959.

National Center for Health Statistics. (1974). Mortality trends for leading causes of death, U.S., 1950–1969. *Vital and Health Statistics.* Series 20, No. 16 (DHEW Publication No. HRA 74-1853). Washington, DC: U.S. Government Printing Office.

Olness, K., McParland, F. A., & Piper, J. (1980) Biofeedback: A new modality in the management of children with fecal soiling. *Journal of Pediatrics, 96,* 505–509.

Palmer, R. L., Stonehill, E., Crisp, A. H., Waller, S. L., & Misiewicz, J. J. (1974). Psychological characteristics of patients with the irritable bowel syndrome. *Postgraduate Medical Journal, 50,* 416–419.

Pazulinec, R., & Sajwaj, T. (1983). Psychological treatment approaches to psychogenic vomiting and rumination. In R. Hoelzl & W. E. Whitehead (Eds.), *Psychophysiology of the gastrointestinal tract: Experimental and clinical applications* (pp. 43–63). New York: Plenum Press.

Peterson, W. L., Sturdevant, R. A. L., Frankl, H. D., Richardson, C. T., Isenberg, J. I., Elashoff, J. D., Sones, J. Q., Gross, R. A., McCallum, R. W., & Fordtran, J. S. (1977). Healing of duodenal ulcer with an antacid regimen. *New England Journal of Medicine, 297,* 341–345.

Pflanz, M. (1971). Epidemiological and sociocultural factors in the etiology of duodenal ulcer. *Advances in Psychosomatic Medicine, 6,* 121–151.

Reboa, G., Piccardo, A., Giusto, F., & Riboli, E. R. (1982, September). *Biofeedback: A new method for the recovery of continence in patients with permanent colostomy.* Paper presented at The First European Symposium on Gastrointestinal Motility, Bologna, Italy.

Reboa, G., Piccardo, A., Frascio, M., Pitto, G., & Riboli, E. B. (1983). The biofeed-back: A new method for the recovery of continence in patients with permanent colostomy. In G. Labo & M. Bortolotti (Eds.), *Gastrointestinal motility.* Verona, Italy: Cortina International.

Richard, W. C., & Fell, R. D. (1974). Health factors in police job stress. In W. H. Kroes & J. J. Hurrell (Eds.), *Job stress and the police officer: Identifying stress reduction techniques.* (HEW Publication No. NIOSH 76-187). Washington, DC: U.S. Government Printing Office.

Rubin, J., Nagler, R., Spiro, H. M., & Pilot, M. L. (1962). Measuring the effect of emotions on esophageal motility. *Psychosomatic Medicine, 24,* 170–176.

Schaefer, C. E. (1979). *Childhood encopresis and enuresis: Causes and therapy.* New York: Van Nostrand Reinhold.

Schiller, L. R., Santa Ana, C., Davis, G. R., & Fordtran, J. S. (1979). Fecal incontinence in chronic diarrhea. Report of a case with improvement after training with rectally infused saline. *Gastroenterology, 77,* 751–753.

Schneider, C. (1983, March). *Biofeedback treatment of irritable bowel syndrome.* Paper presented at the annual meeting of the Biofeedback Society of America, Denver, CO.

Scheurer, U., Witzel, L., Halter, F., Keller, H.-M., Huber, R., & Galeazzi, R. (1977). Gastric and duodenal ulcer healing under placebo treatment. *Gastroenterology, 72,* 838–841.

Schuster, M. M. (1975). The riddle of the sphincters. *Gastroenterology, 69,* 249–262.

Schuster, M. M. (1977). Constipation and anorectal disorders. *Clinics in Gastroenterology, 6,* 643–657.

Schuster, M. M., Nikoomanesh, P., & Wells, D. (1973). Biofeedback control of lower esophageal sphincter contraction. *Rediconti di Gastroenterologia, 5,* 14–18.

Shay, S. S., Rosenthal, R., & Johnson, L. F. (1983, March). Biofeedback therapy of patients with chronic dyspepsia and gastroesophageal reflux. Paper presented at the Fourth Annual Meeting of the Society for Behavioral Medicine, Baltimore, MD.

Siegel, D., Tucker, H., Enck, P., Whitehead, W., & Schuster, M. M. (1984). Symptoms differentiating irritable bowel syndrome (IBS) from other G.I. disorders. *Gastroenterology, 86,* 1251.

Singh, N. N. (1981). Rumination. In N. R. Ellis (Ed.), *International Review of Research in Mental Retardation, Vol. 10*. New York: Academic Press.

Snape, W. J., Jr., Carlson, G. M., & Cohen, S. (1976). Colonic myoelectric activity in the irritable bowel syndrome. *Gastroenterology, 70*, 326–330.

Spiegel, M. K., Johannes, R. S., Shapiro, M., Malley, J., & Hendrix, T. R. (1984). A prospective study of the symptom complex of irritable bowel syndrome. *Gastroenterology, 86*, 1263.

Spiegelman, M., & Erhardt, C. L. (1974). Mortality in the United States by cause. In E. L. Erhardt & J. E. Berlin (Eds.), *Mortality and morbidity in the United States*. Cambridge: Harvard University Press.

Stacher, G., Steinringer, H., Blau, A., & Landgraf, M. (1979). Acoustically evoked esophageal contractions and defense reaction. *Psychophysiology, 16*, 234–241.

Svedlund, J., Sjodin, I., Ottosson, J-O., & Dotevall, H. (1983). Controlled study of psychotherapy in irritable bowel syndrome. *Lancet, 2*, 589–592.

Taylor, I., Darby, C., & Hammond, P. (1978). Comparison of rectosigmoid myoelectric activity in the irritable colon syndrome during relapses and remissions. *Gut, 19*, 923–929.

Thomas, T. M., Plymat, K. R., Blannin, J., & Meade, T. W. (1980). Prevalence of urinary incontinence. *British Medical Journal, 281*, 1243–1245.

Thompson, W. G., & Heaton, K. W. (1980). Functional bowel disorders in apparently healthy people. *Gastroenterology, 79*, 283–288.

Thompson, W. G., & Heaton, K. W. (1982). Heartburn and globus in apparently healthy people. *Canadian Medical Association Journal, 126*, 46–48.

van Baal, J. G., Leguit, P. Jr., & Brummelkamp, W. H. (1984). Relaxation biofeedback conditioning as treatment of a disturbed defecation reflex: Report of a case. *Diseases of the Colon and Rectum, 27*, 187–189.

Van Nostrand, J. F., Zappolo, A., Hing, E., Bloom, B., Hirsch, B., & Foley, D. J. (1979). The national nursing home survey: 1977 summary for the United States. (DHEW Publication No. PHS 79-1794). Washington, DC: U.S. Government Printing Office, Statistics Series 13–43.

Wald, A. (1981a). Biofeedback therapy for fecal incontinence. *Annals of Internal Medicine, 95*, 146–149.

Wald, A. (1981b). Use of biofeedback in treatment of fecal incontinence in patients with meningomyelocele. *Pediatrics, 68*, 45–49.

Wald, A. (1983). Biofeedback for neurogenic fecal incontinence: Rectal sensation is a determinant of outcome. *Journal of Pediatric Gastroenterology and Nutrition, 2*, 302–306.

Wald, A., & Tunuguntla, A. K. (1984). Anorectal sensorimotor dysfunction in fecal incontinence and diabetes mellitus: Modification with biofeedback therapy. *New England Journal of Medicine, 310*, 1282–1287.

Walker, B. B., Lawton, C. A., & Sandman, C. A. (1978). Voluntary control of electrogastric activity. *Psychosomatic Medicine, 40*, 610–619.

Watson, W. C., Sullivan, S. N., Corke, M., & Rush, D. (1974). Hypertonicity of the cricopharyngeal sphincter: A cause of globus sensation. *Lancet, 2*, 1417–1419.

Weinstock, S. A. (1976). The reestablishment of intestinal control in functional colitis. *Biofeedback and Self-Regulation, 1*, 324.

Welgan, P. R. (1974). Learned control of gastric acid secretions in peptic ulcer patients. *Psychosomatic Medicine, 36*, 411–419.

Welgan, P. R. (1977). Biofeedback control of stomach acid secretions and gastrointestinal reactions. In J. Beatty & H. Legewie (Eds.), *Biofeedback and behavior*. New York: Plenum Press.

Welgan, P., Meshkinpour, H., & Hoehler, F. (1985). The effect of stress on colon motor and electrical activity in irritable bowel syndrome. *Psychosomatic Medicine, 47*, 139–149.

Wesley, J. R., Coran, A. G., Sarahan, T. M., Klein, M. D., & White, S. J. (1981). The need for evaluation of gastroesophageal reflux in brain-damaged children referred for feeding gastrostomy. *Journal of Pediatric Surgery, 16,* 866–871.

Whitehead, W. E. (1978). Biofeedback in the treatment of gastrointestinal disorders. *Biofeedback and Self-Regulation, 3,* 375–384.

Whitehead, W. E. (1985). Psychotherapy and biofeedback in the treatment of irritable bowel syndrome. In N. E. Read (Ed.), *Irritable bowel syndrome.* New York: Academic Press.

Whitehead, W. E., & Drescher, V. M. (1980). Perception of gastric contractions and self-control of gastric motility. *Psychophysiology, 17,* 552–558.

Whitehead, W. E., & Schuster, M. M. (1983). Manometric and electromyographic techniques for assessment of the anorectal mechanism for continence and defecation. In R. Hoelzl & W. E. Whitehead (Eds.), *Psychophysiology of the gastrointestinal tract: Experimental and clinical applications* (pp. 311–329). New York: Plenum Press.

Whitehead, W. E., & Schuster, M. M. (1985). *Gastrointestinal Disorders: Behavioral and Physiological Basis for Treatment.* New York: Academic Press.

Whitehead, W. E., Renault, P. F., & Goldiamond, I. (1975). Modification of human gastric acid secretion with operant-conditioning procedures. *Journal of Applied Behavior Analysis, 8,* 147–156.

Whitehead, W. E., Engel, B. T., & Schuster, M. M. (1980). Irritable bowel syndrome: Physiological and psychological differences between diarrhea-predominant and constipation-predominant patients. *Digestive Diseases and Sciences, 25,* 404–413.

Whitehead, W. E., Orr, W. C., Engel, B. T., & Schuster, M. M. (1981). External anal sphincter response to rectal distention: Learned response or reflex. *Psychophysiology, 19,* 57–62.

Whitehead, W. E., Parker, L. H., Masek, B. J., Cataldo, M. F., & Freeman, J. M. (1981). Biofeedback treatment of fecal incontinence in patients with myelomenigocele. *Developmental Medicine & Child Neurology, 23,* 313–322.

Whitehead, W. E., Winget, C., Fedoravicius, A. S., Wooley, S., & Blackwell, B. (1982). Learned illness behavior in patients with irritable bowel syndrome and peptic ulcer. *Digestive Diseases and Sciences, 27,* 202–208.

Whitehead, W. E., Burgio, K. L., & Engel, B. T. (1985) Biofeedback treatment of fecal incontinence in geriatric patients. *Journal of the American Geriatric Society, 33,* 320–324.

Whitehead, W. E., Parker, L. H., Bosmajian, L. S., Morrill-Corbin, E. D., Middaugh, S., Garwood, M., Cataldo, M. F., & Freeman, J. (1986) Treatment of fecal incontinence in children with spina bifida: Comparison of biofeedback and behavior modification. *Archives of Physical Medicine and Rehabilitation, 67,* 218–224.

Winship, D. H. (1978). Cimetidine in the treatment of duodenal ulcer: Review and commentary. *Gastroenterology, 74,* 402–406.

Wolf, S., & Almy, T. P. (1949). Experimental observations on cardiospasm in man. *Gastroenterology, 13,* 401–421.

Young, G. C. (1973). The treatment of childhood encopresis by conditioned gastroileal reflex training. *Behavior Research and Therapy, 11,* 499–503.

Young, S. J., Alpers, D. H., Norland, C. C., & Woodruff, R. A., Jr. (1976). Psychiatric illness and the irritable bowel syndrome: Practical implications for the primary physician. *Gastroenterology, 70,* 162–166.

6

Biofeedback in the Management of Chronic Pain Syndromes

Francis J. Keefe and Timothy J. Hoelscher

Chronic pain is a major medical problem. Treatments for chronic pain represent a major portion of medical costs. Costs include payments for hospitalization and outpatient treatments, workmen's compensation and disability payments, and time lost from work. These costs are staggering and growing rapidly. The estimated cost in the United States for only one of these disorders, low back pain, is one billion dollars per year (Bonica, 1980).

Chronic pain is defined as pain of at least 6 months' duration that is nonmalignant in etiology. Patients suffering from chronically painful conditions often develop behavioral and psychological problems (Keefe, 1982). These include a sedentary life-style with a very limited range of activities, excessive dependence on spouse and family, narcotic addiction, anxiety, depression, and hypochrondriasis. Chronic pain patients can basically be described as failures of traditional medical and surgical treatment (Urban, 1982). Most patients have undergone extensive treatment aimed at removing underlying somatic pathology that may be responsible for their pain. In most cases, further medical and surgical intervention is ruled out either because these treatments would have negative iatrogenic effects or because they are unlikely to help (Urban, 1982).

Preparation of this manuscript was supported by a National Institute of Mental Health Grant Number 1 R03 MH38407-01 entitled "Behavioral Assessment of Chronic Low Back Pain."

Francis J. Keefe and Timothy J. Hoelscher • Department of Psychiatry, Box 3926, Duke University Medical Center, Durham, NC 27710.

There is growing recognition of the importance of behavioral and psychological factors in the maintenance of chronic pain (Keefe, 1982). Primary-care physicians as well as medical and surgical specialists are beginning to incorporate psychological and behavioral techniques as a routine part of assessment and management of chronic pain patients. Specialized behavioral treatment programs also have been developed to treat chronic pain. Although these programs use a variety of treatment methods, almost all have a biofeedback component.

The purpose of this chapter is to review critically the status of bio-feedback as a technique for the management of chronic pain syndromes. We describe the application of biofeedback methods to the following populations: low back pain, central pain, rheumatoid arthritis, dysme-norrhea, and mixed chronic pain syndromes. For each pain disorder, a brief description of symptoms, etiology, and traditional treatment methods is provided. We then review published studies in which biofeedback has been used as a treatment. The rigor and methodological sophistication of research in that area is evaluated. Each section concludes with a statement regarding the efficacy of biofeedback. This chapter ends with a discussion of relevant conceptual, practical, and research issues.

LOW BACK PAIN

Introduction

Low back pain is one of the most common types of chronic pain (Nagi, Riley, & Newby, 1973). Estimates indicate that nearly 80% of adults in Western societies will have back pain severe enough to warrant at least one week of bed rest at some point in their adult life (Dega, 1983). The etiology of low back pain is varied and complex (Caillet, 1968; Flor & Turk, 1984). Possible sources of low back pain include disease processes (e.g., metastatic, visceral, or vascular), degenerative disorders (e.g., spondylosis, osteoarthritis), trauma, and muscular and ligamentous dysfunction. Patients referred for biofeedback or behavioral pain management often present with back pain secondary to a combination of mechanical, degenerative, and discogenic problems.

Mechanical low back pain is related to misuse of the low back musculature during static postures and/or dynamic activities. Reactions such as protective guarding and splinting, which first occur in response to injury, may become habitual and lead to chronic muscle contraction. Treatment typically involves education in proper body mechanics, abdominal strengthening exercises, and exercises designed to stretch the low back, hamstrings, hip flexors, and heel cords. In most cases, mechanical low back pain resolves within a fairly short period of time. In some cases, however, postural abnormalities persist, leading to chronic discomfort.

Another common cause of persistent low back pain is disc disease. Degenerative changes in the intervertebral discs can produce compression of nerve roots. Lumbar disc herniation produces symptoms of pain in the lower back radiating down the legs. Neurological examination is required for diagnosis. Treatment is usually conservative and initially consists of bed rest, minor analgesics, and muscle relaxants. Patients who have motor weakness or who display progressive neurologic signs are candidates for surgical treatments, such as laminectomy. The success rates of laminectomies varies greatly (Caillet, 1968). Hirsch (1956) estimates that only 15% obtain complete, permanent pain relief following lumbar disc surgery. Patients having positive neurological findings on examination typically have the best response to surgical treatment (MacNab, 1977).

Many patients presenting with persistent pain in the low back region have had a course of numerous surgical treatments and a full range of conservative approaches. It needs to be emphasized that this group of patients differs greatly from those suffering from mechanical low back pain of a much less chronic nature. The precise etiology of chronic low back pain is unknown. Chronic pain is perhaps best viewed as resulting from a variety of interacting somatic and psychological factors (Flor & Turk, 1984; Turk & Flor, 1984). Patients who suffer from intractable pain unrelieved by surgery, the so-called failed back syndrome, exhibit entrenched behavioral problems that are extremely difficult to modify (Keefe, 1982).

The BSA Task Force Report, "Biofeedback in Physical Medicine and Rehabilitation," published in 1978 (Fernando & Basmajian, 1978) reviewed only two studies in which biofeedback was used in the treatment of low back pain. They concluded that in the treatment of "low back pain due to muscle spasms, EMG biofeedback techniques are an acceptable part of treatment." As can be seen in Table 1, numerous studies examining the efficacy of biofeedback for low back pain have been conducted since the last Task Force Report.

Clinical Efficacy

All of the published biofeedback studies have utilized electromyographic (EMG) biofeedback. This is not surprising given the incidence of mechanical low back pain and the frequent finding of mechanical problems even in those patients presenting with pain due to lumbar

TABLE 1. Low Back Pain

Authors	Research design	Population	Treatments	Duration of treatment	Outcome	Follow-up	Comments
Seres & Newman (1976)	Single-group outcome study	100 consecutive low back pain patients with a mean duration of pain of 5.7 years	Operant conditioning, flexion exercises, EMG biofeedback, relaxation training, transcutaneous electrical nerve stimulation (TENS), education and psychotherapy	Inpatient treatment averaging 21 days; EMG-biofeedback sessions 3–5 times per week	Large reductions in pain medication and increased mobility and exercise tolerance	Improvement maintained at 3-month follow-up	Pain diaries not used; EMG electrode placement not specified
Gentry & Bernal (1977)	Systematic case studies	*Case 1:* 42-year-old male with chronic back pain (duration unspecified) *Case 2:* 39-year-old female with chronic neck and left shoulder pain of 5 years duration	EMG-biofeedback and relaxation training; Electrode placement: Case 1 = frontalis, Case 2 = trapezius	Case 1: 13, 25-minute sessions Case 2: 9, 25-minute sessions	Both patients showed decreases in pain intensity and EMG levels	Both patients maintained improvement at 6-week follow-up	

Study	Design	Subjects	Treatment	Treatment length	Results	Follow-up	Comments
Gottlieb et al. (1977)	Single-group outcome study	72 unemployed low back pain patients averaging 43 years of age with a mean duration of pain of 3.6 years; 97% were diagnosed as having organic involvement and 60% had pending litigation	EMG biofeedback, psychotherapy, self-medication reduction program, physical reconditioning, vocational counseling, education, and therapeutic milieu	Inpatient treatment averaging 45 days	50 of the 72 patients were judged to have shown significant functional and clinical improvement	Improvement was maintained by 33 of 40 patients evaluated at 1-month follow-up; 8 patients obtained employment and 23 entered job training programs	EMG electrode placement not specified
Newman, Seres, Yospe, & Garlington (1978)	Follow-up study of Seres & Newman, 1976 (above)	23 men and 13 women averaging 44.6 years of age with a mean duration of pain of 6.3 years; patients had a mean history of 2.1 surgeries				At 18-month follow-up, patients maintained reductions in medication intake and increased mobility and exercise tolerance	Follow-up data collected on only 36 of the 100 patients treated in the Seres and Newman (1976) study
Belar & Cohen, 1979	Systematic case study	71-year-old female with a 3-year history of pain in her right upper back with paravertebral muscle spasms in the area of the right inferior scapular angle	Progressive relaxation and EMG biofeedback training of the involved musculature	17 sessions over 9 weeks	Marked decrease in EMG levels and frequency of backaches	Improvement was maintained 12 weeks after the last training session	

Continued

TABLE 1. (*Continued*)

Nouwen & Solinger (1979)	Controlled group outcome study	15 males and 11 females averaging 34.5 years of age with a mean duration of low back pain of 6.3 years	Group 1 (n = 19): biofeedback training of the erector spinae muscles Group 2 (n = 7): Waiting list control group	20, 45-minute sessions over 4 weeks	Only Group 1 showed significant decreases in reported pain and EMG levels	At 3-month follow-up, Group 1 maintained improvement in reported pain though EMG measures returned to baseline levels	Patients were asked not to use medication during the experimental period
Freeman, Calsyn, Paige, & Halar (1980)	Single-group outcome study	8 male low back pain patients; average age and mean duration of pain not given	EMG biofeedback training of the lumbosacral musculature	2, 30-minute sessions per week until patient showed a 50% reduction in baseline levels; maximum of 10 sessions	4 patients reached EMG training criterion and globally reported less pain; of the remaining 4 patients, 2 showed improvement	6 patients maintained lower EMG levels at 3-month follow-up; no pain data reported	Pain diaries not used.
Jones & Wolf (1980)	Systematic case study	35-year-old male with a 2-year history of low back pain	EMG biofeedback training of the lumbar paraspinals while standing and during trunk movement	15 sessions over 5 weeks	Increased range of motion, decreased EMG levels during movement, reduced pain intensity, and decreased medication intake	Improvement was maintained at a 10-week follow-up	

Nigl & Fischer-Williams (1980)	Anecdotal case reports	2 females (ages 34 and 35) and 2 males (ages 51 and 44) with histories of low back pain ranging from 9–16 months	Imagery-based relaxation procedures and EMG biofeedback training of the lumbosacral musculature	15–18 sessions	All cases showed decreased EMG levels and reductions in pain intensity	1-year follow-up of 1 patient revealed maintenance of improvement	Pain diaries not used
Todd & Belar (1980)	Systematic case study	44-year-old male with a 2-year history of low back pain	Progressive relaxation, stress inoculation training, and EMG biofeedback of the lumbosacral musculature	16 sessions over 10 weeks	No change in pain intensity or EMG levels; subjective feelings of depression improved	No follow-up	
Keefe, Block, Williams, & Surwit, 1981	Single-group outcome study	111 chronic low back pain patients averaging 39.4 years of age and 1.3 lumbar surgeries; mean duration of pain not given; 35% were receiving disability or other financial compensation	Progressive relaxation, EMG biofeedback from the frontalis, trapezius, and/or lumbar paraspinals, self-paced reduction of pain medications, psychotropic medication, and physical therapy	Average of 10.6 sessions	Mean decreases of 29% in pain intensity, and 31% in EMG levels; 49%of the patients decreased their pain medication intake and 63% reported increases in activity	No follow-up	Patients who experienced the greatest pain relief rated the pain as initially more severe, had continuous pain for fewer years, and were less likely to be on disability or have had multiple surgical procedures.

Continued

TABLE 1. (*Continued*)

Keefe, Schapira, Williams, Brown, & Surwit (1981)	Single-group outcome study	18 chronic low back pain patients averaging 37.2 years of age with a mean duration of pain of 4.7 years; patients averaged 1.9 surgeries	Progressive relaxation and frontalis EMG biofeedback	6–19 training sessions.	Significant within and between session decreases in EMG levels and subjective ratings of tension; significant within session reduction in pain intensity; non-significant decreases in pain intensity outside the laboratory	On a 1-year follow-up questionnaire, 9 of 13 patients responding reported improvement	
Wolf, Nacht, & Kelly (1982)	Systematic case study (A-B-A-B-A design)	22-year-old woman with low back pain of 5 months' duration	EMG biofeedback training of the lumbar paraspinals during movement	7 weeks	During the course of training, the patient showed more normal EMG levels during trunk rotation and a reduction in pain intensity	No follow-up	Normative data was obtained from Wolf Basmajian, Russe, and Kutner (1979)

Study	Design	Sample	Treatment	Sessions	Results	Follow-up	Notes
Flor, Haag, Turk, & Koehler (1983)	Controlled group outcome study	4 male and 20 female inpatients averaging 49.5 years of age with a mean duration of back or neck pain of 12.9 years	Group 1 (r = 8): Specific site EMG biofeedback plus conventional medical treatment (e.g., physical therapy). Group 2 (n = 8): Pseudotherapy plus conventional medical treatment Group 3 (n = 8): Conventional medical treatment only	12, 30–40 minute sessions over 2 weeks	Group 1 showed significantly greater decreases in pain intensity and duration, qualitative pain rating decreases on the cognitive and affective dimensions, and decreased EMG levels than Groups 2 and 3	At 4-month follow-up, Group 1 maintained improvement and Groups 2 and 3 remained unchanged	No difference in treatment credibility ratings; EMG decreases in the biofeedback group were significantly correlated with reductions in pain
Nouwen (1983)	Controlled group outcome study	10 males and 10 females averaging 42.1 years of age with a mean duration of low back pain of 11.8 yers	Group 1 (n = 10): EMG biofeedback training of the lumbar paraspinals while stancing Group 2 (n = 10): Waiting list control group	15 sessions over 3 weeks	Group 1 showed significantly greater decreases in EMG levels than Group 2; however, there were no significant group differences in daily pain diaries	No follow-up	Patients were forced to stand for the 30-minute training periods, though they were always given 2, 2–5 minute breaks during which they were allowed to sit

disc disease (discogenic low back pain). Three major biofeedback treatment approaches are evident in the literature. First, EMG biofeedback has been used to assist patients in learning generalized muscular relaxation. Two investigations conducted in our laboratory exemplify this approach (Keefe, Block, Williams, Surwit, 1981; Keefe, Schapira, Williams, Brown, & Surwit, 1981). In these studies, patients were taught relaxation skills and then encouraged to practice them in a variety of daily tasks that they found painful. Feedback was provided from the frontal region or muscles in the upper back, such as the cervical paraspinals or trapezii. EMG-assisted relaxation approaches are often utilized with those patients who are extremely anxious or who have had prior surgery on the lumbar paraspinal musculature that produces artifacts that render feedback from these regions invalid. The second major biofeedback approach involves specific training of the lumbosacral skeletal muscles during static activities. A good example of this approach is a study by Nouwen and Solinger (1979) in which patients were provided with feedback from electrodes placed over the erector spinae muscles. The patients remained in the prone position throughout training. Training in a static position is most likely to benefit those patients who have mechanical low back pain secondary to static postural abnormalities. The third approach involves training with EMG biofeedback during dynamic movement. Wolf, Basmajian, and their colleagues (Wolf, Basmajian, Russe, & Kuntner, 1979) have developed a treatment protocol based on their research on normative patterns of muscle activity in the low back region. The recent report of Wolf, Nacht, and Kelly (1982) summarizes the protocol. Briefly, EMG electrodes are placed bilaterally over the erector spinae muscles, and recordings are taken both during rest and during dynamic movements, such as flexion, rotation, and trunk extension. Although some patients display abnormal patterns at rest, many show abnormalities only when required to perform certain trunk movements (Wolf *et al.*, 1979). EMG biofeedback is then provided to teach patients more normal muscular patterns. EMG biofeedback training during dynamic activity is probably most appropriate for those patients having a significant mechanical component to their pain.

The basic characteristics of biofeedback studies with low back pain patients are presented in Table 1. As can be seen, a total of 15 published studies have been conducted. Six studies have employed single-subject designs. The results of these studies generally indicate improvement in pain and reduction of EMG levels across training. The best of these case studies is that of Wolf *et al.* (1982) in which an A-B-A-B-A design was employed. This study found consistent reductions in pain and improvements in appropriate use of back musculature during EMG-feedback training phases.

Several single group outcome studies have been conducted. In this design, outcome measures are taken during and after treatment. In most cases, EMG biofeedback was used as an adjunct to a comprehensive treatment program. Other elements of treatment include operant techniques, assertiveness training, psychotropic medications, physical therapy, and time-contingent pain medication reduction schedules. Virtually all of these studies have reported on patients suffering from intractable low back pain, with most patients having multiple surgeries, long histories of pain, and a high percentage of patients receiving disability or financial compensation payments. Despite these negative prognostic factors, most studies found significant improvements in areas of functioning and in measures of subjective and muscular tension. Pain reductions of 20% to 40% were obtained with very few patients experiencing total pain relief.

Three recent studies used controlled group designs to evaluate the specific effects of EMG biofeedback in back pain. Nouwen and Solinger (1979) compared EMG biofeedback to a waiting list control group with 26 outpatients. Based on pain diaries, the biofeedback patients showed a 40% decrease in pain intensity and duration that was largely maintained at a 3-month follow-up. In contrast, the controls showed a slight increase in pain ratings. A subsequent study by Nouwen (1983) reported no significant pain reductions using EMG biofeedback. However, subjects in this study were required to stand during the 30-minute biofeedback sessions. Nouwen noted that the prolonged duration of standing may have caused protracted ligamentous strain and increased discomfort. In the only study to control for placebo factors, Flor, Haag, Turk & Kochler, (1983) compared EMG biofeedback with a credible pseudotherapy, and conventional medical treatment with 24 inpatients. Biofeedback patients showed a 66% decrease in daily pain ratings compared to a 30% reduction in the placebo group and no change in the medical treatment alone condition. Improvement was maintained at a 4-month follow-up. Thus, two of the three controlled studies supported the effectiveness of EMG biofeedback for low back pain. It should be noted that along with a study by Turner (1982) utilizing progressive relaxation, they are among the few controlled studies examining any behavioral technique for chronic pain.

In conclusion, recent studies suggest that EMG biofeedback is superior to both conventional treatment alone and to placebo control in the management of low back pain. Follow-up data collected up to 4 months following treatment revealed good maintenance of treatment gains. Taken together, the available studies support the efficacy of EMG biofeedback in the treatment of mechanical low back pain. Although initial results are positive, further research is needed to confirm this conclusion and to clarify the precise role that EMG biofeedback may play in the management of intractable low back pain in patients having a history of lumbar disc disease. Also, studies using longer follow-up periods are clearly needed.

Specificity of Effect

In most of the studies reviewed above, biofeedback techniques were used in the context of a comprehensive treatment program. Thus, little is known about the specific effects of biofeedback in the treatment of low back pain. Specificity of effect can be better determined in studies that only used biofeedback. The study by Flor & Turk (1983) is especially noteworthy in this regard. As stated earlier, this study used a placebo control as well as a routine medical treatment control. The pain reductions in the biofeedback group doubled those achieved by patients in the placebo condition. These results tentatively suggest that biofeedback does have a specific treatment effect. However, these data are based on a single investigation, and replication studies are clearly needed.

Mechanism of Action

The precise mechanisms by which biofeedback can improve low back pain are unknown However, there are several possibilities. First, patients may improve with biofeedback by learning to reduce excessive levels of muscle tension in specific regions where pain is experienced. Evidence to support this mechanism of action would arise from significant correlations between decreases in EMG activity and reductions in subjective pain. Flor, Haag, Turk, and Koehler (1983) reported that EMG decreases were significantly correlated with pain reductions. However most other studies have not found significant correlations between these two parameters (e.g., Keefe, Schapira, et al., 1979; Nouwen & Solinger, 1979).

A second possible mechanism of action for biofeedback in the treatment of low back pain is that patients learn to produce more appropriate muscular activity in targeted muscles. Patients may be experiencing pain not simply because there is elevated EMG activity in a targeted muscle but because an abnormal *pattern* of activity in several related muscle groups is occurring. Patients with low back pain, for example, often assume guarded pain-avoidance postures in which very little muscle activity occurs in the area where they feel pain, and extremely high levels of muscle activity are evident in muscles on the opposite side of the spine. Wolf *et al.* (1982) attempted to address this mechanism of pain in their studies. Patients were taught to procedure more appropriate patterns of muscle activity during static and dynamic activities, and substantial reductions in pain were reported. Unfortunately, there is only one case study in the literature in which this approach has been used. It does appear to be a promising method for further investigation, however.

A third explanation for the efficacy of biofeedback in treating low back pain is that it helps patients by reducing anxiety and tension. Patients with chronic low back pain often learn to fear specific activities that are painful, for example, sitting for prolonged periods of time, walking, or going down stairs. Increased anxiety associated with these activities may increase both pain and pain behavior. For patients who have this type of problem, a combination of EMG biofeedback and relaxation training may be quite helpful. The target with these patients is not simply pain reduction but also a resumption of a more functional life-style. Thus, patients may learn that they no longer need to fear and avoid simple daily activities, such as sitting or walking for limited periods of time. During treatment, patients can be trained to walk or sit for progressively longer periods of time without experiencing increased pain.

A fourth and final possibility is that biofeedback helps low back pain patients by increasing their sense of control or mastery of pain. A lack of control is known to heighten pain severity and lower pain tolerance. Patients may benefit from biofeedback because it enables them to better exert control over muscle responses that they believe are related to pain. This cognitive based mechanism has received increased attention from biofeedback researchers during the past few years (e.g., Nouwen & Solinger, 1979).

There are a variety of mechanisms by which biofeedback may help low back pain patients. It is important that future researchers keep in mind the multiple mechanisms by which biofeedback may work. Judging this approach solely on the basis of its ability to reduce pain by reducing EMG levels is unnecessarily restrictive. If biofeedback works via behavioral and cognitive mechanisms, then other target responses are equally important. These targets include reductions in subjective tension, emotional distress, intake of sedative/hypnotic agents or narcotics, and a resumption of well behaviors.

CENTRAL PAIN

Introduction

Central pain is defined as "pain associated with a lesion of the central nervous system" (Bonica, 1977). Lesions occurring in the spinal cord, thalamus, and corticol regions can produce persistent pain. Examples are the pain suffered by paraplegics and patients suffering from thalamic pain syndromes. Phantom limb pain is believed to be due to abnormalities in the peripheral and central portions of the somatosensory system. The symptoms of central and peripheral-central pain vary greatly depending on the location of the lesion. Patients with central pain secondary to paraplegia often complain of pain that is aching or burning in quality, dysesthesias, hyperalgesia, and unusual sensations (grinding, twisting, crawling). Low level stimuli often bring on prolonged reactions of pain and other distressing somatic sensations. Patients having phantom limb pain typically report a severe cramping and crushing sensation in the phantom limb.

Treatments for central and peripheral-central pain typically consist of medications and neurosurgical ablative procedures. Narcotic medications have not been found useful, but anticonvulsive medications are sometimes helpful. Nerve blocks or electrical stimulation designed to alter somatic input are helpful in the treatment of phantom limb pain because these increase sensory input and may restore the central biasing mechanism to a more normal balance (Bonica, 1977). However, these methods have not been found useful in pain that is strictly central in origin. Neurosurgical techniques designed to interrupt pain pathways also frequently fail to produce lasting therapeutic effects and patients must be carefully screened to ensure success.

Clinical Efficacy

Given that phantom limb pain is probably the most frequent cause of persistent pain of peripheral-central or central origin, it is not surprising that this syndrome has received the most attention from biofeedback researchers and clinicians (see Table 2). Sherman and colleagues have published two studies (Sherman, 1976; Sherman, Gall, & Gormly, 1979) in which EMG biofeedback was used to treat phantom limb pain. In these studies, EMG biofeedback was provided to patients from both a frontal and stump muscle placement. Patients were also taught progressive relaxation. This treatment program attempts to alleviate pain by modifying two target responses: anxiety and muscle spasm. Feedback from the stump muscle placement is used to reduce pain due to localized muscle spasm. Sherman et al. (1979) reported dramatic results in the treatment of 16 patients having phantom limb pain. Patients received an average of only four training sessions, though chronic patients received an average of six treatments. Follow-ups ranging from 6 months to 3 years indicated highly significant reductions in pain and pain medication intake. These results are quite impressive, particularly in light of the failure of conventional medical and surgical approaches for this same group of patients and their long histories of pain complaints. Given the promising results achieved, this area certainly warrants further attention. Replication by other investigators is needed to evaluate whether similar results can be achieved in other laboratories.

Blanchard (1979) is the only investigator who has reported on the efficacy of biofeedback in the management of reflex sympathetic dystrophy. This persistent pain problem, believed to be of peripheral-central origin, is characterized by disturbances in the autonomic nervous system. Chronic, burning pain often is associated with reduced blood flow into the affected limb. In the case reported by Blanchard (1979), a 30-year-old man received temperature biofeedback from the finger on the affected side and was trained to produce increases of 1.0 to 1.5 degrees C. Based on pain diaries, large reductions in pain intensity were observed. Although this report is interesting and the results encouraging, it remains the only published report in the literature.

In summary, few studies have examined biofeedback as a treatment approach for the management of central and peripheral-central pain. Data that are available suggest that patients with phantom limb pain or central pain may respond to this approach. Although these findings are intriguing, they come mainly from single cases or collections of single-case reports. The efficacy of biofeedback in comparison to other traditional approaches has not been examined. Given the incidence and refractory nature of certain peripheral-central pain conditions, such as phantom limb pain, further investigation of the effects of biofeedback appears warranted.

Specificity of Effect

It is impossible to determine whether biofeedback has specific effects for phantom limb pain because only single group outcome studies have been reported. Only a single case study (Blanchard, 1979) is available for the other central pain condition we reviewed—reflex sympathetic dystrophy. The only evidence that biofeedback was specific in its effects was that this treatment had no effect on the patient's complaints of persistent back pain whereas substantial improvements in pain due to the reflex sympathetic dystrophy were obtained. This may suggest that the observed improvement was not due to placebo factors. In summary, insufficient data prevents us from making even preliminary conclusions regarding the specific effects of biofeedback for central pain problems.

Mechanism of Action

Data collected by Sherman et al. (1979) suggest that biofeedback approaches for phantom limb pain work primarily through a reduction of anxiety. Sherman notes that in many patients emotional stress in-

TABLE 2. Central Pain

Study	Research design	Population	Treatments	Duration of treatment	Outcome	Follow-up	Comments
Sherman, 1976 (abstract)	Ancedotal case reports	5 males with phantom limb pain	EMG biofeedback from stump and progressive relaxation	Unknown	Reported that all patients showed sharply reduced EMG levels and elimination of pain at the end of the one 50-minute session	No follow-up	Abstract proved no objective outcome data
Blanchard, 1979	Systematic case study	30-year-old male with a 5-month history of reflex sympathetic dystrophy in one arm and post-traumatic back pain	Finger skin temperature biofeedback	18 sessions over 2 months	Almost total pain relief in arm by the end of treatment; no change in back pain	Improvement was maintained at 2-week and 3-month follow-ups; global self-report at 1-year follow-up revealed maintenance of improvement	Mean finger skin temperature increases of 1.0 – 1.5°C

| Sherman, Gall, & Gormly, 1979 | Single-group outcome study | 16 males with phantom limb pain in leg ($n = 14$) or arm ($n = 2$); pain was of recent onset ($M = 3$ weeks) in 2 cases and chronic in 14 ($M = 13.4$ years) | EMG biofeedback from stump and/or frontalis and progressive relaxation | Average of 4, 30-minute sessions; chronic patients required an average of 6 treatments | Pain of both recent amputees eliminated in 3 sessions; chronic patients showed mean reductions of 80% in pain intensity and 66% in self-reported anxiety | Follow-ups ranging form 6 months to 3 years revealed maintenance of improvement according to global self-report | No physiological data presented; pain diaries not used |

creases phantom pain. In his research, a high correlation ($r = .67$) between patients' ratings of pain and anxiety was noted. Another possible mechanism of action is that muscle spasms in stump muscles are reduced with EMG biofeedback. Unfortunately, EMG levels have not been reported, and it is impossible to comment on this. Patients who have reflex sympathetic dystrophies often note a definite correlation between the temperature of the affected limb and pain. In the study by Blanchard (1979), increases in finger temperature were in fact correlated with significant reductions in pain intensity. This suggests that biofeedback for this condition may work by increasing peripheral blood flow. This possibility needs to be explored in subsequent controlled research using a larger number of subjects.

Rheumatoid Arthritis

Introduction

Rheumatoid arthritis is a chronic disease characterized by inflammation of the peripheral joints producing progressive destruction of articular and periarticular structures. Typical complaints include swelling and stiffness in the joints and pain. Treatments include rest, salicylates, anti-inflammatory agents, corticosteroids, and gold compounds. Flexion contractures develop in some patients secondary to avoidance of painful activities. Physical therapy, and instruction about self-care can reduce the problems of contracture and help patients remain active. Surgical intervention is used in only a small minority of cases and usually involves replacement of joint parts.

Clinical Efficacy

Biofeedback approaches to arthritis have attempted to modify complaints of stiffness and pain by teaching patients to produce general body relaxation and to alter peripheral skin temperature. Table 3 summarizes the characteristics of studies conducted in this area. Wickramasekera, Truong, Bush, and Orr (1976) reported that a combination of frontalis EMG biofeedback and autogenic training significantly reduced pain in two rheumatoid arthritis patients. The more recent study of Achterburg, McGraw, and Lawlis (1981), however, is the only controlled study published in this area. Two clinical trials are reported. In the first, all patients were trained to relax, with half of the patients taught to produce skin temperature increases, and the other half taught to produce skin temperature decreases using temperature biofeedback. Results indicated that both groups improved in terms of pain and complaints of stiffness. Both groups of patients showed a trend toward increasing temperature over sessions, which is characteristic of vasodilation accompanying general relaxation. In the second clinical trial, results achieved with patients from both groups in the first study were compared to a control group of patients undergoing a physical therapy regimen involving use of modalities such as heat, cold, exercise, and training in body mechanics. In terms of pain relief, patients in the two biofeedback conditions combined did better than patients in physiotherapy alone. Both groups also showed significant improvements in measures of functional status, such as 50-foot walk time and performance during activities of daily living. Although these data suggest that combined relaxation and temperature biofeedback training program is superior to a control condition, it should be noted that patients were not randomly assigned to the two treatment conditions. Although statistical analyses were not reported, it appears that the physiotherapy and biofeedback groups differed on measures of activity level and pain intensity prior to treatment, suggesting that patients in the physiotherapy condition may have had more severe arthritis.

Rheumatic diseases such as arthritis are common age-related conditions that affect a large segment of the population. Given the prevalence of these disorders, it is surprising that so little controlled research on biofeedback applications has been conducted. The work of Achterberg et al. (1981) is noteworthy primarily because it is the only study in this area that has used some control procedures. Based on the limited information available, it appears that a combination of relaxation and skin temperature biofeedback may be as effective as conventional physical therapy in the management of chronic rheumatoid arthritic pain. EMG biofeedback both as an aide to relaxation and as a method of reducing excessive muscle tension in those muscles surrounding affected joints should be examined more fully in subsequent studies. Future research should use randomized assignment to treatment conditions and long-term follow-ups to control for spontaneous remissions of symptoms characteristic of arthritic disorders.

Specificity of Effect

In the area of management of arthritic pain, there are no studies in which placebo controls have been used, and therefore, it is impossible to comment on the specific effects of biofeedback in the treatment of this condition.

TABLE 3. Rheumatoid Arthritis (RA)

Study	Research design	Population	Treatments	Duration of treatment	Outcome	Follow-up	Comments
Wickramasekera, Truong, Bush, & Orr, 1976	Systematic case studies	2 females, ages 30 and 61, with a history of diagnosed RA of 15 and 12 years, respectively	Frontalis EMG biofeedback and autogenic training	Unknown number of sessions over 26 and 28 weeks	Both patients showed decreases in pain intensity and EMG levels	No follow-up	Daily medication records revealed that medication consumption remained constant in both patients throughout the study
Achterberg, McGraw, & Lawlis, 1981	*Experiment 1:* Uncontrolled group outcome study	24 females with at least 1-year history of diagnosed RA and maintained on a stable medication regimen; average age and mean duration of RA not given	All patients received relaxation training followed by skin temperature biofeedback: *Group 1:* Trained in temperature increase; *Group 2:* Trained in temperature decrease	12, 30-minute sessions over 6 weeks	Both groups showed significant and comparable improvement in pain, muscle tension, and hours slept at post-treatment as measured by global self-reports and decreased EMG levels	No follow-up	Both groups showed increases in finger skin temperature; pain diaries not used

| Experiment 2: Nonrandomized group outcome study | 23 patients averaging 50.2 years of age; mean duration of RA not given | Group 1 (n = 15): Relaxation training followed by finger skin temperature biofeedback (some trained in temperature increase, others in temperature decrease); Group 2 (n = 8): Physiotherapy—consisting of hot packs, cryotherapy, paraffin, home exercise program, and counselling on proper body mechanics and posture | 12, 30–40 minute sessions | Both groups showed significant and comparable improvement in 50-foot walking time and in activities of daily living; Group 1 showed significantly greater improvement in global self-reports of pain and physical activity and decreased number of involved joints than Group 2 | No follow-up | Pain diaries not used |

Mechanism of Action

The work of Achterberg *et al.* (1981) provides the only clues as to the possible mechanisms by which biofeedback may help arthritic patients. This study found that over treatment patients trained to either decrease or increase skin temperature showed gradual increases in finger temperature. The pattern of results is consistent with that achieved with general relaxation. It is not clear, however, whether the increases in peripheral temperature can account for the observed improvements in pain.

DYSMENORRHEA

Introduction

The etiology of dysmenorrhea is not clearly understood, but cervical obstruction, hypoplagia, hypocontractility of the uterus, vasoconstriction and nerve pathology have been implicated. When dysmenorrhea occurs as a result of endometriosis, pubic inflammatory disease, strictures of the cervix, abnormal position of the uterus, or uterine or ovarian tumors, it is termed secondary dysmenorrhea. Secondary dysmenorrhea is treated with appropriate medical or surgical interventions. Primary dysmenorrhea, that is, painful menstruation in the absence of underlying organic factors, is typically treated with a combination of psychological support, education, and minor analgesics. Narcotic medications are rarely used in the management of this condition. Clinical observations suggest that emotional and psychological factors do influence the symptoms of primary dysmenorrhea. Although precise incidence figures are unavailable, estimates suggest that 7% to 26% of women suffer from this condition.

The major symptoms of primary dysmenorrhea are sharp cramping or steady, dull, aching pain localized in the legs and suprapubic area. Abdominal distension, nausea and vomiting, tension, painful breasts, and irritability are also common complaints.

The previous BSA Task Force Report on dysmenorrhea (Fotopoulos & Sunderland, 1978) concluded (a) "biofeedback has a potential as a treatment for this disorder" and (b) "efficacy of any of these (biofeedback) modalities has not yet been convincingly demonstrated."

Clinical Efficacy

Table 4 summarizes the published literature in which biofeedback techniques were used in the treatment of dysmenorrhea. As can be seen, two major treatment approaches have been utilized. The first involves biofeedback-assisted relaxation training. This training approach is designed to help patients learn to control their responses to stressful emotional stimuli that may exacerbate symptoms of dysmenorrhea. An example of this training approach is the study by Balick, Elfner, May, and Moore (1982). In this study, subjects were given a combination of finger skin temperature and trapezius EMG biofeedback along with autogenic training instructions. Major decreases in symptoms of dysmenorrhea and changes in functional measures were reported. The second major training approach has been to provide patients with feedback of physiological responses presumed to be directly involved in symptomatic complaints. For example, Bennink, Hulst, and Benthlem (1982) examined whether EMG feedback from abdominal muscles combined with relaxation training was more effective than relaxation training alone in reducing symptoms of dysmenorrhea. Patients who received the combined treatment showed significant improvements relative to the relaxation training only and no treatment control groups.

A total of five clinical research studies have been published examining the efficacy of biofeedback in the treatment of dysmenorrhea since the last BSA Task Force Report (Fotopoulos & Sunderland, 1978). The status of this field, however, remains relatively unchanged. Biofeedback and related methods of self-control do appear to show some promise in the treatment of this painful condition. Unfortunately, a review of the published literature reveals a complete absence of large-scale, well-controlled studies with long-term follow-ups. The most promising controlled study is that of Bennink et al. (1982), which suggests that biofeedback adds considerably to effects that can be obtained with relaxation training alone. Given the prevalence of this disorder, it would appear that further research on biofeedback is not only necessary, but also practical.

Specificity of Effect

Two studies have indirectly addressed the specific effects of biofeedback in the treatment of dysmenorrhea. Heczey (1980) reported that finger and vaginal temperature biofeedback added to the treatment effects obtained with autogenic training alone. Bennink et al. (1982) also reported that abdominal EMG biofeedback adds considerably to the effects obtained with relaxation alone. If we assume that relaxation/autogenic training approaches produce expectancy of improvement ratings equivalent to biofeedback, then these studies suggest that specific site (i.e., abdominal EMG and vaginal temperature) biofeedback has specific effects in the treatment of dysmenorrhea. However, further research is needed to test this assumption.

TABLE 4. Dsymenorrhea

Study	Research design	Population	Treatments	Duration of treatment	Outcome	Follow-up	Comments
Tubbs & Carnahan, 1976 (abstract)	Single-group outcome study	8 subjects averaging 21.3 years of age with a mean duration of dysmenorrhea of 6.8 years	Finger skin temperature biofeedback and EMG biofeedback	7 sessions of finger skin temperature biofeedback and 2 sessions of EMG biofeedback	Two subjects showed no improvement, two showed moderate improvement, and four learned the skill readily and reported the ability to abort menstrual cramps within minutes of onset	Improvement reportedly maintained at 2- and 5-month follow-up	No objective outcome data reported in abstract; EMG electrode placement not specified
Sedlacek & Haczey, 1977 (abstract)	Ancedotal case reports	3 subjects; ages and duration of dysmenorrhea not given	Vaginal and finger skin temperature biofeedback with frontalis EMG biofeedback	12–16 sessions	Reported that treatment was successful; subjects were able to increase vaginal temperature by .2–.4°F	No follow-up	No objective outcome data reported in abstract

Dietvorst & Osborne, 1978	Systematic case study	29-year-old with an 18-year history of primary dysmenorrhea	Finger skin temperature biofeedback and autogenic training	8, 50-minute sessions	Subject showed a 35% reduction on the Symptom Severity Scale in the 2 months following treatment compared to a 2-month baseline	No follow-up	
Heczey, 1980	Nonrandomized group outcome study	44 students subjects averaging 26 years of age; years duration of dysmenorrhea unknown	*Group 1* (n = 11): Relaxation and autogenic training and both finger and vaginal temperature biofeedback *Group 2* (n = 11): Individual, autogenic training only *Group 3* (n = 12): Group autogenic training only *Group 4* (n = 10): No treatment control group	8, 30-minute sessions	All treatment groups showed significantly greater improvement than the control group; Group 1 showed significantly greater reductions in dysmenorrheic symptoms than Groups 2 and 3	No follow-up	2-month baseline; biofeedback subjects showed a mean increase of 2.7°F in vaginal temperature

Continued

TABLE 4. (*Continued*)

Study	Design	Subjects	Treatment	Sessions	Results	Follow-up	Comments
Hart, Mathisen, & Prater, 1981	Uncontrolled group outcome study	11 subjects averaging 26.9 years of age; years duration of dysmenorrhea unknown	*Group 1* (n = 5): Frontalis EMG biofeedback; *Group 2* (n = 6): Finger skin temperature biofeedback	Average of 12.9, 30-minute sessions	Both groups showed significant and comparable reductions in symptom severity scores at 0-2 months post-treatment	No follow-up	2-month baseline
Balick, Elfner, May, & Moore, 1982	Multiple baseline design across subjects and treatments	9 subjects ranging from 20-33 years of age with a duration of dysmenorrhea ranging from 5-21 years	Finger skin temperature and trapezius EMG biofeedback with autogenic training	Unknown	Substantial reductions in dysmenorrheic symptoms, medication, hours spent in bed, and interference in daily activities in 8 subjects; improvement did not appear to be specific to type of treatment	No follow-up	No significant relationship between physiological measures and symptom reduction

| Bennink, Hulst, & Benthlem, 1982 | Controlled group outcome study | 15 subjects averaging 19.2 years of age; mean duration of dysmenorrhea unknown | Group 1 (n = 5): Relaxation training and EMG biofeedback from lower abdominal muscles Group 2 (n = 5): Relaxation training only Group 3 (n = 5): No treatment control group | 5, 30-minute sessions; 3 sessions were conducted prior to menstruation and the last 2 sessions were conducted on the first 2 days of menstrual flow | Only Group 1 showed a significant reduction in severity of symptoms; both Groups 1 and 2 were able to decrease abdominal EMG levels before menstrual period; however, only Group 1 was able to maintain decreased EMG on Day 1 of menstruation | No follow-up | Results based on one menstrual period |

Mechanism of Action

In the study by Balick *et al.* (1982) cited earlier, the authors were unable to identify any significant relationships between physiological indexes of relaxation and changes in symptomatology. Thus, the precise mechanism for the efficacy of their biofeedback-assisted relaxation approach is unclear. In the study by Bennink *et al.* (1982), the combined relaxation and EMG feedback group and the relaxation-only group showed reductions in EMG levels prior to their menstrual period. However, only the biofeedback group maintained reduced EMG levels on their first day of menses, suggesting that their superior performance could be attributed to self-control of a specific physiologic response. Thus, it appears that biofeedback given from specific sites, such as abdominal muscles, may account for symptom improvement in this population. This is a very preliminary conclusion that needs to be buttressed by further investigation.

HETEROGENEOUS PAIN SYNDROMES

Introduction

In this section, we consider studies that report outcome data collected from groups of patients presenting with a variety of different chronic pain complaints. Although these patients are heterogeneous as to the possible site of their pain, all had very long histories of continuous daily pain. These patients are an extremely difficult and frustrating group for primary-care physicians to manage. There is growing recognition that over time they develop unique behavioral, psychological, and psychophysiologic responses that make them resistant to traditional treatment approaches (Keefe, 1982). Specialized multidisciplinary programs designed to work with this difficult group of patients have been developed at several medical centers. In these programs, patients having pain due to a variety of etiologic factors (e.g., lumbar disc disease, rheumatoid arthritis, cancer, etc.) and whose pain occurs at different body sites are exposed to intensive treatment designed to help them manage pain more effectively. Realistic goals in treatment with these patients include (a) a reduction in narcotic intake, (b) an increase in general activity, (c) a return to enjoyable recreational, social, and vocational pursuits, and (d) a modest reduction in pain. Most specialized pain management programs incorporate biofeedback as a treatment technique. In some instances, biofeedback is the major treatment modality used whereas in others, biofeedback is an adjunct to other somatic and behavioral treatments.

Table 5 summarizes the results of published studies in which bio-feedback has been used with heterogeneous groups of patients suffering from intractable pain. The largest outcome study is that of Swanson, Maruta, and Swenson (1979). They reported on results achieved from a diverse group of 200 patients having very persistent pain. Biofeedback and relaxation training were combined with many other treatments. Reductions in pain and pain medication intake and increases in activity were obtained in the majority of patients, with maintenance of treatment gains over one year reported by many patients. Very little detail is provided, however, on the specific biofeedback methods utilized with this diverse group of patients, and no data are presented on changes in physiologic responding. Two studies, however, have provided a detailed description of their biofeedback treatment protocol for use with diverse samples of intractable pain patients (Hendler, Derogatis, Avella, & Long, 1977; Peck & Kraft, 1977). For example, Peck and Kraft (1977) describe EMG biofeedback methods used with headache, back, and jaw pain patients. Changes in EMG activity were also presented. EMG biofeedback was most effective for the headache patients and least effective for the back pain patients.

The studies previously cited are important in that they demonstrate that patients with long protracted histories of pain can respond to treatment. The results obtained are promising, and most specialized pain management programs are now carrying out active programs of research to examine the mechanisms underlying therapeutic change. At this point, however, it is impossible to determine the precise contribution that biofeedback makes to the results reported. At best, biofeedback may be a useful adjunct to a multidisciplinary treatment package for mixed groups of chronic pain patients. One question facing clinicians working with biofeedback in these settings is how to conduct controlled research on their treatment approach. Single-subject designs in which biofeedback is systematically introduced at specific points in treatment may be quite helpful. A good example of this design is a recent report by Sanders (1983) in which a multiple baseline design was used to evaluate the effects of relaxation, assertiveness training, functional pain-behavioral analysis, and social reinforcements of increased activity. With each patient, a substantial improvement in symptomatology was obtained concomitant with the introduction of relaxation training.

Specificity of Effect and Mechanism of Action

Due to the wide variety of pain syndromes included in this section, it is impossible to comment on either specificity of effect or mechanism of action. Data collected from patients having pain in a variety of different

TABLE 5. Heterogenous Pain Syndromes

Authors	Research design	Population	Treatments	Duration of treatment	Outcome	Follow-up	Comments
Melzack & Perry (1975)	Group outcome study	6 males and 18 females averaging 48 years of age; mean duration of pain not given	*Group 1 (n = 12)*: hypnosis and alpha EEG biofeedback *Group 2 (n = 6)*: Alpha EEG biofeedback only *Group 3 (n = 6)*: hypnosis only	8–14 sessions	Only Group 1 showed significant decreases in pain	Interviews at 4–6 months follow-up with 11 patients revealed maintenance of improvement	Pain syndromes included back, peripheral nerve injury, cancer, arthritis, phantom limb and stump pain, post-traumatic and head pain
Swanson, Swenson, Maruta & McPhee (1976)	Single-group outcome study	27 female and 23 male inpatients averaging 47.9 years of age with a mean duration of pain of 7.2 years; patients averaged 2.2 surgeries and 60% were receiving compensation	Behavior modification, physical therapy, medication management, family participation, group discussion, biofeedback and relaxation techniques	Average of 3–4 weeks	Significant improvement in pain intensity, uptime, medication intake, and pain behaviors in the 34 patients who completed the program	No follow-up	Pain syndromes included back, neck, extremity, chest wall, phantom limb and stump pain, abdominal and head pain; type of biofeedback not specified
Hendler, Derogatis, Avella, & Long (1977)	Single-group outcome study	11 females and 2 males with a mean duration of pain of 1.9 years; patients averaged 2.6 surgeries	Frontalis EMG biofeedback	5, 1-hour sessions over a 1-week period	6 of the 13 patients reported less pain following at least 4 of the 5 biofeedback sessions	1-month follow-up revealed the 6 patients maintained improvement	Sites of pain included low back, leg, neck, shoulder, and arm; pain diaries not used

Peck & Kraft (1977)	Single-group outcome study	13 females and 6 males with durations of pain ranging from 1–42 years	Specific site EMG biofeedback training	2 sessions per week for 9–15 weeks	All patient groups showed EMG decreases; 67% of head and neck pain patients showed significant improvement compared to 13% of the back pain and 33% of the TMJ patients	No follow-up	Sites of pain included head, neck, back, and jaw
Khatami & Rush (1978)	Single-group outcome study	3 females and 2 males averaging 43 years of age with a mean duration of pain of 11.6 years	Relaxation training and EMG biofeedback, cognitive therapy, and operant conditioning	Average of 35.8 sessions	Significant improvement in pain intensity, depression, and medication intake	6- and 12-month follow-ups revealed maintenance of improvement	Sites of pain included head, rectal/bowel, low back, and leg; EMG electrode placement not specified
Khatami, Woody, & O'Brien (1979)	Single-group outcome study	5 males averaging 45.6 years of age with durations of pain ranging rom 8–24 years	Relaxation training EMG biofeedback, antidepressant medication, cognitive therapy, and operant conditioning	Average of 31.2 sessions	Significant reductions in pain intensity, depression, and anxiety	No follow-up	Sites of pain included low back, head, upper back, hand, and neck; EMG electrode placement not specified

Continued

TABLE 5. (*Continued*)

Swanson, Maruta, & Swenson (1979)	Single-group outcome study	200 inpatients averaging 44.9 years of age with a mean duration of pain of 7 years; 56% were receiving compensation	Relaxation and biofeedback, operant conditioning, medication management, physical therapy, group discussion and family participation	Average hospital stay of 20.3 days	Global ratings revealed that 59% showed moderate to marked improvement	Based on questionnaires, 75% of the initial responders maintained improvement at 3-month follow-up and 65% at 1-year follow-up	Sites of pain included back, neck, extremities, chest wall, head, face, and abdomen; type of biofeedback not specified
Cinciripini & Floreen (1982)	Single-group outcome study	121 inpatients averaging 43.8 years of age with a mean duration of pain of 8.3 years; 41% were receiving compensation	Relaxation training, frontalis EMG biofeedback, medication reduction, physical behavioral group therapy, operant conditioning, self-monitoring, contracting, and family training	4 weeks	Significant decreases in pain intensity, medication, and pain behaviors; significant increases in activity, physical therapy measures and assertion	Based on questionnaires at 6- and 12-month follow-up, a majority of respondents maintained improvement	Sites of pain included head, neck, face, low back, extremities, chest, abdomen, and groin

| Khatami & Rush (1982) | Single-group outcome study | 16 female and 7 male outpatients averaging 43.8 years of age; 74% had a duration of pain > 1 year | Relaxation training, EMG biofeedback, cognitive therapy, and operant conditioning | Average of 22.9 sessions for those who completed the program; patients who dropped out averaged 6.4 sessions | 14 of the 23 patients completed the program; no posttreatment data presented | At 1-year follow-up, those who completed the program showed significant decreases in pain, medication intake, anxiety, depression, hostility, and somatization; drop-outs showed significant reductions in pain and depression only | Sites of pain and EMG electrode placement unspecified |

sites are analyzed as a group, making it impossible to address the issues of specificity of effect or mechanism of action. It should be noted, however, that evidence regarding biofeedback as a treatment for specific pain disorders is presented in other sections of this review.

COST-EFFECTIVENESS

The relative costs of medical and biofeedback approaches to chronic pain have not been systematically evaluated in any research study. However, there are a number of reasons to suspect that biofeedback treatments may reduce the medical costs attendant to managing chronic pain conditions. First, several of the studies reviewed above have reported that patients treated with biofeedback reduced their intake of medications and use of health-care resources. Second, many chronic pain patients treated with biofeedback have exhausted available medical and surgical options for their condition. When left untreated, these patients tend to return repeatedly for evaluations and rehospitalizations. The success of biofeedback even with this chronic group of patients is encouraging and raises the possibility that it is a cost-effective approach. Third, biofeedback and related procedures are relatively inexpensive and can be delivered by technicians operating under supervision. Relative to other treatment approaches, such as nerve blocks, neurostimulators, and surgical approaches, biofeedback methods are much less costly.

A great deal of attention has been given to the relative effectiveness of general relaxation approaches versus biofeedback in the management of a wide variety of conditions. It is often argued that relaxation is much more cost-effective than biofeedback because no instrumentation is needed. However, in our opinion, it is unlikely that the cost of biofeedback instrumentation will add significantly to the cost of relaxation therapy in the long run because a single biofeedback unit can be used with hundreds of patients. A more important consideration is the amount of therapist time. A cost-effectiveness issue that has received little attention is the extent to which biofeedback approaches for chronic pain can be delivered in the context of group sessions in order to reduce the amount of therapist time per patient. Patel (1975) has demonstrated that biofeedback procedures can be used for hypertensives in group settings, and there is no reason to believe that a similar approach could not be used for chronic pain patients.

CLINICAL LORE

In the course of preparing this chapter, letters were received from a number of biofeedback researchers and clinicians. Several important points were raised in these letters. First, in many research reports, undergraduate students with little training in biofeedback are used as therapists. Obviously, the limited clinical experience of these individuals may significantly lessen the impact of the treatment they deliver. Although there is no research in the area of chronic pain that compares the effectiveness of experienced versus inexperienced therapists, Taylor, Agras, Schneider, and Allen (1983) found that in the treatment of hypertension, experienced therapists obtain higher compliance levels with home-practice instructions for relaxation than inexperienced therapists. A second point raised in correspondence was that in clinical practice, procedures can be individually tailored to meet the unique problems that a particular chronic pain patient presents. In controlled research studies, treatment procedures are typically standardized, and every patient is provided with a highly similar training protocol. It may well be that better results are obtained when individually tailored programs are used. Future research should compare individually tailored biofeedback treatment approaches to standard approaches for different chronic pain syndromes.

A final question is the degree to which there is a discrepancy between results achieved by clinicians and clinical researchers in the treatment of chronic pain conditions. Some of the clinicians reported success rates of 70% of 90%. This is much higher than that typically reported in controlled studies. It is very difficult to compare these improvement rates because of differences in patient selection, treatment procedures, etc. The most definitive statement we can make at this time is that whereas clinical reports and research studies support the use of biofeedback in the management of chronic pain, clinicians typically report higher improvement rates. Thus, there does appear to be mild-to-moderate discrepancy between results achieved by clinicians and clinical researchers. Although we have mentioned some possible reasons for this discrepancy, research comparing clinical programs with research laboratories is needed to identify the factors accounting for this apparent discrepancy.

FUTURE RESEARCH

The literature reviewed suggests that biofeedback methods may be useful in the management of chronic pain syndromes. Several factors limit our ability to make stronger statements about the efficacy of biofeedback with this diverse population of patients. If the scientific rigor of the biofeedback literature is to advance, several issues need attention in future research.

Patient Characteristics

A critical issue in evaluating any biofeedback study for chronic pain is the nature of the subject population treated. Chronic pain patients are not a homogenous group. A complaint of pain in the low back region, for example, may be the result of a diverse set of factors including muscle spasm, scar tissue, depression, postural abnormalities, hypochondriacal tendencies, or secondary gain factors. Most clinical programs and clinical research studies use stringent inclusion and exclusion criteria. Unfortunately, these criteria are often unspecified in the research reports. Patients may be excluded from a study on the basis of medical status variables, such as having had prior surgery or showing no current organic findings, because of social environmental variables (e.g., narcotic addiction, pending disability, and litigation issues) or for psychological reasons (e.g., severe depression or definite conversion symptoms). Adequate attention has also not been given to specifying patient diagnoses. For example, in studies on low back pain, patients are simply described as having "low back pain" and little or no information is given on how many patients have pain that is discogenic, mechanical, or spondylogenic in origin. The lack of diagnostic sophistication makes these reports much less appealing to the medical community. To the extent that patient characteristics are unspecified, our ability to characterize the efficacy of biofeedback is impaired.

Throughout the review, we have strongly emphasized the difference between patients having acute or intermittent pain and those having intractable, persistent daily pain. In evaluating any report of biofeedback, the duration of pain and its daily temporal characteristics are extremely important. Patients who suffer from persistent daily pain for months or years exhibit many behavioral and psychological problems that patients who have intermittent pain for several months do not show. These problems include narcotic addiction, extreme inactivity, depression, dependency on others, and physical deconditioning. Biofeedback and other self-control modalities are most likely to be effective as a single treatment in patients whose pain problems are less chronic. It is recommended that research reports on biofeedback routinely include information on the duration and temporal characteristics of pain so that the reader can better understand the patient population treated.

Extending Biofeedback to Other Chronic Pain Syndromes

Biofeedback has been applied to a limited range of chronic pain syndromes. Although a great deal of work has been done with low back pain syndromes and a moderate amount of work with arthritis and central pain and dysmenorrhea, there are no published reports on the use of biofeedback with other common chronic pain populations. Biofeedback clinicians often are called on to treat a wide range of pain problems, including fibromyalgia or fibrositis, angina, pain secondary to cancer, coccydynia, abdominal pain, and pain in burn victims. As we prepared this chapter, several members of the Biofeedback Society commented on their success with one or another of these pain problems. Unfortunately, published data are not currently available. We recommend that biofeedback clinicians present case study or single-group outcome material on these patient populations for publication or at national meetings. Such data are likely to be beneficial not only to clinicians but also to future research efforts in these important areas.

Target Responses

Many of the studies reviewed utilized either biofeedback-assisted relaxation methods or attempted to teach patients self-control of a specific physiological response presumed to mediate their reports of pain. However, it is not clear how best to determine which procedure should be used. Assessment and evaluation protocols are being developed for use with a variety of pain problems, and some of these incorporate psychophysiologic monitoring. An excellent example of this type of assessment protocol is that developed by Wolf et al. (1979) in which measurements of electromyographic activity are taken from the lumbar paraspinal musculature in patients suffering from low back pain. EMG activity recorded during a series of static and dynamic activities are compared to readings obtained from a normative population. Cram and Steger (1983) have also described a protocol in which EMG measures are taken from multiple muscle sites as part of a diagnostic evaluation of muscle tension in chronic pain patients. On the basis of such evaluation protocols, a rational decision as to a target physiological response and series of tasks needed to be learned through biofeedback training can be made. Other examples of this type of assessment protocol are available for patients suffering from myofascial dysfunction syndrome or headaches.

How can one determine whether biofeedback-assisted relaxation training might be useful? A number of authors have described self-monitoring and objective-monitoring devices that can be used for purposes of behavioral assessment with chronic pain patients (Keefe, 1982). Patients whose pain shows a definite relationship to self-recorded anxiety, muscle tension, stress, or fatigue may be good candidates for general relaxation training. It is recommended that further work be done on methods for identifying patients likely to respond to specific biofeedback approaches.

The measurement and specification of treatment outcome is a major problem for the entire field of pain research. It is clear from the previous review that the goals of treatments vary for different types of pain problems. Realistic goals for intractable pain patients may be a reduction in pain medication and return to greater function whereas a realistic goal for a patient suffering from intermittent muscle spasms in the neck would be total pain relief. It is naive to judge the efficacy of biofeedback solely on the basis of pain response. Placebo factors are known to affect the perception and report of pain. Thus, we recommend that future studies include appropriate placebo controls and a comprehensive set of dependent measures. This should include a measure of subjective pain (for example, the Adjective Checklist of the McGill Questionnaire; Melzack & Torgerson, 1971), a measure of the impact of pain on functioning and behavior (for example, a daily activity diary, Fordyce, 1976; uptime monitor, Sanders, 1980; or score on the Sickness Impact Profile, Bergner, *et al.*, 1976) a measure of health-care utilization (for example, narcotic intake, number of hospital visits, days lost from work, etc.), and a measure of appropriate physiological responding (for example, muscle activity exhibited during a task that previously induced pain). Research that uses such a varied assessment approach can help clarify the mechanisms responsible for biofeedback effectiveness.

Generalization and Maintenance of Treatment Gains

Another important issue in evaluating biofeedback studies for chronic pain is the degree to which treatment effects obtained in a laboratory environment generalize across different settings and are maintained over time. Studies that evaluate biofeedback solely on the basis of data gathered in a laboratory session in which patients are reclining in a comfortable position are of questionable validity because most pain syndromes are exacerbated by movement. The generalization of biofeedback effects can be best assessed when multiple dependent measures, such as those described earlier in this discussion, are used. Particular training approaches also can be used to enhance generalization across settings. For example, Wolf et al. (1982) trained low back pain patients with electromyographic biofeedback to make proper use of the lumbar paraspinal musculature during daily tasks that caused increased pain (e.g., picking up a basket of laundry, bending, or stooping). Portable biofeedback devices also permit training in a variety of naturalistic settings. The major obstacle to generalization, however, in most chronic pain patients is their poor compliance with treatment instructions. Kremer, Block, and Gaylor (1981) found that patients who regularly participated in behaviorally oriented treatments and complied with instructions to practice skills on an inpatient ward environment had much better therapeutic outcomes. Compliance with home practice instructions in biofeedback training is more difficult to evaluate, and almost no data on compliance is available. However, recent research utilizing objective, unobtrusive measures of relaxation compliance indicate a high degree of noncompliance in anxiety (Hoelscher, Lichstein, & Rosenthal, 1984) and hypertensive (Hoelscher, Lichstein, & Rosenthal, 1986; Taylor, Agras, Schneider, & Allen, 1983) populations. Information on compliance to biofeedback instructions with pain populations would help researchers ascertain the relative importance of home practice in determining treatment efficacy.

Follow-up data gathered from large-scale, behaviorally oriented pain management programs suggest that anywhere from 30% to 40% of the patients relapse after one year. Obviously, maintenance is a critical issue in the treatment of chronic pain. Patients often present for treatment at the time their pain is most severe, and therapeutic results may simply be due to remission of presenting symptoms with the passage of time. Although long-term follow-ups on multidisciplinary programs have been conducted for periods ranging up to 5 years (Toomey, Taylor, Skelton, & Carron, 1982), similar data on biofeedback interventions alone are unavailable.

CONCLUSIONS

This review examined data on the efficacy of biofeedback with a wide range of chronic pain syndromes. The current status of the field for each syndrome can be summarized as follows:

Low Back Pain. Biofeedback appears to be an effective treatment of muscularly based low back pain when compared to appropriate control procedures.

Central Pain. Promising data are available from case studies and single-group studies, suggesting that biofeedback may be helpful. However, controlled research is lacking.

Rheumatoid Arthritis. Initial results suggest that biofeedback and related relaxation methods may be useful but further controlled research is needed.

Dysmenorrhea. There is limited data suggesting that biofeedback may be effective in reducing pain when compared to no treatment or relaxation training only. Further controlled research is needed to confirm this preliminary conclusion.

Heterogeneous Pain Syndromes. Biofeedback may be a useful component in multidisciplinary treatment programs for patients having intractable pain. However, component analyses are required to identify the specific effects of biofeedback treatment.

ACKNOWLEDGMENTS

The authors wish to thank the following members of the Biofeedback Society of America who provided suggestions, advice, and helpful input into the Task Force Report: Drs. Carol J. Schneider, Gary Jay, Robert Grove, Jeffrey Cram, Patricia Lawson, Carl J. Michels, Cathryn Holt, Kenneth Appelbaum, and Gloria Abad.

The authors also wish to thank Ms. Linda Jackson for her extensive work in preparation of the manuscript.

REFERENCES

Achterberg, J., McGraw, P., & Lawlis, G. F. (1981). Rheumatoid arthritis: A study of relaxation and temperature biofeedback training as an adjunctive therapy. *Biofeedback and Self-Regulation, 6,* 207–223.

Balick, L., Elfner, L., May, J., & Moore, J. D. (1982). Biofeedback treatment of dysmenorrhea. *Biofeedback and Self-Regulation, 7,* 499–519.

Belar, C. D., & Cohen, J. L. (1979). The use of EMG feedback and progressive relaxation in the treatment of a woman with chronic back pain. *Biofeedback and Self-Regulation, 4,* 345–353.

Bennink, C. D., Hulst, L. L., & Benthem, J. A. (1982). The effects of EMG biofeedback and relaxation training on primary dysmenorrhea. *Journal of Behavioral Medicine, 5,* 329–341.

Bergner, M., Bobbitt, R. A., Kressel, S., Pollard, W. E., Gilson, B. S., & Morris, J. R. (1976). The sickness impact profile: Conceptual formulation and methodology for the development of a health status measure. *International Journal of Health Services, 6,* 393–415.

Blanchard, E. B. (1979). The use of temperature biofeedback in the treatment of chronic pain due to causalgia. *Biofeedback and Self-Regulation, 4,* 183–188.

Bonica, J. J. (1977). Neurophysiological and pathologic aspects of acute and chronic pain. *Archives of Surgery, 112,* 750–761.

Bonica, J. J. (1980). Introduction. In J. J. Bonica (Ed.), *Pain* (pp. 1–17). New York: Raven Press.

Caillet, R. (1968). *Low back pain syndrome.* Philadelphia, PA: F. A. Davis.

Cinciripini, P. M., & Floreen, A. (1982). An evaluation of a behavioral program for chronic pain. *Journal of Behavioral Medicine, 5,* 375–389.

Cram, J. R., & Steger, J. C. (1983). EMG scanning in the diagnosis of chronic pain. *Biofeedback and Self-Regulation, 8,* 229–242.

Dega, R. A. (1983) Conservative therapy for low back pain. *Journal of the American Medical Association, 250,* 1057–1062.

Dietvorst, T. F., & Osborne, D. (1978). Biofeedback-assisted relaxation training for primary dysmenorrhea: A case study. *Biofeedback and Self-Regulation, 3,* 301–305.

Fernando, C. K., & Basmajian, J. V. (1978). Biofeedback in physical medicine and rehabilitation. *Biofeedback and Self-Regulation, 3,* 435–455.

Flor, H., Haag, G., Turk, D. C., & Koehler, H. (1983). Efficacy of EMG biofeedback, pseudotherapy, and conventional medical treatment for chronic rheumatic back pain. *Pain, 17,* 21–31.

Flor, H. & Turk, D. C., & Koehler, H. (1984). Etiological theories and treatments for chronic back pain: 1. Somatic models and interventions, *Pain, 19,* 105–122.

Fordyce, W. E. (1976). *Behavioral methods for chronic pain and illness.* St. Louis, MO: C. V. Mosby.

Fotopolous, S. S., & Sunderland, W. P. (1978). Biofeedback in the treatment of psychophysiologic disorders. *Biofeedback and Self-Regulation, 3,* 331–361.

Freeman, C. W., Calsyn, D. A., Paige, A. B., & Halar, E. M. (1980). Biofeedback with low back pain patients. *American Journal of Clinical Biofeedback, 3,* 118–122.

Gentry, W. D., & Bernal, G. A. A. (1977). Chronic pain. In R. B. Williams & W. D. Gentry (Eds.), *Behavioral approaches to medical treatment* (pp. 173–182). Cambridge, MA: Ballinger.

Gottlieb, H., Strite, L. C., Koller, R., Madorsky, A., Hockersmith, V., Kleeman, M., & Wagner, J. (1977). Comprehensive rehabilitation of patients having chronic low back pain. *Archives of Physical Medicine and Rehabilitation, 58,* 101–108.

Hart, A. D., Mathisen, K. S., & Prater, J. S. (1981). A comparison of skin temperature and EMG training for primary dysmenorrhea. *Biofeedback and Self-Regulation, 6,* 367–373.

Heczey, M. D. (1980). Effects of biofeedback and autogenic training on dysmenorrhea. In D. A. Grahan & E. Beecher (Eds.), *Menstrual cycle: Synthesis of inter-disciplinary research.* New York: Springer.

Hendler, N., Derogatis, L., Avella, J., & Long, D. (1977). EMG biofeedback in patients with chronic pain. *Diseases of the Nervous System, 38,* 505–509.

Hirsch, C. (1965). Efficacy of surgery in low back disorders. *Journal of Bone and Joint Surgery, 47,* 991–1000.

Hoelscher, T. J., Lichstein, K. L., & Rosenthal, T. L. (1984). Objective vs subjective assessment of relaxation compliance among anxious individuals. *Behaviour Research and Therapy, 22,* 187–193.

Hoelscher, T. J., Lichstein, K. L., & Rosenthal, T. L. (1986). Home relaxation practice in hypertension treatment: Objective assessment and compliance induction. *Journal of Consulting and Clinical Psychology, 54,* 217–221.

Jones, A. L., & Wolf, S. L. (1980). EMG biofeedback training during movement. *Physical Therapy, 60,* 58–63.

Keefe, F. J. (1982). Behavioral assessment and treatment of chronic pain: Current status and future directions. *Journal of Consulting and Clinical Psychology, 50,* 896–911.

Keefe, F. J., Block, A. R., Williams, R. B., & Surwit, R. S. (1981). Behavioral treatment of chronic low back pain: Clinical outcome and individual differences in pain relief. *Pain, 11,* 221–231.

Keefe, F. J., Schapira, B., Williams, R. B., Brown, C., & Surwit, R. S. (1981). EMG-assisted relaxation training in the management of chronic low back pain. *American Journal of Clinical Biofeedback, 4,* 93–103.

Khatami, M., & Rush, A. J. (1978). A pilot study of the treatment of outpatients with chronic pain: Symptom control, stimulus control, and social system intervention. *Pain, 5,* 163–172.

Khatami, M., & Rush, A. J. (1982). A one year follow-up of the multimodal treatment for chronic pain. *Pain, 14,* 45–52.

Khatami, M., Woody, G., & O'Brien, C. (1979). Chronic pain and narcotic addiction: A multitherapeutic approach—a pilot study. *Comprehensive Psychiatry, 20,* 55–60.

Kremer, E., Block, A., & Gaylor, M. (1981). Behavioral approaches to chronic pain: The inaccuracy of patient self-report measure. *Archives of Physical Medicine and Rehabilitation, 62,* 188–191.

MacNab, I. (1977). *Backache.* Baltimore, MD: Williams & Wilkins.

Melzack, R., & Perry, C. (1975). Self-regulation of pain: The use of alpha-feedback and hypnotic training for the control of chronic pain. *Experimental Neurology, 46,* 452–469.

Melzack, R., & Torgerson, W. S. (1971). On the language of pain. *Anaesthesiology, 34,* 50–59.

Nagi, S. Z., Riley, L. E., & Newby, L. C. (1973). A social epidemiology of back pain in a general population. *Journal of Chronic Disease, 26,* 769–779.

Newman, R. I., Seres, J. L., Yospe, L. P., & Garlington, B. (1978). Multidisciplinary treatment of chronic pain: Long-term follow-up of low-back pain patients. *Pain, 4,* 283–292.

Nigl, A. J., & Fischer-Williams, M. (1980). Treatment of low back strain with electromyographic biofeedback and relaxation training. *Psychosomatics, 21,* 492–499.

Nouwen, A. (1983). EMG biofeedback used to reduce standing levels of paraspinal muscle tension in chronic low back pain. *Pain, 17,* 353–360.

Nouwen, A., & Solinger, J. W. (1979). The effectiveness of EMG biofeedback training in low back pain. *Biofeedback and Self-Regulation, 4,* 103–111.

Patel, C. H. (1975). Yoga and biofeedback in the management of "stress" in hypertensive patients. *Clinical Science and Molecular Medicine, 48,* 171–174.

Peck, C. L., & Kraft, G. H. (1977). Electromyographic biofeedback for pain related to muscle tension. *Archives of Surgery, 112,* 889–895.

Sanders, S. H. (1980). Toward a practical instrument for the automatic measurement of "uptime" in chronic pain patients. *Pain, 9,* 103–109.

Sanders, S. H. (1983). Component analysis of a behavioral treatment program for chronic low back pain. *Behavior Therapy, 5,* 697–705.

Sedlacek, K., & Heczey, M. (1977). A specific biofeedback treatment for dysmenorrhea. *Biofeedback and Self-Regulation, 2,* 294.

Seres, J. L., & Newman, R. I. (1976). Results of treatment of chronic low back pain at the Portland Pain Center. *Journal of Neurosurgery, 45,* 32–36.

Sherman, R. A. (1976). Case reports of treatment of phantom limb pain with a combination of electromyographic biofeedback and verbal relaxation techniques. *Biofeedback and Self-Regulation, 1,* 353.

Sherman, R. A., Gall, N., & Gormly, J. (1979). Treatment of phantom limb pain with muscular relaxation training to disrupt the pain-anxiety tension cycle. *Pain, 6,* 47–55.

Swanson, D. W., Swenson, W. M., Maruta, T., & McPhee, M. C. (1976). Program for managing chronic pain. I. Program description and characteristics of patients. *Mayo Clinic Proceedings, 51,* 401–408.

Swanson, D. W., Maruta, T., & Swenson, W. M. (1979). Results of behavior modification in the treatment of chronic pain. *Psychosomatic Medicine, 41,* 55–65.

Taylor, C. B, Agras, W. S., Schneider, J. A., & Allen, R. A. (1983). Adherence to instructions to practice relaxation exercises. *Journal of Consulting and Clinical Psychology, 51,* 952–953.

Todd, J., & Belar, C. D. (1980). EMG biofeedback and chronic low back pain: Implications of treatment failure. *American Journal of Clinical Biofeedback, 3,* 114–117.

Toomey, T. C., Taylor, A. G., Skelton, J. A., & Carron, H. (1982). Five year follow-up status of chronic low back pain patients. In M. Stanton-Hicks and R. A. Boas (Eds.). *Chronic low back pain* (pp. 25–38). New York: Raven Press.

Tubbs, W., & Carnahan, C. (1976). Clinical biofeedback for primary dysmenorrhea. A pilot study. *Biofeedback and Self-Regulation, 1,* 323.

Turk, D. C. & Flor, H. (1984). Etiological theories and treatments for chronic backpain. 2. Psychological models and intervention. *Pain, 19,* 209–234.

Turner, J. A. (1982). Comparison of group progressive-relaxation training and cognitive-behavioral group therapy for chronic low back pain. *Journal of Consulting and Clinical Psychology, 50,* 757–765.

Urban, B. J. (1982). Therapeutic aspects in chronic pain: Modulation of nocioception, alleniation of suffering, and behavioral analysis. *Behavior Therapy, 13,* 430–437.

Wickramasekera, I., Truong, X. T., Bush, M., & Orr, C. (1976). The management of rheumatoid arthritic pain: Preliminary observations. In I. Wickramasekera, S. T. Truong,

M. Bush, & C. Orr (Eds.). *Biofeedback, behavior therapy, and hypnosis: Potentiating the verbal control of behavior for clinicians* (pp. 47–55). New York: Nelson-Hall.

Wolf, S. L., Basmajian, J. V., Russe, C. T. C., & Kutner, M. (1979). Normative data on low back motility and activity levels: Implications for neuromuscular reeducation. *American Journal of Physical Medicine, 58,* 217–229.

Wolf, S. L., Nacht, M., & Kelly, J. L. (1982). EMG feedback training during dynamic movement for low back pain patients. *Behavior Therapy, 13,* 395–406.

7

Behavioral Treatment of Raynaud's Syndrome

RICHARD S. SURWIT AND JOHN S. JORDAN

INTRODUCTION

Raynaud's Disease is a syndrome of disrupted peripheral bloodflow first described by Maurice Raynaud in 1862. A triphasic color change, usually exhibited in the digits of the hands or feet, is the hallmark of the disorder: sudden blanching and numbness of the affected part, due to localized arteriolar constriction; cyanosis, in which the pallor previously observed evolves into a blue color, characteristic of deoxygenated tissue and attributed to retarded blood flow in dilated capillaries and venules; and reactive hyperemia, characterized by the spread of red oxygenated blood through the upper level of the epidermis. This last phase is often accompanied by burning and tingling and lasts until the skin returns to its normal pink color. Only a minority of patients actually exhibit the classic triphasic color change, however, isolated pallor or cyanosis are much more likely (Porter, Rivers, Anders, & Baur, 1981). Typically, ischemia starts in the fingertips and progresses proximally to a variable degree, but rarely involves the palm. Occasionally, the earlobes, cheeks,

Portions of this manuscript were adapted from *Behavioral Approaches to Cardiovascular Disease* by R. S. Surwit, R. B. Williams, Jr. and D. Shapiro. New York: Academic Press, 1982, and from Behavioral Treatment of Raynaud's Syndrome in Peripheral Vascular Disease by R. S. Surwit. *Journal of Consulting and Clinical Psychology*, 1982, 50(6), 922–932. Preparation of this was supported by National Institutes of Health Grants RO1 AM29989 and National Institute of Mental Health Research Scientist Development Award KO1 MH00303 as well as by funds from the John D. and Catherine T. MacArthur Foundation.

RICHARD S. SURWIT AND JOHN S. JORDAN • Behavioral Physiology Laboratory, Department of Psychiatry, Duke University Medical Center, Durham, NC 27710.

and tip of the nose may also be affected (Hoffman, 1980). Attacks may last from minutes to hours and usually involve a local sensation of coldness, a loss of manual dexterity and considerable pain that can result in the interruption of routine activity. In severe cases, patients experience chronic vasoconstriction or such frequent episodes of cyanosis that gangrene or small nutritive lesions and ulcerations can appear at the distal end of the digits. Although cold stimulation is the most reliable eliciting stimulus, emotional stress has also been reported to produce these attacks (e.g., Mittlemann & Wolff, 1939).

The term Raynaud's *disease* has historically been used to connote the *idiopathic* syndrome involving no observable organic pathology. When this syndrome results from an identifiable pathological processes, it is known as Raynaud's *phenomenon* (Spittell, 1972). Raynaud's phenomenon can occur secondary to trauma as an occupational occlusive disease of the hand or occupational acro-osteolitis; with neurogenic lesions, such as carpal tunnel syndrome or shoulder girdle compression syndrome; with occlusive arterial disease, such as arteriosclerosis obliterans, thromboangiitis, embolisms and thromboses; with heavy metal or ergotamine intoxication; and with numerous rheumatological conditions, such as scleroderma, lupus erthematosus, and rheumatoid arthritis (Spittell, 1972).

Allen and Brown (1932) produced one of the first attempts to improve on the nosological categories established by Maurice Raynaud. They suggested the following criteria for the diagnosis of true idiopathic Raynaud's disease: (a) intermittent attacks of discoloration of the extremities, (b) absence of evidence of organic arterial occlusion, (c) symmetrical or bilateral distribution, (d) trophic changes, when present, limited to skin and never consisting of gross gangrene, (e) disease present for at least 2 years and (f) no evidence of any other disease that could produce the symptoms secondarily. Gifford and Hines (1957) and DeTakats and Fowler (1962) cautioned that a period of at least 16 years may separate the first evidence of vasospasm from the appearance of scleroderma. Thus the 2-year requirement proposed by Allen and Brown is probably insufficient to rule out other pathology. Although some rheumatologists argue that all Raynaud's disease is a precursor to some latent rheumatological condition, Surwit and colleagues (Surwit, 1982) have seen many cases of people with a 40-year history of symptoms that have not been progressive. Nonetheless, Porter and colleagues (e.g., Porter *et al.*, 1981) note that more sophisticated and sensitive laboratory procedures for the evaluation of immunologic abnormalities have revealed that over half of patients with Raynaud's-like vasospasms have an associated systemic disease process. They suggested that the distinction between Raynaud's disease and Raynaud's phenomenon be abandoned and that all patients who show these vasospastic symptoms be characterized as having Raynaud's syndrome. Nevertheless, proper differentiation of patient subgroups may well have important medical treatment implications. Conversely, disputes as to the efficacy of various behavioral interventions for Raynaud's syndrome—as well as its etiology—may be partially attributable to diagnostic confusion.

Pathophysiology

The pathophysiology of Raynaud's disease is not completely understood (Halperin & Coffman, 1979). Whereas Raynaud himself attributed the malady to sympathetic nervous system (SNS) overreactivity, Lewis (1949) maintained that the problem resulted from a local fault in the peripheral digital vessels. Lewis collected evidence showing that changes in environmental temperature could have specific effects on the part of the digits stimulated by cold. Furthermore he did not believe that the patients he examined were abnormally nervous, leading him to downplay the contribution of emotional and central nervous system (CNS) activity to the manifestations of this disorder.

Mittelmann and Wolff (1939) demonstrated that emotional stress could reduce the digital bloodflow as measured by skin temperature in both normals and Raynaud's patients. In Raynaud's patients, however, these changes in temperature were also accompanied by pain and the pallid-cyanotic-edemic color change. They reported that vasospastic attacks seemed to occur most reliably when emotional stress and low ambient temperature interacted. Additionally, they failed to find emotional stimuli effective in producing this reaction after sympathectomy. Peacock (1959) reported increased levels of plasma catecholamines in the venous blood of patients with Raynaud's disease, indicating that sympathetic overreactivity may indeed play a role in this disorder. However, Kontos and Wasserman (1969) were unable to replicate Peacock's results. Graham (1955) was also able to demonstrate the vasoconstrictive effects of disturbing interviews on the skin temperature of both patients with Raynaud's disease as well as normal subjects. In addition, he was able to isolate hostility and anxiety as the emotions most responsible for this reaction. In a subsequent study, Graham, Stearn, and Winokur (1958) demonstrated that, by suggesting these emotions to normal subjects under hypnosis, vasoconstriction in the digits could be produced.

Although this evidence strongly implies that emotional stimuli are at least a contributing factor in the elicitation of Raynaud's disease, the local-fault hypothesis of Lewis cannot be immediately ruled out. Mendlowitz and Naftchi (1959) suggested that Raynaud's disease might be dichotomized into two separate disorders: one in which the vasculature is normal and vasomotor tone is heightened by sympathetic overreactivity, and another in which normal vasomotor tone produces an overreaction in pathological local vasculature. More recently, Surwit and colleagues (Surwit, Allen, *et al.*, 1983) suggested that idiopathic Raynaud's disease is associated with a different neuroendocrine response to cold than Raynaud's phenomenon. Whereas the neuroendocrine response to cold of patients with Raynaud's phenomenon is essentially normal, patients with idiopathic Raynaud's disease show significantly lower levels of plasma norepinephrine in response to cold in the presence of high cortisol levels. Thus, idiopathic Raynaud's disease may be related to excess adrenal cortical rather than sympathetic nervous system activity.

Although there is substantial agreement about the existence of one or more active vasodilatory mechanisms in the proximal portions of the limbs, vascular control of the peripheral vessels of the digits is thought to be mostly a result of sympathetically mediated vasoconstriction. Although the primary function of this sympathetically mediated vasoconstriction system is thermoregulatory, the system is exquisitely responsive to higher cortical activity. In fact, any stimulus to which an animal attends can produce a vasoconstrictive response in these peripheral vessels. Sokolov (1963) describes this reaction as part of the "orienting reflex" that occurs in response to all stimuli that have a "signal value" to the organism. That the central nervous system (CNS) can affect this otherwise "reflexive" response system is crucial to the understanding of how behavior interacts with peripheral vascular disease.

The tendency of the peripheral vasculature to respond to environmental stimulation can be traced to anatomical and neuroendocrine factors. First, as large arteries branch into smaller ones, the ratio of neurally innervated musculature to noninnervated elastic tissue gradually increases to reach a maximum at the arteriolar level. A similar relationship is found in the venous system. Whereas the veins have a larger lumen and usually a thinner wall, the ratio of smooth muscle fiber to total tissue mass increases as the veins get smaller and smaller down to the level of the venules. Unlike the arteries, veins also contain a number of valves that prevent retrograde flow in this relatively low-pressure system. Neuromuscular control of blood flow is thus most effective at the distal branches of the vascular tree (Surwit, Shapiro, & Williams, 1982).

Post-ganglionic axons that control the digital vessels are continuously active and maintain a constant vasomotor tone that is apparently modulated by increases and decreases in both alpha and beta adrenergic activity. The alpha adrenergic receptors in the vascular smooth muscle produce vasoconstriction whereas new evidence suggests the presence of a beta adrenergic vasodilatory mechanism as well (Cohen & Coffman, 1981). Thus, central activation of the SNS produces direct stimulation through post-ganglionic fibers and humoral stimulation through release of epinephrine by the adrenal medulla. Cortisol, secreted by the adrenal cortex, can potentiate this effect by sensitizing adrenergic receptors to catecholamines (Goldie, 1976, Schmid, Eckstein, & Abboud, 1967). The importance of these humoral mechanisms in the control of vasoconstriction is underscored by the fact that digital vasoconstriction can still occur following sympathectomy (Patton, 1965).

Coordination and intergration of these autonomically mediated vascular responses takes place at medullary, diencephalic, and cortical levels. The hypothalamus and areas in the medulla have been shown to be crucial in this process (Folkow, 1955). The powerful regulatory effect of the CNS was demonstrated by Rapaport, Fetcher, and Hall (1948). The showed that when the body was sufficiently heated, bare hands and feet would remain warm even when exposed to ambient temperatures as low as $-34°C$. Therefore, although the effects of bradykinen, the axon reflex, and the other vasoregulatory mechanisms are important to thermoregulation, the effect of the SNS on the peripheral vasculature is paramount (Burton & Edholm, 1954). This powerful centrally mediated phenomenon makes digital blood flow an appropriate target for behavioral control.

Epidemiology

Although a satisfactory epidemiologic survey of Raynaud's syndrome in the general population has not been conducted, Lewis (1949) has estimated that Raynaud's syndrome affects approximately 20% of most young people in its mildest forms. Similarly, Olsen & Nielson (1978) surveyed women aged 21–50 years in a cold environment in Copenhagen and found that 22% reported cold sensitivity. Clinical Raynaud's syndrome is found to occur five times more often in women than in men, with onset usually occurring in the first and second decades of life. Women are also more likely to have either idiopathic Raynaud's disease or associated connective tissue disease; men tend to present at an older age with a much greater incidence of associated atherosclerosis (Porter et al., 1981).

Although serve manifestations of Raynaud's syndrome in the general population are not common, certain occupational groups, particularly those who are exposed to cold temperatures or who routinely use vibrating equipment, seem especially vulnerable to the development of Raynaud's syndrome. For example, it has been estimated that 50% of workers exposed to alternating hot and cold in fish processing plants and as many as 90% of loggers and 50% of mine workers may eventually become affected (e.g., Chatterjee, Petrie, & Taylor, 1978; Mackiewisz &

Piskorz, 1977). A survey of 1540 forestry workers in Quebec revealed a prevalence of Raynaud's phenomenon of 30.5% among chain saw users and 8.7% among nonusers, with prevalence directly related to duration of chainsaw use. After 20 years of chainsaw use, over 50% of the population had Raynaud's syndrome. It is also noteworthy that the relative risk of Raynaud's syndrome for smokers was found to be nearly twice that for nonsmokers after 10 years of chainsaw use (Thériault, DeGuire, Gingras, & Laroche, 1980).

Medical Treatment of Raynaud's Disease

Until recently, medical treatment of Raynaud's syndrome was largely prophylactic. Characteristically, patients have been instructed to dress warmly, avoid exposure to cold, and avoid use of tobacco, birth control pills, beta-adrenergic blocking agents, and ergotamine preparations; with severe conditions, patients have been admonished to move to a warmer climate (Porter, et al., 1981; Pratt, 1949). Surgical treatment via sympathectomy, although effective in reducing vasospasms in the lower extremities has yielded unreliable results in the upper extremities (Spittell, 1972) and leaves permanent side effects (Patton, 1965). Drugs that block autonomic ganglia, act on peripheral or central adrenergic receptors, interfere with the action of norepinephrine, or directly relax vascular smooth muscle are the most common form of treatment (Coffman, 1979).

Since the 1960s, orally administered reserpine has been shown to decrease both the frequency and severity of vasospastic attacks in patients with Raynaud's syndrome (Abboud, Eckstein, Lawrence, & Hoak, 1967; Kontos & Wasserman, 1969; Romeo, Whalen, & Tindall, 1970). Even given in small doses, reserpine can have a profound effect on the CNS and produces a severe depression and even suicidal behavior, increased appetite, weight gain, as well as gastrointestinal complications (Nickerson, 1970). During the last decade, there had been hope that intra-arterial reserpine therapy would have a beneficial effect on the injected limb without the adverse systemic reactions commonly seen with oral administration. However, a recent double-blind study by Surwit, Gilgore, Duvic, Allen, and Neal (1983) determined that there was no indication that reserpine provided clinical improvement or changed vasomotor reactivity in the treated patients. Furthermore, intra-arterial reserpine did produce systemic cardiovascular effects lasting up to 6 weeks.

Kontos and Wasserman (1969) reported that positive results could also be obtained by administration of guanethadine and therefore concluded that therapeutic benefit resulted from a catecholamine-depleting effect and consequent decrease in adrenergic activity. Varadi and Lawrence (1969) used methyldopa to prevent vasospastic attacks in 42 patients who were exposed to experimental cold. Spittell (1972) reported that doses of 25mg to 50mg of tolazoline (a vasodilator with alpha-adrenergic blocking potential) three to four times a day is helpful in the management of mild Raynaud's disease. The combined results generally support the notion that decreasing adrenergic activity is important in producing clinical improvement. Other medications, such as papaverine, nicotinic acid, isoxsuprine, cyclanelate, and phenoxybenzamine have all been tried with varying degrees of success (Coffman, 1979; Halperin & Coffman, 1979). Most recently, Surwit, Gilgor, Allen, and Duvic (1984) demonstrated that prazosin, and alpha blocking agent, appeared effective in reducing vasospasms in patients with Raynaud's phenomenon associated with scleroderma. Several studies suggest that the new calcium channel blocking agents may also be useful (e.g., Conner, 1983; Smith & McKendry, 1982). In general, however, prazosin and calcium channel blockers can cause orthostatic hypotension. As the severity of the disease increases, however, the side effects produced by these medications begin to outweigh therapeutic benefit. Methyldopa can also provoke depression and gastrointestinal complications as well as lactation, extrapyramidal signs, and liver damage (Nickerson, 1970). Tolazoline can cause tachycardia, cardiac arrhythmias, anginal pain, and gastrointestinal disturbance and may even be a participating factor in myocardial infarction (Nickerson, 1970). In general, drug therapy has been hampered by the unavailability of any agent that specifically dilates only the vessels of the digits (Halperin & Coffman, 1979). Although certain drugs may produce temporary, symptomatic relief of Raynaud's disease, pharmacotherapy often causes intolerable side effects, especially when symptom severity demands vigorous treatment. More importantly, because most of these agents tend to work by reducing alpha-adrenergic activity, either locally or centrally, it is plausible that a behavioral intervention resulting in a central decrease in sympathetic activity could have equal therapeutic benefit.

CLINICAL EFFICACY

The previous BSA task force report on biofeedback in the treatment of vasoconstrictive syndromes (Taub & Stroebel, 1978) summarized research involving approximately 130 patients with pathological conditions of the peripheral vascular system. The majority of studies, however, were single-case report and limited group outcome studies that did not permit careful assessment of the mechanisms by which the effect of behavioral interventions is presumed to occur. A lack of adequate long-term follow-up data was also recognized. Questions were raised as to the adequacy of self-report data as a means of obtaining reliable information about Raynaud's symptom reduction, and the need for objective verification of the efficacy of thermal biofeedback through cold stress tests or similar means was emphasized. Although several controlled group outcome studies have been conducted since the last task force report, we shall see that certain key ambiguities and contradictions remain unresolved.

Voluntary Control of Peripheral Vasomotor Responses

Most of the research concerning voluntary control of digital bloodflow utilizes skin temperature as the dependent variable. However, the relationship of skin temperature to bloodflow is nonlinear. Temperature rises with bloodflow until it approaches core temperatures (36°–37°C). At that point, bloodflow can increase markedly whereas skin temperature will not change. Therefore, there are distinct limitations to this variable. Nevertheless, because skin temperature is easily measurable as well as quantifiable, it has been used in the majority of studies investigating voluntary control of digital bloodflow. As long as one keeps in mind the ceiling effect that confounds this measure, the results of studies utilizing skin temperature as a measure of bloodflow are usually interpretable.

There is ample evidence that peripheral vasomotor activity can be controlled to some extent through voluntary CNS activity. Hadfield (1920) and Barber (1970) reported control of skin temperature using eidetic imagery. When subjects were told to imagine that their hands were warm or cold, corresponding changes in skin temperature of the digits was observed. Maslach, Marshall, and Zimbardo (1972) demonstrated that subjects could learn to control digital temperature through the use of hypnosis. All hypnotized subjects demonstrated an ability to produce bilateral increases and decreases in skin temperature. Temperature decreases were easier to produce and were generally larger than temperature increases, however. The biofeedback paradigm brought renewed interest in voluntary control of autonomic functions and many demonstrations of skin temperature control (e.g., Keefe, 1975; Roberts, Schuler, Bacon, Zimmerman, & Patterson, 1975; Surwit, Shapiro, & Feld, 1976; Taub & Emurian, 1976). In most of these studies, voluntary skin temperature increases were smaller than temperature decreases.

The relative difficulty that subjects have in learning to vasodilate may be due to the primary role of active neural vasoconstrictive mechanisms in the digits (Surwit 1982). Hence most if not all vasodilation must take place by the reduction in ongoing alpha-adrenergic activity.

Furthermore, Surwit *et al.* (1976) hypothesized that because an orienting reflex to the biofeedback stimulus situation typically heightens sympathetic tone, increases in sympathetic activity are easier to learn with biofeedback than decreases in sympathetic activity. This hypothesis is consistent with results of studies on voluntary control on blood pressure and heart rate (Blanchard & Young, 1973), salivation (Wells, Feather, & Hedrich, 1973) and occipital alpha control (Paskowitz & Orne, 1974). Thus, nonstimulating relaxation strategies would seem to have an advantage over biofeedback in achieving a general sympatholytic effect. Biofeedback might, however, be advantageous in producing localized and specific alterations in blood flow.

In the previous BSA task force report, Taub and Stroebel (1978) noted that because Raynaud's disease symptoms are episodic, self-regulation strategies need only be implemented for short periods of time in order to be effective—perhaps just long enough to terminate or prevent an attack. Unlike the control of a chronic condition, which would involve continuous self-regulation over long periods of time, this is a much simpler requirement to place on a self-regulation task. Based on research with normals and Raynaud's patients, it is also a task that seems feasible.

Case Studies

In the first study in which patients suffering with Raynaud's disease were trained to increase peripheral bloodflow, Shapiro and Schwartz (1972) provided two patients suffering from primary Raynaud's disease with biofeedback of blood volume changes from a photoplethysmograph. The treatment was moderately successful for one patient, who reported a reduction in the severity of Raynaud's symptoms. Surwit (1973) reported the first systematic use of temperature feedback in the treatment of Raynaud's disease. Using a combination of autogenic and progressive relaxation techniques followed by a series of 52 laboratory biofeedback sessions over a 9-month period, the patient demonstrated a basal digital temperature rise from 23.3° to 26.6°C and a concomitant decrease in the frequency of vasospastic attacks. Jacobson, Hackett, Surman, and Silverberg (1973) explored the utility of hypnosis in temperature feedback. In this case, the patient showed very little improvement during the hypnosis portion of training; however, when biofeedback training was introduced, and the patient was instructed to increase finger temperature in relation to that of the forehead, a marked reduction in the frequency of vasospasms was observed.

The most systematic and controlled single-case study published to date was reported by Blanchard and Haynes (1975). Changes in skin temperature and the frequency of vasospastic attacks were evaluated under three conditions: a no-treatment baseline, a self-control technique, in which the patient was asked to try to increase her hand temperature in any way that she could, and biofeedback training to increase hand temperature in relation to that of the forehead. Only during the biofeedback sessions did the patient show an ability to increase her hand temperature, with reductions in the frequency of vasospastic attacks achieved concurrently with temperature biofeedback training alone.

In an effort to provide a more stringent measure of learned control of peripheral vasodilation, a number of researchers have suggested that one examine the ability of the patients to maintain hand temperature under cold stress. Taub (1977) described such a procedure with a patient who was fitted with a "cold suit" in which cold water could be rapidly circulated, exposing the patient's entire body to cold stress. Taub reported that this patient was able to increase hand temperature from 88°F to 89.5°F while the temperature of the cold suit was decreased from 80°F to 60°F. Unfortunately, no data were provided on the clinical changes observed in this patient.

Although these case studies did suggest that biofeedback might be clinically efficacious in the treatment of Raynaud's, their lack of appropriate methodological controls precluded attribution of the obtained benefits strictly to biofeedback. Recently, controlled group outcome studies have attempted to address more systematically the potential contribution particular behavioral techniques may provide.

Controlled Group Outcome Studies

Surwit, Pilon, and Fenton (1978) compared simple autogenic training exercises practiced at home with more elaborate biofeedback procedures and laboratory training in the treatment of Raynaud's syndrome. Thirty patients with vasospasms characteristic of Raynaud's syndrome were trained in either autogenic training or a combination of autogenic training and skin-temperature feedback. Training was conducted either in a laboratory or in three group sessions supplemented by extensive home practice. To assess the effects of training, all subjects were exposed to an initial cold challenge during which time the ambient temperature of a special chamber was dropped from 26°C to 17°C. Skin temperature was monitored continuously during a temperature change. This procedure was given to one half of the subjects before and following the 4-week training sequence. The remaining one half of the sample was initially not treated. They were exposed to two cold challenges 4 weeks apart without receiving any behavioral training. Following this control period, they were also trained and retested once again. All subjects, regardless of which condition they were trained in, showed a significant improvement in their ability to maintain digital temperature relative to both their initial cold challenge and to the second cold challenge given to the half of the sample not initially treated. Patients who served as no-treatment controls not only failed to show improvement during the second test but actually deteriorated in performance. In addition, all treated patients reported significant reductions in the frequency of vasospastic episodes over the 4-week episode. However, no additional benefits were observed for those subjects receiving skin-temperature biofeedback or the laboratory training course.

Similar findings were obtained by Keefe, Surwit, and Pilon (1980). Their study attempted to provide a more rigorous task of home-biofeedback training by having patients on a home-practice regimen use more sophisticated and sensitive feedback equipment than Surwit *et al.* (1978) used. In addition, this study compared the efficacy of autogenic training (which focuses specifically on sensations of warmth and heaviness in the hands) to general-relaxation training (which focuses on reducing muscular tension gradually throughout the body). Four laboratory cold challenges, like those described in the previous study, were given at Week 1 of a 4-week baseline and during Weeks 1, 3, and 5 of training. Twenty-one patients were randomly assigned to one of three treatment conditions. The first group received progressive muscle-relaxation and taped home-practice instructions; the second group received autogenic training and taped home instructions; and the third group received autogenic training, taped instructions, and a sophisticated electronic temperature-feedback device for home practice (a Cyborg J42 feedback thermometer). The results confirmed those of Surwit *et al.* (1978) that the effect of treatment was nonspecific and was not related to skin-temperature feedback *per se*. Data gathered from the cold challenges indicated that subjects improved gradually and significantly over the four challenges and that learning was taking place, despite the fact that ambient temperature was falling during this period. In addition, all treated patients experienced a 40% reduction in the frequency of vasospastic attacks.

Jacobson, Manschreck, and Silverberg (1979) reported similar results. They treated 12 patients suffering from Raynaud's syndrome with 12 sessions of muscle-relaxation training over a 6-week period. One half of the patients were also given auditory and visual skin-temperature feedback. Skin temperature during training as well as self-reports of improvements were monitored. Both groups showed significant increases in skin temperature during training, with larger skin-temperature increases shown by the group not receiving feedback. All subjects rated themselves moderately to markedly improved at one month, with seven subjects continuing to report improvement at 2 years. No data were collected on objective hand-temperature changes at follow-up.

To date, the only controlled group outcome study to demonstrate significantly greater reduction in Raynaud's symptom frequency following temperature feedback versus other relaxation strategies was reported by Freedman, Ianni, and Wenig (1983). In their study, 32 subjects with idiopathic Raynaud's disease were randomly assigned to receive finger-temperature feedback (TEMP), finger-temperature feedback under cold stress (TEMPCS), frontalis electromyographic feedback (EMG) or autogenic training (AUTO). In addition, because emotional stress has been implicated as a cause of Raynaud's attacks, cognitive stress management (Meichenbaum, 1977) was concurrently employed with one half of the patients in each treatment group. During all phases of assessment subjects' finger temperature, relaxation (EMG level, heart rate, respiration rate, and skin conductance level) and subjective stress ratings were recorded. All groups participated in two pretreatment sessions, one in which subjects were told to increase the temperature of their fingers as much as possible using any mental means, and a second in which subjects were exposed to a cold stress. Each subject received 10 biweekly training sessions consisting of 10 minutes of adaptation, a 16-minute resting baseline, and 16 minutes of feedback or instructions. One week and one year after the last training session, each subject was given posttraining voluntary control and cold stress tests.

During training, the TEMP and TEMPCS subjects showed significant finger temperature increases whereas the EMG and AUTO subjects did not. Whereas EMG and AUTO groups showed significant declines in muscle tension and stress ratings, the other groups did not. During the initial posttraining voluntary control and cold stress tests, TEMP subjects demonstrated finger temperatures significantly higher than the other three groups. One year later, however, TEMPCS subjects showed the best performance with TEMP subjects also showing a significant but smaller temperature increase. Decrements in reported symptoms were 92.5% for the TEMPCS group, 66.8% for the TEMP group, 32.6% for the AUTO group, and 17.0% for the EMG group. Tonic skin temperature levels measured in the natural environment were not altered in these patients, but following TEMP or TEMPCS treatment, colder temperatures were needed to produce vasospastic attacks. The addition of cognitive stress management had no significant effects on any procedure.

In an attempt to discern the contribution of nonspecific factors (e.g., placebo or seasonal changes) to therapeutic outcomes, Guglielmi, Roberts, and Patterson (1982) recently conducted a group outcome study employing the double-blind design. In this study neither the subjects nor the experimenters were aware of whether the subjects were getting skin-temperature feedback or EMG feedback. There was also a third no-treatment control group (however, due to attention periodically given to these subjects by the experimenters, this group may also have benefited from nonspecific or placebo effects). Although both auditory and visual feedback was given to both groups receiving laboratory training, subjects were not told about the nature of the physiological change upon which feedback was contingent. Not all subjects who received laboratory training over 20 sessions actually learned to produce reliable physiological training in the prescribed direction (indeed, some actually learned the opposite response). Although all patients showed a marked decrease in the number of vasospastic attacks, no significant differences were found among the three treatment groups on any of the clinical measures used to assess symptomatic relief. Although Guglielmi et al. (1982) argued that any therapeutic benefit therefore must be ascribed to nonspecific factors, Surwit and Keefe (1983) noted that the failure to find positive results could be directly attributed to their double-blind experimental design. Surwit and Keefe contended that major problems arise when the double-blind is applied to research on self-regulation as a behavioral treatment of disease. Research on self-regulation attempts to test whether learned control over physiological response is clinically efficacious. Methods of enhancing this learned control (e.g., biofeedback, autogenic training, progressive relaxation) are based on the notion that increasing awareness of the physiological response will lead to improved voluntary control of those responses. If patients are unaware of the response being trained, less learning takes place.

Long-Term Effectiveness

There are few systematic evaluations of the long-term effectiveness of behavioral techniques in Raynaud's syndrome. As stated earlier, Jacobson et al. (1979) reported that 7 of their 12 subjects were symptomatically improved 2 years after behavioral treatment. Recall that in the Freedman et al. (1983) study, one year after treatment with finger temperature feedback (with or without cold stress), subjects reported symptom reductions of 92.5% and 66.8%, respectively. A 3-year followup of 81.3% ($N = 13$) of the subjects in these two treatment conditions (Freedman, Ianni, & Wenig, 1985) revealed that significant symptom reductions were maintained—despite the fact that subjects no longer showed significant temperature control during the 2-year follow-up voluntary temperature control test.

A similar contradiction between self-reported symptomatic relief and objective assessment measures was found by Keefe, Surwit, and Pilon (1979). Keefe et al. (1979) reevaluated 19 patients who had participated in the study of Surwit *et al.* (1978). One year following their initial training, patients were again asked to record the number and severity of vasospasms as well as the number of times they practiced self-control techniques. They also were given another cold challenge to reassess objectively their vasomotor response to cold. Although all patients reported continued improvement in the number of vasospasms they were experiencing, their digital temperatures during the cold challenge returned to pretreatment levels. Also, most patients were practicing voluntary-control procedures much less frequently than immediately following treatment. The discrepancy between self-reports of improvement and cold performance has two explanations. First, it is possible that subjects were simply trying to please the investigators by reporting fewer vasospastic attacks. It is also reasonable to believe that subjects actually did retain some vasomotor control—enough to prevent vasospasms but not enough to maintain higher temperature during the cold challenge. Mittelmann and Wolff (1939) demonstrated that a drop in digital temperature alone is not sufficient to bring on vasospasms. They noted that low digital temperature is a precursor to vasospasms only if the subject is autonomically aroused.

Raynaud's Syndrome in Severe Vascular Disease

Several investigators have examined the application of behavioral techniques in the treatment of Raynaud's phenomenon in severe peripheral vascular disease (e.g., scleroderma, carpal tunnel syndrome, vibrating tool injury). May and Webber (1976) treated four patients having Raynaud's phenomenon and scleroderma or systemic lupus erythematosus with 16 sessions of skin-temperature biofeedback, autogenic training, and progressive relaxation. These patients reported fewer vasospastic attacks over the 8-week training period and showed increased finger-temperature during biofeedback. Unfortunately, these findings were not statistically tested. Adair and Theobald (1978) treated one severe case of scleroderma and Raynaud's phenomenon with finger-temperature feedback and imagery techniques. The patient's baseline and maximum finger temperatures increased over the 10 training sessions and these gains were partially maintained at 6-month follow-up. The patient also showed reduced digital ulceration and required less pain medication. Freedman, Lynn, Ianni, and Hale (1981) trained six patients with apparent idiopathic Raynaud's disease and four patients with Raynaud's phenomenon with 12 sessions of finger-temperature biofeedback. The mean frequency of vasospastic attacks was reduced to 7.5% of what was reported during the pretreatment baseline and was maintained for a one-year follow-up. All trained patients demonstrated a significant control of digital temperature during laboratory training sessions, with the Raynaud's phenomenon patients showing greater temperature increases during feedback than the Raynaud's disease patients. Freedman, Ianni, and Wenig (1984) randomly assigned 24 patients with scleroderma and Raynaud's phenomenon to three groups (temperature feedback, EMG feedback, and autogenic training). Only subjects receiving temperature biofeedback showed increased finger temperatures. However, they were unable to maintain these changes during cold stress, and none of the groups showed significant clinical improvement. Finally, Keefe, Surwit, and Pilon (1981) reported on one patient with severe Raynaud's syndrome and mixed connective tissue disease who was treated with both autogenic and biofeedback techniques. In addition to fewer reported vasospasms, this patient showed a gradual increase in resistance to repeated cold procedures over a 7-month training period. By the end of this period, the patient was able to demonstrate a 7°C increase in digital temperature in response to a 20°C ambient cold exposure. These data make a strong case for the utility of training even when vascular disease is extensive.

Individual Differences and Response to Treatment

There is an extensive literature on the use of psychometric tests to predict success with various forms of behavioral treatment (e.g., Lanyon, 1966). Another literature identifies variables that seem to predict success with electromyographic (EMG)-feedback-assisted relaxation training. Several studies have suggested that subjects with an internal locus of control are better able to relax with EMG biofeedback than subjects with an external locus of control (Carlson, 1977; Fotopoulos & Binegar, 1977; Reinking, 1977). Most recently Surwit, Bradner, Fenton, and Pilon (1979) identified several variables as important in predicting the response of patients to a behavioral program designed to treat Raynaud's syndrome. These investigators found that subjects improvements as measured by increases in skin temperature between a pre- and posttreatment cold challenge, could be predicted by subjects' responses to a simple paper-and-pencil test. Thirty patients with Raynaud's syndrome who were treated with autogenic training were given the Psychological Screening Inventory (Lanyon, 1973). Subjects scoring high in the Alienation scale of this inventory were found to show no improvement in skin temperature in response to cold following training, whereas subjects who scored low in Alienation scored net increases of 4.5°C during the challenge after training. According to Lanyon (1973), high scores on the Alienation scale are associated with high scores on those Minnesota Multiphasic Personality Inventory scales related to psychopathology (schizophrenia, infrequency, paranoia, and hypermania). People with high scores on this scale perceive themselves as not responsible for (or not in control of) their own lives. Thus, this scale appears sensitive to a feeling of self-control, which seems important for success in treatment based on the exercise of self-control.

The Combined Effect of Behavioral and Pharmacologic Interventions

As previously described, current pharmacotherapy provides only limited relief because full benefit is often prevented by averse reactions that limit dosage (Coffman, 1979). Theoretically, relaxation techniques should augment the effects of medication and enhance their therapeutic efficacy without increasing the adverse reactions accompanying most medication. Surwit and colleagues (Surwit, Allen, Gilgore, & Duvic, 1982) demonstrated that autogenic training could facilitate the action of a peripherally acting sympathetic blocking agent in raising digital skin temperature during cold exposure in patients with Raynaud's syndrome and scleroderma. Eighteen female and two male patients with sclero-derma and prominent Raynaud's syndrome of at least 2 years duration were given a cold challenge similar to that described elsewhere (see Surwit et al., 1978). Subjects were then given either 1 mg three times a day of prazosin hydrochloride, which is a presynaptic alpha one blocking agent, or a matched placebo. All subjects and investigators were blind to the experimental condition of the subjects. Four weeks following initiation of drug treatment, the cold challenge was repeated. At that time, all subjects were given autogenic training. Four weeks later, the cold challenge was repeated again. It was found that only the combination of autogenic training and prazosin hydrochloride was effective in raising digital temperature during the ambient cold challenge. Neither prazosin nor autogenic training alone was effective in altering finger temperature during cold in this patient population. Thus, it appears as though autogenic training can work in concert with an alpha blocking agent to produce an additive effect. Whether relaxation training or biofeedback also augment pharmacological treatment has not yet been investigated.

Summary on Clinical Efficacy

By 1977, at least five widely quoted case studies using biofeedback in combination with other instructional techniques in the treatment of Raynaud's syndrome has been published. In each of the studies, however the number of subjects was small and no statistical treatment of the data was presented. Because only cases in which such treatment techniques are successful tend to be published, the number of failures has gone unreported. Moreover, without a no-treatment or other appropriate control group, the therapeutic gains reported cannot be attributed to biofeedback. Finally, in each study multiple treatment techniques were used. When treatment effects are analyzed over such a long time period the possibility of carry-over effects from one treatment to another is strong. Although patients may show change during temperature biofeedback sessions, these changes may be mediated by a cognitive strategy previously taught to the patient, for example, self-hypnosis or autogenic training.

Controlled group outcome studies (e.g., Jacobson et al., 1979; Keefe et al., 1980; Surwit et al., 1978) utilizing various behavioral training procedures—autogenic training and progressive muscle relaxation, with and without skin temperature biofeedback—have typically reported symptom reduction in the 30% to 40% range. A notable exception is the study by Freedman et al. (1983), which showed 60% to 90% symptom reduction in patients receiving temperature feedback alone. Minimally, these results equal the best efforts of surgical and pharmacologic intervention. Furthermore, these benefits seem to be maintained up to 3 years after follow-up and occur without side effects. It also appears that combined pharmacologic and behavioral interventions may be particularly efficacious (Surwit, Allen, et al., 1982).

Clinical Experience

The significant but somewhat modest symptom reductions reported in most controlled group outcome studies contrast sharply with the treatment benefits described in many clinical reports. For example, Sedlacek (1979) reports that biofeedback affords relief in 70% to 80% of "properly selected" patients. No controlled group outcome study has reported similarly striking results. However, it must be kept in mind that most clinical interventions are more intensive and comprehensive than those used in controlled outcome studies so it is not completely surprising that better results are obtained in practice than in research. On the other hand, clinical results are often not objectively verified and success rates eminating from clinical programs are probably somewhat inflated due to placebo effects and demand characteristics of the clinical setting acting on patient self-reports of improvement.

SPECIFICITY OF EFFECT

Most of the controlled research does not support the notion that biofeedback per se is the essential ingredient in a successful behavioral intervention for Raynaud's. Research by Surwit et al. (1978), Keefe et al. (1980), and Jacobson et al. (1979) failed to demonstrate any substantial symptom decrement attributable to the inclusion of skin-temperature biofeedback. Autogenic training and muscle relaxation training appeared to produce effects equivalent to temperature biofeedback alone or in combination with other behavioral approaches.

Two recent studies do point to a difference in therapeutic efficacy between biofeedback-assisted and non-biofeedback-assisted relaxation procedures. Surwit and Fenton (1980) compared the performance of subjects during autogenic training both with and without skin-temperature feedback. Eight subjects received eight sessions of feedback-assisted autogenic instructions and eight subjects received eight sessions of autogenic training alone. Typically, all subjects showed a .3°C rise from baseline temperature levels during the 5-minute interval when they were given autogenic instructions. Following the playing of the tapes, subjects were asked to recite the autogenic phrases to themselves over a 72-minute period. All subjects demonstrated a decrease in digital skin temperature over this period. However, those subjects receiving skin-temperature feedback were able to maintain higher levels of digital temperature throughout the course of the session. Thus, although the autogenic instructions or suggestions were seen as responsible for the initial changes in vasomotor tone, feedback did seem to be some help in allowing subjects to maintain these changes. The previously described study by Freedman et al. (1981) was the first to demonstrate that biofeedback training without autogenic training or other relaxation strategies could be effective in the treatment of vasospastic diseases. Only these two studies (Freedman et al., 1983; Surwit & Fenton, 1980) demonstrated a possible specific contribution superiority of temperature feedback over other relaxation strategies.

Mechanism of Action

Whereas there is substantial evidence to support the notion that Raynaud's disease may be treated effectively by a variety of behavioral techniques, the mechanism by which these techniques act to reduce vasospastic frequency is completely open to question. Do autogenic procedures, biofeedback procedures, and progressive relaxation work via similar mechanisms? Unfortunately, there is little data available on this question. Although one may speculate that all these techniques work to reduce SNS activity, the neuroendocrine consequences of these procedures have not been identified. If, as some have speculated (e.g., Taub, 1977), biofeedback is capable of producing very localized vasomotor responses, it would operate via a different neuroendocrine mechanism than general relaxation. Furthermore, autogenic training, which involves the use of very specific postural cues, may operate via a different mechanism than progressive muscle relaxation. One mechanism that does not seem to account for symptomatic improvement following temperature feedback training is an increase in the overall tonic level of finger temperature. Freedman *et al.* (1985) found no differences between their four treatment groups at one-year follow-up in finger temperature measured over a 24-hour period.

Both increased autonomic arousal and low digital temperature have been implicated in the production of vasospastic attacks (Mittlemann & Wolff, 1939). It is possible that the therapeutic effect of autogenic and relaxation training results from a decreased adrenal cortical activity (Surwit, 1982), whereas the effect of temperature feedback may result from increased beta adrenergic activity (Freedman *et al.*, 1983). Although it had generally been thought that vascular control of digital blood flow resulted solely from sympathetically mediated alpha adrenergic vasoconstriction (Surwit, Williams, & Shapiro, 1982), a beta adrenergic vasodilating mechanism has recently been identified in the finger (Cohen & Coffman, 1981). As Freedman *et al.* (1983) pointed out, a different physiological mechanism may therefore exist to explain increased digital bloodflow in the absence of decreased sympathetic activity.

COST-EFFECTIVENESS

Even if one uses the potentially conservative success rates claimed by most controlled research (i.e., 30%–40%), the efficacy of behavioral treatment of Raynauds' compares very favorably to pharmacologic and surgical intervention. If for the moment we assume that extensive (i.e., 15–20 sessions) of laboratory biofeedback training sessions are warranted, the overall expense is still far less than for surgical intervention, without the risk of even more costly iatrogenic effects. Now we are also beginning to see evidence suggesting sustained long-term effectiveness of behavioral treatment (e.g., Freedman *et al.*, 1985). Should such results be confirmed, it is likely that initial biofeedback training costs would compare favorably to the cost of ongoing pharmacologic therapy.

Note, however, that substantial numbers of laboratory biofeedback training sessions may not be necessary. A careful review of the literature reveals that biofeedback training *per se* probably is not an essential ingredient. Alternative, potentially less costly inventions, such as muscle relaxation and autogenic training, often achieve equivalent results. Furthermore, Keefe *et al.* (1980) have demonstrated the efficacy of home training for some patients.

FUTURE RESEARCH

The previously reviewed studies provide strong support for the use of behavioral techniques in the treatment of vasospasms characteristic of Raynaud's syndrome. The reductions in symptoms reported by patients immediately after treatment and up to one year later are impressive and parallel the best clinical effects of many medical and surgical interventions. Moreover, these benefits accrue without known side effects. Only recently, however, have any controlled studies (Freedman *et al.* 1981, 1983) demonstrated that biofeedback procedures have any advantage over simpler, less costly relaxation-training methods. It is not completely clear what may account for the discrepancies between these results and those of other investigations (e.g., Guglielmi *et al.*, 1982; Keefe *et al.*, 1980; Surwit *et al.*, 1978).

Although the double-blind design as employed by Guglielmi *et al.* (1982) has serious flaws (Surwit & Keefe, 1983), their study does highlight the potentially important contribution of nonspecific factors (especially placebo effects) to Raynaud's syndrome treatment studies. Indeed, in one early study (Lipkin, McDevitt, Schwartz, & Duryee, 1945), some Raynaud's patients showed excellent objective and subjective symptomatic improvement after treatment with saline injections and a sham iontophoresis procedure. Further research involving wait-list groups, multiple baselines, and other appropriate controls is clearly warranted. Guglielmi *et al.* (1982) also raised important questions concerning the adequacy of baseline periods and carefulness of control for ambient outdoor temperature. It has been demonstrated that hand temperatures tend to increase when a patient moves from the cool outdoors and into a comfortable ambient temperature. Whereas it may be obvious that Raynaud's patients report significantly greater vasospastic attacks in colder months than warmer months, it is unclear what effects weekly, daily, diurnal, or hourly variations in outdoor temperature may have on indoor symptom severity and frequency, adaptation periods, cold stress test, or training sessions.

Although attempts have been made to distinguish the impact of biofeedback from that of other behavioral techniques (e.g., autogenic training and progressive muscle relaxation) it may not be a simple task to disentangle these processes. Several authors (Blanchard & Haynes, 1975; Schwartz, 1973) reported that in order to get the desired effect from the feedback apparatus, a number of subjects spontaneously evolved strategies of picturing themselves at a hot setting such as the beach. Although concurrent physiological recordings of heart rate, skin conductance level, and EMG levels may help discern any general relaxation effect, it is difficult to reliably discern the cognitive strategies subjects may use to augment biofeedback. It is also possible that feedback may serve to reinforce other strategies, such as use of imagery.

Several studies (e.g., Keefe *et al.*, 1979) have revealed an apparent contradiction between patients inability to demonstrate voluntary vasomotor control while reporting substantial symptom decreases. These findings do confirm other reports (see Keefe, Kopel, & Gordon, 1978) that indicate discrepancies between verbal report and observable behavior. They also call into question previous clinical research on the medical treatment of Raynaud's disease that relies heavily on patient reports on improvement for data (e.g., Kontos & Wasserman, 1969; Willerson, Thompson, Hookman, Herdt, & Decker, 1970). Furthermore, it appears that different researchers may be employing different criteria for a self-reported Raynaud's attack. Average frequency of attacks per month ranges from approximately 24 (Guglielmi *et al.*, 1982) to over 80 (Freedman *et al.*, 1981) during pretreatment phases of several studies.

The greatest impediment to the development of a successful treatment for Raynaud's disease has been our ignorance of its pathophysiology. Raynaud's phenomenon is differentiated from Raynaud's disease only on the basis of history. Whether or not the same mechanism is responsible for both conditions is open to question. In certain cases, in which the mechanism of disease is understood, effective treatments have been devised (e.g., surgical release of a trapped nerve in carpal tunnel syndrome). Surwit *et al.* (1981) suggested that idiopathic Raynaud's disease may be associated with elevated plasma cortisol. If this is the case, the nonspecific relaxation techniques, which may lower plasma cortisol (DeGood & Redgate, 1982; Jevning, Wilson, & Davidson, 1978; Surwit & Feinglos, 1984) should be as useful as the more specific biofeedback and autogenic procedures. Indeed, much of the existing literature supports this contention (Jacobson *et al.*, 1979; Keefe *et al.*, 1979; Surwit *et al.*, 1978).

Conclusions

Controlled research studies involving over 160 patients have demonstrated that behavioral treatment of Raynaud's Syndrome can be very effective, paralleling the best clinical effects of many medical and surgical interventions. In these studies, patients have typically reported reductions in symptom frequency of between 30% and 90%. Furthermore, these benefits occur without side effects. There are 10 studies that demonstrate that behavioral treatment benefits are long lasting. Poor treatment durability has been related to poor compliance. Behavioral treatment benefits have not only been obtained for patients with idiopathic

Raynaud's disease, but also with the more severe peripheral vascular diseases often seen in Raynaud's phenomenon. Research has produced conflicting reports as to whether skin temperature biofeedback procedures have any significant advantage over simpler relaxation training methods, such as autogenic training. Although biofeedback procedures are generally more costly than the simpler methods, both can be made to be extremely cost-effective and in many cases can be largely self-administered by the patient. Overall, especially in light of the inadequacies of current medical and surgical treatments for Raynaud's Syndrome, behavioral interventions seem to have much to add to the care of patients with this problem.

REFERENCES

Abboud, F. M., Eckstein, J. W., Lawrence, M. S., & Hoak, J. C. (1967). Preliminary observations on the use of intra-arterial reserpine in Raynaud's phenomenon. *Circulation, 36* (no. 4, Suppl. II) 11–49, (Abstract).

Adair, J., & Theobald, D. (1978). Raynaud's phenomenon: treatment of a severe case with biofeedback. *Journal of the Indiana State Medical Association, 71,* 990–993.

Allen, E. V., & Brown, G. E. (1932). Raynaud's disease: A critical review of the minimal requisite for diagnosis. *American Journal of Medical Sciences, 183,* 187–200.

Barber, T. X. (1970). *LSD, marihuana, yoga, and hypnosis.* Chicago, IL: Aldine.

Blanchard, E. B., & Haynes, M. R. (1975). Biofeedback treatment of a case of Raynaud's disease. *Journal of Behavior Therapy & Experimental Psychiatry, 6,* 230–234.

Blanchard, E. B., & Young, L. D. (1973). Self-control of cardiac functioning: A promise as yet unfulfilled. *Psychology Bulletin, 79,* 145–163.

Burton, A. C., & Edholm, O. G. (1954). *Man in a cold environment: Physiological and pathological effects of exposure to low temperatures.* Baltimore, MD: Williams & Wilkins.

Carlson, J. G. (1977). Locus of control and frontal electromyographic response training. *Biofeedback and Self-Regulation, 2,* 259–271.

Chatterjee, D. S., Petrie, A., & Taylor, W. (1978). Prevalence of vibration-induced white finger in flourspar mines in Weardale. *British Journal of Industrial Medicine, 35,* 208–218.

Coffman, J. D. (1979). Vasodilators in peripheral vascular disease. *New England Journal of Medicine, 300,* 232–236.

Cohen, R., & Coffman, J. D. (1981). Beta adrenergic vasodilator mechanism in the finger. *Circulation Research, 49,* 1196–1201.

Conner, C. S. (1983). Nifedipine: Two new uses. *Drug Intelligence and Clinical Pharmacy, 17,* 457–458.

DeGood, D. E., & Redgate, E. S. (1982). Interrelationship of plasma cortisol and other activation indices during EMG biofeedback training. *Journal of Behavioral Medicine, 5,* 213–224.

DeTakats, E., & Fowler, E. F. (1962). Raynaud's phenomenon. *Journal of the American Medical Association, 179,* 1–8.

Folkow, B. (1955). Nervous control of the blood vessels. *Physiological Review, 35,* 629–663.

Fotopoulos, S. S., & Binegar, G. A. (1977). Differences in baseline and volitional control of EEG (8-12Hz and 13-20Hz), EMG and skin temperature: Internal versus external orientation. (Abstract). Biofeedback and Self-Regulation 2, 357–358.

Freedman, R., Lynn, S., Ianni, P. & Hale, P. (1981). Biofeedback treatment of Raynaud's disease and phenomenon. *Biofeedback and Self-Regulation, 6,* 355–364.

Freedman, R. R., Ianni, P. & Wenig, P. (1983). Behavioral treatment of Raynaud's disease: Long-term follow-up. *Journal of Consulting and Clinical Psychology, 53,* 136.

Freedman, R. R., Ianni, P. & Wenig, P. (1984). Behavioral treatment of Raynaud's phenomenon in scleroderma. *Journal of Behavioral Medicine 1,* 343–354.

Freedman, R. R., Ianni, P. & Wenig, P. (1985). Behavioral treatment of Raynaud's disease. *Journal of Consulting and Clinical Psychology, 51,* 539–549.

Gifford, R. W., & Hines, E. A. (1957). Raynaud's disease among women and girls. *Circulation, 16,* 1012–1021.

Goldie, R. G. (1976). The effects of hydrocortisone on responses to and extraneuronal uptake of (−)-isoprenaline in rat and guinea-pig atria. *Clinical and Experimental Pharmacology and Physiology, 3,* 225–233.

Grahm, D. T. (1955). Cutaneous vascular reactions in Raynaud's disease and in states of hostility, anxiety, and depression. *Psychosomatic Medicine, 17,* 200–207.

Grahm, D. T., Stern, J. A., & Winokur, C. (1958). Experimental investigation of the specificity of attitude hypothesis in psychosomatic disease. *Psychosomatic Medicine, 20,* 446–457.

Guglielmi, R. S., Roberts, A. H., & Patterson, R. (1982). Skin temperature biofeedback for Raynaud's disease: A double-blind study. *Biofeedback and Self-Regulation, 7,* 99–120.

Hadfield, A. (1920). The influence of suggestion on body temperature. *Lancet, 2,* 82–89.

Halperin, J. L., & Coffman, J. D. (1979). Pathophysiology of Raynaud's disease. *Archives of Internal Medicine, 139,* 89–92.

Hoffman, G. S. (1980). Raynaud's disease and phenomenon. *American Family Physician, 21,* 91–97.

Jacobson, A. M., Hackett, T. P., Surman, O. S., & Silverberg, E. L. (1973). Raynaud's phenomenon: Treatment with hypnotic and operant technique. *Journal of the American Medical Association, 225,* 739–470.

Jacobson, A. M., Manschreck, T. C., & Silverberg, E. (1979). Behavioral treatment for Raynaud's disease: A comparative study with long-term follow-up. *American Journal of Psychiatry, 136,* 844–846.

Jevning, R., Wilson, A. F., & Davidson, J. M. (1978). Adrenocortical activity during meditation. *Hormone Behavior, 10,* 54–60.

Keefe, F. J. (1975). Conditioning changes in differential skin temperature. *Perceptual and Motor Skills, 40,* 283–288.

Keefe, F. J., Kopel, S., & Gordon, S. (1978). *A practical guide to behavioral assessment.* New York: Springer.

Keefe, F. J., Surwit, R. S., & Pilon, R. N. (1979). A one-year follow-up of Raynaud's patients treated with behavioral therapy techniques. *Journal of Behavioral Medicine, 2,* 385–391.

Keefe, F. J., Surwit, R. S., & Pilon, R. N. (1980). Biofeedback, autogenic training and progressive relaxation in the treatment of Raynaud's disease. *Journal of Applied Behavior Analysis, 13,* 3–11.

Keefe, F. J., Surwit, R. S., & Pilon, R. N. (1981). Collagen vascular disease: Can behavior therapy help? *Journal of Behavior Therapy and Experimental Psychiatry, 12,* 171–175.

Kontos, H. A., & Wasserman, A. J. (1969). Effects of reserpine in Raynaud's phenomenon. *Circulation, 3,* 259–266.

Lanyon, R. I. (1966). The MMPI and prognosis in stuttering therapy. *Journal of Speech and Hearing Disorders, 31,* 186–191.

Lanyon, R. I. (1973). *Psychological Screening Inventory Manual.* Goshen, N.Y.: Research Psychologist Press.

Lewis, T. (1949). *Vascular disorders of the limbs: Described for practitioners and students.* London: Macmillan.

Lipkin, M., McDevitt, E., Schwartz, M., & Duryee, A. (1945). On the effects of suggestion in the treatment of vasospastic disorders of the extremities. *Psychosomatic Medicine, 7,* 152–159.

Mackiewisz, A., & Piskorz, A. Raynaud's phenomenon following long-term repeated action of great differences of temperature. *Journal of Cardiovascular Surgery, 18,* 151–154.

Maslach, C., Marshall, G., & Zimbardo, P. G. (1972). Hypnotic control of peripheral skin temperature: A case report. *Psychophysiology, 9,* 600–605.

May, D., & Weber, C. (1976). Temperature feedback training for symptoms reduction in primary and secondary Raynaud's disease. *Biofeedback and Self-Regulation, 1,* 317.

Meichenbaum, D. (1977). *Cognitive-behavior modification.* New York: Plenum Press.

Mendlowitz, M., & Naftchi, N. (1959). The digital circulation in Raynaud's disease. *American Journal of Cardiology, 4,* 580–584.

Mittelmann, B., & Wolff, H. G. (1939). Affective states and skin temperature: Experimental study of subject with "cold hands" and Raynaud's syndrome. *Psychosomatic Medicine, 1,* 271–292.

Nickerson, M. Vasodilator drugs. (1970). In L. S. Goodman & A. Gilman (Eds.), *The pharmacologic basis of therapeutics.* New york: Macmillan.

Olsen, N., & Nielsen, S. L. (1978). Prevalence of primary Raynaud's phenomenon in young females. *Scandanavian Journal of Clinical Laboratory Investigation, 37,* 761–764.

Paskowitz, D. A., & Orne, M. T. (1974). Visual effects on alpha feedback training. *Science, 181,* 360–363.

Patton, H. D. (1965). The autonomic nervous system. In T. C. Ruch, H. D. Patton, J. W. Woodbury, & A. L. Towe (Eds.), *Neurophysiology* (pp. 226–235). Philadelphia, PA: W. B. Saunders.

Peacock, J. H. (1959). Peripheral venous blood concentration of epinephrine and norepinephrine in primary Raynaud's disease. *Circulation Research, 7,* 821–827.

Porter, J. M., Rivers, S. P., Anderson, C. J., & Baur, G. M. (1981). Evaluation and management of patients with Raynaud's syndrome. *The American Journal of Surgery, 142* 183–189.

Pratt, G. H. (1949). *Surgical management of vascular disease.* Philadelphia, PA: Lea & Febiger.

Rapaport, S. I., Fetcher, E. S., & Hall, J. F. (1948). Physiological protection of the extremities from severe cold. *Federal Proceedings, 7,* 99.

Raynaud, M. (1862). *De l'asphyxie locale et de la gangrène symétrique des extremités.* Paris: Rignoux.

Reinking, R. H. (1977). The influence of internal-external control and trait anxiety on acquisition of EMG control. (Abstract). *Biofeedback and Self-Regulation, 2,* 357–358.

Roberts, A. H., Schuler, J., Bacon, J. R., Zimmerman, R. L., & Patterson, R. (1975). Individual differences and autonomic control: Absorption, hypnotic susceptibility, and the unilateral control of skin temperature. *Journal of Abnormal Psychology, 84,* 272–279.

Romeo, S. G., Whalen, R. E., & Tindall, J. P. (1970). Intra-arterial administration of reserpine. Its use in patients with Raynaud's disease or Raynaud's phenomenon. *Archives of Internal Medicine, 125,* 825–829.

Schmid, P. G., Eckstein, J. W., & Abboud, F. M. (1976). Comparison of effects of deoxycorticosterone and dexamethasone on cardiovascular responses to norepinephrine. *Journal of Clinical Investigation, 46,* 590–597.

Schwartz, G. E. (1973). Biofeedback as therapy: Some theoretical and practical issues. *American Psychologist, 28,* 666–673.

Sedlacek, K. (1979), Biofeedback for Raynaud's disease. *Psychosomatics, 20,* 535–541.

Shapiro, D., & Schwartz, G. E. (1972). Biofeedback and visceral learning: Clinical applications. *Seminars in Psychiatry, 4,* 171–184.

Smith, C. D., & McKendry, R. J. R. (1982). Controlled trial of nifedipine in the treatment of Raynaud's phenomenon. *Lancet, 2* (8311), 1299–1301.

Sokolov, Y. N. (1963) *Perception and the conditioned reflex*. London: Pergamon.

Spittell, J. A. (1972). Raynaud's phenomenon and allied vasospastic condition. In J. F. Fairbairn, J. C. Juergens, & A. Spittell (Eds.), *Allen-Barker Hines peripheral vascular diseases* (4th ed., pp. 387–420). Philadelphia, PA: W. B. Saunders.

Surwit, R. S. Raynaud's disease. (1973). In L. Birk (Ed.), *Biofeedback: Behavioral Medicine* (pp. 123–130). New York: Grune & Stratton.

Surwit, R. S. (1982). Behavioral treatment of Raynaud's syndrome in peripheral vascular disease. *Journal of Consulting and Clinical Psychology, 50,* 922–932.

Surwit, R. S., & Feinglos, M. N. (1984). Relaxation induced improvement in glucose tolerance is associated with decreased plasma cortisol. *Diabetes Care, 7,* 203–204.

Surwit, R. S., & Fenton, C. H. (1980). Feedback and instruction in the control of digital skin temperature. *Psychophysiology, 17,* 129–132.

Surwit, R. S., & Keefe, F. J. (1983). The blind leading the blind: problems with the "double-blind" design in clinical biofeedback research. *Biofeedback and Self-Regulation, 8,* 1–8.

Surwit, R. S., Shapiro, D., & Feld, J. L. (1976). Digital temperature autoregulation and associated cardiovascular changes. *Psychophysiology, 13,* 242–248.

Surwit, R. S., Pilon, R. N., & Fenton, C. H. (1978). Behavioral treatment of Raynaud's disease. *Journal of Behavioral Medicine, 1,* 323–335.

Surwit, R. S., Bradner, M. N., Fenton, C. H., & Pilon, R. N. (1979). Individual differences in response to the behavioral treatment of Raynaud's disease. *Journal of Consulting and Clinical Psychology, 47,* 363–367.

Surwit, R. S., Allen, L. M., Gilgor, R. S., & Duvic, M. (1982). The combined effect of prazosin and autogenic training on cold reactivity in Raynaud's phenomenon. *Biofeedback and Self-Regulation, 7,* 537–544.

Surwit, R. S., Williams, R. B., & Shapiro, D. (1982). *Behavioral approaches to cardiovascular disease*. New York: Academic Press.

Surwit, R. S., Allen, L. M., Gilgor, R. S., Schanberg, S., Kuhn, C., & Duvic, M. (1983). Neuroendocrine response to cold in Raynaud's syndrome. *Life Sciences, 32,* 995–1000.

Surwit, R. S., Gilgor, R. S., Allen, L. M., & Neal, J. A. (1983). Intra-arterial reserpine for Raynaud's syndrome, *Archives of Dermatology, 119,* 733–735.

Surwit, R. S., Gilgor, R. S., Allen, L. M., & Duvic, M. (1984). A double-blind study of prazosin in the treatment of Raynaud's phenomenon in scleroderma. *Archives of Dermatology, 120,* 329–331.

Taub, E. (1977). Self regulation of human tissue temperature. In G. E. Schwartz & J. Beatty (Eds.), *Biofeedback: Theory and research* (pp. 265–300). New York: Academic Press.

Taub, E., & Emurian, C. S. (1976). Feedback-aided self-regulation of skin temperature with a single feedback locus. I. Acquisition and reversal training. *Biofeedback and Self-Regulation, 1,* 147–168.

Taub, E., & Stroebel, C. F. (1978). Biofeedback in the treatment of vasoconstrictive syndromes. *Biofeedback and Self-Regulation, 3,* 363–373.

Therault, G., DeGuire, L., Gingras, S., & Laroche, G. (1982). Raynaud's phenomenon in forestry workers in Quebec. *Canadian Medical Association Journal, 126,* 1404–1408.

Varadi, D. P., & Lawrence, A. M. (1969). Suppression of Raynaud's phenomenon by methyldopa. *Archives of Internal Medicine, 124,* 13–18.

Wells, D. T., Feather, B. W., & Headrick, M. W. (1973). The effects of immediate feedback upon voluntary control of salivary rate. *Psychophysiology, 10,* 501–509.

Willerson, J. T., Thompson, R. H., Hookman, P., Herdt, J., & Decker, J. L. (1970). Reserpine in Raynaud's disease and phenomenon: Short-term response to intra-arterial injection. *Annals of Internal Medicine, 72,* 17–27.

8

The Biofeedback Treatment of Tension Headache

FRANK ANDRASIK AND EDWARD B. BLANCHARD

INTRODUCTION

Epidemiology

Leviton (1978), in commenting on the epidemiology of headache, believes it is helpful to identify the *unrecognized need,* or the extent to which headache is distributed among the population at large, and the *recognized need,* or the proportion of individuals reporting to health care facilities seeking treatment for headache. Community studies conducted in the United States and elsewhere reveal nearly all individuals can be expected to experience a headache within a given one-year period. As many as 15% of males and 30% of females will experience headaches during this period that are fairly frequent or intense. Headache is the primary complaint in from 1% to 8% of patients seeking outpatient health care.

The clear majority of headaches can be termed tension, migraine, or mixtures of both. Studies of patient files at headache specialty clinics reveal approximately equal proportions of migraine and tension headache, with these two types of headaches accounting for nearly all patients seen (85% to 95%) (e.g., Lance, Curran, & Anthony, 1965). In community prevalence studies tension headache is rarely identified as a distinct

Preparation of this report was supported by grants RO1 NS-15235, RO1 NS-16891, and KO4 NS-00818, awarded by the National Institute of Neurological and Communicative Disorders and Stroke.

FRANK ANDRASIK • Pain Therapy Centers, Greenville Hospital System, Greenville, SC 29601. EDWARD BLANCHARD • Center for Stress and Anxiety, State University of New York at Albany, 1535 Western Avenue, Albany, NY 12203.

entity, so it is not possible to determine precisely its distribution in the community at large. Most experts (e.g., Dalessio, 1980; Diamond & Dalessio, 1982) suspect that a majority of headaches are tension based and that only those individuals experiencing tension headache in its severe and frequent form are motivated to seek treatment. It is further believed that a majority of individuals may treat their tension headaches quite effectively by rest, vacation, and over-the-counter preparations. So far as can be determined, tension headache knows no social, racial, educational, or intellectual boundaries.

Epidemiological studies of tension headache in children have not been conducted, but there is reason to believe this type of headache is highly prevalent during childhood. Bille's (1962) study of nearly 9,000 school children, aged 7 through 15, found that 7% of them experienced frequent nonmigraineous headache, whereas another 48% reported the presence of infrequent nonmigraineous headache; the majority of these headaches are likely to be tension. Another suggestion of an increased prevalence of tension headaches is the fairly high percentage of adults who report their tension headaches as beginning during childhood (e.g., Friedman, Von Storch, & Merritt, 1954; Lance *et al.*, 1965).

Description and Pathophysiology

The Ad Hoc Committee on Classification of Headache (1962) defined tension (or muscle contraction, psychogenic, depression, or nervous) headache as:

> Ache or sensations of tightness, pressure, or constriction, widely varied in intensity, frequency, and duration, sometimes long-lasting, and commonly suboccipital. It is associated with sustained contraction of skeletal muscles in the absence of permanent structural change, usually as part of the individual's reaction during life stress. (page 718)

The prototypical tension headache is experienced as a dull, steady, bilateral or band-like pain or ache, which has an insidious onset and resolution. Typically, it is devoid of accompanying phenomena (nausea, vomiting, etc.) and prodromes. The pain is less intense than that of a migraine, but many individuals experience this type of headache on a daily or near-daily basis. The pain is attributed to stimulation of pain receptors in the contracted muscles and ischemia produced by compression of intramuscular arterioles (Robinson, 1980).

The proposed pathophysiological account is rather straightforward and seems to imply the following: (a) sustained contraction of key muscles is a necessary condition for headache, (b) pain severity and EMG activity levels should be highly correlated, (c) the muscular abnormality is a tonic dysfunction, (d) reductions in EMG levels will be accompanied by reductions in headache severity (Philips, 1978), and (e) stress is a prime precipitant.

The etiological role of muscle contractions in the genesis of tension headache (assumptions a–d) has received much research attention to date. Recent reviews of this literature, however, reveal no clear or consistent support for the proposed muscle tension pathophysiology (Andrasik, Blanchard, Arena, Saunders, & Barron, 1982; Haynes, Cuevas, & Gannon, 1982; Philips, 1978). Some speculate the negative findings are due to limitations of existing methods and procedures for assessing EMG activity (Van Boxtel, Goudswaard, & Janssen, 1983), whereas others suggest that heightened muscle activity may be of etiological significance for only a small subset of individuals now ending up diagnosed as tension headache (Adams, Brantley, & Thompson, 1982). Adams *et al.* (1982) believe it may be more meaningful to reclassify individuals revealing normal levels of muscle tension, but otherwise meeting criteria for tension headache, as having psychogenic headache. Whether improving psychophysiological assessment methodologies and varying current classification practices will lead to more clear-cut findings is uncertain.

The clinical literature readily acknowledges stress as a major factor in etiology of tension headache, but few researchers have conducted rigorous empirical tests of this notion. Although a sizable proportion of tension headache sufferers report emotional stress as a common precipitant of their headaches (Friedman, 1979; Howarth, 1965), the number of major stressful life events experienced by tension headache sufferers is not all that different from the amount reported by matched controls (Andrasik, Blanchard, Arena, Teders, *et al.* 1982; Holm, Holroyd, Hursey, & Penzien, 1984). Holm *et al.* (1984) did find that tension headache sufferers reported a much greater level of everyday stress or "daily hassles" than their matched counterparts. How stress serves to promote or exacerbate tension merits further careful investigation and refinement.

A curious omission in the Ad Hoc Committee's definition is any reference to a vascular component to tension headache, as research existing prior to the committee's report had implicated vascular involvement (Philips, 1977). An additional alternative view of tension headache is that it is not qualitatively different from migraine; rather, that both forms of headache share a common underlying pathology (i.e., aberrations in vascular and muscular tone). Bakal (1982) terms this the severity model of headache. In this model, differences in symptom presentation that occur for the two types of headache are attributed only to variations in the degree of pathology present; tension headache is assumed merely to be a less severe form of headache. This view is highly appealing because of its parsimony, but much additional research is needed to determine whether this alternative view is indeed more viable. Positive support for this viewpoint would have far-reaching implications for research and clinical practice.

Conventional Treatment

Conventional treatment for tension headache consists of palliative agents (ranging from over-the-counter analgesics to narcotics), muscle relaxants, antidepressants (which seem to work irrespective of whether the patient has significant depressive symptomatology), and physical therapy (Diamond & Dalessio, 1982; Raskin & Appenzeller, 1980). Tricyclic antidepressants are thought to have analgesic effects as well when used with headache sufferers. Rates of improvement for these various treatments range from approximately 30% to approximately 80%.

Emerging evidence suggests overreliance on analgesics can lead to paradoxical effects and serve actually to increase headache pain, a condition termed analgesic rebound headache. Kudrow (1982) speculates frequent use of analgesics may sustain pain by suppressing central serotonergic pathways concerned with regulation of dull pain. Preliminary results from Kudrow's (1982) clinic and similar research elsewhere (Rapoport, Sheftell, Baskin, & Weeks, 1984) suggest a substantial proportion of headache sufferers who have been abusing analgesics can undergo marked improvement following withdrawal of analgesics alone. Kudrow's data suggest, also, that allowing patients to continue analgesics at abusive levels can interfere with medical treatment known to be effective. Similar adverse effects may be expected for analgesic abusers receiving biofeedback therapy for tension headache. In related fashion, Jay, Renelli, and Mead (1984) reported that certain medications can impede the progress of patients being administered EMG biofeedback. They found that patients taking amitriptyline proceeded less rapidly towards meeting established biofeedback training criteria. Whether this translates to slower or reduced patient symptom improvement was not addressed in the study, unfortunately.

Previous Task Force Report Conclusions and Recommendations

The previous task force report, chaired by Budzynski and published in 1978, offered eight specific conclusions and, just as importantly, identified 10 particular areas in need of attention in future research. The conclusions and recommendations are restated here as they serve as a meaningful starting point for this updated review.

The 1978 report offered the following conclusions.

1. Frontal EMG feedback is an effective procedure for the alleviation or elimination of muscle-contraction (tension) headache.
2. Frontal EMG feedback training appears to produce a faster reduction in frontal EMG levels and headache activity than do the nonbiofeedback relaxation procedures.
3. Nonbiofeedback relaxation procedures also may be effective in reducing tension headaches.
4. Cognitive skills training appears to be helpful in alleviating these headaches.
5. Discrimination training can be an important addition to the training.
6. Placebo effects occur in headache patients; however, these effects are not as powerful alone as those produced with biofeedback or relaxation procedures.
7. Augmentation through regular relaxation practice outside the clinic is important for the maintenance of a headache-free condition.
8. Augmentation through monthly group meetings may facilitate positive follow-up results (Budzynski, 1978, p. 428).

The following suggestions were offered as ways to help consolidate the next stage of research on tension headache.

1. Careful screening to rule out types of headache other than muscle contraction. Mixed or combined headache cases and those with nausea or vomiting also should be ruled out.
2. Baseline durations of at least 4 weeks because many headache conditions appear to follow a periodic course.
3. Attempts to instill positive expectancy in all subjects regardless of treatment or control condition.
4. Assessment before, during, and after treatment of the credibility (degree of positive expectancy) for each subject.
5. Assessment of the degree of compliance with home practice instructions during treatment and in follow-up periods.
6. Assessment of the type and degree of secondary gain or payoff factors operative. Consider eliminating those subjects who show evidence of these factors that are best handled by nonbiofeedback therapies.
7. Consideration of a design that separates the subjects into high and low frontal EMG groups.
8. The use of charting of headaches (for 4 weeks) and several lab sessions plus interviews at follow-up points (suggest 3, 6, 12, and 24 months).

9. The use of a multiple-baseline design with small N studies (Barlow, Blanchard, Hayes, & Epstein, 1977).
10. In the data collection look at frequency, intensity, duration, and a global index separately. A given treatment may reduce any one or a combination of these parameters (Budzynski, 1978, pp. 428–429).

CLINICAL EFFICACY

Biofeedback Modalities

The dominant biofeedback treatment for tension headache remains the electromyographic (EMG) procedure pioneered by Budzynski, Stoyva, and colleagues in the early seventies (Budzynski, Stoyva, & Adler, 1970; Budzynski, Stoyva, Adler, & Mullaney, 1973). In their treatment procedure three sensors were placed horizontally across a subject's forehead and feedback, in the form of an audible tone, was made available to the subject to assist in learning ways to decrease tension levels in the affected muscles. Basmajian (1976) pointed out that when electrodes are placed in this manner they are sensitive to muscle activity emanating not just from the frontalis, but from the entire scalp, neck, and down to about the first rib. Rather than refer to this procedure as frontalis EMG biofeedback, we prefer to use the terms suggested by Basmajian, either forehead or frontal EMG biofeedback. Budzynski *et al.* augmented biofeedback by relaxation training exercises. Whether relaxation is necessary for biofeedback or exerts an independent effect continues to be a focus of research. In a subsequent paper, Stoyva and Budzynski (1974) speculated that frontal EMG biofeedback training led to a generalized state of relaxation, which they termed cultivated low arousal. This notion suggests that frontal EMG biofeedback has therapeutic potential for a wide variety of problems linked to excessive arousal. However, a recent review of investigations testing for such generalization effects was not supportive of this claim (Thompson, Haber, & Tearnan, 1981).

Clinical efficacy has been explored in very preliminary fashion for two additional biofeedback modalities. McKenzie, Ehrisman, Montgomery, and Barnes (1974) describe the successful use of alpha enhancement biofeedback in the treatment of several selected cases and Daly, Donn, Galliher, and Zimmerman (1983) report thermal biofeedback as being efficacious for tension headache as well. Whether these other biofeedback approaches will stand the test of time is unknown. Our report is restricted to investigations of EMG biofeedback because of the extremely limited data base for these other biofeedback approaches.

Review of the Literature

Outcome investigations abound for self-regulatory treatment of tension headache, making it impractical to review each study. Fortunately, two meta-analytic comparisons have appeared over the past few years for studies employing EMG biofeedback by itself, relaxation training by itself, or the combination of the two procedures in the treatment of tension headache. In a meta-analysis, outcomes for an entire group of subjects given a common treatment become the data point in an overall statistical analysis. Hence, it is an analysis of studies rather than individual subjects, and this approach allows one to quantify results from a large body of literature in a rather efficient fashion. Both meta-analytical analyses confined themselves to prospective studies containing at least five subjects per condition and employed similar criteria for quantifying symptom improvement per treatment condition.

Results from the first meta-analysis (Blanchard, Andrasik, Ahles, Teders & O'Keefe, 1980) revealed nearly identical posttreatment improvement rates for biofeedback alone, relaxation alone, or both combined (see Table 1). This meta-analysis included several control conditions and the statistical comparisons revealed all three active treatments to be superior to psychological placebo (mean improvement = 35.3%), pharmacological placebo (mean improvement = 34.8%), and symptom monitoring alone (mean improvement = −4.5%). Although on average, biofeedback (as well as relaxation training) revealed a high overall rate of improvement, considerable variability in range of improvement was found across the studies. For example, at least one study employing biofeedback by itself found an improvement rate as low as 12%, which is certainly not clinically meaningful. The meta-analysis of Blanchard *et al.* (1980) was not conducted in a manner that permitted examination of possible reasons for lowered outcomes. This was rectified in part in the subsequent analysis conducted by Holroyd and Penzien (1985).

This more up-to-date analysis included approximately double the number of investigations appearing in the earlier analysis, which is an indicant of the continued and growing interest in biofeedback and other self-regulatory treatments for tension headache. This second metanalysis yielded smaller magnitude rates of improvement for EMG biofeedback alone (a drop from 60.9% to 46.0%, which is a decrease of approximately 1/4) and relaxation training alone (a decrease from 59.2% to 44.6%, which is a decrement of again approximately 1/4). Interestingly, rate of improvement for biofeedback combined with relaxation remained essentially as reported in the analysis by Blanchard *et al.* (1980). Although not statistically significant, the quantitative difference between the combined treatment and either treatment by itself ranged from 11.1% to 12.5%.

TABLE 1. Meta-Analytic Evaluations of EMG Biofeedback and Relaxation Training for Tension Headache

Authors		EMG biofeedback	Treatment conditions Relaxation training alone	EMG biofeedback combined with relaxation training
Blanchard, Andrasik, Ahles, Teders, & O'Keefe (1980)	Average Improvement (%)	60.9	59.2	58.8
	Range of Improvement (%)	12 to 81	14 to 100	28 to 79
	Number of Treatment Groups	12	9	6
Holroyd & Penzien (1985)	Average Improvement (%)	46.0	44.6	51.1
	Range of Improvement (%)	13 to 87	17 to 94	29 to 88
	Number of Treatment Groups	26	15	9

All three active treatments were superior to the two control conditions also included in the analysis: noncontingent biofeedback (mean improvement = 15.3%) and headache monitoring alone (mean improvement = −3.9%).

This analysis, too, revealed considerable variability in outcome. Holroyd and Penzien classified each study on several dimensions to help isolate factors accounting for the varied improvements. These dimensions concerned characteristics of the clients (number per condition, dropout rate, gender, age, and referral source), therapy (duration in terms of hours of therapist contact and whether procedures were included to enhance transfer, such as incorporating regular home practice or testing a subject's ability to control EMG response in the absence of feedback), and the research design (use of unbiased procedures to assign subjects to experimental conditions, degree of internal validity, and specification of diagnostic criteria). Many of these, it should be noted, were suggested as important to consider in the earlier Task Force Report.

The client characteristic age served to explain the greatest proportion of the variance in treatment response, 30%; two other client variables (sample size and dropout rate) were significantly, but weakly, related to outcome, as well. Client samples having a mean age of less than 35 achieved a significantly better response to treatment (regardless of type) than those whose average age exceeded 35: 55% reduction in headache activity versus 34% reduction in headache activity. None of the therapy or research design characteristics correlated in any meaningful way with outcome. Holroyd and Penzien also noted the trend for there to be a decreased overall response in studies conducted more recently. The recent studies were characterized by inclusion of samples with an older mean age, a larger proportion of males, and a larger proportion of referred rather than solicited clients. However, these variables did not completely account for the decreased overall response in the more recently conducted studies, indicating that other variables not coded in this analysis need to be examined. It is difficult at this time for us to speculate just what these other variables might be.

Tension headache may be highly prevalent in children, but little is known about its course over time or how it responds to any type of treatment. Two small-scale investigations have recently reported very positive results for biofeedback treatment of childhood tension headache (see Table 2). Whether the very high rates of improvement found for children treated by Andrasik, Blanchard, Edlund, and Attanasio (1983) and Werder and Sargent (1984) will hold up to increased scrutiny awaits the future.

Results from both comprehensive meta-analytic evaluations indicate that biofeedback, either alone or in combination with relaxation training,

TABLE 2. Biofeedback Treatment of Childhood Tension Headache

Authors	No. of subjects	Age	Study design	Treatment procedure	Results
Andrasik, Blanchard Edlund, & Attanasio (1983)	1	11	Systematic Case Study	EMG BF	79% reduction in HA Sum at 1-yr. follow-up; 75% reduction in HA frequency at 1-yr. follow-up
Werder & Sargent (1984)	10	7–11	Single-group outcome	Thermal BF, EMG BF, autogenic TR, relaxation TR, self-awareness, & guided imagery	80% of children seen for 2–3 yr. follow-up ($n = 5$) could "successfully regulate their headaches"

continues to remain an efficacious treatment for managing symptoms of tension headache; however, the magnitude of the effect does not appear to be as substantial as earlier thought. The review by Holroyd and Penzien suggests that client variables may be more important than design or procedural variables in determining response to treatment. More is said about this at a later point.

Results from Biofeedback Clinics

From the summer of 1983 to the summer of 1984 a number of individuals directing biofeedback clinics were asked to make input to a panel commissioned by the American College of Physicians to evaluate the clinical efficacy of biofeedback for selected disorders, one of which was tension headache. Available responses were forwarded to us as well by Dr. Patricia Norris for possible inclusion in the present chapter. This section summarizes the comments provided by the 49 respondents, most of whom were physicians.

Every individual commenting about biofeedback treatment of tension headache responded favorably, but quantitative summaries of outcome were not always provided. Table 3 summarizes results from centers providing actual numerical estimates of improvement rates, along with the number of patients upon which this figure is based and the particular treatment modalities incorporated if specified. Seven of the nine respondents reported improvement rates equal to or exceeding 70%; one reported a slightly lowered rate of improvement (60%) based on a very extensive sample of 120 patients; whereas the remaining respondent reported a much lower overall rate, with improvement being in the neighborhood of 1/3 to 1/4 of treated patients. With the exception of the results described by Packard, these rates of improvement stand in marked contrast to those obtained in the majority of published accounts of biofeedback as shown in the two meta-analytic reviews of literature. In fact, the improvement rates reported by seven of the nine respondents exceed those of the Holroyd and Penzien meta-analysis by from 30% to 40%. A salient question becomes: How does one account for these discrepant outcomes?

Although we have no definitive explanations, we can advance some hypotheses that may be worthy of consideration.

1. Improved results from clinical settings may be due in part to varied patient selection. Many of the respondents reported on the importance of screening patients for biofeedback. Comments such as the following were not uncommon: "We carefully select patients for biofeedback conditioning; eliminating those patients who are not highly motivated, are depressed, or have overt psychological mechanisms." In the typical research study patients are rarely excluded for these reasons.

TABLE 3. Results from Clinical Settings

Setting	Number of patients	Biofeedback modality	Adjunctive techniques	Results
Menninger Foundation—Biofeedback and Psychophysiology Center (Norris, July, 1984)	32	?	?	80% of patients clinically improved through follow-up to 11 yrs.
Georgetown University Hospital—Biofeedback Program (Rosenbaum, June, 1984)	48	?	?	75% of patients clinically improved
Montefiore Hospital and Medical Center— Headache Unit (Solomon, September, 1983)	?	?	?	80% of patients are greatly improved
Packard— Pensacola, Florida (Packard, August, 1983)	?	?	?	33% to 40% of patients experience a marked reduction in headache frequency and/or severity
Pet—Manchester, Connecticut (Pet, September, 1983)	?	EMG	Relaxation training Autogenic training	85 to 95% reduction in symptoms
Remington—Pittsford, New York (Remington, September, 1983)	?	?	Psychotherapy Medication	80%–85% of patients totally or markedly relieved of headache
Santa Barbara Medical Foundation Clinic (Permut, August, 1983)	?	?	?	70% of patients attain moderate to excellent levels of benefit
Shealy Pain & Health Rehabilitation Institute—Springfield, Missouri (Shealy, August, 1983)	?	Thermal	EMG EEG	72% of patients obtain 50% or greater improvement
Stress Regulation Institute— New York, NY (Sedlacek, April, 1984)	120	EMG	Thermal Antidepressants (with approx. 25% of patients)	60% of patients have a good to excellent result

2. Improved results may be due in part to increased competence and experience of clinic biofeedback therapists. Respondents again frequently attributed their enhanced success rates to increased competence and experience of staff. Respondents seemed to be in agreement that therapists in research studies often possess a less than desirable level of biofeedback expertise. Elsewhere we review the limited data bearing on this point.

3. Improved results may be due in part to the fact that treatment tends to be much more intensive, to be supplemented by more adjunctive techniques, and to encompass longer intervals and include a greater number of treatment sessions in clinical settings. Although few respondents described the actual number of sessions for the typical patient, those that did reported as many as 30 or so training sessions were often needed. Number of treatment sessions for studies included in the Holroyd and Penzien (1985) meta-analysis ranged from 3 to 18 ($M = 9.8$). Within this range, however, number of sessions bore no relationship to outcome. It is assumed, but not stated, that many of the approaches included conventional medical management in addition to training in self-regulation skills.

4. Improved results may be due in part to subtle measurement bias. Only one of the nine respondents reported how improvement was assessed, and this individual reported systematic use of headache charting. His results (Sedlacek, personal communication, April, 1984) are not too dissimilar from Holroyd and Penzien's meta-analysis of improvement for combined treatment (57.6%). If the remaining investigators used interviews or global questionnaires to obtain retrospective estimates of improvement, then it is possible that the greater improvements found in clinical settings may be due in part to a systematic bias to overstate level of improvement. Review of a study conducted by Cahn and Cram (1980) shows why this may be so.

Daily ratings of headache pain made in a pocket-size diary have become the gold standard for evaluating outcome in published investigations of headache treatment. In some situations, such as collection of long-term follow-up data, it has not always been possible/feasible to obtain this same type of data, so some investigators/clinicians resort to telephone interviews, in-person interviews, or global questionnaires for data collection. Cahn and Cram's investigation examined the correspondence between data collected by these various procedures. In one sample of patients, telephone interview data and daily diary records were collected prior to treatment and at intermediate follow-up. This same basic procedure was replicated in a second sample except that the follow-up interview was done in person rather than via the telephone.

Several interesting findings emerged from this study (see Figure 1).

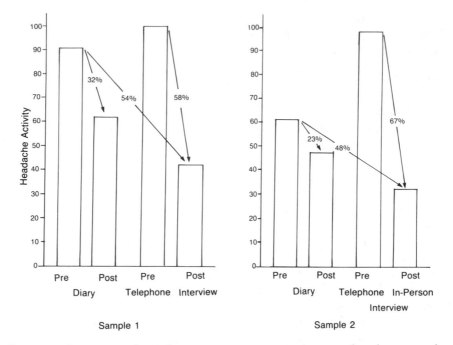

FIGURE 1. Comparison of varied ways to assess treatment outcome (based on research described in Cahn & Cram, 1980).

First, interview-based measures and diary-based measures differed considerably. At pretreatment, the interview measures overestimated or overstated headache activity relative to the diary, whereas at follow-up the interview-based measures understated headache activity relative to the diary. If one calculates symptom reduction from pretreatment to follow-up for each set of data, improvement rates vary quite markedly depending on which measure is used. For Sample 1, diary measures show the sample as a whole to be improved by 32%, whereas interview measurers reveal the sample to be improved by an amount nearly twice that of the diary-generated improvement. An even greater discrepancy occurs for Sample 2 (23% rate of improvement versus 67% rate of improvement). The posttreatment in-person interview led to the lowest estimate of headache activity suggesting it may be the most biased measure of all. Determining the percentage of improvement utilizing the diary for the pretreatment value and the interview for the follow-up value (a mixture of measures that commonly occurs in retrospective follow-up evaluations) yields a percentage improvement rate of 54% for Sample 1 and 48% for Sample 2. These later outcome determinations are of smaller magnitude than the ones based entirely on the interview measures, but they still appear to overstate actual improvement by a considerable degree.

Blanchard, Andrasik, Neff, Jurish, and O'Keefe (1981) found that patients and significant others serving as evaluators similarly overestimated improvements (relative to diary results) when completing questionnaires. More information is needed about methods used to assess outcome in clinical settings in order to judge the tenability of this hypothesis.

Biofeedback versus Relaxation: Does Equivalent Outcome Mean the Procedures are Interchangeable?

Results from both meta-analyses reveal nearly identical improvement rates for subjects treated by frontal EMG biofeedback or relaxation training, as does a box score tally for the individual studies conducting these "horse race" comparisons (Chesney & Shelton, 1976, Cott, Goldman, Yavloski, Kirschberg, & Fabich, 1981; Cox, Freundlich, & Meyer, 1975; Daly et al., 1983; Gray, Lyle, McGuire, & Peck, 1980; Haynes, Griffin, Mooney, & Parise, 1975; Hutchings & Reinking, 1976; Janssen, 1983; Martin & Mathews, 1978; Schlutter, Golden, & Blume, 1980). This mathematical equivalence in outcome has led some researchers (Silver & Blanchard, 1978) to conclude the two treatments are interchangeable and work by similar change mechanisms, and thus to advocate for relaxation instead of biofeedback due to the reduced cost and technical sophistication required for administering relaxation therapy.

Such conclusions, however, are based on flawed logic. Equivalent statistical outcomes could occur for very different reasons, two of which are illustrated in Figure 2. It could be the case that the treatments are truly interchangeable and that a given patient on a given day would have an equally likely chance to succeed at biofeedback as at relaxation. Alternatively, it could be the case that certain patient types are responding uniquely to biofeedback whereas other patient types are responding uniquely to relaxation, but that the overall response levels happen to be similar. Thus, it is possible that group statistics may be masking important patient-by-treatment interactions. Most existing studies do not adequately test for this possibility.

Blanchard et al. (1982) compared frontal EMG biofeedback and progressive muscle relaxation training in a sequential design (or a partial-crossover design) as one way to evaluate the differential, rather than the comparative, effectiveness of the two treatments. In this study, patients diagnosed as tension headache were first offered an 8-session, 10-week course of progressive muscle relaxation training. At the end of treatment the patients were classified as successful if their diary records

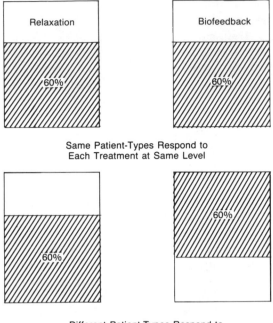

FIGURE 2.   Alternative explanations for equivalent group outcomes.

revealed 60% or greater level of improvement. Patients not meeting this criterion were termed unsuccessful and then offered a second course of treatment involving 12-sessions of frontal EMG biofeedback spaced over 6 weeks. Although the protocol called for twice-weekly appointments, some patients took as long as 12 weeks to complete this course of treatment. Fourteen tension headache patients (3 males, 11 females) entered this second stage of treatment and at the completion of treatment, 5 of these individuals (36%) now met the clinical criterion for success. Heightened levels of baseline headache activity, depression, and anxiety were associated with continued failure to respond to treatment. Although this study has some limitations (primarily that it did not offer continued relaxation therapy to a subset of the treatment failures, which is needed to rule out the possibility that additional practice at relaxation training is the main reason for the five patients becoming treatment successes), the data suggest that relaxation and biofeedback may not be interchangeable, and that biofeedback may offer different advantages to a certain subset of patients.

Billings, Thomas, Rapp, Reyes, and Leith (1984) used a similar sequential methodology to determine if hand temperature biofeedback could enhance treatment response following a course of frontal EMG biofeedback with four tension headache subjects. They concluded there was no advantage to this practice.

The data from Blanchard *et al.* (1982) suggest it is premature to conclude that frontal EMG biofeedback and relaxation training are equivalent in outcome and mechanism. The data suggest further that biofeedback may be of unique benefit for certain tension patients; although the design problems mentioned earlier and the limited sample size demand further replication before stronger claims can be made. We see no need at this point for researchers to conduct continued direct group comparisons of these two procedures without taking into account client variables.

Biofeedback versus Other Treatments

Our search uncovered a few published reports describing results from comparisons of biofeedback treatment to cognitive therapy, medical therapy, and psychotherapy.

Biofeedback versus Cognitive Therapy

Cognitive, stress-coping treatments are gaining in popularity and a number of studies have appeared since publication of the original task force report. Some (i.e., Meichenbaum, 1976) believe that cognitive or cognitive-behavioral treatments might be especially suited for stress-related disorders, such as headache, because these treatments take a more expanded focus, incorporating in treatment the cognitive, affective, sensory, and behavioral components of the disorder, as well as the physiological component. We located nine investigations of cognitive treatments for tension headache, but only one included a direct comparison of biofeedback and cognitive therapy. In this investigation, Holroyd, Andrasik, and Westbrook (1977) randomly assigned 31 community residents experiencing recurrent tension headache to a waiting-list control condition ($n = 10$), frontal EMG biofeedback treatment ($n = 11$), or cognitive stress-coping training ($n = 10$). Biofeedback was administered in a manner similar to that employed in other studies. Cognitive therapy focused on helping subjects to identify and subsequently modify maladaptive cognitive responses assumed to mediate headache. Specifically, subjects were taught to identify (a) cues that triggered tension and anxiety, (b) their response when becoming tense and anxious, (c) their thoughts prior, during, and subsequent to becoming tense, and (d) the relationship between cognitions, tension, and headache. Subjects were next taught to interrupt the dysfunctional cognitive sequence as soon as it was recognized. Subjects were instructed to use three specific cognitive techniques—cognitive reappraisal, attention deployment, and fantasy. Both active treatments were administered in eight 45-min. individual treatment sessions spaced over 4 weeks. Counterdemand instructions (Steinmark & Borkovec, 1974) were administered at the end of treatment session one in order to neutralize unintended experimental demands for improvement.

Subjects receiving cognitive therapy revealed marked improvement for every measure of headache activity assessed; 89% of the subjects achieved reductions of headache activity in excess of 50%, or a clinically meaningful degree of improvement. Statistically, biofeedback treated subjects were indistinguishable from controls, but inferior to patients receiving cognitive therapy. Holroyd *et al.*, in attempting to account for the poor results for biofeedback, speculated that "strong implicit demands" might be a "necessary condition, at least for some clients, for the therapeutic effectiveness of biofeedback" (p. 131). If this notion is correct, it raises some questions about factors mediating treatment effectiveness in biofeedback therapy. There is one potential confound in this study, however, which may lessen the significance of the findings. Biofeedback and cognitive therapy were administered by different therapists. Although treatment credibility ratings provided by patients revealed both treatments were perceived as highly credible by patients, it is possible that therapist differences accounted in part for the lack of significance for biofeedback therapy. Effects due to the counterdemand instructional set have yet to be replicated; such replication would be helpful to determine whether this was a spurious finding.

Five of the eight remaining investigations employed a combination of cognitive therapy and frontal EMG biofeedback. Most of these investigations included exceedingly small sample sizes (Reeves, 1976, $N = 1$; Mitchell & White, 1976, $N = 1$; Kremsdorf, Kochanowicz, & Costell, 1981, $N = 2$; Steger & Harper, 1980, $N = 9$). The only investigation to include a large sample (Bakal, Demjen, & Kaganov, 1981, $N = 17$) did not differentiate tension headache subjects from other headache subjects when evaluating outcome. Although all five studies reported fairly positive outcomes from the combination of biofeedback and cognitive therapy, the limited samples used in four studies and the limited information available in the remaining study do not permit us to make any strong claims about the clinical efficacy of this treatment combination.

Biofeedback versus Medical Therapy

Two published studies describe results from comparisons of frontal EMG biofeedback and medical therapy. In the first, Bruhn, Olesen, and Melgaard (1979) assigned subjects either to standard frontal EMG biofeedback or to the "most suitable alternative therapy," which was individualized for patients and consisted of either physical therapy, medication (analgesics, sedatives, antidepressants, or muscle relaxants), or the combination of the two. Biofeedback patients showed significant declines for headache intensity, duration, and medication intake. No significant changes were observed for patients assigned to medical therapy. Seven of 13 biofeedback subjects achieved improvements greater than or equal to 50%; only one of the 10 subjects receiving medical therapy improved to this degree. These results continued through the 3-month follow-up. Of the various predictor variables studied, only initial frontal EMG level correlated with treatment response; the nature of the relationship was such that patients evidencing lower initial levels obtained an enhanced response.

Paiva *et al.* (1982) compared frontal EMG biofeedback to Diazepam to false EMG biofeedback and to drug placebo. Percentage symptom improvement found at immediate posttreatment and one-month follow-up for the various conditions for two separate measures of headache activity are summarized in Table 4. Diazepam resulted in the greatest level of improvement during treatment, but at the brief follow-up Diazepam-treated patients revealed a sizable return of symptoms. At this brief follow-up the biofeedback-treated subjects now revealed substantial treatment gains. Table 4 reveals a surprisingly large percentage change for patients receiving biofeedback placebo. Patients receiving the false biofeedback unintentionally showed large decreases in frontal EMG levels that may have accounted for this improvement. It is unfortunate that longer-term follow-up data were not obtained to see whether the pattern at brief follow-up endured. The authors did not report whether use of

TABLE 4. Results from Paiva *et al.* (1982)

| | Percentage improvement | | | | | | | |
| | Treatment | | | | One-month follow-up | | | |
Headache measure	BF	BF-P	DZ	DZ-P	BF	BF-P	DZ	DZ-P
Frequency	36.4	24.0	41.9	25.8	65.3	40.5	26.7	8.8
Intensity	36.6	43.6	54.9	25.6	79.9	47.8	33.3	22.2

other medications was controlled for all groups, so this remains as a
potential confound.

Biofeedback versus Psychotherapy

Bell, Abramowitz, Folins, Spensley, and Hutchinson (1983)
compared "broad-gauged" biofeedback (frontal EMG biofeedback plus
a variety of adjunctive techniques), eclectic psychotherapy (cognitive-
behavioral procedures combined with psychodynamic techniques),
the two combined, and no-treatment for 24 individuals experiencing
tension headache.

Biofeedback was delivered in 12 one-half-hour sessions spaced over
6 weeks, whereas psychotherapy was delivered in 6 weekly one-hour
sessions. All treatments led to similar changes in EMG activity, and all
were perceived as highly credible by patients. Percentage reductions
from pre- to posttreatment for most of the outcome measures included
in this study are presented in Table 5. A curious finding occurred for
headache frequency in that the no-treatment control obtained improvements equal to or greater than all active treatments. The authors offered
no speculation for this curious finding. Psychological status was monitored across time and participants undergoing biofeedback revealed
greater improvement in this dimension than individuals receiving psychotherapy or no treatment. Changes for some psychological dimensions, most notably depression, anxiety, obsession-compulsion, and
repression-sensitization, were quite substantial. Bell et al. (1983) speculated that "the incongruity between the demands of psychotherapy
and the personality structure of the headache patient, the brevity of the
psychotherapy offered and the differential therapeutic impact of nonspecific placebo effects" (p. 171) were among the possibilities for this
occurrence.

TABLE 5. Percentage Symptom Reduction from Pre- to Posttreatment for Each
Treatment Condition (from Bell et al., 1983)

Measure	Treatment condition			
	Biofeedback	Psychotherapy	Combined	No treatment
Headache duration in hours	87	59	75	5
Headache intensity	36	27	42	6
Headache frequency per day	36	14	69	69
Medication potency	74	56	78	17

In summary, the only direct comparison found cognitive therapy to be superior to frontal EMG biofeedback therapy. Data from two reports are suggestive of an enhanced response for biofeedback compared to medical treatment. Although one study found fairly similar outcomes for EMG biofeedback and psychotherapy, biofeedback produced greater positive side effects in terms of improved psychological status. All of these conclusions remain tentative because of the very limited data base.

Long-Term Follow-Up Evaluation of Biofeedback Therapy

The meta-analyses mentioned earlier reveal a large number of studies have been conducted to examine the short-term outcome effectiveness of biofeedback, relaxation, and related procedures. The number of studies reporting follow-up 12 months or more beyond the end of treatment is very sparse and stands in marked contrast to the data set available for short-term outcome. Long-term follow-up evaluations consist of two types: retrospective and prospective.

Four large-scale (Diamond & Montrose, 1984; Diamond, Medina, Diamond-Falk, & DeVeno, 1979; Sargent, Solbach, & Coyne, 1980; Solbach & Sargent, 1977; two moderate size (Adler & Adler, 1975; Satinsky & Frerotto, 1981), and two small-scale (Kondo & Canter, 1977; Libo & Arnold, 1983) retrospective follow-up investigations have appeared in the literature for time spans ranging from 1 to 5 years. All of these published reports describe high levels of maintenance, but many of them did not distinguish between various headache types, which makes it impossible to discuss improvement rate for tension headache patients alone. Further, nearly all of the treatments provided to subjects incorporated multiple modalities, making it difficult to determine with any precision the role EMG biofeedback played in accounting for these results. The paper by the Adlers included psychotherapy as well. Although findings from these studies suggest that gains evidenced at the end of treatment are maintained for extended follow-up periods, these results need to be viewed with a certain amount of caution because of problems inherent in retrospective research methodology (refer to earlier discussion on the study of Cahn & Cram, 1980).

Our search uncovered five prospective evaluations of long-term effectiveness of biofeedback, and these are summarized in Table 6. The improvement rates reported for frontal EMG biofeedback range from lows of 18% to 39% to highs of 68% to 85% for varied intervals. The only study we could find evaluating the long-term efficacy of a nonbiofeedback approach revealed a high level of improvement for cognitive therapy at 2 years (Holroyd & Andrasik, 1982). Attrition, where reported, was sizable. If one assumes that many of the individuals who

TABLE 6. Summary of Prospective Follow-up Investigations of Self-Regulation Treatment for Tension Headache

| Authors | Subjects | | | Treatment procedure | Follow-up interval | Level of maintenance |
	Number completing treatment	Number completing follow-up	Percentage completing follow-up			
Reinking & Hutchings (1981)	10	?	?	Frontal EMG Biofeedback	1 yr.	
	10	?	?	Relaxation Training	1 yr.	
	10	?	?	Biofeedback + Relaxation	1 yr.	
	30	18	60			39% of sample treatment successes
Holroyd & Andrasik (1982)	14	11	79	Cognitive Therapy	2 yr.	75% reduction for overall headache activity
						64% of sample clinically improved
	10	8	80	Frontal EMG Biofeedback	2 yr.	18% reduction for overall headache activity
						38% of sample clinically improved
Andrasik & Holroyd (1983)	10	7	70	Frontal EMG Biofeedback	3 yrs.	68% reduction for overall headache activity[a]
Ford, Stroebel, Strong & Szarek (1983)	?	33	?	Quieting Response Training[b]	2 yrs.	39% of sample treatment successes
Andrasik, Blanchard, Neff, & Rodichok (1984)	20	14	70	Relaxation or Relaxation + Frontal EMG Biofeedback	1 yr.	87% of sample clinically improved

[a] Extrapolated from Figure 1, page 635.
[b] Consisted of EMG and thermal biofeedback, autogenic training, progressive relaxation, breathing exercises, mental imagery, and generalization training.

were unwilling to participate in follow-up were not improved, then the success rates revealed in Table 6 may represent overestimates of improvement.

There is a problem in interpreting these long-term follow-up results as reflecting "maintenance" of treatment effects. None of the studies performed careful analyses of individual patients across time, making it impossible to determine how many of the patients who were successful at the end of treatment remained successful at follow-up. We know only that improvement rates for the groups as a whole were "maintained." An idiographic analysis is needed to give a better idea of maintenance of individual gains.

The varied rates of improvement during follow-up indicate that additional attention needs to be given to ways to make initial treatment effects more durable. One of the follow-up evaluations reported in Table 6 attempted to do just that. At the completion of treatment, Andrasik, Blanchard, Neff, and Rodichok, (1984) randomly assigned treatment successes either to intensive booster treatments (six 1-hour treatments held at monthly intervals) or to periodic contacts (brief, monthly-in-person contacts designed primarily to facilitate data collection). Statistical analyses revealed high levels of maintenance for both conditions but no differences between them, indicating that intensive care during follow-up is not warranted. The high level of maintenance obtained for subjects assigned to the periodic contact condition suggests that some form of contact during follow-up may be helpful, however.

In conclusion, the limited data suggest that long-term treatment effectiveness is variable. Brief, regular contacts following treatment completion may help insure continued success. Clearly, further evaluations of the long-term effectiveness of biofeedback and ways to enhance durability are needed. These evaluations should study the course of individual patients to determine the number and characteristics of patients maintaining, improving, or regressing relative to end of treatment.

Factors Affecting Outcome

Procedural Variables

Recording Sites. It has become standard practice to use a frontal sensor placement when treating individuals who have tension headache. Pain is not localized solely or predominantly in the frontal area for many individuals with tension headache, and, because of this, some researchers (Belar, 1979) suggest it may be more useful to select the sensor placement identified by the patient as corresponding to the locus of the pain or by objective measurement as being the primary source of heightened muscle activity. Only a handful of studies have tested this notion.

Key methodological features and findings from these five studies are summarized in Table 7.

Results from these five studies suggest there is no particular advantage for one recording site versus another, and this seems to hold irrespective of the amount of control the patient gains over the relevant response. Hudzniski (1983) solicited preferences of patients, and six out of six patients whose headaches emanated from the neck area expressed a preference for this recording site, whereas 8 out of 10 patients whose

TABLE 7. Studies on Tension Headache Comparing Frontal EMG Biofeedback to EMG Biofeedback from Other Sites

Author(s)	No of pts.	Length of training	Muscle sites studied	Results	
				HA activity	EMG levels
Philips (1977)	5	12	BF from frontalis or temporalis, whichever had higher resting EMG level	Sig. reduct. in HA freq. (27%) and HA intensity (30%)	EMG reduced to "normal"
Philips & Hunter (1981)	8 (high EMG levels)	6	same as Philips, 1977	no sig. reduction	EMG reduced by 47%
Martin & Mathews (1978)	12	12	BF from forehead (6 sessions) then neck (6 sessions) or vice versa	sig. reduct. regardless of site (no diff. from relaxation)	no sig. reduction in resting EMG levels
Hart & Cichanski (1981)	20	7–15 ave. = 13	BF from forehead ($n = 10$) or back of neck ($n = 10$)	sig. reduct. in HA activity for forehead (45%) & neck (57%): no diff. between sites	
Hudzinski (1983)	16	10	BF alternated between forehead and back of neck at each session; Subjects selected preferred site at sessions 8 & 9	headaches "markedly reduced" for 81% of subjects; Patients pref. BF from origin of pain	forehead EMG reduced by 30%; neck EMG reduced by 54%

headaches emanated from other areas of the head expressed a preference for a frontal sensor placement.

Available evidence, which is by no means conclusive, indicates no unique advantage to either a forehead or a neck recording site. Most of the studies (with the exception of Hart & Cichanski, 1981) used designs that did not allow for adequate tests of the notion (separate sites were not compared directly or feedback was frequently altered between sites). An acid test of the relative benefits may be obtained by extending the procedures employed by Philips (1977). Philips pretested EMG activity at the forehead and neck and then provided feedback to patients from the site revealing the highest resting EMG level. A strategy to provide a more definitive answer would involve pretesting patients and grouping them into high forehead involvement or high neck involvement (as done by Philips) and *then* treating half of the patients in each group by either forehead or neck biofeedback. One can only speculate as to the results of this study prior to its being conducted.

Discrimination Training. The previous Task Force Report concluded that discrimination training might be an important addition to biofeedback, but this notion was not tested directly by any studies prior to the publication of that report. Jacobsen (1938) long ago concluded that enhanced discrimination was of critical importance to learning how to relax the musculature. The procedure of systematic tensing and relaxing of muscles developed by Jacobsen was intended to facilitate a sense of awareness of tension levels that would then lead to relaxation. More recently, Epstein and Blanchard (1977) likewise speculated that discrimination training may be a key component to effective use of self-regulation strategies. Some data attesting to the value of discrimination training are now available.

Hudzinski (1984) assigned patients to either standard EMG biofeedback (feedback alternated between the forehead and neck and combined with relaxation therapy) or to the standard EMG combined with muscle discrimination exercise training. This training consisted of having subjects engage in a series of tension and release exercises for the neck, scalp, and facial muscles, for approximately 10 minutes per session, while they observed the biofeedback display. At the completion of the 10-session treatment program, subjects were exposed to a stressful mental arithmetic task for 10 minutes, after which subjects provided estimates of their absolute level of muscle tension and then were instructed to reduce their tension levels as much as possible. Individuals assigned to that discrimination-augmented training procedure revealed greater discrimination abilities at the end of the stressor, and a greater portion of these individuals were able to reduce their EMG level by 25% or more following exposure to the stressor. Eighty-one percent of the patients receiving the discrimination training reported marked improvement in headache activity that, although 10% better than subjects receiving the standard protocol (71%), was not significantly different from the standard group. It may be that the high level of improvement found for the standard group exerted a ceiling effect, making it difficult for discrimination training to show a significant edge.

Results from Hudzinski's study exceed the level of improvement shown in the more recent meta-analysis of Holroyd and Penzien (46%). Because his subjects made global determinations about improvement in headache activity following completion of treatment it is possible that results for both treatments are somewhat inflated. Hudzinski's results, nonetheless, are encouraging and suggest that attempts at replication that employ more stringent measures for evaluating treatment outcome could be helpful. At present, the value of discrimination training remains only suggestive.

Training to Criterion.   Researchers are becoming increasingly aware of the need to establish the integrity of treatment administration (was biofeedback administered as intended, did the patient actually learn to control the relevant response, etc.) before one can conduct a careful examination of outcome effectiveness (Belar, 1979; Steiner & Dince, 1981). One way this need has been addressed is by analyzing change in EMG levels during and across sessions. Belar, and Steiner and Dince, among others, believe this approach must be taken one step further, and draw upon pharmacological evaluation methodology to support their suggestion. Pharmacologic evaluation of a drug, it is argued, makes no particular sense unless it can be demonstrated that the patient has a specifiable level of the chemical in the blood stream. Hence, they argue that biofeedback researchers need to demonstrate that patients have achieved a certain level of physiological control or that they have been "trained to a criterion" prior to evaluating outcome.

Although this is a laudable recommendation, there are theoretical and practical problems with adhering to this suggestion in the frontal EMG biofeedback treatment of tension headache. First, as earlier discussed, heightened levels of EMG activity have not been shown unequivocally to be the key distinguishing characteristic of individuals who end up being diagnosed as having tension headache. We really do not know what EMG level is excessive and therefore likely to cause symptoms or even if this is in fact the cause of tension headache. Second, there are many different machines available for measuring EMG activity and several ways to quantify results. These practical problems make it difficult to compare findings across laboratory settings.

Nonetheless, at least one study describes an initial test of this notion (Libo & Arnold, 1983). Patients discussed in this report presented with a variety of problems, but five of them were diagnosed as having tension headache. EMG biofeedback was administered by an Autogen 1700 with the bandpass set at 100–200 Hz. Thermal biofeedback and other adjunctive relaxation strategies were included in the treatment package delivered to patients. After treatment, the authors retrospectively reviewed patient records to determine which individuals receiving frontal EMG biofeedback had met or exceeded a specifiable criterion (i.e., a microvolt integral average reading of 1.1 or below). Ninety-three percent of all patients who met their established EMG criterion were found to be markedly improved at follow-up versus 65% for those who did not achieve the criterion level. Unfortunately, results were not reported for individual patient types; whether tension patients satisfying the criterion obtained greater benefit cannot be determined. The authors report one additional shortcoming of their study—that it was not designed to be a prospective test of the training to criterion notion.

> The shortcoming is that it does not test the hypothesis that *training* patients to a specific, stringent criterion, as a task of the therapist, is efficacious, though this study provides indirect support for recommending this strategy. (p. 402–403)

We agree with Libo and Arnold's cautious optimism and believe that the training to criterion notion merits a priority for future research.

Home Practice. Extratherapeutic practice of self-regulation techniques is an integral part of biofeedback therapy and nearly all practitioners urge their patients to engage in regular daily home practice. Intuitively this makes a lot of sense, yet, like much of our clinical wisdom, the empirical base supporting its merits is scarce.

In an analog study (Kotses & Weiner, 1982), 40 undergraduates were randomly assigned to contingent or noncontingent frontal EMG biofeedback; one half of the subjects in each condition completed home practice exercises whereas the remaining subjects did not. Individuals randomly assigned to home practice were instructed to practice 15 minutes per day for a one-week evaluation period. Subjects were asked to mail the experimenters completed compliance cards for each practice period. All subjects then returned to the laboratory for a no-feedback monitoring session. Subjects who engaged in regular home practice were able to keep their forehead EMG activity at low stable levels during this monitoring session, whereas those individuals not practicing revealed higher EMG levels that steadily increased over the recording session.

The relationship between regularity of home practice of self-regulation skills and maintenance of therapeutic effects was investigated in two of the prospective long-term follow-up evaluations mentioned previously. Reinking and Hutchings (1981) noted that 86% of their subjects who remained successes at one year reported they continued to practice on a regular basis. It is difficult to know what to make of this finding because the authors did not report practice patterns for individuals who had not remained successful. Also, they did not report any data summarizing the amount of practice engaged in by successful patients. Andrasik *et al.* (1984) found no relationship between regularity of home practice and maintenance of treatment gains for tension headache patients receiving either relaxation alone or relaxation combined with frontal EMG biofeedback.

Two of the published retrospective follow-up evaluations reported on this relationship, as well. Sargent *et al.* (1980) reported that 85% of their long-term treatment successes continued regular home practice where as only one half of those whose headache activity remained unchanged or deteriorated reported continuation of home practice. However, these authors did not break their data down by headache types, so it cannot be determined if this relationship was present for tension patients.

Libo and Arnold (1983) conducted a careful analysis of the importance of posttherapy practice for a diverse group of patients (individuals experiencing chronic pain, anxiety, and hypertension, in addition to headache). A significant relationship was present but it is best thought of from a threshold rather than a dose-response perspective. Patients who continued to practice at any level maintained improvement at a rate higher than those who had stopped their practice altogether; occasional practice was just as effective as frequent practice. Practice patterns were not examined for individual disorders, so it cannot be determined whether this relationship held equally for all groups under study. These results fit with clinical observations that patients engage in home practice only on an as needed basis once they have acquired the necessary skills.

It must be remembered, however, that all of the above findings are correlational and do not support statements of causality. The study by Kotses and Weiner (1982) was the only investigation to manipulate prospectively home practice. Replication of this approach with a clinical population and concurrent examination of clinical endpoints is needed before stronger statements can be made about the benefits of home practice.

Therapist Variables

Individuals providing input to the American College of Physicians frequently commented that therapist variables bore an important relationship to clinical success. We are aware of two articles that address this topic; one directly and the other indirectly.

Following a course of either relaxation alone or relaxation combined with biofeedback treatment, Blanchard *et al.* (1983) analyzed the response of approximately 100 chronic headache patients to see whether outcome was related to therapist experience level (Study 1) or particular therapist characteristics (Study 2). The seven treating therapists (3 females and 4 males) were all at the doctoral level; three were relative novices, three had one full year of prior clinical experience, and one had 2 years prior experience. These seven individuals served as therapists for 2 consecutive years, which allowed the investigators to assess whether success rates improved over time as well. No systematic relationship was found for therapist prior experience or sex of therapist and outcome for either Year 1 or Year 2 of treatment. One shortcoming to this study is that it did not include therapists with extensive prior experience; it may be concluded, though, that level of experience appears to have minimal bearing on treatment outcome for beginning to intermediate level clinicians.

The second study reported by Blanchard *et al.* (1983) examined the relationship between patients' ratings of competence, warmth, and helpfulness of treating therapists and outcome. All therapist ratings were made on visual analog scales, anchored at one end "extremely incompetent," "extremely unhelpful," "extremely cold and aloof," and at the other end "extremely competent," "extremely helpful," and "extremely warm and friendly." Correlations between these three therapist ratings did not achieve statistical significance. Although there was a trend for perceived warmth of therapist to be negatively associated with outcome ($r = -0.28$, $p < .10$), this correlation accounted for less than 8% of the explained variance. Classifying patients into success or failure and then analyzing therapist ratings revealed no differences as well.

Although this study suggests that the personality of the therapist does not affect outcome, one study suggests that the way a therapist behaves may impact effectiveness. Borgeat, Hade, Larouche, and Bedwani (1980) randomly assigned 16 patients experiencing pure tension headache or tension headache combined with migraine to conditions where the therapist was present and quite active or to a condition where the therapist was virtually absent from the therapy setting. In the active-presence condition the therapist coached, encouraged, provided information about overall progress, and looked with the patient for causes for poor performance. In the therapist-absent condition the therapist remained in an adjacent room and did not communicate during actual delivery of feedback. The therapist interacted with the patient only at the beginning and ending of the experimental phases. The conditions of therapist-absent and therapist-present were rotated midway during treatment. Baseline recordings of EMG activity were significantly higher in the therapist-present condition versus the therapist-absent condition (magnitude of difference = .85 microvolts). A similar trend was evident during provision of feedback and during probe tests in the absence of feedback; however, the magnitudes of these differences were smaller (.59 microvolts during feedback and .53 microvolts during no feedback) and they did not reach conventional levels of statistical significance. Unfortunately, by rotating the two conditions the authors were not able to assess whether the differences in EMG activity exerted any effect on clinical outcome. These data suggest that therapists remaining in the treatment room should avoid being intrusive and refrain from making extensive comments to patients until biofeedback proper is concluded.

Client Variables

Results from the meta-analysis conducted by Holroyd and Penzien suggest that client variables may account for a large part of the variance in treatment outcome and that increased age is a primary indicant of a reduced response to treatment. A similar effect for age has shown up in additional studies as well, although the age that best divides the groups into success and failure has varied somewhat, ranging from 30 to 40 (Blanchard et al., 1986; Diamond et al., 1979; Werder, Sargent, & Coyne, 1981). It is difficult to pin down this seemingly straightforward relationship, however. Older individuals are likely to have experienced headaches for a greater length of time, but none of the studies controlled for chronicity. Variables associated with increased chronicity, such as a greater number of failed treatments, decreased motivation, and increased abuse of analgesics, may be more important than age per se. Future research needs to tease out whether age alone is the main factor accounting for the diminished effectiveness or whether correlated variables are more critical.

Baseline EMG level is a logical variable to consider in examinations of prediction of treatment response. Unfortunately, only a couple of investigators have evaluated this variable and both found that increased levels of muscle tension were associated with decreased improvement (Bruhn et al., 1979; Epstein & Abel, 1977). This is a rather surprising finding because it was for such individuals that frontal EMG biofeedback was developed.

Another variable receiving consistent support across studies is depression. Depressive symptomatology is often present in individuals experiencing chronic tension headache, and this has led some investigators to conclude that a sizable percentage of tension headaches may be secondary to an underlying depression (Diamond, 1964, 1983). Even subclinical scores on scales measuring depression (e.g., score on Beck Depression Inventory of 7 or higher) have been shown to be predictive of a diminished response to biofeedback treatment (Blanchard et al., 1985; Cox, Lefebvre, & Hobbs, 1982; Jacob, Turner, Szekely, & Eidelman, 1983).

A final variable reliably predictive of a poor response to treatment is baseline headache values that reveal high and unremitting levels of pain (Bakal, Demjen, & Kaganov, 1981; Blanchard et al., 1982; Jacob et al., 1983). It may be speculated that individuals who show invariant headache pain may be experiencing significant secondary gain or may be more properly diagnosed as hypochondriacal headache. Respondents from biofeedback clinics frequently mentioned that the presence of secondary gain was a poor predictor of response to treatment, but there is no systematic empirical evidence addressing this topic.

Other predictor variables have been identified in isolated studies, but they have either failed to hold upon further study or have yet to be replicated. For example, Diamond et al. (1979) found that females had a better response relative to males, and that a history of drug habituation was associated with reduced benefits. Werder et al. (1981) were unable to document similar relationships.

Identification and cross validation of client variables reliably predictive of response to treatment is an exceedingly important area for researchers. If it is assumed that the meta-analytic findings of Holroyd and Penzien are most representative of expected outcomes from biofeedback and related self-regulation treatments, then it is seen that a sizable number of individuals remain unimproved following treatment. Identification of predictor variables could help conserve therapist time, patient time, and patient expense.

Other Changes Associated with Biofeedback Therapy

One of the distinct advantages of biofeedback often voiced by experimenters and practitioners alike is its absence of nocuous side effects. Recent research has shown that biofeedback and related self-regulation strategies can lead to positive changes in untargeted psychological variables, chief among these being depression and anxiety (Andrasik et al., 1984; Bell et al., 1983; Blanchard et al., 1986; Cox & Thomas, 1981; Cox et al., 1982; Gerber, Miltner, Birbaumer, & Lutzenberger, 1983). Blanchard et al. (1986) found significant change on certain psychological tests even for individuals whose headache activity did not change measurably following self-regulation treatment. Hence, participation in biofeedback self-regulation therapy may have a positive psychological effect somewhat independent of outcome.

One negative side effect of EMG biofeedback must be acknowledged even though it did not concern a patient seeking treatment for headache

(DeGood & Williams, 1982). The patient was referred for chronic low back and leg pain and received an EMG-assisted relaxation training program combined with autogenic exercises and integrative counseling. The patient, who prior to treatment was headache free, reported experiencing a severe headache and nausea of several hours duration immediately upon leaving the first training session. This pattern continued for a few additional treatments at which point it was overcome. The authors attributed this to "vagal rebound" or "parasympathetic over compensation" as a response to EMG biofeedback. To our knowledge, this type of effect has not been mentioned in the treatment of headache patients; its presence should be monitored nonetheless.

SPECIFIC EFFECTS AND MECHANISMS OF BIOFEEDBACK

The meta-analysis by Holroyd and Penzien showed biofeedback to be superior to headache monitoring alone (essentially no treatment or wait-list controls: average improvement across 10 separate studies $= -1.8\%$) and biofeedback control procedures employing noncontingent biofeedback (average rate of improvement $= 18.5\%$ for 6 separate investigations). Thus, EMG biofeedback, either alone or in combination with relaxation training, is both arithmetically and clinically superior to symptom monitoring and noncontingent biofeedback control procedures. Likewise, biofeedback has been found to be statistically and clinically superior to drug placebo in two separate investigations: 19% symptom improvement for placebo in Cox et al. (1975) and 9% symptom improvement for Paiva et al. (1982). Finally, biofeedback has been shown to be statistically and clinically superior to nonbiofeedback pseudo-therapies of equivalent credibility (Carrobles, 1981; Cram, 1980; Holroyd, Andrasik, & Noble, 1980). Thus, all evidence indicates that biofeedback is superior to no treatment, medication placebo, biofeedback placebo, and psychotherapy placebo.

How frontal EMG biofeedback produces these efficacious results is not all that clear, however. Budzynski et al. (1973) noted a highly significant correlation ($r = .90$) between amount of reduction in forehead muscle tension level and amount of symptom improvement for subjects undergoing biofeedback therapy, and interpreted this as strong evidence that learning to reduce EMG activity was the chief mechanism or mediator of symptom improvement. Subsequent idiographic analyses of the association between change in EMG level and change in headache activity failed to find significant positive relationships on a subject-by-subject basis (Epstein & Abel, 1977; Hart & Cichanski, 1981).

Andrasik and Holroyd (1980) compared standard biofeedback to two biofeedback control procedures and a no-treatment control in an effort to isolate better the role learned reductions in forehead EMG level played in treatment. Subjects in one biofeedback control condition were taught to increase forehead tension, whereas subjects assigned to the other biofeedback control procedure were taught to stabilize their forehead muscle tension activity. Feedback presented to subjects in the biofeedback control conditions was contingent, but it either emanated from an irrelevant site (forearm for the EMG stability group) or was presented in a direction opposite to that of the standard treatment (increase rather than decrease). All subjects receiving biofeedback were instructed in a similar manner and were led to believe they were learning to decrease forehead tension. EMG readings made during and following treatment sessions revealed subjects had learned to decrease, stabilize, or increase their muscle tension levels as intended. At brief and 3-year follow-up (Andrasik & Holroyd, 1983) all three biofeedback conditions revealed similar-size significant reductions in headache activity; no treatment controls remained unchanged. The authors proposed that cognitive and behavioral changes stimulated by participating in treatment may have been most responsible for the improvements noted, although they acknowledged the design of the study did not permit a test of this hypothesis. Other studies employing EMG stability training (Cram, 1980) or EMG increase training (Philips & Hunter, 1981) have found no relationships between change in EMG activity and outcome.

Holroyd *et al.* (1984) examined more directly the role cognitions play in mediating outcome in biofeedback treatment of tension headache. Two conditions replicated Andrasik and Holroyd (1980)—standard biofeedback and biofeedback to increase forehead tension levels (as before, subjects were led to believe they were actually relaxing forehead tension levels). One half of the subjects in each condition were provided feedback designed to convince them they were being highly successful at the biofeedback task, whereas the remaining subjects were led to believe they were being much less successful. Subjects provided high-success feedback achieved greater improvement (headache activity reduced by 53%) than subjects administered low-success feedback (mean reduction of 26%). Actual performance, as assessed by change in EMG activity, was unrelated to outcome. Holroyd *et al.* concluded:

> our results suggest that the reduction of frontal EMG during biofeedback training may be neither necessary nor sufficient for bringing about headache reduction in many tension headache sufferers. Instead, cognitive changes mobilized by performance feedback appear to play a central role in mediating headache improvement. (p. 1052)

Results from Andrasik and Holroyd (1980), Cram (1980), Holroyd *et al.* (1984), and Philips and Hunter (1981) indicate the early explanations of the therapeutic benefits of frontal EMG biofeedback are oversimplified and inaccurate. Future research on mechanisms of biofeedback treatment needs to take an expanded focus to include the interplay between physiological and cognitive variables.

COST-EFFECTIVENESS

We could not locate any studies addressing the cost-effectiveness of biofeedback treatment for tension headache. The need for such examinations is apparent.

SUGGESTIONS FOR FUTURE RESEARCH

1. Further study of the epidemiology and course of tension headache by targeting it as a specific entity in child and adult populations in community and treatment settings.

2. Further analysis of factors causing or exacerbating tension headache, the outcome of which should have important implications for diagnosis and treatment.

3. Further direct comparisons of biofeedback and relaxation in and of themselves are not needed. However, research attempting to identify which patients are best suited for biofeedback and which for relaxation are of considerable importance.

4. Attempt to account empirically for the differences in outcome obtained in research studies and that observed in clinical settings.

5. Further analysis of the independent and combined effects of biofeedback and cognitive therapy.

6. Further analyses of the long-term benefits of treatment and ways to make long-term gains more durable.

7. Further study of treatments for childhood headache.

8. Further study of the potential advantages of providing feedback from alternate muscle sites and incorporating discrimination exercises and training to criterion in biofeedback treatment.

9. Further study of the need for and benefits of regular home practice during and following treatment. The availability of compact home biofeedback training devices may facilitate more refined analyses of the value of practicing and applying biofeedback in the patient's home or work environment.

10. Further study of effects due to varied therapist characteristics.

11. Further study of predictors of outcome.

12. Further study of mechanisms of biofeedback treatment.

13. Begin to evaluate the cost effectiveness of biofeedback relative to other treatments.

14. Further study of the comparative and interactive effects of medication and biofeedback treatments.

CONCLUSIONS

1. Frontal EMG biofeedback remains an efficacious treatment for tension headache, with end of treatment improvement averaging approximately 46% for biofeedback alone and 57% for biofeedback combined with relaxation training (Holroyd & Penzien, 1985). This contrasts with an average rate of improvement of approximately 45% for relaxation training by itself. These levels of improvement are not statistically different.

2. Effects for biofeedback exceed those for no treatment, medication placebo, biofeedback placebo, and psychotherapy placebo.

3. Preliminary evidence suggests although biofeedback and relaxation produce similar magnitudes of improvement on a group-by-group basis, the two treatments may not be interchangeable. Rather, biofeedback may offer unique benefits to a subset of patients.

4. Data are too limited to support any conclusions about biofeedback treatments other than EMG biofeedback.

5. Long term benefits of biofeedback treatment are less well documented, with improvements ranging from approximately 20% to 87%. Preliminary evidence suggests that continued, limited contact during follow-up may make improvements more durable.

6. Cognitive therapy, either alone or combined with biofeedback, appears to be an efficacious treatment for tension headache. The only direct comparison found cognitive therapy to be more effective than biofeedback therapy.

7. Preliminary (limited) evidence suggests biofeedback may be more effective than some medical therapies.

8. Several client variables, most notably younger age, absence of depression, lower EMG level, and lower overall headache activity, appear to be associated with a more favorable response to treatment.

9. There is no conclusive evidence at present that selecting recording sites other than the forehead and incorporating discrimination training enhance outcome.

10. Preliminary, indirect evidence suggests that patients trained to a criterion level of performance may achieve better outcome.

11. The value of frequent, sustained, daily home practice of self-regulatory skills is questioned. Data suggest that even small amounts of practice may be adequate for maintaining treatment gains.

12. There is no conclusive evidence that experience level or personal characteristics of therapists relate to outcome. Preliminary evidence suggests overinvolvement by a therapist may impede therapy, however.

13. Mechanisms underlying the effectiveness of biofeedback are not clear. Preliminary evidence suggests cognitive variables may be as important as physiological variables in explaining treatment effects.

ACKNOWLEDGMENTS

Appreciation is expressed to Charles Burgar, Donald J. Dalessio, Kenneth A. Holroyd, and Clare Philips for carefully reviewing and critically commenting on an early draft of this report.

REFERENCES

Ad Hoc Committee on Classification of Headache. (1962). Classification of headache. *Journal of the American Medical Association, 179,* 717–718.

Adams, H. E., Brantley, P. J., & Thompson, K. (1982). Biofeedback and headache: Methodological issues. In L. White & B. Tursky (Eds.), *Clinical biofeedback: Efficacy and mechanisms* (pp. 358–367). New York: Guilford.

Adler, C. S., & Adler, S. M. (1975). Biofeedback-psychotherapy for the treatment of headaches: A 5-year follow-up. *Headache, 16,* 189–191.

Andrasik, F., Blanchard, E. B., Arena, J. G., Saunders, N. L., & Barron, K. D. (1982). Psychophysiology of recurrent headache: Methodological issues and new empirical findings. *Behavior Therapy, 13,* 407–429.

Andrasik, F., Blanchard, E. B., Arena, J. G., Teders, S. J., Teevan, R. C., & Rodichok, L. D. (1982). Psychological functioning in headache sufferers. *Psychosomatic Medicine, 44,* 171–182.

Andrasik, F., Blanchard, E. B., Edlund, S. R., & Attanasio, V. (1983). EMG biofeedback treatment of a child with muscle contraction headache. *American Journal of Clinical Biofeedback, 6,* 96–102.

Andrasik, F., Blanchard, E. B., Neff, D. F., & Rodichok, L. D. (1984). Biofeedback and relaxation training for chronic headache: A controlled comparison of booster treatments and regular contacts for long-term maintenance. *Journal of Consulting and Clinical Psychology, 52,* 609–615.

Andrasik, F., & Holroyd, K. A. (1980). A test of specific and nonspecific effects in the biofeedback treatment of tension headache. *Journal of Consulting and Clinical Psychology, 48,* 575–586.

Andrasik, F., & Holroyd, K. A. (1983). Specific and nonspecific effects in the biofeedback treatment of tension headache: 3-year follow-up. *Journal of Consulting and Clinical Psychology, 51,* 634–636.

Bakal, D. A. (1982). *The psychobiology of chronic headache.* New York: Springer.

Bakal, D. A., Demjen, S., & Kaganov, J. A. (1981). Cognitive behavioral treatment of chronic headache. *Headache, 21,* 81–86.

Barlow, D. H., Blanchard, E. B., Hayes, S. C., & Epstein, L. H. (1977). Single-case designs and clinical biofeedback experimentation. *Biofeedback and Self-Regulation, 2,* 221–239.

Basmajian, J. V. (1976). Facts versus myths in EMG biofeedback. *Biofeedback and Self-Regulation, 1,* 369–371.

Belar, C. D. (1979). A comment on Silver and Blanchard's (1978) review of the treatment of tension headaches by EMG feedback and relaxation training. *Journal of Behavioral Medicine, 2,* 215–220.

Bell, N. W., Abramowitz, S. I., Folkins, C. H., Spensley, J., & Hutchinson, G. L. (1983). Biofeedback, Brief psychotherapy and tension headache. *Headache, 23,* 162–173.

Bille, B. (1962). Migraine in school children. *Acta Paediatrica, 51* (Suppl. 136), 1–151.

Billings, R. F., Thomas, M. R., Rapp, M. S., Reyes, E., & Leith, M. (1984). Differential efficacy of biofeedback in headache. *Headache, 24,* 211–215.

Blanchard, E. B., Andrasik, F., Ahles, T. A., Teders, S. J., & O'Keefe, D. (1980). Migraine and tension headache: A meta-analytic review. *Behavior Therapy, 11,* 613–631.

Blanchard, E. B., Andrasik, F., Neff, D. F., Jurish, S. E., & O'Keefe, D. M. (1981). Social validation of the headache diary. *Behavior Therapy, 12,* 711–715.

Blanchard, E. B., Andrasik, F., Neff, D. F., Teders, S. J., Pallmeyer, T. P., Arena, J. B., Jurish, S. E., Saunders, N. L., Ahles, T. A., & Rodichok, L. D. (1982). Sequential comparisons of relaxation training and biofeedback in the treatment of three kinds of chronic headache or, the machines may be necessary some of the time. *Behaviour Research and Therapy, 20,* 1–13.

Blanchard, E. B., Andrasik, F., Neff, D. F., Saunders, N. L., Arena, J. G., Pallmeyer, T. P., Teders, S. J., Jurish, S. E., & Rodichok, L. D. (1983). Four process studies in the behavioral treatment of chronic headache. *Behaviour Research and Therapy, 21,* 209–220.

Blanchard, E. B., Andrasik, F., Evans, D. D., Neff, D. F., Appelbaum, K. A., & Rodichok, L. D. (1985). Behavioral treatment of 250 chronic headache patients: A clinical replication series. *Behavior Therapy, 16,* 308–327.

Blanchard, E. B., Andrasik, F., Appelbaum, K. A., Evans, D. D., Meyers, P., & Barron, K. D. (1986). Three studies of the psychological changes in chronic headache patients associated with biofeedback and relaxation therapies. *Psychosomatic Medicine, 48,* 73–83.

Borgeat, F., Hade, B., Larouche, L. M., & Bedwani, C. N. (1980). Effect of therapist's active presence on EMG biofeedback training of headache patients. *Biofeedback and Self-Regulation, 5,* 275–282.

Bruhn, P., Olesen, J., & Melgaard, B. (1979). Controlled trial of EMG feedback in muscle contraction headache. *Annals of Neurology, 6,* 34–36.

Budzynski, T. (1978). Biofeedback in the treatment of muscle-contraction (tension) headache. *Biofeedback and Self-Regulation, 4,* 409–434.

Budzynski, T., Stoyva, J. M., & Adler, C. S. (1970). Feedback-induced muscle relaxation: Application to tension headache. *Journal of Behavior Therapy and Experimental Psychiatry, 1,* 205–211.

Budzynski, T., Stoyva, J. M., Adler, C. S., & Mullaney, D. J. (1973). EMG biofeedback and tension headache: A controlled outcome study. *Psychosomatic Medicine, 35,* 484–496.

Cahn, T., & Cram, J. R. (1980). Changing measurement instrument at follow-up: A potential source of error. *Biofeedback and Self-Regulation, 5,* 265–273.

Carrobles, J. A. I., Cardona, A., & Santacreu, J. (1981). Shaping and generalization procedures in the EMG biofeedback treatment of tension headaches. *British Journal of Clinical Psychology, 20,* 49–56.

Chesney, M. A., & Shelton, J. L. (1976). A comparison of muscle relaxation and electromyogram biofeedback treatments for muscle contraction headache. *Journal of Behavior Therapy and Experimental Psychiatry, 7,* 221–225.

Cott, A., Goldman, J. A., Pavloski, R. P., Kirschberg, G. J., & Fabich, M. (1981). The long-term therapeutic significance of the addition of electromyographic biofeedback to relaxation training in the treatment of tension headaches. *Behavior Therapy, 12,* 556–559.

Cox, D., & Thomas, D. (1981). Relationship between headaches and depression. *Headache, 21,* 261–263.

Cox, D. J., Freundlich, A., & Meyer, R. G. (1975). Differential effectiveness of electromyographic feedback, verbal relaxation instructions, and medication placebo with tension headaches. *Journal of Consulting and Clinical Psychology, 43,* 842–898.

Cox, D. J., Lefebvre, R. C., & Hobbs, W. R. (1982). Ancillary symptoms in the biofeedback treatment of headaches. *Headache, 22,* 213–215.

Cram, J. R. (1980). EMG biofeedback and the treatment of tension headaches: A systematic analysis of treatment components. *Behavior Therapy, 11,* 699–710.

Dalessio, D. J. (1980). A clinical classification of headache. In D. J. Dalessio (Ed.), *Wolff's headache and other head pain* (4th ed., pp. 1–8). New York: Oxford.

Daly, E. J., Donn, P. A., Galliher, M. J., & Zimmerman, J. S. (1983). Biofeedback applications to migraine and tension headache: A double-blinded outcome study. *Biofeedback and Self-Regulation, 8,* 135–152.

DeGood, D. E., & Williams, E. M. (1982). Parasympathetic rebound following EMG biofeedback training: A case study. *Biofeedback and Self-Regulation, 7,* 461–465.

Diamond, S. (1964). Depressive headaches. *Headache, 4,* 255–259.

Diamond, S. (1983). Depression and headache. *Headache, 23,* 123–126.

Diamond, S., & Dalessio, D. J. (1982). *The practicing physician's approach to headache* (3rd ed.). Baltimore, MD: Williams & Wilkins.

Diamond, S., & Montrose, D. (1984). The value of biofeedback in the treatment of chronic headache: A four-year retrospective study. *Headache, 24,* 5–18.

Diamond, S., Medina, J., Diamond-Falk, J., & DeVeno, T. (1979). The value of biofeedback in the treatment of chronic headache: A five-year retrospective study. *Headache, 19,* 90–96.

Epstein, L. H., & Abel, G. G. (1977). An analysis of biofeedback training effects for tension headache patients. *Behavior Therapy, 8,* 37–47.

Epstein, L. H., & Blanchard, E. B. (1977). Biofeedback, self-control, and self-management. *Biofeedback and Self-Regulation, 2,* 201–211.

Ford, M. R., Stroebel, C. F., Strong, P., & Szarek, B. L. (1983). Quieting response training: Long-term evaluation of a clinical biofeedback practice. *Biofeedback and Self-Regulation, 8,* 265–278.

Friedman, A. (1979). Nature of headache. *Headache, 19,* 163–167.

Friedman, A. P., Von Storch, T. C., & Merritt, H. H. (1954). Migraine and tension headaches: A clinical study of two thousand cases. *Neurology, 4,* 773–788.

Gerber, W. D., Miltner, W., Birbaumer, N., & Lutzenberger, W. (1983). Cephalic vasomotor feedback therapy: A controlled study of migraines and normals, in K. Holroyd, B. Schlote & H. Zenz (Eds.), *Perspectives in Research on Headache.* New York: C. J. Hogrefe.

Gray, C. L., Lyle, R. C., McGuire, R. J., & Peck, D. F. (1980). Electrode placement, EMG feedback, and relaxation for tension headaches. *Behavior Research and Therapy, 18,* 19–23.

Hart, J. D., & Cichanski, K. A. (1981). A comparison of frontal EMG biofeedback and neck EMG biofeedback in the treatment of muscle-contraction headache. *Biofeedback and Self-Regulation, 6,* 63–74.

Haynes, S. N., Griffin, P., Mooney, D., & Parise, M. (1975). Electromyographic biofeedback and relaxation instructions in the treatment of muscle contraction headaches. *Behavior Therapy, 6,* 677–678.

Haynes, S. N., Cuevas, J., & Gannon, L. R. (1982). The psychophysiological etiology of muscle contraction headache. *Headache, 22,* 122–132.

Holm, J. E., Holroyd, K. A., Hursey, K. G., & Penzien, D. G. (1984). *Tension headache versus headache-free subjects: An evaluation of stressful events, cognitive appriasal, and coping strategies.* Philadelphia, PA: Society of Behavioral Medicine.

Holroyd, K. A., & Andrasik, F. (1982). Do the effects of cognitive therapy endure? A two-year follow-up of tension headache sufferers treated with cognitive therapy or bio-feedback. *Cognitive Therapy and Research, 6,* 325–334.

Holroyd, K. A., & Penzien, D. B. (1985). *Client variables and the behavioral treatment of recurrent tension headache: A meta-analytic review.* Unpublished manuscript.

Holroyd, K. A., Andrasik, F., & Westbrook, T. (1977). Cognitive control of tension head-ache. *Cognitive Therapy and Research, 2,* 121–133.

Holroyd, K. A., Andrasik, F., & Noble, J. (1980). A comparison of EMG biofeedback and a credible pseudotherapy in treating tension headache. *Journal of Behavioral Medicine, 3,* 29–39.

Holroyd, K. A., Penzien, D. B., Hursey, K. G., Tobin, D. L., Rogers, L., Holm, J. E., Marcille, P. J., Hall, J. R., & Chila, A. G. (1984). Change mechanisms in EMG bio-feedback training: Cognitive changes underlying improvements in tension headache. *Journal of Consulting and Clinical Psychology, 52,* 1039–1053.

Howarth, E. (1965). Headache, personality, and stress. *British Journal of Psychiatry, 111,* 1193–1197.

Hudzinski, L. G. (1983). Neck musculature and EMG biofeedback in treatment of muscle contraction headache. *Headache, 23,* 86–90.

Hudzinski, L. G. (1984). The significance of muscle discrimination training in the treatment of chronic muscle contraction headache. *Headache, 24,* 203–210.

Hutchings, D. F., & Reinking, R. H. (1976). Tension headaches. What form of therapy is most effective? *Biofeedback and Self-Regulation, 1,* 183–190.

Jacob, R. G., Turner, S. N., Szekely, B. C., Eidelman, B. H. (1983). Predicting outcome of relaxation therapy in headaches: The role of "depression." *Behavior Therapy, 14,* 457–465.

Jacobson, E. (1938). *Progressive relaxation.* Chicago, IL: University of Chicago Press.

Janssen, K. (1983). Differential effectiveness of EMG-feedback versus combined EMG-feedback and relaxation instructions in the treatment of tension headache. *Journal of Psychosomatic Research, 27,* 243–253.

Jay, G. W., Renelli, D., & Mead, T. (1984). The effects of propranolol and amitriptyline on vascular and EMG biofeedback training. *Headache, 24,* 59–69.

Kondo, C., & Canter, A. (1977). True and false electromyographic feedback: Effect on tension headache. *Journal of Abnormal Psychology, 86,* 93–95.

Kotses, H., & Weiner, H. (1982). Effects of home practice exercises on EMG activity subsequent to biofeedback training. *American Journal of Clinical Biofeedback, 5,* 103–109.

Kremsdorf, R. B., Kochanowicz, N. A., & Costell, S. (1981). Cognitive skills training versus EMG biofeedback in the treatment of tension headaches. *Biofeedback and Self-Regulation, 6,* 93–102.

Kudrow, L. (1982). Paradoxical effects of frequent analgesic use. In M. Critchley, A. Friedman, S. Gorini, & F. Sicuteri (Eds.), *Headache: Physiopathological and clinical concepts* (Advances in Neurology, Vol. 22, pp. 335–341). New York: Raven Press.

Lance, J. W., Curran, D. A., & Anthony, M. (1965). Investigations into the mechanism and treatment of chronic headache. *Medical Journal of Australia, 2,* 909–914.

Leviton, A. (1978). Epidemiology of headache. In V. S. Schoenberg (Ed.), *Advances in Neurology* (Vol. 19, pp. 341–352). New York: Raven Press.

Libo, L. M., & Arnold, G. E. (1983). Does training to criterion influence improvement? A follow-up study of EMG and thermal biofeedback. *Journal of Behavioral Medicine, 6,* 397–404.

Libo, L. M., & Arnold, G. E. (1983). Relaxation practice after biofeedback therapy: A long-term follow-up study of utilization and effectiveness. *Biofeedback and Self-Regulation, 8,* 217–227.

Martin, P. R., & Mathews, A. M. (1978). Tension headaches: Psychophysiological investigation and treatment. *Journal of Psychosomatic Research, 22,* 389–399.

McKenzie, R. E., Ehrisman, W. J., Montgomery, P. S., & Barnes, R. H. (1974). The treatment of headache by means of electroencephalographic biofeedback. *Headache, 14,* 164–172.

Meichenbaum, D. (1976). Cognitive factors in biofeedback therapy. *Biofeedback and Self-Regulation, 1,* 201–216.

Mitchell, K. R., & White, R. G. (1976). Self-management of tension headaches: A case study. *Journal of Behavior Therapy and Experimental Psychiatry, 7,* 387–389.

Paiva, T., Nunes, S., Moreira, A., Santos, J., Teixeira, J., & Barbosa, A. (1982). Effects of frontalis EMG biofeedback and diazepam in the treatment of tension headache. *Headache, 22,* 216–220.

Philips, C. (1977). The modification of tension headache pain using EMG biofeedback. *Behavior Research and Therapy, 15,* 119–129.

Philips, H. C. (1978). Tension headache: Theoretical problems. *Behaviour Research and Therapy, 16,* 249–261.

Philips, C., & Hunter, M. (1981). The treatment of tension headache—I. Muscular abnormality and biofeedback. *Behavior Research and Therapy, 19,* 485–498.

Rapoport, A., Sheftell, F., Baskin, S., & Weeks, R. (1984, September). *Analgesic rebound headache.* Paper presented at the annual meeting of the Migraine Trust, London.

Raskin, N. H., & Appenzeller, O. (1980). *Headache.* Philadelphia, PA: Saunders.

Reeves, J. L. (1976). EMG-biofeedback reduction of tension headache: A cognitive skills-training approach. *Biofeedback and Self-Regulation, 1,* 217–225.

Reinking, R. H., Hutchings, D. (1981). Follow-up to: "Tension headaches: What form of therapy is most effective?" *Biofeedback and Self-Regulation, 6,* 57–62.

Robinson, C. A. (1980). Cervical spondylosis and muscle contraction headaches. In D. J. Dalessio (Ed.), *Wolff's headache and other head pain* (4th ed., pp. 362–380). New York: Oxford.

Sargent, J. D., Solbach, P., & Coyne, L. (1980). Evaluation of a 5-day non-drug training program for headache at the Menninger Foundation. *Headache, 20,* 32–41.

Satinsky, D., Frerotte, A. (1981). Biofeedback treatment for headache: A two-year follow-up study. *American Journal of Clinical Biofeedback, 1,* 62–65.

Schlutter, L. G., Golden, C. J., & Blume, H. G. (1980). A comparison of treatments for perfrontal muscle contraction headache. *British Journal of Medical Psychology, 53,* 47–52.

Silver, B. V., & Blanchard, E. B. (1978). Biofeedback or relaxation training in the treatment of psychophysiologic disorders: Or, are the machines really necessary? *Journal of Behavioral Medicine, 1,* 217–239.

Solbach, P., & Sargent, J. D. (1977). A follow-up evaluation of the Menninger pilot migraine study using thermal training. *Headache, 17,* 198–202.

Steger, J. C., & Harper, R. G. (1980). Comprehensive biofeedback versus self-monitored relaxation in the treatment of tension headache. *Headache, 20,* 137–142.

Steiner, S. S., & Dince, W. N. (1981). Biofeedback efficacy studies: A critique of critiques. *Biofeedback and Self-Regulation, 6,* 275–288.

Steinmark, S., & Borkovec, T. (1974). Active and placebo treatment effects on moderate insomnia under counterdemand and positive demand instruction. *Journal of Abnormal Psychology, 83,* 157–163.

Stoyva, J., & Budzynski, T. (1974). Cultivated low arousal—An antistress response? In L. V. DiCara (Ed.), *Limbic and autonomic nervous systems research* (pp. 369–394). New York: Plenum Press.

Thompson, J. K., Haber, J. D., & Tearnan, B. H. (1981). Generalization of frontalis electromyographic feedback to adjacent muscle groups: A critical review. *Psychosomatic Medicine, 42,* 19–24.

Van Boxtel, A., Goudswaard, P., & Janssen, K. (1983). Absolute and proportional resting
EMG levels in muscle contraction and migraine headache patients. *Headache, 23,* 215–222.

Werder, D. S., & Sargent, J. D. (1984). A study of childhood headache using biofeedback
as as treatment alternative. *Headache, 24,* 122–126.

Werder, D. S., Sargent, J. D., & Coyne, L. (1981, October). *MMPI profiles of headache patients
using self-regulation to control headache activity.* Presented at the 1981 meeting of the
American Association of Biofeedback Clinicians, 1981, Kansas City, MO.

9

Guidelines for Controlled Clinical Trials of Biofeedback

JOHN P. HATCH

INTRODUCTION

The authors of the foregoing chapters have assembled a tremendous amount of data pertaining to the clinical efficacy of biofeedback. Their evaluations of the evidence lead to the conclusion that significant progress is being made in the quality as well as the quantity of biofeedback research. In spite of these very positive and encouraging findings, however, the research in the area is not flawless, and it is important to ask how even stronger evidence could be generated in the future. In other words, what features should be incorporated into the next generation of clinical biofeedback studies? The authors of each chapter were instructed to address this question from the perspective of their own area of expertise. One conclusion, common to all areas, was that more studies are needed that could be described as controlled clinical trials. The purpose of this chapter is to provide a guide to some of the issues that should be considered in conducting controlled clinical trials used to evaluate biofeedback as a treatment modality. The emphasis on the word *guide* is important because research is largely a creative endeavor, and it is impossible to provide a formula applicable to all situations.

Many of the issues that I will discuss will be rudimentary to established researchers. Nonetheless, I will try to cover all important aspects

Preparation of this chapter was supported in part by PHS Grant No. HL27698

JOHN P. HATCH • Department of Psychiatry, The University of Texas Health Science Center at San Antonio, 7703 Floyd Curl Drive, San Antonio, TX 78284.

of the research process. Sometimes, seemingly elementary procedures, if performed improperly, can jeopardize an entire study. For example, the randomization of subjects to treatment groups, although conceptually quite simple, is a critically important step in the research process, and there are many ways that subjects can be randomized improperly.

My aim is to write mainly for those people who are familiar with research in biofeedback, but whose training is not primarily in research. These people from applied settings are very important to biofeedback research, and they could play a much more active role than they currently do because they have access to the patient populations that are most appropriate for research. They also are highly knowledgeable about clinical applications of biofeedback and have experience in truly clinical settings. Thus, they are in an excellent position to generate many researchable questions, and provide advice as to how biofeedback should be utilized in clinical research. For this reason, collaboration between expert clinicians and expert researchers should be encouraged.

For those who decide not to become actively involved in clinical trials involving biofeedback, I hope to provide insight into what functions clinical trials can and cannot serve for the field of biofeedback. I also hope to provide a frame of reference that will help consumers of current and future research to evaluate critically the many offerings that are provided.

What Are Controlled Clinical Trials?

A useful definition that highlights the critical features defines a controlled clinical trial as "a *prospective* study comparing the effect and value of *intervention(s)* against a *control* in *human* subjects" (Friedman, Furberg, & DeMets, 1981, p. 1, emphasis added). Let us examine each of these features. First, the study must be *prospective*. This means that patients are followed foreward in time from whenever they enter the study. Although some retrospective data may be collected as well, the primary data concerning response to treatment must be collected subsequent to a well-defined point in time. That the study must involve *interventions* distinguishes controlled clinical trials from observational studies. A well-defined intervention must be involved. By *control* is usually meant a group that either does not receive the intervention, or else receives an alternate intervention, but is sufficiently similar to the intervention group prior to treatment that posttreatment differences may be reasonably attributed to actions of the intervention. Finally, the study must be performed using *human subjects*. If the aim of the study is to evaluate therapy then the subjects must be actual clinical patients; they cannot be college students or people with subclinical forms of the disorder. These points are all critically important. The absence of any one of these features would constitute a major flaw in a clinical trial.

What Can Be Accomplished through Controlled Clinical Trials?

Research is a process of acquiring knowledge by adhering to certain rules of evidence. These rules demand objective measurements and comparisons that are open to public verification. The general objective of controlled clinical trials, like all research, is to acquire new knowledge about a problem. Whether or not your particular objectives can be accomplished through research will depend on many factors that should be given careful consideration before you begin. A clinical trial is a major undertaking, and there are a seemingly endless number of things that can go wrong. The main reason for performing controlled clinical trials of biofeedback therapy is to demonstrate its effectiveness relative to a known standard therapy, a placebo therapy, or no therapy. This information is needed not only to justify the clinical use of biofeedback, but also to enable clinicians to make better therapeutic decisions regarding its use. A controlled trial offers two important advantages over one that is uncontrolled. First, it allows a comparison to be made between biofeedback and some alternate treatment. Second, it allows the exclusion of certain nonspecific factors as the cause of the observed therapeutic effect and controls threats to the validity of the study.

Another important purpose of clinical trials is to discover any potential risks or hazards associated with the therapy. Biofeedback is considered safe, but certain negative side effects may exist. Clinical trials are well suited to assist in the identification of risks, even when they are mild or rare. In fact, the more uncommon a side effect is, the more important it is to search systematically for it. It is unlikely that rare or mild side effects will be discovered through casual clinical observation, and even if they are noted, they may not be attributed to a treatment that is already accepted as safe. On the other hand, when side effects are systematically monitored, they are more likely to be detected. Furthermore, when side effects are disproportionately observed in one group compared to another, it is more likely that they will be attributed to the treatment rather than to some uncontrolled aspect of the patients' lives. If biofeedback can be proven to have fewer or less severe risks and side effects than other therapies, then this would be a major advantage.

Besides usefulness in assessing effectiveness and risk of a therapy, there are other reasons for performing controlled clinical trials. For example, clinical trials are sometimes performed to understand better the mechanism of action of a treatment. An understanding of the mechanism of action is not necessary for the clinical justification of therapy, however, it usually allows wiser clinical decisions to be made. If we had a better understanding of how biofeedback works we might be better able to predict when and for whom it will work. The identification of prognosticators of therapeutic success and failure is frequently another aim of clinical trials. Another reason for conducting clinical trials is to evaluate the practical aspects of the therapy, such as cost-effectiveness, time requirements, and acceptability to patients. Sometimes clinical trials are conducted to evaluate the possible interactions of one treatment with other concomitant forms of therapy, or to determine whether a new treatment technique has value as an adjunct to a more conventional therapy. Finally, clinical trials can be used to establish the specifics that would allow the optimization of treatment efficacy. In the case of biofeedback this might involve determining optimal length, frequency, and number of treatment sessions or the optimal amount of home practice that should be prescribed. A well planned, controlled clinical trial can address several of the issues discussed in this section, however, it is unusual for a single study to address more than a few in any depth.

When Should Controlled Clinical Trials Be Attempted?

In this section, I will discuss an issue that I think is of particular importance to the area of biofeedback now. The issue is the proper timing of clinical trials in order to achieve maximum benefit. The primary aim of clinical trials is to gain knowledge about the effectiveness of a new therapy. If the treatment is proven to be effective, with acceptable risk, the new therapy is put into use. If, on the other hand, it is found to be ineffective or hazardous, the new therapy is rejected. Ordinarily, it makes sense to go through this process as quickly as possible. However, the decision to conduct a trial implies that the new therapy is understood well enough to make conducting an adequate clinical trial feasible. When new medicines are proposed for human use they are put through a series of tests culminating with large-scale, clinical trials. It has been suggested that research in biofeedback might profit by following a similar model (Miller, 1978). In the case of a new medicine, the preliminary phases of research will typically have provided a considerable amount of information regarding such things as mechanism of action, toxicity, dosage range, and magnitude of expected response. Knowledge of these factors in the case of biofeedback is incomplete at best, and biofeedback techniques have not become highly standardized. Therefore, before elaborating the details of clinical trials research, I think it is important to consider whether the science of biofeedback is mature enough to take this step.

Perhaps the issue can be clarified by considering the recent experiences of two other clinical areas, psychopharmacology and psychotherapy. There are vast differences in the results of research efforts in these two areas. Part of the difference is economic. The pharmaceutical industry has supported hundreds of clinical trials to evaluate new products, and support for psychotherapy research is small in comparison. However, the main reasons for the discrepancy relate to the appropriateness of the questions asked, preparedness to do the research, and the quality and productivity of the studies performed. Whereas clinical-trials research in psychopharmacology continued to prosper, clinical-trials research in psychotherapy became confused and conflict ridden. In retrospect, it appears that a lot of time was wasted in psychotherapy research by asking the wrong questions, applying techniques inconsistently, specifying diagnoses imprecisely, using inappropriate outcome measures, and failing to take into account important individual differences in patients. At the completion of an enormous review of the psychotherapy research literature (Bergin & Strupp, 1972), Strupp was left with such questions as "What is psychotherapy?" "What does it try to accomplish" and "By what criteria do we evaluate changes as desirable or undesirable, healthy or unhealthy, good or evil?" (p. 449). Many of these problems are currently being corrected (see Williams & Spitzer, 1984), and a new generation of psychotherapy studies will soon begin to appear. The frustrating outcome of all this was that only very weak effects of psychotherapy were demonstrated. The researchers failed to achieve their objectives using research methods. Furthermore, most psychotherapists would agree that psychotherapy research had little, if any, impact on how they practice psychotherapy. Has biofeedback research had a significant impact on biofeedback therapy? Is it likely to in the future? I think we need an honest answer to these questions before we launch large-scale clinical trials in the area. The question we must come to grips with now is whether the area of biofeedback is at a stage of development where large-scale, controlled clinical trials would be productive, or is biofeedback more like psychotherapy, still trying to ask the right questions? If biofeedback is a valuable therapy, then we have a responsibility to prove this quickly in the most convincing way possible. On the other hand, it would be imprudent to launch prematurely expensive studies that are incapable of achieving their intended purpose. One obvious lesson to be learned from the experiences of psychotherapy researchers is that it will not be productive to design studies to test the general effects of global treatments on ill-defined response variables. Instead of asking "Does biofeedback work?" we will make more progress by asking "*What* treatment, by *whom*, is most effective for *this* individual with *that* specific problem, and under *which* set of circumstances?" (Paul, 1967, p. 111).

Let us assume that biofeedback treatments for a certain disorder are, or soon will be, developed and specified to the point where controlled clinical trials are necessary. What do you do next? If you decide that your objectives can be achieved through research you must: (a) plan the study, (b) execute the study, (c) analyze the data, and (d) interpret the results. Each of these phases of the research process will be discussed in turn.

PLANNING THE STUDY

Adequate planning of a study is at least as important as any other phase. If you do not have a good plan, you probably will not achieve your objective. One of the first questions to ask is who should do the study?

Who Should Attempt Controlled Clinical Trials?

A person with limited research experience may be quickly overwhelmed by the responsibility of directing a large-scale clinical trial. The principal investigator must be a competent researcher who thoroughly understands the disorder, its treatment, the research question, and the research methodology to be used. He or she should also understand how the experiment fits into the overall frame of reference in the area. He or she must be able to organize a huge data base and coordinate many different aspects of the study. He or she will constantly be called on to resolve ambiguities and to resolve conflicts and problems. If collaboration with other scientists will be involved, and this will probably be the case, it is important that they are carefully screened to make sure that they can fulfill the responsibilities assigned to them. Collaborators should be identified as early as possible in the planning phase and should have input at this time. A clear-cut division of labor should be established. Who will treat the patients? Who will analyze the data? Who will write the progress reports? Who will provide resources? Who will get publication credit?

Stating the Primary Research Question

Once it is established who will be doing the research, all concerned parties should understand and agree on why the research is being done. There must be a clearly and explicitly stated primary hypothesis or research question. Every study should be planned so that it can answer one question that is designated as primary. There will, of course, be secondary questions that also will be asked of the data, but during planning, decisions should be made to ensure that one primary question will receive the most credible answer possible. Do not compromise the design of a study in any way that will jeopardize the primary question, even if it means not being able to answer a secondary question. These priorities may have to be negotiated, but once stated, everyone must understand that the study is being planned, first and foremost, to answer the primary question.

How do you arrive at your primary question? It will usually require an intimate familiarity with the literature in your area. Your familiarity with the literature will determine how extensive a literature review you must undertake. A good place to start a literature review is with some of the computerized literature searches available in most major academic libraries. If you are not highly familiar with the literature in the area, pick several recent comprehensive review articles on the topic and read these first. This should give you an idea of who is doing the major work in the area and what some of the current issues being researched are. Next, begin to limit your scope and read several of the original research articles cited in the reviews. As you do this, begin to make notes about issues and methodologies you think are particularly appropriate, and begin to assemble a file of references. In science, a piece of information is generally not acceptable without supporting documentation. Also, read some of the classics in the field; they will give you a valuable historical perspective on your problem. This retrospective literature review is relatively easy because you have a system of interrelating reference citations to guide you. However, you will also want to know what has been done in the area more recently, and a "prospective" literature search can be more tedious. Here again, computerized searches and abstract services can be helpful, but to cover thoroughly the most recent 12 to 24 months nothing can substitute for searching the indexes or tables of contents of the journals that frequently publish articles in your area. Abstracts published in the proceedings of various scientific organizations is another good source of recent information.

Once you complete your literature review you should be able to state your primary research question. Next, ask yourself: Can I answer this question through research? Can it be answered with the facilities available? Is it the right question, or am I asking "does biofeedback work"? Is it worth answering? Has it already been answered? When you are satisfied with your research question you are ready to continue the planning of your study.

Relating the Question to the Research Process

To go beyond the planning stage requires a shift in thinking from the abstract to the pragmatic. To achieve your objective, you must translate your idea into concrete actions. For some reason, many people seem to have difficulty relating an idea to the research process. Good clinical research must begin with good clinical work. This point cannot be overemphasized. A study that involves a contrived, restricted, or abbreviated form of biofeedback cannot be generalized to actual clinical practice. If standard clinical practice is to provide 15 to 20 biofeedback training sessions in treating a particular disorder, it is not acceptable to plan on using fewer sessions for research purposes unless the aim is to evaluate a brief form of the treatment technique. However, whereas good clinical work often involves adapting therapy to individual patient characteristics, clinical research aims to standardize treatment. The primary distinctions between clinical practice and clinical research relate to the rules of evidence adhered to by the scientific community. The first of these rules is that events must be *measurable*, so the goal is not simply to produce a good clinical effect but rather to produce a good and measurable clinical effect. Inherent to the concept of measurement is comparison to a standard. Suppose you develop a new treatment for some disorder and are eager to spread the news of how effective your technique is. Eventually a critic will ask "compared to what?" If you cannot answer this question, your claims will not be as persuasive as they would be if you could answer "compared to treatments A, B, and C." Therefore, clinical trials should contain a standard against which the intervention can be compared. This is the primary function of the control group. In addition, your research should be publicly verifiable. This means that if your critic asks you to "prove it" you can repeat your results or explain your methods in sufficient detail that anyone wishing to could repeat the experiment and obtain the same results.

Another question that will be asked about your research is whether or not the comparison was *biased*. In order for your research question to receive a fair and honest answer, the study must not be biased. A study is said to be biased if there are any extraneous factors operating in such a way as to unfairly favor one outcome over another. Bias can have a great many sources, and it can enter an experiment at any stage from inception to interpretation. Anyone involved in handling the data in any way can introduce a bias. This includes the investigator, the patients, the technicians, and the data analyst. Therefore, the researcher must be continuously vigilant of this potential problem. In the ideal experiment, all treatments should be identical except for the controlled manipulation of one precisely defined variable, the independent variable. Manipulation of this one variable introduces a known bias into the system. The effects of this manipulation are measured as changes in the patient's clinical condition as reflected by the dependent variable. If all other sources of bias are successfully controlled, then it is assumed, with a reasonable degree of confidence, that differences among treatment groups are caused by the effects of the controlled bias that was introduced. Conversely, it is also assumed that if the intervention did not occur, then the treatment groups would differ only to a degree expected by chance. Sometimes asking the question both ways is helpful in identifying a source of bias.

Of course, the discussion of bias in such an ideal experiment is only useful as a guide to be followed in designing a real experiment, and certain qualifiers are needed. First, in biofeedback research, treatments can seldom be precisely manipulated in such specific ways. It is far more likely that the test in applied research will actually be between rather broadly defined treatment strategies than between precisely defined treatments. Second, many extraneous factors that could bias the study will be unknown or uncontrollable. Third, unless a factor is successfully controlled, it will not have been eliminated as a source of bias. Finally, it should be acknowledged that there is much debate as to whether or not any science can prove a causal relation between variables. This is a complex philosophical question, but in pragmatic terms an experiment will generally be easier to interpret if as many competing explanations as possible have been reasonably ruled out by reducing bias to a minimum. I will repeatedly return to the important issue of reducing bias throughout the remainder of this chapter.

Besides reducing bias, another major concern in planning an experiment is maximizing *statistical power*. I will also return to this topic and cover it in greater detail in a later section on the determination of sample size, but I will introduce the idea here because important decisions made very early in planning can have a major impact on power. Statistical power sets limits on your ability to detect a true difference when one does in fact exist. Because this will be the principal aim of many studies, it is wise to make certain that the influences that certain actions will have on power are taken into account during planning. Power is determined by the following factors: (a) the alpha level, (b) the sample size, (c) the size of the effect sought, and (d) the variance of the measure in the population of interest. Alpha levels are usually set by convention, so any decisions made will have to consider the remaining three factors. Power increases with the size of the difference actually observed, and it makes very good intuitive sense that one can be more confident of a large difference between treatments than a small one. It may go without saying, but it is, therefore, important to plan a study to produce a relatively large and meaningful effect. A researcher should have a fairly good idea how large a difference would be meaningful and plan a study to produce an effect at least that large. It is usually a mistake to plan an experiment not knowing what to expect and just hoping for the best.

Another way to increase power is to increase sample size. Therefore, researchers should begin early in planning to ask: Are appropriate patients readily available? How much will it cost to run each subject in time, effort, and money? In most biofeedback applications, it will quickly be appreciated that procedural economics set very severe practical limits on sample size. Only when the cost of running a single subject in a clinical trial of biofeedback is realistically calculated can the importance of increasing power through means other than adding patients be fully appreciated.

Fortunately, there is another factor affecting power over which an investigator has some control. Statistical power increases as the variance in the measurements decreases. Therefore, power can be increased by reducing extraneous variability. Extraneous variability can enter an experiment from many sources, including subject heterogeneity, equipment malfunction, poorly designed questionnaires, and carelessness in collecting and recording data. Reducing extraneous variance is usually a sound investment.

Before leaving the topic of statistical power, it should also be noted that some test statistics are inherently more sensitive than others. Therefore, in planning an experiment, consideration should be given to characteristics of the data that are likely to be generated. If you can plan a study so that the data will conform to assumptions required for the use of parametric statistics, then you will be able to take advantage of the greater power these techniques provide relative to nonparametric techniques when it comes time to analyze your data.

Returning to the problem of relating your research question to a series of actions that constitute the research process, it may be helpful to keep the following points in mind. The foundation of good clinical research is good clinical work. In addition to this, however, the clinical effect produced must be objectively measurable, implying comparison to a standard. The study design must provide for the control of extraneous factors so that the outcome is reasonably free of bias. Finally, the study design must provide sufficient statistical power so that a treatment effect of a specified magnitude will be reliably detected if in fact it does occur. Many of the decisions made and actions taken later on will be justified by these principles.

Identifying the Variables

Identification and definition of the variables will determine what type of data will be collected and at what times during the experiment. Every piece of data collected should have a known purpose, and the decision to include a variable should be made to advance the purpose of the research. Sometimes this requires quite a bit of thought. Too often variables are included arbitrarily. Once you have stated your research question, the selection of all variables should be based on a known or suspected relationship to the processes being studied.

One important class of variables in a clinical trial are the outcome or response variables. It is in these units that you will attempt to measure the effectiveness of your biofeedback intervention. Response variables will vary greatly from study to study, but in every case you will want to use the best response variable that you can. In general, a nominal response variable does not give as much information as a quantifiable response variable. Therefore, more observations and a larger sample size will usually be required when a nominal response variable is used. For example, simple countings of patients who are improved or unimproved at the completion of therapy will not provide as much information as if the therapeutic response can be quantitatively measured on a continuous scale. With proper care, blood pressure can be objectively measured with resonable validity on a continuous scale composed of calibrated units. On the other hand, if you are using biofeedback to treat a pain disorder you may have to rely on patient's subjective reports of the pain experience on a much more restricted and uncalibrated scale.

Besides being measurable on a continuous and quantitative scale, what other features should a desirable response variable possess? It should allow the therapeutic response to be measured accurately, that is with a small measurement error. Measurement error contributes extraneous variability to an experiment and reduces statistical power. Therefore, in choosing between available response variables the standard deviation of the measure should be investigated. Of course, a good response variable should have high reliability and validity. A good response measure will also demonstrate a high degree of *sensitivity*. This means that falsely negative results will be minimized because changes in patients' conditions will always be reflected by the measure. The response variable should also show high specificity. *Specificity* refers to the ability to avoid falsely positive results that can occur if the response variable is responsive to influences besides those of the intervention being investigated.

In biofeedback research there will generally be more than one possible way to measure the patient's response to treatment. For example, in research using biofeedback to treat headaches it is common to report response to treatment in terms of headache frequency, intensity, duration, and/or medication use. This is important because any or all of several dimensions of the disorder can respond differently to the treatment. If enough subjects are available, then the multiple hypotheses that each of several dimensions will respond to treatment can be tested. A multivariate test of the effect of treatment on multiple response variables can also be performed. Unfortunately, what sometimes happens is that investigators use the available degrees of freedom over and over again to test for possible effects of treatment on several response variables. The problem with this analysis strategy is that the alpha level established for rejecting the null hypothesis is inflated as the number of hypotheses tested increases. This is unfair because it capitalizes on an increasing probability of finding a significant difference by chance. This dilemma has never been adequately resolved in biofeedback research; however, it is clearly unacceptable to analyze several response variables and then report that selected ones were significant at the .05 level. Results are usually more easily interpreted if only one response variable is used.

Another approach is to designate one response variable as primary and others as secondary. In this case, any decision regarding the efficacy of the treatment relative to the control would be based on the primary response variable. The null hypothesis is not rejected unless this analysis proves significant. Secondary response variables would also be analyzed but would not have a direct bearing on the primary hypothesis under study. The analysis of secondary response variables may help in the interpretation of the study, but the reliability of such secondary results must be questioned unless statistical adjustments are made.

Yet another technique for analyzing multiple response variables in biofeedback research is to combine individual variables into a derived conglomerate measure. The Headache Index, which combines intensity, frequency, and duration information is an example of such a measure. The Headache Index has been shown to be sensitive to the effects of biofeedback, but its clinical meaningfulness has been questioned (Blanchard, Theobald, Williamson, Silver, & Brown, 1978). If conglomerate response measures are used, investigators should realize that the various dimensions of behavior that are represented in the measure are probably not independent, and it may be difficult to discern exactly how the patient's condition has changed following treatment. It is even possible that one component of a conglomerate response measure will cancel the effect of another component.

Using only one primary response variable also eliminates the interpretation problems that can occur when various response variables favor different treatments. Of course, this can legitimately occur, but it can also occur by chance alone. If it is decided, during the planning phase, which response variable must show a significant difference between treatments for rejection of the null hypothesis, this problem is avoided. Supplementary, exploratory analyses of secondary response variables can still be performed, but these results are reported tentatively.

In addition to the clinical response to the treatments used, other information about the patients and the therapeutic context will be of value in interpreting the results of the study. Therefore, planning should include the identification of concomitant variables. For example, such things as a patient's age, race, sex, exercise habits, use of alcohol, or recent life stress may help to determine his or her clinical response to biofeedback therapy. Compliance with instructions for home practice is another important dimension of biofeedback therapy that deserves further study.

One class of concomitant variables that are of critical importance in clinical trials of biofeedback are those that are used to document that learned control over the targeted physiological response actually is achieved. Because the aim of biofeedback is almost universally to help the patient acquire voluntary control over biological function, it is necessary to demonstrate clearly that this has occurred. This requirement is especially important when the patient is given biofeedback training to modify one response system (e.g., digital vasodilation) and outcome is measured in another response system (e.g., verbally reported Headache Index). There are a number of ways in which change in the targeted physiological system can be indexed. For example, change can be measured within treatment sessions, between treatment sessions, and/or from pretreatment to posttreatment periods. Showing change in the targeted physiological response system in clinical trials of biofeedback is as important as showing changes in blood levels of drugs given in clinical trials of pharmacological agents. Without this concomitant information changes in clinical status may be difficult to explain. In some studies it may, therefore, be necessary to continue the therapy phase until some criterion of self-regulatory ability is demonstrated. Unfortunately, acceptable criteria have not become standardized in the biofeedback literature.

Another area where information is often lacking in biofeedback research is cost-effectiveness. This can be difficult to evaluate because the cost of a therapy and the benefit received are not always measurable in the same units. Depending on the disorder being treated, benefits might include avoidance of more costly or invasive procedures, prolongation of life, reduced hospital stays, reduced loss of work, improved quality of life, or reduced need for drug therapy. These are very important issues, and they may represent some of the most valuable advantages of biofeedback. Cost and efficacy play a role in determining what form of therapy is most appropriate in a given situation, and a cost-effectiveness analysis would be a valuable addition to clinical trials research in biofeedback.

Instrumentation and Methodology

Experimentation in biofeedback requires behavioral and biological research skills. The variance in physiological behavior during biofeedback training is due to many factors in addition to the biofeedback itself. Some of these factors can be controlled, whereas others cannot. It is important to realize that all uncontrolled variance in the experiment will reduce statistical power and reduce the likelihood of discovering a significant treatment effect. Therefore, great care should be taken to ensure that all apparatus is in excellent condition, and that laboratory procedures have been worked out in sufficient detail to allow accurate data collection under standardized conditions. One noteworthy example is the failure of investigators using EEG and EMG biofeedback to employ standardized amplifier bandpass filter settings. Excellent discussions are available on recording techniques for heart rate (Jennings et al., 1981), electrodermal activity (Fowles et al., 1981), skin temperature (Taub & School, 1978), blood pressure (Kirkendall, Feinleib, Freis, & Mark, 1981), and electromyography (Basmajian & Blumenstein, 1980). Another excellent source of information on psychophysiological recording techniques is a book edited by Martin and Venables (1980).

Careful attention must also be paid to the use of psychological and behavioral measurement techniques. If psychological tests are used, they must be administered in standardized format if their reliability and validity are to be preserved. The more data that are available about a psychometric instrument that define the construct measured and document its scientific value, the more easily interpreted and widely accepted will be the obtained results. Nonstandardized behavior checklists and patient questionnaires can also be useful, but it is the experimenter's responsibility to justify and defend their use. Unreliable instruments can be expected to produce unreliable results.

When patients are required to record information about themselves and their disorder for research purposes, the problems can be greatly compounded. Patients are usually not trained in research methods, and their reasons for participating in the study are much different from those of the investigator. Therefore, patients should be instructed very carefully and completely, and the investigator should devise a method to monitor their compliance with recording procedures. One potential problem is that patients sometimes change their motivation to record information during an experiment. During a pretreatment, baseline period, patients are usually enthusiastic and eager to please. They want to qualify for therapy and tend to believe that the information requested will somehow help the investigator perform a cure of their particular problem. During posttreatment follow-up, however, the situation can be quite different. At this time, keeping records or diaries can become a nuisance, and compliance may suffer. With some measures, such as headache frequency, failure to record properly all headaches could easily be misinterpreted as improvement. To minimize such problems patients should be well educated in the methods to be used. The recording method should be simple, convenient, and standardized, and compliance should be regularly monitored and encouraged.

When possible, it is often helpful to have patients monitor and record information on a trial basis, before formalized baseline data collection begins. In this way, they can be given corrective feedback and can improve their understanding or compliance before any important data are lost. During the study, it is a good policy to routinely discuss the data collection process with patients and give corrective feedback as required. If the experimenter tries to uncover problems, they can often be discovered and improvements can be made, but if they are not discovered, patient compliance problems can seriously jeopardize an otherwise well-designed experiment.

Finally, before leaving the topic of research instrumentation and methodology, I would like to comment briefly on the importance of a properly designed data collection form. A properly designed form can be much more than a passive data storage device; it can guide and facilitate the data collection process. The layout of the form should be simple, uncluttered, highly structured, and exact in what it requires. A good form will include clear definitions of variables, and understandable coding instructions. It should specify the measurement units that are to be used and the accuracy to which coding should be performed. A data form should also logically follow the sequence in which data items will be collected, and it should minimize the need for later recopying or editing data.

Identifying the Study Population

In identifying the study population, the main issue to be thought out is to whom the results of the experiment are to be generalized. The study population is then defined by stating objective inclusion and exclusion criteria. If an experiment were open to all patients having the disorder, then the results would potentially be generalizable to anyone who has the disorder. Unfortunately, this is never possible. Participants must live near the study center, they must be physically and mentally able to participate, and they must decide to volunteer for the study. All these factors are largely outside the experimenter's control, yet they do exert an undeniable source of bias, and they do limit the generalizability of results. Many other factors will, however, be within the experimenter's control, and he or she will have to decide whether or not the benefit to be achieved by excluding any subgroup of the population will be outweighed by the disadvantage of limiting generalizability.

One reason for excluding certain subgroups of patients is to achieve a more homogeneous study sample. If a particular type of patient is expected to increase the population variance to a large degree, the researcher may decide to exclude such patients in order to avoid the attendant loss of statistical power. Another common reason for setting exclusion criteria is to maximize the treatment effect. If the experimental treatment is expected to be highly effective in treating one type of patient but highly ineffective in another type, then the researcher may decide to focus his or her efforts where success is most likely. Here again, the basic issue relates to statistical power because power increases as the magnitude of the treatment effect increases. Finally, exclusion criteria are usually set to protect vulnerable patients from possible hazards of the treatment procedure or participation in the experiment. This is commonly the rationale for excluding very young or old patients, pregnant women, or those who are otherwise either physically or psychologically at high risk. Of course, whenever exclusion criteria are set, the researcher assumes the responsibility of clearly defining the population to which the results may reasonably be generalized. A highly selected treatment population can seriously limit the external validity of the study.

If a researcher decides that exclusion of certain patients is needed, then the next step is to state the inclusion and exclusion criteria. These criteria must be specified precisely and objectively so that a decision to include or exclude any potential patient can be made easily. Once the criteria are specified there should be no exceptions made. To be admitted to the study a patient must clearly satisfy all inclusion criteria and none of the exclusion criteria. Frequently, inclusion and exclusion criteria will take into account such things as age, availability of reliable diagnostic information, disease severity and duration, prior experience with therapy, pregnancy, concomitant medical or psychological disorders, and likelihood of cooperativeness and compliance with therapy.

Identifying the Appropriate Experimental Design: Eliminating Bias

Another important aspect of planning an experiment is the selection of an appropriate experimental design. Based on the definition of a controlled clinical trial stated earlier, we can immediately rule out certain types of experiments. First, we can rule out all case studies and single-subject experimental designs. These approaches can be useful to investigate rare disorders where large groups of patients are not available, or to explore the effectiveness of new treatments or exceptions to established clinical conventions, or to monitor formally patient progress for clinical reasons, but they are not controlled clinical trials. Another class of designs that can immediately be ruled out are analogue studies. Analogue studies are carried out under restricted, simplified, or contrived conditions, and therefore do not constitute true clinical trials. For example, analogue studies may investigate very restricted but readily available forms of a disorder or use so-called student therapists rather than experienced, practicing clinicians. Analogue studies can be helpful in exploring the processes that underlie biofeedback effects and in generating hypotheses to be tested in later clinical trials, but they cannot substitute for controlled clinical trials. A third class of studies that can be ruled out are retrospective cohort studies. Because the primary variable of interest is not manipulated in retrospective cohort studies they usually provide data that must be considered correlational. Furthermore, adequate controls are seldom available in retrospective data.

Controlled clinical trials will always contain one or more experimental groups, which will receive the therapy that is being investigated, and one or more control groups. Therefore, all single group outcome studies can be ruled out. Sometimes a repeated-measures design is used in which the same patients receive the experimental and control treatments sequentially. This can be an efficient design, because fewer total subjects are required. Also, because the various treatments are evaluated on the same group of patients, any difference in the response can more confidently be attributed to characteristics of the treatments as opposed to characteristics of the subjects. A particularly effective special case of the repeated-measures design is the crossover design. In a crossover design patients begin therapy with one treatment and then, at some time during therapy, some or all of them are "crossed over" and receive another treatment from that time on. The crossover design can be used effectively in biofeedback research as recently demonstrated by Blanchard et al. (1982). This study showed that some headache patients who failed to improve during relaxation training did improve after being crossed-over to biofeedback. This experiment is important for its demonstration that relaxation training and biofeedback are not equally effective in treating headaches in all patients, and it is an example of the effective use that can be made of a crossover design.

A problem with crossover designs, however, is the fact that results can be contaminated by order effects and by carryover effects. It cannot be assumed, for example, that a patient crossed-over from relaxation training to biofeedback is equivalent to a patient given biofeedback first. To control this, the order of treatments is usually randomized or counterbalanced in crossover designs, and the order effects are evaluated. If an order effect is found, the results may be difficult to interpret. It is also a good policy in a crossover study to continue some patients on one therapy without crossing over, in order to control for effects due to the duration of treatment with one type of therapy. Unfortunately, controlling for all these temporal variables may require that additional subjects be included, a requirement that would reduce the efficiency advantage of the repeated measures design.

Regardless of whether subjects will serve as their own controls in a repeated-measures design, or whether a separate sample control group will be used, the purpose will be the same—to perform an unbiased contrast of alternative treatments. The treatment provided the experimental group will be designed primarily to maximize a therapeutic effect; designing the control treatment may not be so straightforward. The basic question the researcher must ask in designing a control treatment is, What should the control group control for? To answer this question it is necessary to consider the possible sources of bias in the experiment being planned. An experiment is biased when any factor, other than a manipulated variable, occurs disproportionately in any of the comparison samples. In reality there are many factors that can occur disproportionately in the comparison samples, and the investigator must decide, during planning, which are meaningful and which are trivial. Any factor that is not considered trivial should be controlled to the extent possible.

One type of bias that an experiment must not contain is sampling bias. There are two broad categories of sampling bias with which the investigator should be concerned. In one instance, one treatment group is biased with respect to another treatment group. This limits the external validity of the study. In the other instance, the study sample is biased with respect to the population from which it was drawn. This limits the internal validity of the study. If the former case is true, then the affected group is probably also biased with respect to the population. Sampling bias is an extremely serious violation of the tenets of good experimentation. Fortunately, it can almost always be avoided if subjects are randomized to treatments. I will have more to say about randomization in a later section. If subjects do not represent the population that is of interest in an unbiased manner, then errors may be made in generalizing the results of the clinical trial.

In addition to sampling bias, there are many other sources of bias that must be considered in designing a control group. Among the most important of these are placebo effects, regression effects, seasonal trends, patient compliance, and treatment credibility. Moreover, bias can be introduced through equipment malfunction, improper data analysis, and even computer errors. It is the primary function of the control group to make certain that the influences of these many nonspecific factors are not erroneously attributed to the experimental treatment. Such an error could be extremely costly if it is undetected, and a form of treatment is erroneously recommended based on distorted or prejudiced data.

I have criticized biofeedback research for not having clearly established what factors need to be controlled, and what factors different types of control groups actually can and cannot control for (Hatch, 1982). Most biofeedback studies completed to date can be roughly classified into the following classes, according to the type of control group used.

Untreated Control Group. The untreated control group is probably more of an illusion than a reality. Just because a researcher assigns a patient to a waiting list or a no-treatment condition does not mean that the patient will not take independent action to improve his or her condition. For this reason, the untreated or waiting-list control is a very weak control condition. Furthermore, once any treatment is effectively shown to be superior to no treatment at all, it is unnecessary to redocument this fact in every subsequent study. Once it is determined that biofeedback is effective to any degree and for any reason, then it is time to move on to experiments that use controls that are capable of providing information about its effectiveness relative to more standard forms of treatment and placebos.

Comparison with an Alternate Therapy. If there is an established therapy in use for treating the disorder in question, then it is important to evaluate the effectiveness of biofeedback against that of the established therapy. The effectiveness of biofeedback cannot be meaningfully discussed unless it is compared to something that is already accepted as clinically meaningful. Moreover, the comparisons must be unbiased. This means that all competing therapies must be administered in a clinically acceptable manner and must be given every chance to produce a maximum therapeutic response. This will usually require collaboration among researchers. Only clinicians who have comparable levels of expertise with the techniques being evaluated should participate. In addition, the many nonspecific variables that are likely to distinguish the competing therapies must be considered potential sources of bias. For example, there are innumerable differences between the acts of prescribing ergotamine tartrate for a migraine patient and administering multiple sessions of thermal biofeedback training. Because the two treatments differ in so many respects, there are many competing explanations for the different results that might be obtained. For example, a difference between the groups of patients treated with medication and biofeedback might be related to (a) the chemical properties of the drug, (b) the patients' skill level at temperature control, or (c) the amount of time spent talking with the clinician. Similar problems may be raised concerning the comparison of biofeedback with relaxation training or autogenic training. In spite of their many substantial problems, however, direct comparisons between biofeedback and established alternative forms of therapy must occur. If there is not strong evidence from small scale clinical studies that biofeedback can realistically compete with established therapies, then careful consideration should be given to the question of whether controlled clinical trials of biofeedback would be premature.

Studies that compare biofeedback versus no treatment or verus an established therapy are superior to uncontrolled studies because they can control for many nonspecific effects that could bias the results. Both these designs may control for such things as initial therapeutic contact and intake procedures, the passage of time, spontaneous recovery, effects of symptom monitoring, subject history, maturational processes, regression artifacts, and uncontrolled aspects of patients' lives. Depending on the type of therapy against which biofeedback is compared, however, the alternate treatment design may also control for periodic therapist attention, and interaction with data collection procedures, recording equipment, and personnel. Additionally, the alternate treatment, like biofeedback, will probably generate some degree of patient motivation and expectancy for improvement.

A serious weakness of the no treatment control design is that it does not control for placebo effects. In the alternate treatment design, biofeedback and the comparison treatments can be expected to have their individual placebo effects, although these might be quite different. If the primary research objective is to compare the effectiveness and safety of the respective treatment packages, including all their inherent specific and nonspecific effects, then controlling placebo effects is probably unnecessary. However, if the primary objective is to compare the respective treatments only in terms of the specific contribution of biofeedback, then an alternate treatment design will not suffice because specific and nonspecific effects will be confounded. To the extent that nonspecific effects occur disproportionately in the comparison groups the experiment is biased, and the comparisons are unfair. If the research objective is to compare the clinical effectiveness of biofeedback and some other treatment, and to attribute any observed difference to the biofeedback, then it is necessary to design an unbiased control group. The experiment can be considered unbiased if the various treatment groups can be assumed to differ only because of the action of biofeedback. Of course in practice, no experiment is ever completely free of bias. Nonetheless, in choosing an experimental design the investigator must anticipate as many potentially confounding conditions as possible and include controls for all those that are judged capable of limiting the interpretability of the results.

All biofeedback theories assume, in one form or another, that biofeedback facilitates self-regulation of physiological function because it conveys information about some targeted biological process. This information can be defined as a contingency between physiological activity and a sensory signal that the subject is able to perceive. I have argued (Hatch, 1982) that this contingency can be considered the critical specific feature of biofeedback that is necessary for any unique therapeutic effect. It follows from this argument that if the contingency was eliminated, so that the biofeedback no longer conveyed meaningful information, then any clinical effect would be attributable either to nonspecific or chance events. In biofeedback research three basic strategies have been used to study the specific effects of the biofeedback–behavior contingency. These are attention placebo groups, pseudofeedback groups, and altered contingency groups.

Attention Placebo Groups. An attention-placebo group is a better control treatment than a no-treatment or waiting-list group because subjects are at least exposed to many of the nonspecific conditions and procedures that are involved in biofeedback therapy. Unfortunately, the treatment that attention-placebo groups generally receive is seldom made very realistic or credible. Therefore, like the alternate treatment design, the treatment given to an attention placebo group will differ in many ways from that given to a group that is receiving biofeedback. Attention-placebo treatments have included such techniques as presenting subjects with a constant tone, a recorded stimulus, feedback from another subject, or a random signal. Subjects are usually instructed to attend to these signals, but they are not told that they are receiving biofeedback. Sometimes cover stories are devised that include instructions and suggestions designed to make the attention placebo treatment seem more therapeutic.

Attention placebo groups are probably effective in controlling for some of the nonspecific effects embedded in the biofeedback treatment package, such as attention to a stimulus, sensory intake, and physiological monitoring. I must say "probably" because there has been practically no attempt made actually to evaluate the effectiveness of any control procedures used in biofeedback research. The effectiveness of cover stories in generating levels of patient motivation, expectancy for improvement, credibility, and compliance equal to the levels generated by biofeedback, however, is doubtful.

Pseudofeedback Groups. The chief distinction to be made between attention placebo and pseudofeedback groups is that in the latter case an effort is made to deceive subjects into believing that they are receiving true biofeedback when actually, they are not. With pseudofeedback, it would be theoretically possible to keep all experimental procedures identical with the exception of the contingency between the feedback and subject's physiological response. For instance, the rationale for treatment, the instructions given to subjects, and other important elements of the treatment context can be exactly the same in both conditions. If subjects were successfully deceived into believing that the pseudofeedback is true biofeedback, then this design would be analogous to a single-blind design. Furthermore, if both subjects and therapist were prevented from knowing whether biofeedback or pseudofeedback was being used, then the design would be analogous to a double-blind design. If this were possible, then the pseudofeedback condition might also control for experimenter bias.

There have been few biofeedback experiments in which single- or double-blind designs have been used, and little is known about the effects of pseudofeedback on physiological self-regulation ability or on any disorder that is commonly treated with biofeedback. Therefore, much additional preliminary research on the effects of pseudofeedback must occur before this design could be recommended for controlled clinical trials. An important technical concern about the use of pseudofeedback controls is whether or not subjects can be successfully deceived into believing that they are receiving biofeedback. The ethical concerns will be discussed in a later section. If control subjects are allowed to discover that they are not receiving true biofeedback they may feel angry or betrayed. These emotions would certainly be counterproductive to therapy, and would bias the study. Even the act of informing subjects in advance, which certainly must be done in a clinical study, that they stand a change of being treated with pseudofeedback may raise doubts or create suspicions that would be countertherapeutic.

A recently published study (Hatch, Klatt, Fitzgerald, Jasheway, & Fisher, 1983) compared the effects of true EMG biofeedback and three different patterns of pseudofeedback that were generated by a computer and were independent of the subject's EMG activity. The subjective responses of the subjects to the various types of pseudofeedback were different, showing that all types of noncontingent feedback do not necessarily produce equivalent nonspecific effects. Different types of pseudofeedback can make a unique contribution to the treatment effect. Therefore, the relative difference between the effectiveness of biofeedback and pseudofeedback may depend on the particular type of pseudofeedback selected as well as the presence or absence of a contingency on physiology. Many questions remain unanswered regarding the appropriateness of pseudofeedback as a control for nonspecific effects in biofeedback research, and it appears that much work remains to be done before a satisfactory biofeedback placebo could be developed.

Altered Contingency Groups   Whereas pseudofeedback is independent of physiological activity, and, therefore, is presumed not to convey any information about performance of a self-regulation task, altered contingency feedback conveys information that has been distorted or that is presented in a manner that would be expected to produce a less than optimal effect. Studies that have utilized this design have provided control subjects feedback for stabilizing the targeted response (Cram, 1980), for responding in the opposite direction (Andrasik & Holroyd, 1980), or for relaxing an irrelevant muscle (Gray, Lyle, McGuire, & Peck, 1980). Techniques such as these have the advantage of exposing control subjects to a biofeedback signal that really is contingent on some aspect of their physiological behavior. Therefore, altered contingency biofeedback does allow control subjects to experience the immediate feedback of true information and might foster the development of a sense of self-control. However, it cannot be assumed that these control subjects would find altered contingency feedback as credible as true biofeedback, or that they would be as motivated for treatment as a group that was given true biofeedback. Just as with pseudofeedback, additional research will be required before the value of altered contingency feedback can be evaluated as a control procedure.

Designing a proper control treatment for a clinical trial requires the investigator to know what factors, if uncontrolled, could bias the experiment. In other words, the investigator must know what potentially confounding factors the control group should control for and be able to evaluate whether or not any particular factor has or has not been adequately controlled. Designing a proper control group is a challenging and critically important step in planning an unbiased experiment. Therapeutic effects can be magnified or diminished in relation to different control groups, and the results of a study can be influenced as much by the selection of a comparison group as by the actual effectiveness of the treatments used. In biofeedback research there is no standard placebo that can be administered to control patients, so the researcher who designs the study is responsible for making sure that the control group does indeed control important confounding factors. There are advantages and disadvantages to all kinds of designs. The choice will depend on theoretical, empirical, clinical, and pragmatic considerations. The choice will also depend on the level of research sophistication that has been achieved in the particular area and on acquired knowledge about the actions of biasing factors. Bradford Hill (Bulpitt, 1983) emphasized the importance of designing control groups capable of removing bias from clinical trials as follows, "the judgements must be made without any possiblity of bias, without any overcompensation for a possible bias, and without any possibility of accusation of bias"(p. 56).

Determining the Appropriate Sample Size

In an earlier section, I introduced the idea of statistical power, and commented on the researcher's obligation to make sure that sufficient power is available to achieve the primary research objective. In this section, I return to this important topic. In clinical-trials research, statistical analysis has the primary function of helping the investigator avoid two very serious types of errors. First, statistical analysis helps avoid wrongly rejecting a truly valuable therapy. Second, statistical analysis helps avoid wrongly accepting a truly worthless therapy. No ethical clinician or researcher would want to make either error; yet many people seem to view statistical techniques as very unfriendly things. It is disappointing to complete a laborious research effort and then find that the results are considered suspect because an arbitrary level of statistical significance was not met, and it is difficult to feel grateful for possibly having been prevented from making an error. Unfortunately, nothing can be done to remedy such a situation once the study has reached the analysis stage. The time to take positive steps to prevent such a situation is while the experiment is still in the planning stage. If an experiment is planned so that sufficient power is available, and if a treatment effect of the predicted magnitude is achieved, then statistical significance is also likely to be achieved.

The only mechanism that determines statistical power over which the experimenter has complete control is the number of patients included in the study. Acceptable statistical power can always be theoretically achieved by increasing sample size. However, the expense involved in doing so may be prohibitive, and other options should be explored. For example, reducing the standard error of a critical response variable by technician training, proper equipment calibration, or searching the literature for best available measurement scale may also determine whether or not statistical significance is achieved. Once these options have been explored, the researcher should formally determine the sample size that will be required.

Although a statistical sample size determination for a simple study involving one experimental group and one control group is not difficult, power analysis involving more complicated designs quickly becomes complex. The reason for this is that as the dimensions of the study design increase, the number of alternate hypotheses and interaction effects multiply rapidly. Therefore, the advice I will give here is to consult a professional biostatistician for help in determining sample size. The interested reader who would like to pursue the issue of sample size determination more thoroughly is referred to Cohen (1977) or Donner (1984).

If you do consult a biostatistician for help in determining sample size, there are several pieces of information that you should be prepared to provide. You should be prepared to state your primary research question or hypothesis, describe your independent and dependent variables, and outline the basic layout of your experimental design. You will also probably wish to discuss the measurement scale and probable distribution characteristics of the variables, and decide what inferential test statistic would be most appropriate.

Once your consultant understands your objective and how you plan to accomplish it, you will have to set alpha and beta levels. This establishes the degree of protection you will have against committing the two types of errors described earlier. Alpha is conventionally set at .05 in behavioral research; however, if a decision error would be very serious or costly, then alpha is set equal to .01 or even lower. In the same manner the experimenter must set the value of beta, the degree of risk you are willing to take that you will erroneously conclude that a truly valuable therapy is no more effective than a control treatment. Setting alpha and beta levels can be conceived as taking out insurance against committing a serious error in interpreting the results of the experiment you have planned. Like most types of insurance, the higher the level of protection you select, the greater will be the cost. In biofeedback research the cost of protection is calculated in numbers of research subjects.

In addition to setting alpha and beta levels, you will also need to provide information about the variance of the primary response variable in the study population. This information can be obtained from previously published reports of studies that used inclusion and exclusion criteria similar to your own, but read carefully to make sure recording procedures were not drastically dissimilar to those you plan to use. A pilot study designed to collect variability data can also be helpful. If you cannot locate a variance measure that you feel is appropriate to your situation, you can make a rough estimate by hypothesizing mean values in the various cells of your design layout. If you can specify the largest range of mean values that you could reasonably anticipate and divide this range by four, the result can be used as a variance estimate for the purpose of determining sample size.

The only other information that will be needed is an estimate of the size of the clinical effect that you reasonably expect to achieve using the treatment procedures that you have selected. This estimate can also be achieved simply by hypothesizing mean values for each of the cells of your design layout.

Given all this information you, or your biostatistical consultant, will be able to estimate the number of subjects that will be required to achieve economically your research objective. The economics involved in conducting clinical trials research cannot be overemphasized. Biomedical research is extremely expensive, and research budgets to perform controlled clinical trials in biofeedback might easily exceed $1,000 per patient. With costs so high, funding agencies must look very closely at the justification provided for research budgets. If an investigator proposes to attempt a controlled clinical trial without enough subjects to achieve his or her objective, then the time and money spent on such a project might be wasted. On the other hand, if the investigator proposes to use more patients than are required, then the time and money spent by running the extra patients might be more productively spent on another project. These factors must be considered very carefully in the planning of a clinical trial.

STATISTICAL SIGNIFICANCE VERSUS CLINICAL SIGNIFICANCE

The term *significant*, when used to describe an experimental result, can have a connotation quite different from that implied when the term is used nontechnically. Inferential statistics were developed to enable researchers to quantify the reliability of inferential judgments made about functional relationships among variables. *Statistical significance* implies that the measured relationship between variables has an arbitrarily low probability of having occurred by chance alone; it is an index of reliability. In other words, when researchers report that $p < .05$, all they arc saying is that the result is probably not random. Statistical signficance implies nothing about the magnitude of a clinical effect or the proportion of variance in the real world that is accounted for by the relationship described. Establishing statistical significance is a necessary but very preliminary step in evaluating a clinical procedure. Clinical significance must take into account not only reliability, but also the meaningfulness of the therapy to the society in which it is used. Both statistical and clinical significance are important and should be maximized.

Researchers investigating biofeedback have sometimes been criticized for emphasizing statistical significance rather than clinical significance. For example, biofeedback-assisted reductions in systolic blood pressure of 3 or 4 mmHg from baseline can be statistically significant under controlled laboratory conditions, but an effect of this size may have little clinical value. In such a case, statistical significance overestimates clinical significance. At other times, statistical significance can underestimate clinical significance. Biofeedback is not equally effective with all patients affected with a particular disorder. One subgroup of a treated population may make remarkable improvement, whereas another subgroup may show no improvement at all. Even though the improvement may be highly significant in clinical terms for the subgroup that improves, the treatment effect for the group as a whole may not be statistically sigtnificant. Such a heterogenous response to treatment is expected in clinical work, but the same individual differences in response to therapy are treated as error in experimental work.

Statistical or clinical significance will be emphasized in an experiment depending on the stated research objective. Many biofeedback studies are designed to investigate some process or phenomenon other than therapeutic effectiveness. In such studies it is the reliability of the effect that is of interest, and statistical significance is emphasized. It would be a mistake to try to infer clinical significance from reported statistical significance levels in such a study. In controlled clinical trials, however, the primary objective is to document the relative clinical value of the treatments being evaluated. Therefore, in planning clinical trials investigators should make certain that the requirements for clinical and statistical significance are met. The study should be planned so that a statistically significant result would also be clinically meaningful. This can be accomplished during sample size determination.

Recall that in order to determine the needed sample size, it is necessary to state the anticipated magnitude of the various treatment effects. Also, recall that statistical power increases proportionately with the anticipated difference between treatment conditions. This means that if you compute the required sample size based on a small anticipated difference between treatments, a statistically signficant effect is likely to occur if a difference that large is actually achieved. However, such a small difference in therapeutic efficacy may be clinically meaningless. In planning a clinical trial it would be much more desirable to compute a sample size based on an anticipated treatment effect that would also be clinically meaningful. To decide how large an effect would be clinically meaningful, ask several experienced clinicians in the field to specify the minimal difference between two therapies that they would consider relevant in making a therapeutic choice between the two therapies. Ask them to take into account such things as expense to patients, therapist time, equipment needed, and possible risks and side effects. If there are standard medical or surgical treatments in use for treating the disorder that have documented efficacy, these facts should be considered. If you plan the experiment so that the sample size is sufficient to yield a statistically significant effect given a clinically meaningful difference between experimental treatment conditions, then the result is likely to be viewed as both clinically and statistically significant.

A clinical trial in which a relatively large advantage for the experimental treatment (presumably biofeedback) over the control treatment is anticipated will require fewer subjects to achieve a given level of statistical power than one in which a relatively small effect is anticipated. Therefore, there is an economic advantage in specifying the largest effect that one could reasonably expect to achieve. However, if an investigator becomes overly optimistic and specifies an unrealistic advantage for the experimental treatment, then he or she runs the risk of overestimating statistical power and failing to achieve statistical significance. This decision is of the utmost importance in determining the success or failure of an experiment, and it is only during the planning phase that an investigator can have an influence. If a wise decision is made, then the investigator can procede with the experiment economically and with some confidence that the primary research question will receive a credible answer. If proper consideration is not given to the determination of statistical power when the experiment is planned, and the investigator decides to just cross his or her fingers and hope for the best, then he or she runs a greater risk of producing results that are neither statistically nor clinically significant.

CONDUCTING THE STUDY

If the study has been carefully planned, execution becomes primarily a matter of carrying out the planned procedures in a consistent and timely fashion. Inevitably, however, unanticipated problems will develop that require plans to be changed. Fortunately, there is seldom an absolute right or wrong way to carry out any experimental procedure, so most of these problems can be resolved without significantly compromising the study. It is important, however, that the problems be discovered as early as possible and that whatever changes are made be followed consistently from that time on. For this reason, the first several patients are sometimes placed on the protocol to debug procedures, with no intention of using them in the final analysis. Once everything is running smoothly, it is time to begin recruiting the actual study patients.

Recruiting Patients

Many of the problems that plague clinical trials during the execution phase involve patient recruitment. It is easy to overestimate the availability of appropriate patients who are also willing to volunteer for a study. It is usually good practice to set a date and to try and start on that day if at all possible. Delays in starting patient recruitment are sometimes difficult to overcome even if patient availability was correctly estimated. Interim goals should be set and an effort made to adhere to them. The best way to avoid patient recruitment problems is to have done the necessary planning in advance. This may involve identifying primary and secondary sources of patients, making the necessary contacts with referral sources, negotiating collaborative agreements, or securing permission to use a subject pool.

Once the appropriate subject pool has been defined and adequate numbers of eligible patients have been located, the next step is to begin contacting individuals for screening and possible inclusion in the study. How this is done will be determined by the needs of the particular study. If patients are to be drawn from the general population, then information about the study should be made widely available so as not to bias the study by limiting access to people who read a certain newspaper or listen to a certain radio station. If patients are to be recruited from some more restricted source, such as a hospital population, your own practice, or from a certain school or company, then different procedures will be required.

Any delay in a clinical trial is expensive. Expenses continue whether the study is running at full capacity or not. Delays can be converted into other problems as well. For example, the longer a study runs, the greater the likelihood of equipment malfunction and personnel changes. Delays also affect the timeliness of the results.

Randomization of Patients

Patients must be assigned to receive treatments on a random basis. Random assignment is the only way to guarantee that an experiment is free of selection bias. If patients are assigned to treatments by any nonrandom process, the experiment will be biased. Randomization also tends to balance the treatment groups for many confounding conditions, whether or not these conditions are known. Random assignment of subjects is a necessary condition for the validity of commonly used statistical techniques. Random assignment means that every patient has a statistically equal chance of receiving each treatment being offered. Haphazard assignment, or assignment according to date of entry into the study, a precreated list, alphabetical order, or patient's wishes are not random. Each patient should be assigned to receive treatment according to a truly random process, such as flipping a coin or using a table of random digits.

Patients should be randomized only after all inclusion and exclusion criteria have been met and documented, and after they have given informed consent to participate in the study. The patient who is not willing to participate in any of the treatments being offered should be excluded. If possible, randomization should also be delayed until after baseline data have been collected. If an investigator knows in advance that the next patient will be assigned to receive biofeedback or some other treatment, he or she may inadvertently alter screening or baseline data collection procedures in subtle ways that would bias the study.

It can sometimes make a difference who performs the randomization. Although it is possible for a researcher to randomize the patients, it may be preferable to have a statistician or a colleague who does not know the details of the study perform this task. The researcher then remains blind with respect to treatment assignments. If this method is used, the researcher simply calls the randomizer when a patient is accepted into the study and asks for a patient assignment. The assignment is then made with no further discussion involved. This avoids any temptation the researcher might have to assign the patient in a biased manner. If a double-blind design is to be used, then someone other than the researcher or therapist must randomize the patients.

If the sample size to be used in the experiment is relatively large, then it is unlikely that disproportionalities of any important subject variable will occur among treatment groups under randomization. However, when sample sizes are small important variables can get disproportionately distributed among treatment groups by chance. If a confounding variable is known to exist, and the researcher decides that he or she is not willing to run the risk of a chance disproportionality, then the rules of strict randomization are sometimes relaxed. For example, in some studies patients are matched according to some concomitant variable and assigned to pairs. One member of the pair is then randomized to receive either the experimental or control treatment, and the remaining member of the pair is arbitrarily assigned to the remaining treatment. Such forms of restricted randomization can serve a useful purpose, but they are best reserved for situations where their use is clearly indicated. Matching or stratifying patients on more than one or two variables becomes cumbersome. In some instances where strict randomization does result in a chance disproportionality, a statistical adjustment can be applied during the analysis phase to compensate for the effect.

Randomization is a very simple procedure to carry out. In spite of this simplicity, however, randomization should never be taken for granted. Adherence to the rules of randomization, perhaps more than any other action that can be taken, will help to guide an experiment to a successful conclusion. Some extremely serious errors can be made in interpreting studies in which proper attention is not paid to randomization. As an example, consider the following statement by T. C. Chalmers (1982):

> I have made many mistakes in my life practicing medicine. A major one was my acceptance of a trial in cirrhosis comparing high-protein diets with a *nonrandomized* control group. It was on this basis that many of us began to treat cirrhotic patients with a high-protein diet. When patients went into a coma we put a tube down into their stomachs to give them the diet homogenized. When they died in coma we said that we must not have given them enough. (p. 13)

Data Collection and Study Monitoring

Before treatment commences, there should be a period of baseline-data collection. Baseline data convey information about the patient sample prior to the initiation of therapy. They also allow others to compare the patients used in different studies and to evaluate the likelihood of obtaining similar results with other groups of patients. Baseline data also help to document the extent to which randomization and stratification strategies were successful in equally distributing patients having various characteristics across groups. Many of these characteristics, if measured prior to therapy, can be evaluated as prognosticators of treatment efficacy. If there are confounding subject variables that may not be experimentally controlled through randomization, these should be measured during the baseline period so that they can be statistically controlled during analysis.

Most importantly, the primary and secondary response variables must be documented before therapy is begun if any change in the patient's condition is to be meaningfully assessed. For this reason it is desirable not only to document the patient's condition prior to therapy, but also to show that his or her condition is reasonably stable. This may require that baseline data be collected over a period of time. It is also not uncommon for a patient's behavior or condition to change simply in response to being entered into a study or being exposed to data collection procedures. This has been referred to as the Hawthorne or placebo effect. Investigators should expect these nonspecific reactions, and they should realize that they can contribute an unwanted source of variance. Finally, the baseline period should end as close as possible to the time when treatment begins. If there is a lengthy delay, there is a greater risk of some change in the patient's condition that cannot be accounted for by any of the treatments provided.

When therapy begins, there should be a smooth transition from the baseline phase to the treatment phase of the study. Many of the same variables that were measured during baseline will continue to be measured during treatment and follow-up phases. The emphasis in all phases must be on objectivity, accuracy, and standardization. Someone should be made specifically responsible for monitoring the accumulating data to make sure that they are of the highest quality. Missing data should be kept to a minimum because missing values are always an aggravating problem during analysis.

All data collection procedures should be designed to be as objective as possible. Also, data should be collected in a standardized manner. For maintaining standardization there is no substitute for keeping a detailed procedural manual. People tend to develop idiosyncratic methods of doing things. Therefore, people, as well as equipment, should be "calibrated" from time to time against the procedural manual to make sure treatments are being applied and measurements are being made as they should be.

Where accuracy of data collection is concerned a deliberate monitoring program is usually required. At selected intervals during a study a number of cases should be selected at random and a detailed audit of data accuracy should be made on a point by point basis. If errors of recording or coding in excess of an established limit (e.g., 2%–3%), are discovered then further inquiry should be made to uncover and correct the problem. This type of quality control is laborious, but it will pick up many types of errors that computer programs for data editing will miss. More important, however, errors will be discovered at a time when problems can still be remedied. More useful information on data management and quality control techniques can be found in an article by Marinez, McMahan, Barnwell, and Wigodsky (1984).

Deciding to Stop the Study

Ordinarily it is best to end a study when all planned subjects have completed the treatment protocol. This may seem like an obvious piece of advice, but there are many circumstances in which experiments are terminated either earlier or later than planned. Preliminary data analyses are usually done in clinical trials for preparing progress reports, monitoring data collection procedures, and determining the frequency of negative effects of treatments. Based on the results of these interim analyses an investigator may decided to terminate the study earlier than planned. For example if interim analysis shows a group that is receiving one form of treatment to be improving far more than a group receiving another type, then the investigator may decide that it is unethical to continue treating patients with the inferior treatment. Another occasion where a trial must be terminated early is when evidence indicates that one of the treatments is having a harmful effect on patients. If a study is halted prematurely on ethical grounds, the results obtained up to that time may have limited value in terms of evaluating treatment efficacy. Because almost no negative side effects of biofeedback have been reported, it seems highly unlikely that a study would ever need to be abandoned on these grounds. However, with some diseases, a relative lack of clinical effect with biofeedback, compared with other available treatments, might place patients in some types of studies at unacceptable risk.

It is far more likely in the case of biofeedback research that an investigator will decide to terminate a study prematurely because a preliminary data analysis suggests that the research objective has already been achieved. For example, suppose that an interim data analysis, done after treating only two thirds of the planned subjects, showed one group to be improving at a significantly faster rate than another. It would probably be a mistake to stop the experiment and present the results as if the experiment had been completed as planned. The reason for this is that statistical results that are based on relatively small sample sizes tend to be unstable, and it is possible that the preliminary results would not hold up if the experiment was ended as planned. In general, results based on larger samples are more reliable than those based on smaller samples.

There are also occasions where an investigator may be tempted to extend an experiment beyond the anticipated end point. This temptation usually occurs when results are almost statistically significant, and would be significant if a few more subjects were available to provide the lacking degress of freedom. This temptation to enroll additional subjects should ordinarily be resisted. For one reason, a group of subjects added at the end of an experiment may differ in some important respect from the original sample. More important, however, is the fact that the data will have been analyzed twice following the addition of the extra subjects. The level of significance adopted when an experiment is planned assumes that the data will be analyzed only once. If, after the normal termination of an experiment, additional subjects are added and data are reanalyzed, it is possible that statistical significance would be achieved by chance alone. Because the level of significance adopted, e.g. $p = .05$, no longer offers the stated level of protection against falsely rejecting a true null hypothesis, an error could be made in interpreting the results. Therefore, although adding subjects would increase statistical power, it would also be necessary to adjust the stated alpha level upward to compensate for the additional data analysis. As a result there may be little or no gain in net statistical power, and the analysis would again fail to produce statistically significant results.

If additional subjects must be added in order to achieve the required statistical power, then the decision to do so should be made as early as possible in the experiment. Statistical power depends to a large extent on the variance of the variables measured. Sometimes an investigator must make a very rough estimate of sample variance or rely entirely on variance estimates reported by others. In this case anticipated power may have been underestimated if sample variance turns out to be greater than expected. If available power is investigated early in an experiment, based on preliminary results, and is found to be lower than expected, then a decision can be made to expand the sample size before tests for statistical significance are performed. Obviously, the earlier in an experiment that such an adjustment is made, the better.

DATA ANALYSIS

Statistics are critical to behavioral and biomedical research, but they can be overemphasized. Statistics are tools that can help the investigator avoid certain types of errors and report results in standardized and understandable terms. These tools can be invaluable in helping an investigator design and report an experiment, but statistics should never dictate what is studied or hinder the research process. Statistics should give a researcher greater conceptual freedom and scientific power to understand and describe the complex processes studied. It is unfortunately true that there are many statistical "experts" whose advice, if followed, would result in no research ever being done because designs are never perfect. It is difficult for many people to see much worth in statistical advice that is presented in this way. The good statistical consultant will listen carefully as you explain what you wish to accomplish, and will then suggest techniques that will help.

Although the mathematics involved are sometimes difficult, and the calculations are always tedious, the logic behind most test statistics is straightforward. Essentially, the object is always to base a decision between a null hypothesis and some alternate hypothesis on data collected, while maintaining a low probability of an incorrect decision based on chance events. If certain conditions are met, then the probability of making such an error can be estimated. For example, in the case of the Student's t statistic, the following conditions are assumed before data are collected: (a) errors are normally distributed; (b) errors are independently distributed; (c) errors show equal variance across treatment groups; (d) the null hypothesis is true. If these conditions are true, then it is unlikely that a statistically significant difference will occur between treatment group means. Conversely, when a statistically significant difference does occur it is highly likely that one or more of the assumptions was untrue. When assumptions a to c are known to be true and a statistically significant difference is found, it can be concluded with reasonable confidence that assumption d was untrue. When this occurs the null hypothesis is said to be rejected and the alternate hypothesis is accepted. If any of the first three assumptions are untrue, then the validity of the statistical test may be questioned. From this analysis it should become clear that the key to good experimental design is to make certain that assumptions a to c are likely to be true. Fortunately, these assumptions are likely to be true if the investigator assigns subjects to treatments in a truly random manner, selects outcome variables wisely, and administers treatments uniformly. If one or more of these assumptions turns out to be untrue despite the investigator's best efforts, all is not necessarily lost; there are usually adjustments that can be made to preserve the validity of the analysis. However, if the assumptions are not met and the investigator ignores this fact, the analysis will probably be invalid.

The data analysis should begin with a thorough editing of the data files to eliminate erroneous values. A decision must also be made regarding what to do in the case of missing data. Even the most elegant statistical analysis is invalid if data are inaccurate or missing.

Once all data are coded correctly, the investigator must decide which patients to include in the analysis. Once a patient is randomized he or she should ordinarily be kept in the trial to its completion and be included in the analysis if possible. However, there are many reasons for removing a patient from the analysis. For example, people may die, or move out of the area, or develop other medical conditions that require confounding treatments. They may also be noncompliant with the therapy or refuse to provide certain data. Sometimes a patient who does not meet eligibility criteria is inadvertently admitted to a study, and sometimes a patient will show an extreme reaction that is unlike that of any other patient. All of these situations can introduce undesirable variance into a study, so there is a temptation to remove the patient. On the other hand, patients were randomized to treatments in order to eliminate bias from the study. If some of these patients are now removed on a nonrandom basis, a bias can still be introduced. Patients tend to remove themselves from a study in a nonrandom manner, too. For example, patients decide to drop out of clinical trials because they do not feel that they are improving fast enough, or because they improve before the trial has ended, and do not feel that they require further treatment. Therefore, a bias can actually be caused by the differential effectiveness of the treatments being compared. Because heterogeneity of variance is usually a lesser evil than bias in an experiment, it is advisable to include questionable patients in the analysis if at all possible. Whenever patients are removed from a study, drop out by themselves, or are lost to follow-up for any reason, it is important to compare them to the remaining group to determine whether the missing patients differ from the original group in ways that would be likely to bias the results. The decision to exclude a randomized patient from analysis is one that an investigator should consider very carefully and one that he or she should be prepared to defend. Whenever possible, the final outcomes of all randomized patients should be reported.

An analysis problem that should have been anticipated during the planning phase is the need to perform significance tests on the many variables that will have been collected. Because the experiment-wise alpha level grows larger as the number of statistical tests increases, the investigator must find some way to protect him/herself against committing an alpha error. As a rule of thumb, if k significance tests are performed, then alpha grows approximately alpha times k. Therefore, if 25 significance tests are performed, then the alpha level used for each test would need to be set equal to .002 in order to limit the experiment-wise probability of committing an alpha error to .05. The reduction in power associated with a 25-fold reduction in alpha greatly reduces the likelihood that a true difference of the anticipated size would be detected if indeed it did occur.

The best approach to solving this problem is to have identified one variable, in advance, as the primary response variable of interest. This ensures that the analysis of the most important experimental question will receive a meaningful answer. If the effect of treatments on the primary response variable is statistically significant, then the results can probably be considered positive. On the other hand, if the primary response variable does not reflect a significant treatment effect, it is unlikely that any other significant effects can fully compensate for this.

It can also be helpful to distinguish between confirmatory and exploratory statistical analyses. *Confirmatory* analyses are planned before the experiment is executed to test specific hypotheses. *Exploratory* analyses are usually considered less critical than and supplemental to the confirmatory analysis. An example of a confirmatory analysis might be an analysis of variance to compare the effects of biofeedback and diuretic medication on the systolic blood pressures of two randomized groups of hypertensive patients. Exploratory analyses might involve such things as analyzing baseline characteristics of the two groups, determining whether or not certain personality factors predicted treatment outcome, or comparing the effects of the two treatments on diastolic blood pressure or heart rate. Exploratory analyses are an important dimension of data analysis, and they can help considerably in the interpretation of a confirmatory analysis. However, the distinction between confirmatory and exploratory analyses should be kept quite clear, and the interpretation given to results should reflect this distinction.

Finally, it should be realized that a study can still be biased during the data analysis phase. Although all confirmatory data analyses should be planned before data are actually collected, this is seldom the case. More often, investigators plan their data analyses step by step as they go. When this is done there may be a temptation to omit certain patients or rerun the analysis in a slightly different form if the results are not quite significant or not in the expected direction. If possible, the data should be analyzed by a statistician other than the principal investigator. Furthermore, it would be preferable for the data analyst to be blind with respect to the group membership of the patients. This could be accomplished by simply not telling the data analyst what system is used to code group membership information until data analysis is complete. Of course, the data analyst may eventually guess the correct coding scheme, but by this time the most important confirmatory analyses will be completed, under reduced risk of bias.

INTERPRETING AND REPORTING RESULTS

In research, figures do not "speak for themselves." They require thoughtful interpretation that comes from the investigator's experience and knowledge of the area. The interpretation should consider such things as the following. What are the limitations of the study? What problems occurred and were they resolved? Was patient compliance good or bad? Were the data appropriate for the analysis, or was the analysis complicated somehow? If an effort was made to control potentially confounding variables, how successfully was this done? Was the desired sample size achieved, and was sufficient statistical power available? Did different response variables reflect conflicting results? Do the results support, extend, clarify, or contradict previous findings? What recommendations can be made regarding the clinical use of biofeedback in treating the disorder investigated?

Another important point to consider is the generalizability of the results. Many variables are controlled for research purposes that would be allowed to vary freely under standard clinical conditions. Therefore, the proportion of variance in patient response that can be accounted for by treatments in a controlled, experiment setting might overestimate the effects that would result if treatment occurred in the natural environment. On the other hand, in clinical practice, the clinician is free to modify the treatment procedures and apply multiple treatments as clinical judgment and patient response dictate, whereas in clinical research the researcher usually must sacrifice some degree of clinical freedom in order to rule out the influences of biasing factors. Therefore, it is also possible that greater patient improvement would occur from the actual clinical application of a therapy than from a restricted research application. In this case, the variance accounted for by the treatment variables in an experimental application might underestimate the actual therapeutic gains that are possible with the technique in a real clinical setting.

In reporting results, authors should always try to place the results into the context of already existing knowledge, being careful to present an honest and balanced statement. Conclusions and recommendations must be justifiable from the results, and definitive statements may not always be honestly possible. This situation may be frustrating for the reader who is only interested in the bottom line of whether or not the therapy in question will benefit his or her patients. Some readers may think that the researcher has been overly cautious and should have made a stronger statement. Usually the reason for not making a stronger statement is not a wish to hedge on the part of the researcher; in fact, there is usually a bias toward emphasizing positive results and ignoring negative results in reporting clinical trials. This bias is encouraged by the publication policies of many journals not to publish negative results and replication studies. Although knowledge is usually advanced most rapidly if positive results are emphasized, it is unfortunately true in the case of clinical-trials research that such a policy could lead to a cumulative exaggeration of therapeutic efficacy.

Writing the report of results is the most difficult aspect of the research process for some investigators, and some trials are never reported because the investigator will not or cannot adequately express the findings. To have maximum impact, however, the results must be published, preferably in a refereed journal. Oral presentations at meetings simply cannot provide the detail that is required to properly explain a clinical trial, and these presentations are usually forgotten soon after they are made. There is nothing sacred about refereed journals, and referees are not infallible; however, most research reports are improved and their credibility is enhanced if they are submitted to the peer review process. Another advantage of publishing in refereed journals is that they are archival and are collected more widely by libraries than are nonrefereed journals and books.

ETHICAL PROBLEMS WITH CONTROLLED CLINICAL TRIALS

Much of the preceding discussion has concerned the many pragmatic problems that will face the investigator conducting controlled clinical trials involving biofeedback. Some of these are concrete, such as the need for large numbers of patients having the same diagnosis, the need for financial support, and the need to invest a considerable amount of time. Others are more subtle, such as making certain that the therapeutic impact of the treatments is not reduced when they are transformed from clinical procedures into research procedures. Some of the most difficult problems, however, have not yet been discussed. These involve the ethical questions that must be answered before clinical experimentation on human subjects can occur.

One such ethical question involves the justification for withholding therapy for research purposes. Is it justifiable to withhold therapy for an extended baseline period? Is it justifiable to give medically ill patients placebo therapy or assign them to a waiting-list or no-treatment group when it is likely that they could benefit by receiving treatment? Is it justifiable to charge a fee for an experimental treatment for a baseline period? Is it justifiable to assign randomly patients to treatments when decisions based on clinical knowledge might produce a more desirable response? If a patient's condition becomes worse while receiving a placebo treatment, has he or she been harmed by participating in the research? Do we really know what nonspecific factors need to be controlled for in biofeedback research or what constitutes an acceptable control treatment? If patients are denied therapy or given some sort of placebo therapy, will they develop negative attitudes toward biofeedback or will the patient–therapist relationship suffer? Will any negative attitudes that do develop generalize to other health care settings? These are all very important questions that must be considered with regard to the rights and welfare of the individual patient and those of the society that might benefit from the advancement of knowledge. The central ethical question is whether current knowledge allows a preferred treatment to be chosen, and whether the relative risk to a patient would be greater as a result of assigning treatments randomly versus basing treatment assignments on clinical judgment.

Any research involving human subjects must use an informed consent procedure in recruitment. Patients must be informed of all experimental procedures to be followed, including an assessment of any possible risks, and they must freely consent to participate before any experimentation can begin. Almost all research centers and academic institutions have institutional review boards that meet periodically to review proposed research protocols and to determine whether acceptable ethical standards will be met. Although this process can be time consuming and frustrating for the eager investigator, it does remove some of the burden of making independent decisions about important ethical questions. In general, patients are becoming more informed about their disorders and increasingly want to play a role in making decisions about their treatment. It is easy to plan a study on paper by simply dividing the patients in half to form two groups. However, when patients ask questions, request a recommendation, or express a preference for one treatment over another they must be treated honestly and fairly, even if it means failing to recruit the patient for the study. Informed consent allows the patient to decide the balance between his or her individual need for treatment and his or her obligation or desire to contribute something to society. Where ethical issues are concerned, openness with the patients involved and the solicitation of a variety of outside opinions is advised.

The responsibility for high ethical standards does not end when the final patient completes therapy. Ethical issues continue to arise during data analysis and interpretation of results. When negative results are obtained from relatively small-scale clinical studies, authors should not be allowed to conclude that there is no advantage of the experimental treatment over the control. In the absence of information about statistical power, negative results could be due to inadequate sample size, overestimation of treatment effects, improper choice of an outcome variable or simply sloppy research methods. The reporting of no difference between treatments without examining these possibilities is unethical and can be damaging to future progress in the field. In the absence of evidence of bias, positive results are usually easier to interpret. However, the investigator is not relieved of his or her obligation to discuss the limitations of the results. Consumers of research also have an ethical obligation to be skeptical of claims made for new treatment techniques and should not allow authors to paint a picture that is too positive.

REFERENCES

Andrasik, F., & Holroyd, K. A. (1980). A test of specific and nonspecific effects in the biofeedback treatment of tension headache. *Journal of Consulting and Clinical Psychology,* 48 575–586.
Basmajian, J. V., & Blumenstein, R. (Eds.). (1980). *Electrode placement in EMG biofeedback.* Baltimore, MD: Williams & Wilkins.

Bergin, A. E., & Strupp, H. H. (Eds.). (1972). *Changing frontiers in the science of psychotherapy.* Chicago, IL: Aldine-Atherton.

Blanchard, E. B., Andrasik, F., Neff, D. F., Teders, S. J., Pallmeyer, T. P., Arena, J. G., Jurish, S. E., Saunders, N. L., Ahles, T. A. (1982). Sequential comparisons of relaxation training and biofeedback in the treatment of three kinds of chronic headache or, the machines may be necessary some of the time. *Behavior Research and Therapy, 20,* 469–481.

Blanchard, E. B., Theobald, D. E., Williamson, D. A., Silver, B. V., & Brown, D. A. (1978). Temperature biofeedback in the treatment of migraine headaches. *Archives of General Psychiatry, 35,* 581–588.

Bulpitt, C. J. (Ed.). (1983). *Randomized controlled clinical trials:* The Hague: Martinus Nijhoff.

Chalmers, T. C. (1982). The randomized clinical trial as a basis for therapeutic decisions. In N. Tygstrup, J. M. Lachin, & E. Juhl (Eds.), *The randomized clinical trial and therapeutic decisions.* (pp. 13–20). New York: Marcel Dekker.

Cohen, J. (1977). *Statistical power analysis for the behavioral sciences.* New York: Academic Press.

Cram, J. R. (1980). EMG biofeedback and the treatment of tension headaches: A systematic analysis of treatment components. *Behavior Therapy, 11,* 699–710.

Donner, A. (1984). Approaches to sample size estimation in the design of clinical trials—a review. *Statistics in Medicine, 3,* 199–214.

Fowles, D. C., Christe, M. J., Edelberg, R., Grings, W. W., Lykken, D. T., & Venables, P. H. (1981) Publication recommendations for electrodermal measurements. *Psychophysiology, 18,* 232–239.

Friedman, L. M., Furberg, C. D., & DeMets, D. L. (Eds.). (1981). *Fundamentals of clinical trials.* Boston, MA: John Wright.

Gray, C. L., Lyle, R. C., McGuire, R. J., & Peck, D. F. (1980). Electrode placement, EMG feedback, and relaxation for tension headaches. *Behavior Research and Therapy, 18,* 19–23.

Hatch, J. P. (1982). Controlled group designs in biofeedback research: Ask, "What does the control group control for?" *Biofeedback and Self-Relaxation, 7,* 377–401.

Hatch, J. P., Klatt, K., Fitzgerald, M., Jasheway, L. S., & Fisher, J. G. (1983). Cognitive and physiologic responses to EMG biofeedback and three types of pseudofeedback during a muscular relaxation task. *Biofeedback and Self-Regulation, 8,* 409–425.

Jennings, J. R., Berg, W. K., Hutcheson, J. S., Obrist, P., Porges, S., & Turpin, G. (1981). Publication guidelines for heart rate studies in man. *Psychophysiology, 18,* 226–231.

Kirkendall, W. M., Feinleib, M., Fries, E. D., & Mark, A. L. (1981). Recommendations for human blood pressure determination by sphygmonanometers. *Stroke, 3,* 510A–519A.

Marinez, Y. N., McMahan, C. A., Barnwell, G. M., & Wigodsky, H. S. (1984). Ensuring data quality in medical research through an integrated data management system. *Statistics in Medicine, 3,* 101–111.

Martin, I., & Venables, P. H. (Eds.). (1980). *Techniques in psychophysiology.* Chichester: Wiley.

Miller, N. E., (1978). Biofeedback and visceral learning. *Annual Review of Psychology, 29,* 373–404.

Paul, G. L. (1967). Strategies of outcome research in psychotherapy. *Journal of Consulting Psychology, 31,* 109–118.

Taub, E., & School, P. J. (1978). Some methodological considerations in thermal biofeedback training. *Behavior Research Methods and Instrumentation, 10,* 617–622.

Williams, J. B. W., & Spitzer, R. L. (1984). *Psychotherapy research: Where are we and where should we go?* New York: The Guilford Press.

Index